Thomas Scott

The Book of Job, in English verse

Thomas Scott

The Book of Job, in English verse

ISBN/EAN: 9783337736354

Printed in Europe, USA, Canada, Australia, Japan

Cover: Foto ©ninafisch / pixelio.de

More available books at **www.hansebooks.com**

THE

BOOK of JOB,

IN

ENGLISH VERSE;

TRANSLATED FROM THE ORIGINAL HEBREW;

WITH

REMARKS,

HISTORICAL, CRITICAL, and EXPLANATORY.

By THOMAS SCOTT.

Then Job anfwered the Lord, and faid . . . .
Verily I have uttered that I underftood not, things too wonderful for me that I knew not.
Wherefore I abhor myfelf; and repent in duft and afhes.
Job xlii. 1, 3, 6.

LONDON:
Printed by W. STRAHAN,
And fold by T. CADELL, in the Strand; M. HINGESTON, Temple-Bar; J. and F. RIVINGTON, St. Paul's Church-Yard; J. BUCKLAND, in Pater-nofter-Row; E. and C. DILLY, in the Poultry; and J. SHAVE, Ipfwich.
MDCCLXXI.

PREFACE.

THE *poetry* in this venerable book begins with the second verse of the third chapter; and breaks off, at the end of the sixth verse of the concluding chapter. Those, therefore, are the limits of the *poem:* which presents to us the shades of an illustrious character; a great and good man in the depth of adversity, reduced to despair, and complaining loudly of the ways of God. His three most intimate friends, who came to condole with him, very early insinuate their uncharitable suspicions: and, afterward, openly accuse him of atrocious *wickedness*, as the cause of his afflictions. Accordingly, they exhort him to repentance, that repentance which a *wicked* man needeth, as the only means of his restoration. By thus defending the honour of Providence at their friend's expence, they exasperate his distress, inflame his passions, and hurry him into blameable excesses in the justification of himself, and in expostulations with his Maker about the reason of his sufferings. He is, however, by wiser management in other hands [a], gradually recovered to a becoming temper: And at last acknowledgeth his fault to the Almighty, in the fullest terms of contrition and self-abasement. With this *compleat* confession the poem closeth, *the design* of the *poem* being then accomplished.

The moral of such a poem, formed on the plan of discontent with the measures of Providence, and the issue of that discon-

---

[a] Elihu.

tent in fubmiffion to them, is too obvious to ftand in want of explanation.

The majefty and fublimity of this divine compofition have been admired by writers of the firft rank in genius, tafte, and learning [a]: One of whom, diftinguifhed by his critical fkill in the facred poetry of the Hebrews, is of opinion, that the peculiar character of this poem is a certain air and caft of antiquity [b]: for the language is very old Hebrew, and the manners are thofe of the earlieft ages. It has, however, many other beauties; well known to that fagacious judge, and finely illuftrated by his elegant pen [c]. It excels in concifenefs, force, and fulnefs of expreffion, in mafterly painting both of the violent and tender paffions, in moving reprefentations of human life, great powers of defcription, and the noble fimplicity of its theology and ethics.

Whether the following tranflation has, in general, reached the meaning of this extremely difficult author, and copied his ideas with fufficient clearnefs, brevity, and fpirit; is now fubmitted to the judgement of the public.

---

[a] The whole book of Job, with regard both to fublimity of thought and morality, exceeds beyond all comparifon the moft noble parts of Homer. Mr. Pope's *Tranflation of the Odyffey*, b. xvi. the laft note.

[b] Letter to the Right Reverend Author of the *Divine Legation of Mofes*, by Dr. Lowth.

[c] *De Sacra Poefi Hebræorum.*

LIST of the SUBSCRIBERS.

A

SIR Edward Aſtley, Bart. M. P. for Norfolk.
Mrs. Elizabeth Abney, Stoke Newington.
Mr. Stephen Abbot, Ipſwich.
James Adams, Eſq;
Rev. Edward Aſhburner, A. M.
Anonymous, two Books.

B

Sir Charles Bunbury, Bart. M. P. for Suffolk.
Edward Bacon, Eſq; M. P. for Norwich.
Rev. J. Barney, D. D. Archdeacon of Norwich.
Rev. Richard Barney, Norwich.
Rev. Thomas Bolton, A. M. Rector of Holleſley, Suffolk.
Rev. John Brown, A. M. Rector of Falkenham, Suffolk.
Rev. James Baldwin, Rector of Lyng and Little Brand, Norfolk.
Rev. Thomas Bagſhaw.
Rev. Samuel Bourn, Norwich.
Rev. James Belſham, Bedford.
Rev. ——— Burnet, Hull.
Wadſworth Buſk, Eſq;
John Buxton, Eſq; of Shadwell-Lodge, Norfolk.
Leonard Buxton, Eſq; of Eaſton, Norfolk.
Benjamin Boddington, Eſq; Hackney.
Thomas Boddington, Eſq; ditto.
Benjamin Bond, Junior, Eſq;
W. Bowden, Eſq;
Frederick Bull, Eſq; Wanſted.
Coulſon Bell, Eſq; Oulton, Norfolk.
John Bell, Eſq; ditto, ditto.
Mr. ——— Burgh, Newington-Green.

William

LIST of the SUBSCRIBERS.

William Gregg Barnſton, Eſq;
Gill Baddeley, Eſq; Norwich.
Samuel Badeley, Junior, Eſq; Walpole, Suffolk.
George Buxton, M. D. Chelmsford.
John Baker, Eſq;
Henry Baker, Eſq; Clapton.
Mr. John Baker, Junior.
Miſs Elizabeth Baker.
Mr. Samuel Bolton, Merchant, Ipſwich.
Mr. John Barnard, ditto.
Mr. Nathaniel Bucke, Junior, Surgeon, ditto.
Mr. George Boggis, ditto.
Mr. James Buttal.
Mr. Thomas Brown, Merchant, Rotterdam.
Mr. Cornelius Vanden Boſch, ditto.
Mr. Charles Boutwell, Tittiſhall, Norfolk.
Mr. John Bowles.
Mr. William Buck, Merchant, Halifax, Yorkſhire.

C

Rev. John Clubbe, Rector of Whatfield, Suffolk.
Rev. William Clubbe, Rector of Flouton, ditto.
Rev. Abraham Coveney, Armingland-Hall, Norfolk.
Rev. John Conder, D. D.
Rev. ——— Coppock.
Rev. ——— Clayton, Liverpool.
Richard Cooke, Eſq;
William Cooke, Eſq; two Books, Woodford.
John Chambers, Eſq; Norwich.
Mr. Maſon Chamberlain.
Mr. Joſeph Clarke, Ipſwich.
Mr. John Conder, ditto.
Mr. William Carter, Norwich.
Mr. Edmond Cobb, Merchant, Yarmouth.
Mr. Cotton, Attorney at Law, Hackney.
Mr. Jonathan Clarke, ditto.
Alexander Champion, Eſq; Walthamſtow.

William

LIST of the SUBSCRIBERS.

D

William Dolby, Efq; Hackney.
Rev. William Duke, Barbadoes.
Rev. Benjamin Dawfon, D. D. Rector of Burgh, Suffolk.
Rev. ——— Dean.
Rev. Bernardus Doormborfch, Wormeever, Holland.
Mr. William Donn, Surgeon, Norwich.
Mr. John Dobfon, Merchant, Ipfwich.
Mr. William Dymock, ditto.
Mr. Philip Dikes, ditto.
Mr. John May Dring, ditto.
Mr. Nathaniel Dowding.
Mr. Edward Dyfon, Difs, Norfolk.

E

Rev. William Enfield, Tutor in the Belles Lettres at Warrington Academy.
Rev. David Edwards, Ipfwich.
Mr. John Elfden, ditto.
Mr. John Ely, Bury.
Mr. Jonathan Eade.

F

Thomas Fletcher, Efq; Walthamftow.
John Ffrere, Efq; Roydon, Norfolk.
Rev. Hugh Farmer, Walthamftow.
Rev. John Fuller, A. M.
Rev. John Forfaith, Norwich.
Rev. Theodorus Frretts, Rotterdam.
Peter Finch, Efq; Norwich.
John Ford, M. D.
Mrs. Mary Farr, Ipfwich.
Mr. John Fowler, Merchant, ditto.
Mrs. Fowell.
Mifs Charlotte Finch
Mr. Thomas Field.

LIST of the SUBSCRIBERS.

G

Rev. Thomas Gibbons, D. D.
John Gay, Efq; Norwich.
Rev. Thomas Greaves, Rotterdam.
Rev. William Gordon, Philadelphia.
Mr. James Geldard, of Staples-Inn.
Mrs. Gawfell, Bury.
Mr. John Gravenor, Ipfwich.

H

Sir Harbord Harbord, Bart. M. P. for Norwich.
John Hawkefworth, LL. D.
John Hopkins, Efq; Brittons near Rumford.
Edward Hague, Efq; fix Books.
Thomas Hallum, Efq; Captain in his Majefty's Navy, Ipfwich.
Edward Hopfon, Efq; Norwich.
Rev. Henry Hubbard, B. D. Fellow of Emanuel Colledge, Cambridge.
Rev. —— Humfry, Rector of Thorpe near Norwich.
Rev. Rice Harris, D. D.
Rev. John Hoyle, Norwich.
Rev. Thomas Harmer, Whattisfield, Suffolk.
Rev. —— Howell, Birmingham.
Rev. Philip Holland, Bolton.
Mr. William Hall, Merchant.
Mr. Thomas Henfman, Bedford.
Mr. Ifaac Hoyle, Norwich.
Mr. Stephen Hooker, Druggift, Colchefter.
Homerton Academy.

I

Thomas Jacomb, Efq;
Charles Jackfon, Efq; Layton, Effex.
James Johnfon, Efq;
Jeremiah Ives, Efq; Alderman of Norwich.
John Ives, Efq; Norwich.

LIST of the SUBSCRIBERS.

Mr. Thomas Ives, Merchant, Norwich.
Edward Jeffries, Efq;
Mr. David Jennings.
Mr. Charles Jordein.
Mr. William Jackſon, for Self and Friends, three Books, Ipſwich.

K

Joſhua Kirby, Efq; Kew.
Rev. Benjamin Kennicott, D. D. Canon of Chriſt-Church, Oxford.
Rev. Andrew Kippis, D. D.
Mr. William King, Merchant, Ipſwich.
Mrs. Mary Kell, Woodbridge, Suffolk.
Mr. John Kerridge, Surgeon, Ipſwich.
Mr. Kendal, Colcheſter.
Mr. John Kerſhaw, Merchant, Halifax, Yorkſhire.
Mr. William Kirby, Attorney at Law, Witneſham, Suffolk.

L

Thomas Lucas, Efq; Treaſurer of Guy's Hoſpital.
Robert Lovelace, Efq; Clapham.
Hewling Luſon, Efq; Loweſtoft.
John Lee, Efq;
Mr. Robert Lewin, Hackney.
Rev. Andrew Layton, A. M. Rector of St. Matthew's, Ipſwich.
Rev. Robert Lewin, Liverpool.
Rev. W. Lincolne, Bury.
Rev. —— Lilly.
Mr. John Leggatt, Ipſwich.

M

Robert Marſham, Efq; Stratton-lawleſs, Norfolk.
Jaſper Mauduit, Efq; Hackney, three Books.
Iſrael Mauduit, Efq;
Mr. William Mauduit, two Books.

Robert

LIST of the SUBSCRIBERS.

Robert Mendham, Esq;
Robert Marsh, Esq; Norwich.
Mr. Charles Marsh, ditto.
Mr. Robert Marsh, ditto.
Mr. Philip Meadows, Attorney at Law, Diss, Norfolk.
John Manning, M. D. Norwich.
Rev. Archibald Maclean, D. D. the Hague, two Books.
Rev. Michael Vander Mersch, Rotterdam.
Mr. Samuel Moody.
Mr. William Manning, Yarmouth.

N

Richard Norton, Esq; Ipswich.
John Nuthall, Esq;
Rev. Samuel Newton, Norwich.
Rev. Cornelius Nozeman, Rotterdam.
Mr. Thomas Nasmith, Norwich.
Mr. John Notcutt.
Mr. George Notcutt.
Mr. John Notcutt, Junior.

O

The Right Hon. Lord Orwell, of Orwell-Park.
Mr. John Ollyet, Merchant, Norwich, two Books.

P

Joseph Paice, Esq;
Robert Parish, Esq; Ipswich.
Rev. John Peal, Norwich.
Rev. Richard Price, D. D. F. R. S. Newington-Green.
Rev. Joseph Priestley, LL. D. F. R. S.
Rev. Edward Pickard.
Rev. William Prior.
Rev. John Palmer, Islington.
Rev. Samuel Palmer, Hackney, two Books.

LIST of the SUBSCRIBERS.

Rev. John Palmer, Woodbridge, Suffolk.
Mr. John Phillibrown, two Books.
Mrs. Elizabeth Parish, Walthamstow.
Mrs. Peach, Bengal.
Mr. James Pearson.
Rev. Michael Pope.
Michael Pope, Esq;

R

David Roberts, Esq;
Humphry Rant, Esq; Ipswich.
Thomas Rogers, Esq; Newington-Green.
Samuel Rickards, Esq; ditto.
John Ruggles, Esq; Bury.
John Ryland, Esq;
Miss Ryland.
Rev. Ebenezer Radcliff, Walthamstow.
Rev. John Ralph, Halifax, Yorkshire.
Mr. William Rose, Chiswick, six Books.
Mrs. Elizabeth Radcliff, Walthamstow.
Mr. William Richardson.
Mr. John Roberts.
Mr. John Rodbard, Surgeon, Ipswich.

S

Thomas Staunton, M. P. for Ipswich.
Ralph Smith, Esq; Major in the Norfolk Militia.
Thomas Sims, Esq; Walthamstow.
Samuel Shore, Esq;
Thomas Streatfield, Esq; Stoke-Newington.
Rev. Thomas Stanton, D. D. Colchester.
Rev. Benjamin Sowden, Rotterdam.
Rev. ——— Shaw.
Mr. John Scott, Merchant, Norwich.
Mr. Daniel Scott, Merchant, ditto.
Mr. Thomas Scott, Merchant, ditto.

LIST of the SUBSCRIBERS.

Mr. Thomas Nicol Scott, Attorney at Law, Ipswich.
Mr. John Shave, Bookseller, ditto.
Mr. Henry Seekamp, Druggist, ditto.
Mr. Joseph Shrimpton, Merchant.
Mr. Thomas Shrimpton.
Mr. John Seagrave.
Mr. John Stratton, Bethnal-Green.
Miss Swift.
Mrs. Elizabeth Smith, New-England.
Samuel Sparrow, Esq;
Rev. Samuel Stennet, D. D.

T

Matthew Twogood, Esq; Walthamstow.
Rev. Richard Tapps, Norwich.
Rev. William Turner.
Rev. ——— Thomas
Rev. Thomas Towle, B. D.
Rev. ——— Tayler, Stoke-Newington.
Rev. ——— Toller.
Mr. John Turner, Ipswich.
Mr. Martin Tomkins.
Mrs. Thornton, Clapham.
Mr. John Townsend, Master of an Academy near Spital-Square.
Mr. William Travis, Hull.
Mr. John Travis, ditto.
Mr. Francis Twiss, Rotterdam.
Mr. William Toulmin, Surgeon, Hackney.
Mr. James Tompson, Norwich.
Mr. Stephen Todd.

V

Delme Vanheytheusen, Esq;
Samuel Vaughan, Esq;
Mr. Anthony Van Vollenhoven, Merchant, Rotterdam.

William

LIST of the SUBSCRIBERS.

W

William Wollaston, M. P. for Ipswich.
Jonathan Worrel, Esq; Ipswich, two Books.
Robert Watts, Esq; Stratford by Bow.
Robert Waftfield, Esq;
Miles Wallis, Esq; General Receiver for Suffolk.
John Winter, Esq;
Rev. —— Watson
Rev. —— White
Rev. —— Warren
Rev. Thomas Whitaker
Rev. John Whiteside, Yarmouth.
Rev. —— Walker, ditto.
Rev. Samuel Wilton, Tooting.
Rev. William Wood, Ipswich.
Mrs. Elizabeth Wright, Hackney.
Mr. William Welby.
Mr. John Walton.
Mr. Samuel Wigget, Merchant, Norwich.
Mr. William Worth, Merchant, ditto.
Mr. William Wilton.
Mr. Thomas Wellings.
Mr. Sayer Walker.
Mr. James Webster.
Mrs. Sarah Wilkes.
Mr. Arnold Wife, Surgeon.
Mr. John Warren,
John White, Esq; Stowupland, Suffolk.

ADVERTISEMENT.

The following remarks will be more intelligible, if the reader will pleafe to lay before him our public verfion of this book, to which they are adapted.

THE

BOOK

OF

JOB.

CHAP.
I.
Ver. 1. THERE liv'd an Arab, of diftinguifh'd fame,
In Idumean Uz; and Job his name:
Of fpotlefs manners, with a foul fincere,
Evil his hate, and God alone his fear.
2. Seven

The narration in this, and the following chapter, contains the materials of the Poem. Several of the incidents, and indeed the whole ftory, might have appeared, with advantage, in the drefs of poetry. They could not, however, make a part of the *poem*, without deftroying the finglenefs of its plan. Thefe two chapters, therefore, are cut off from it, by being written in profe: as likewife are, for the fame reafon, the laft eleven verfes in the book; which compleat the *hiftory* of this extraordinary man.

Ver. 1. *Uz*] A territory in the land of Edom[a]. The land of Edom was a portion of Arabia Petræa, lying between Egypt and the fouth boundary of Paleftine[b]. Hence it is reafonable to imagine, that Job was well acquainted with

---

[a] *Lamentat.* iv. 21. Bp. Lowth, in his admirable *Prælectiones de facra pœfi Hebræorum*, p. 414, &c. 8vo, has well fupported this geography of Uz; and anfwered the objections to it.

[b] Exod. xiii. 17. Numb. xx. 14, 17. xxxiv. 3. Reland's *Palæftina*, vol. i. p. 66. Arabia Petræa is a rocky country confifting of mountains, valleys between them, and fandy plains. It lies between the two gulfs of the Red Sea, and extends away to the eaft of the Dead

2. Seven fons his patriarchal fway rever'd,
   His houfhold cares three beauteous daughters cheer'd.
3. His flocks in thoufands brows'd, his camels fed
   In thoufands; o'er his fertile paftures fpread.
   In beeves, and beafts of more ignoble ftrain,
   In rural magazines, and ruftic train,
   His mighty opulence no rival found,
   Among the princes in Arabia's bound.
4. On the glad feafon of each natal day
   Sweet friendfhip call'd, the brother friends obey:
   The feftal in the birth-day houfe was blefs'd,
   And each fair fifter came a bidden gueft.

5. Oft

with Egypt: Hence, alfo, we may account for the mention of the *Jordan* in the poem [c]: The *Euphrates*, doubtlefs, would have been thus honoured, had Job lived in Arabia Deferta near the banks of that river; as many have fuppofed.

Ver. 3. *Three thoufand camels*] The Arabs ufed thefe animals in war [d], in their caravans, and for food [e]. One of their ancient poets, whofe hofpitality grew into a proverb, is reported to have killed yearly in a certain month ten camels every day for the entertainment of his friends [e].

Of all the men of the eaft] The land of Uz, where Job dwelt, lay fouth of Paleftine: But it was in Arabia Petræa: and as a confiderable part of Arabia Petræa formed the eaftern boundary of Paleftine, it was natural for a Jewifh hiftorian to denominate *all* the Petræan Arabians, *men of the eaft*. Bp. Lowth has alfo fhown, that all that tract of land which was between Egypt and the river

---

Dead Sea and the River Jordan. (Pococke's *Defcription of the Eaft.* vol. i. p. 136.) No tillage, no grafs in all this country. *(Ibid* p. 137.) The mountains are rocks of granite marble, mount Sinai being about the centre of them. *(Ibid.)* The vallies are the beds of torrents in winter, but dry in fummer. *Ibid.* 140.

[c] Chap. xl. 23.
[d] Vid. Schultens' *Excerpta* from the *Arabian Anthologia*, p. 315. n.
[e] Pocock: *Specim. hift. Arab.* p. 343. *Togr.* p. 115.

5. Oft as these rounds of social joy expir'd,
The pious father holy rites requir'd:
By due ablutions cleans'd, the filial band
For solemn sacrifice around him stand;
When, rising with the morn, the priestly fire
Dispos'd th' atonement on the hallow'd fire.
For every child a costly victim blaz'd,
For every child the fervid pray'r he rais'd:
" Forgive my childrens sin, all-gracious Pow'r,
" If ought displeas'd thee in their mirthful hour:
" If some loose moment's gaiety of heart
" E'er said to piety and God, depart.

6. Now, on a day in heav'n, before the throne
Supreme th' angelic ministration shone,
Jehovah's

river Euphrates, was called *the east*. He remarks from Mr. Joseph Mede, that the Israelites learned this phraseology while they sojourned in Egypt[f].

Ver. 5. *cursed God in their hearts*] It shocks credulity, that this excellent father should conceive so gross a sentiment of his amiable children. He was only apprehensive, least, in the gaiety of a festival, they had let loose their minds from the restraints of religion. The word constantly signifies *to bless*[g]. It was the term of compliment between friends at their meeting, and at parting[h]: in the latter use of it, it answered, as Bp. Lowth observes, to our english phrase *fare you well*: and probably, like that, came to be used in a bad sense, for *renouncing an acquaintance*. This passage, therefore, might have been turned, and have bidden *farewel to* (or *renounced*) *God in their hearts*.

Ver. 6—12. *Now there was*, &c.] This is not history; but a piece of allegorical scenery, somewhat resembling the councils of the Gods in Homer.
The

---

[f] *Letter to the author of the Divine Legation*, p. 58.

[g] In I *Kings* xxi. 13. it is rendred to *blaspheme: Naboth did blaspheme* (renounce) *God and the king*: that is, he had spoken words which imported a renunciation both of his religion and his allegiance. See the note of Schultens on *Job*, i. 5.

[h] *Gen.* xlvii. 7, 10. II *Sam.* xix. 39.

Jehovah's high-born fons: Among them ftands
7. Satan, of whom the fovereign voice demands;
   From which of my dominions art thou come?
   From earth, he anfwer'd, licens'd there to roam:
   Affiduous in my office, I have run
   Through all its peopled climes from fun to fun.
8. Accufer, haft thou mark'd with hoftile aim
   My fervant Job; on earth a matchlefs name,
   Of blamelefs manners, with a foul fincere,
   Evil his hate, and God alone his fear?
9. Th' accufer anfwer'd: Is the fervice free,
   Rewarded with fuch ample hire by thee?
10. Is not himfelf, his houfe, his all, fecur'd
    From harm; within thy providence immur'd?
    Profper'd by thee, his wealth, increafing ftill,
    Flows from a thoufand fprings in vale and hill.
11. Smite now his all, this feeming fon of grace
    Will, on my head, renounce thee to thy face.

12. Once

The noble inftruction, which it veileth, is; that God governs the world by the inftrumentality of fecond caufes, that the evils of human life are under his direction, and that the afflictions of good men are appointed by him for the illuftration of their virtue, and advancing, by that means, the honour of religion.

Ver. 6. *Satan*] Job himfelf, and the other human fpeakers in the poem, conftantly reprefent his calamities as the immediate act of God. They, therefore, had no idea of this evil being, nor of his agency in human affairs: He is never once mentioned throughout the poem.

Ver. 7. *going*, &c. *walking*, &c.] Thefe expreffions mean, in the Hebrew idiom, vigilant execution of a miniftry, or office. *Zech.* i. 10, 11.

Ver. 11. *he will curfe thee*, &c.] *he will renounce thee to thy face*. The phrafe is ftronger than in ver. 5. *curfed God in their hearts*. It importeth here an utter and public renunciation of religion as a vain thing.

12. Once more Jehovah: Go, invade his all,
   But at thy peril on his perſon fall.
   Swift from the preſence flew the Pow'r of ſpite,
   And prone to earth precipitates his flight.

13. 'Twas now the birth-day of the elder ſon,
    The kindred met, the banquet was begun.

14. When, lo, a ſervant, breathleſs, pale with fear,
    Bare heavy tidings to the maſter's ear:
    Thy aſſes graz'd, thy heifers turn'd the ſoil,

15. Sabean robbers flew upon the ſpoil:
    Thy faithful ſlaves lie ſlaughter'd on the plain,
    I, only I, to bring the tale remain.

16. Him interrupt another's doleful cries:
    The fire of God was darted from the ſkies,
    The flocks and ſhepherds are confum'd. alone,
    I, wretch, furvive to make the miſchief known.

17. A third; The Chaldees, in a triple band,
    Have forc'd the camels to a foreign land.

I only

Ver. 13—19. *And there was*, &c.] The calamitous cataſtrophe deſcribed in theſe verſes, is crowded with events ſo very extraordinary in their nature and coincidence; that, I confeſs, it hath more the air of parable than of matter of fact.

Ver. 17. *The Chaldeans*] Chaldea was, indeed, at a vaſt diſtance from the land of Edom. But theſe were a ſet of profligates, who followed the pilfering life of the wild Arabs: and like them, it is probable, they made excurſions through the Arabian deferts; to any diſtance where there was any hope of plunder [i]. The Arabs eſteemed it heroiſm to make long journeys over pathleſs ſolitudes, in queſt of daring adventures [k].

fell

---

[i] Let the learned reader ſee what is offered in the *Prælectiones* p. 417, towards ſolving this objection to placing Uz in the land of Edom.

[k] *Arab. Anthologia*, p. 397. n.

I only from their cruel sword have fled,
To speak the loss and how the herdsmen bled.

18. Worse message follow'd, follow'd close behind,
The bearer's look spoke horror in his mind:
Thy first-born son, his brethren, sisters—all
Were met, and feasting in his friendly hall:

19. When rushing from the wild, a wheeling blast
Full on the house all ways its fury cast:
Thy children smother'd in the ruin fell,
I only live the fatal blow to tell.

20. Then Job arose; and, father now no more,
He lopt his flowing hair, his robe he tore:
Prone to the dust he bow'd his rev'rent head,
And, worshipping, with humblest accent said:
Peace every murmur, naked into birth
I came, and naked shall return to earth.
The LORD in bounty gave, but gave in trust,
The LORD resumes; resuming, not unjust:

fell upon the camels] The Arabs continued these practices in succeeding generations. The first poem in the *Arabian Anthologia*, published by the learned Schultens, turns upon the loss of ten camels; which the poet had sustained by an incursion of this kind.

Ver. 19. *from the wilderness*] Some desert eminently so called; most probably that deep sandy desert which lies between Egypt and Palestine, mentioned by Josephus and Arrian[1]. It was, therefore, a south wind which overthrew the house, where Job's children were feasting. Zech. ix. 14. *The Lord God .... shall go with whirlwinds of the south.*

Ver. 20, 21. *and worshipped*, &c.] This was behaviour truly sublime; the noblest homage that could be paid by a reasonable being to his great Creator.

---

[1] Vid. Reland's *Palæstina*, vol. i. p. 59.

CHAP. I.   THE BOOK OF JOB.   7

  Giving, refuming, he is ftill the LORD,
  Still be the glories of his name ador'd.
 21. Thus far the blamelefs man his ills fuftain'd,
  Nor one complaint the ways of God arraign'd.

CHAP. II.
Ver. 1. Again the fons of God his throne furround,
  Again th' accufer in the ranks was found.
 2, 3. To him Jehovah: erring was thy aim,
  My fervant Job is ftill a matchlefs name;
  Of blamelefs manners, with a foul fincere,
  Evil his hate, and God alone his fear.
  His virtue ftands, unmeriting he mourns,
  On thy own head thy calumny returns.
 4. Satan reply'd; who that efcapes to fhore,
  Will, though his all be wreck'd, his lofs deplore?
 5. Smite but his *perfon* home, this fon of grace
  Will, on my head, renounce thee to thy face.
 6. God anfwer'd: lo I yield him to thy will;
  Licens'd to wound, at thy own peril kill.

            7. Swift

Ver. 21. *In all this*, &c.] This remark, and the repetition of it chap. ii. 1, warneth us to expect a very different behaviour in the *poem*.

CHAP. II.

Ver. 4. *fkin for fkin*, &c.] This proverbial form of fpeech might have, among the Hebrews, fufficient dignity for profe. But it appeared to me too humble for verfe. I have, therefore, in my tranflation, changed it into another; which, I think, expreffeth its meaning.

Ver. 5. *he will curfe thee*, &c.] See the note ch. i. 11.

7. Swift from the prefence went the Pow'r of fpite,
And prone to earth precipitates his flight.

Job inftant felt the cruel foe, all o'er
Smitten with boils and flung at every pore.
8. Down in the duft he fat, in humble fign
Of forrow paffive to the will divine.
9. 'Twas then, the frail companion of his care
Wounded his foul with words of wild defpair:
What,

Ver. 7. *with fore boils*] This was one of the plagues, with which the Egyptians were fmitten [m]. It was frequently the firft ftage of a leprofy [n]. According to the great Dr. Mead [o], it was that fpecies of leprofy, which had the name of Elephantiafis, *the elephant difeafe*; fo called from its fwelling the mouth, legs, and feet to an enormous fize, although the body at the fame time was emaciated. The very bones, he adds, are injured by it. The learned Michaelis [p] fays " it is an univerfal ulcer; an exceedingly foul, painful, and naufeous diftemper. Thofe who were affected by it, are faid to have been weary of life, and to wifh and hope for nothing fo much as death : It made them impatient, paffionate, difcontented with every thing, wild and defperate."

Ver. 8. *a pot-fherd*] This was a part of the kitchen furniture, and an utenfil of the hearth in thofe days of fimplicity [q]. But the action, here defcribed, feemed to me too low to be admitted into englifh heroic verfe.

he fat down among the afhes] Sitting down on the hearth, and likewife fprinkling duft upon the head, were ancient rites of mourning [r].

Ver. 9. *curfe God*, &c.] The tranflation might have been *bid farewel to*, or *renounce*, *God*, &c. there will be, however, more poignancy in the fpeech, if
we

---

[m] Exod. xi. 10, 11.   [n] Levit. xiii. 10.
[o] *Medica Sacra*, Stack's *tranflation* ch. i. p. 11. ii. 10.
[p] *Not in Lowthi Prælect.* p. 202, 203.
[q] Ifaiah xxx. 14.
[r] Among the Hebrews, II Sam. xiii. 19. Ifaiah lviii. 5. Jerem. vi. 26. Thefe cuftoms obtained alfo among the ancient Greeks : Odyff. vii. 153. xxiv. 315.

CHAP. II.   THE BOOK OF JOB.   9

What, ſtill a faint? go on, and cringing low
Praiſe him once more, and feel his *mortal* blow. .

10. Doſt thou (he ſaid, and caſt a tender look
While zeal deliver'd its ſevere rebuke,)
Even thou thus raſhly ſpeak? in ſuch a ſtyle,
Let a blind paganeſs her gods revile.
Jehovah's hand divides our portion ſtill;
Shall we embrace his good, and not his ill?

Thus far the patient man his lips reſtrain'd
From ſin, and firm in every ſhock remain'd.

11. Lamenting fame now haſten'd from his place
Temanian Eliphaz, of Shuah's race
Bildad, and Zophar of Naamah's line:
Theſe, guided by the voice of friendſhip, join;
Then ſpeedy to their ſuff'ring friend they go,
To mingle tears, and mollify his woe.

12. His

we retain here the proper meaning of the Hebrew term as in ch. i. 21, *bleſs God and die*; a ſevere ſarcaſm on thoſe admirable words of devout adoration, *bleſſed be the name of the Lord*. The raſhneſs of this poor diſtreſſed Lady cannot be altogether excuſed: But candour will make favourable allowances for the frailty of her ſex, and the severity of her trial.

Ver. 10. *the fooliſh*] ſo the Hebrews ſtyled idolaters, Pſ. lxxiv. 18. The Heathens, when any misfortune befel them, were wont to revile their Gods: Thus, in Homer, Achilles and Menelaus blaspheme Jupiter[1].

Ver. 11. *The Temanite*] The intimate friendſhip between Job and thoſe three men implies, ſurely, vicinity of habitation. Teman, the reſidence of Eliphaz, was in the land of Edom[1]: the other two, therefore, dwelt, we may ſuppoſe, in that country, or in its neighbourhood.

[1] Il. i. 353. iii. 365.   [1] Jerem. xlix. 7.

12. His form now opens to their diſtant view,
   But O how alien from the form they knew!
   They ſprinkled duſt upon their heads, they rent
   Their flowing veſture, and aloud lament.
13. Then ſeated near him on the ground, amaze
   Fetter'd their tongues. For ſeven ſucceeding days,
   With mourning rite, their viſit they renew'd,
   But ſilent ſtill. They ſaw; his grief withſtood
   All lenient counſel; for his looks expreſs'd
   Torture, and huge affliction in his breaſt.

CHAP.
III.
1, 2. At length the ſuff'ring man; oppreſt with pain,
   Pour'd out his anguiſh in lamenting ſtrain:
   And thus devoted to eternal ſhame
   His natal day, whence all his ſorrows came.

3. Periſh

Ver. 13. *ſeven days and ſeven nights*] that is, a whole week; which was the cuſtomary ſpace of time for mourning. Eccleſiaſt. xxii. 12. *Seven days do men mourn for him that is dead.* Compare Gen. L. 10.

C H A P. III[u].

The poem opens with that kind of tragical diſtreſs, which is lofty in its conceptions and highly figurative in its language; which labours for the ſtrongeſt images, and moſt energetic words; to expreſs its feelings, and to ſpread over all objects around it its own gloominefs and horror. A paroxyſm of ſuch violent grief vents itſelf in the following imprecations. The paſſion, however, ſubſides a little in the latter part of the ſpeech, and flows in the ſoft complaining
ſtrain

[u] See the beautiful obſervations on this chapter in Bp. Lowth's *Prælectiones*, p. 170—175, 8vo. Alſo, concerning the different ſtyles of grief in its different degrees; p. 212, 213. of the ſame admirable book.

CHAP. III.   THE BOOK OF JOB.

3. Perish the day my hapless years began!
Perish the night, which hail'd the new-born man!
4. Dark, total darkness, be that day; nor eye
Of God, all viewing from his throne on high,
                                                                Its

strain of elegy. This impotence of mind in Job, so inconsistent with his former firmness, may, I think, be accounted for, in part, from the influence of his disease: to which must be added, his not having obtained any abatement of his affliction, notwithstanding his submission; and his suspicion, from the silence of his three friends, that he was to expect no consolation from them.

Ver. 1. *his day*]: his birth-day. here *day* denoteth a space of twenty-four hours: which, for the sake of amplification, is in the third verse divided into its constituent parts; *the day*, or time from sun-rise to sun-set, and *the night*, or time from sun-set to sun-rise again.

Ver. 3. *the day perish . . . and the night.*] The *day*, by being deprived of the light of the sun; the *night*, by losing the light of the moon and stars: to which circumstances he addeth others, to aggravate the horror.

There is a man-child conceived] He is speaking of the night of his *birth*: for he mentions the celebration of its anniversary, ver. 6. the version, therefore, should have been, *a man-child was conceived*". The night of his birth discovered that his mother had been pregnant with a son. The birth of a son was one of the great occasions of festivity among the Arabs: the other two were; the birth of a foal of family, and the rising up of a poetical genius, in any of their tribes*.

Ver. 4. *regard it*] Our public version renders it *to care for*, in Deut. xi. 12. *A land which the Lord thy God careth for.*

God is here represented sitting on his throne in heaven, and surveying the universe; to see that all its movements be carried on according to the laws which he has established. Job wisheth that the day of his nativity may be rejected from the care of that providence, by which the constant vicissitudes of day and night are preserved.

The light] .The sun. so the word signifies in Arabic ʸ.

" הרה It appears, from Gen. iii. 16, that this word includes the whole period of pregnancy: It may denote here the termination of that period in *child-birth*, as in 1 Chron. iv. 17. Some, perhaps, will chuse to adopt the reading which the LXX followed, הרֹה *ecce, ἰδου behold a man child.*
* Pocock. *Spec. Hist. Ar.* p. 160, 337.
ʸ Lockman. *Fab. Sel. et Ventus.*

Its revolution heed; nor orient beam
Revifit, gladd'ning with its golden ftream.
5. Let Death poffefs it with his dreary fhade,
Let ftorm and thund'ring cloud its heav'n invade:
Let boding figns, from all the quarter'd fphere,
Trouble its brow, and terrify the year.
6. That night let darknefs in his realm replace;
Erafe it from the rolls of time, erafe.
7. All through that lonefome night may filence reign,
Nor joy intrude, nor joy-awak'ning ftrain.
8. Curfe

Ver. 5. *ftain it*] in the margin, *challenge it* [a]; as its property.

the blacknefs [b] *of the day*] Whatever can be imagined moft difmal to make a day terrible and abhorred; fuch as deftructive ftorms, lightnings, thundrings, portents, &c. is, I conceive, comprehended in this phrafe.

Ver. 6. *darknefs*] It is a different word in the hebrew from *darknefs* in the foregoing verfe. We tranflate it chap. x. 22. *darknefs it felf*. It there denoteth the utter exclufion of every particle of light.

let it not be joined unto] The marginal verfion, *let it not rejoice among* [c], has an equal claim, is more poetical, and raifes the anniverfary of his birth to the the dignity of a public feftival: an honour from which he now wifheth it may for ever be degraded.

Ver. 7. *folitary*, &c.] That is, let none affemble, to converfe, or to rejoice, in that night. The Arabs had their meetings for converfation in the night [d]: and among the eaftern nations, in general, the night was devoted to feftivity [e]: It is fo ftill among the Moors in Barbary [f].

But

---

[a] Ἀντιποιησαιτο αὑτης, Theodot. Symmachus turns it by a ftill ftronger word, αγχιστευσαιω αυτω *let it redeem it in right of confanguinity*.

[b] בכירי *triftitiæ maximæ*; an augmentative noun fubft. from the verb בכר, in Syriac, *triftis fuit*: as כריך *a very cloudy, rainy day*, from כר, *to fhut up*. In the Syriac Teftament, Matt. xvi. 3. במי-איה *trifté* is the tranflation of στυγναζει lowring.

[c] יהד from חדה *to rejoice*.

[d] Pocock. *in carm. Tgr*. p. 106.

[e] Matt. xxv. 1, &c.   [f] Shaw's *Travels*, p. 203. 4to.

CHAP. III.   THE BOOK OF JOB.   13

8. Curfe ye that night in horror-moving rhime,
All ye, whofe proverbs execrate the time
When wretches, by difaftrous chance mifled,
Roufe fierce Leviathan from his oozy bed.
9. Starlefs and deep eclipfe its twilight be,
Still may it pine one glimm'ring ray to fee:

But

But Mr. Heath, following the learned Schultens, tranflates this member of the verfe; *Lo, that night may it be fruitlefs* [f], that is, Let there be no births in that night: a fentiment full of horror, but withal fublime; not too outrageous for *the fpeeches of one who was defperate* [g]; perfectly anfwering the expectation raifed by the fignal of attention, *Lo*, and correfponding well to the feftivity [h] mentioned in the latter claufe.

That night be childlefs; let no human birth
Break the fad filence with the voice of mirth.

Ver. 8. *their mourning*] In the margin, *leviathan*.
Let them curfe it, that *curfe the day*
Of thofe who fhall awake [i] *leviathan.*

To *ftir up*, or *awake*, Leviathan [k], is reprefented chap. xli. 8—10. to be inevitable deftruction: It was natural to mention fuch a terrible cafualty, in the ftrongeft terms of abhorrence; and to lament thofe who fo miferably perifhed, with moft bitter imprecations on the difaftrous day. Job here calleth for the affiftance of fuch language, to execrate the fatal night of his nativity.

Ver. 9. *Let the ftars*, &c.] Either thofe whofe aid he had juft invoked, are introduced uttering thefe execrations; as Schultens fuppofes: or Job himfelf borroweth their ftyle and manner.

---

[f] *galmúd*. It fignifies in Arabic, *a fmooth, flinty* rock: and is ufed, metaphorically, of flocks and camels which are become barren through age. *Schultens*.

[g] Ch. vi. 26.

[h] The Arabians celebrated the birth of their male children with feafts, dances, and fongs. Pococke. *Spec. Hift. Ar.* p. 160.

[i] עֲתִידִים עֹרֵר, a periphrafis of the future tenfe, in the Syriac idiom. Vid. Schaaf's *Lex. Syr.* p. 441. In profe, indeed, the prepofition ל is prefixed to the infinitive mood in this phrafe; but was omitted by our author, probably, for the fake of the metre.

[k] Moft probably the Crocodile. See the notes on Chap. xli.

But see no glimm'ring ray, nor morn's fair eye,
Half-op'ning, twinkle on its fadden'd sky.
10. That guilty night fulfill'd my mother's throe,
And gave me being but to give me woe.
11. Ah! why not bury'd in the womb? or why
Not favour'd, recent from the womb, to die?
12. Why did the midwife-knee the birth receive?
Or the full pap its fatal nurture give?
13. Else I had lain, at ease, in sleep profound,
In peaceful chambers of the cavern'd ground,

And

Ver. 10. *it shut not up*, &c.] Nothing could shew the distracted state of his mind more forcibly, than such a sentiment as this: His distress had overset reason.

Ver. 11, 12. *Why*, &c.] The pathos in these interrogations very much resembles the distress, which is described in so natural and moving a manner in *Oedipus Tyrannus*:

Ιω Κιθαιρων, &c.   Ver. 1404, &c.

Ah! why, Cithæron, did thy shades receive
Me, or, receiving, not forthwith destroy?
That I had never in the walks of men
Appear'd; the hapless progeny of man.
O Polybus, O Corinth, &c.

Ver. 11. *from the womb*] *in the womb*[1]. Jerem. xx. 17. *Because he slew me not in the womb; that my mother might have been my grave*, &c.

Ver. 13. *For now I should have been still*, &c.] He feels himself miserable: Is it strange, he should wish to be out of misery? Can the clearest hopes of future happiness extinguish these natural desires in the best of men? Death appeared to him his only deliverance: Is it strange that he should passionately long for that deliverance? that he should speak of it with transport? and dwell upon the idea of this negative happiness?

---

[1] LXX. ὁ κοιλια.

14. And sweetly rested; with a princely train,
Whose burial mansions load the desert plain,
15. Vain works of Kings! and fill'd with wealth as vain!
16. Or like th' abortive, I had ne'er begun;
Or, not less happy, ne'er beheld the sun.
The still-born infant's lot had been my own,
A nameless being, and a grave unknown.
17. O land desir'd! where tyrants scourge no more,
Where chiefs repose, and statesmens toils are o'er:
18. The captive's home, who, slumb'ring on his clod,
Hears not the cruel voice nor sounding rod.
19. There

Ver. 14, &c. *With kings,* &c.] This beautiful panegyric, on the grave, contains a fine oblique satire on ambition and avarice.

counsellors of the earth] This is but another appellation for a sovereign, or supreme magistrate; Isaiah ix. 6.

desolate places] sepulchral Grottos [m]; such as those superb monuments of the kings of Thebes [n], which Bp. Pococke saw: Or the famous pyramids, some of which were, probably, older than the times of Job [o]

who filled their houses, &c.] their sepulchral mansions. Is. xiv. 18. *All the kings of the nations lie in glory, every one in his own house.* The sepulchres of the kings of Judah had great treasure deposited in them [p];

Ver. 16. *as an hidden,* &c.] This refers to the first of the two wishes ver. 11. *why died I not in the womb.*

Ver. 17. *the wicked*] let it be observed once for all, that *the wicked* and *the oppressor* are, in this book, terms of the same import. chap. xv. 20.

Ver. 18. *the oppressour*] *the task master* [q]. The account given us of the treatment of the christian slaves in Mequinez, is a lively comment on this passage:
"Their

[m] Prælectiones, p. 87. n.
[n] They are cut in the rocky mountains, on the west side of the Nile; over against Carnack, the ancient Thebes. *Description of the East.* vol. i. 97, &c.
[o] Greaves *on the Pyramids.* p. 41.
[p] Whiston's *Josephus.* vol. i. 517.
[q] Or *driver.* chap. xxxix. 7.

19. There great and small are undistinguish'd mould,
And there the slave's among the free inroll'd.

20. Why o'er the wretched must the day-star roll,
Who nauseate life in bitterness of soul?

21. Who wait the coming of the king of fears,
Who seek the ruthless dart his hand uprears,
Impatient seek; as greedy misers toil
For treasure bury'd in the rocky soil?

22. And when the grave appears, with sparkling eyes
Spring and in rapture seize the blissful prize.

23. Why

" Their respective guardians, or task-masters, deliver them over at night, as
" so many sheep, to another; who is appointed to take charge of all: who se-
" cures them in one house till next morning, and then they hear the doleful
" echo of *come out to work*." '

Ver. 20. *Wherefore*, &c.] These inquisitive expostulations are the beginning of that striving with his Maker, which increases to great boldness in the progress of the poem.

Ver. 21, 22. *Which long for death*, &c.] The utmost power of eloquence is here exerted; to give us an adequate idea of the distress of the speaker: five different words, rising one above the other in significancy', are employed; to express how welcome death would be to him. He even falls into a rapture at the thought of a dissolution, which fills every human breast with horror. The image from avaricious men, in search of hidden treasure, is astonishingly great.

' Account of South-West Barbary. p. 115.

' (1) הכה, *long for*; it denoteth the continuance of desire under delays of the desired good. Hab. ii. 1.

(2) חפר *dig for*; it signifies eager persevering activity to obtain what we desire.

(3) שמח *to rejoice*: this word importeth a pleasure that has no trouble mixed with it, being a metaphor from a smooth reed.

(4) גיל, *joy*, expressing itself by leaping; or rather dancing in a ring, after the eastern mode.

(5) ישיש, *to be in rapture*: it is used for the vivacity and sparkling appearance of the eye, caused by an excessive flow of spirits, in the war-horse. ch. xxxix. 21. See the Comment. of *Schultens*.

CHAP. III.   THE BOOK OF JOB.   17

23. Why muſt I breathe, who ſee no gleam of light;
Whom God environs with deſpair's black night?
24. My daily meal but deepens all my groans,
And like the burſting ſluice I pour my moans.
25. Ah boding fears! I ſuffer'd what I fear'd;
Soon as divin'd, the dreaded ill appear'd:
Still trembling, ſuff'ring, I'm allow'd to know
No eaſe from terror, nor one pauſe in woe.

CHAP.

Ver. 23. *Whoſe way is hid*] by *his way* he means his preſent condition[s]: which he compares to that of a man, who is ſhut up in a ſtrong and dark priſon[t]; out of which there is no poſſibility of eſcape. He could neither ſee the reaſon why God had caſt him into this deplorable ſituation, nor any probability of his deliverance from it.

Ver. 24. *before I eat*] It is in the hebrew, *before*[u] (in the preſence of) *my meat*. The light of his food renewed his diſtreſs; becauſe it was the means of prolonging a miſerable life: or becauſe, as Mr. Peters ingeniouſly conjectures, it brought to his remembrance thoſe happy hours when *his children were about him*[x].

Ver. 25, 26. *For the thing which I greatly feared*, &c.] The expreſſions are much too ſtrong to repreſent the ſtate of his mind in his proſperity: He was under no apprehenſions of a calamitous change; *Then I ſaid, I ſhall die in my neſt*[z]. But upon the ſudden deſtruction of his fortunes and family, he preſaged, no doubt, ſome evil to his perſon: when that *thing which he feared, came upon him*[y]: his alarms, no queſtion, were increaſed: he dreaded ſome new blow. at this very time, it is likely, he apprehended an addition to his afflictions from the unkindneſs of his friends.

Ver. 26. *I was not*, &c.] Mr. Heath's tranſlation is, I think, more juſt to the meaning of the ſacred poet: *I have no more eaſe, my tranquillity is clean gone, neither have I any more reſt: but terror cometh.*

[s] Iſaiah xl. 27.
[t] לפנו *coram.* Vid. Noldium.
[x] Chap. xxix. 18.
[u] Lamentat. iii. 7, 9.
[z] Chap. xxix. 5.
[y] Chap. ii. 7.

D

CHAP.
IV.
1, 2.   The Temanite reply'd: To speak our sense
Shall we presume, and hazard the offence?
But whom can silence hold, or doubt suspend,
To truth unfaithful or displease a friend?

3, 4.   Not such the strain, when grief attentive hung
On the wise lessons of thy pow'rful tongue:
Affliction's palsy'd arm was strung by thee,
The tott'ring step confirm'd and feeble knee;
What numbers, in the conflict half subdu'd,
Arouz'd to courage, strong in patience stood!
5. Now touch'd thyself, and thine the suff'ring part,
Maz'd and unmann'd thou faintest with the smart.
6. Should

CHAP. IV.

The overthrow of Job, so nearly resembling the judgements of God on some notoriously wicked men, had raised in the minds of his three friends a suspicion of his moral character: His intemperate complaint strengthened their suspicion. The following reply kindles a flame of controversy, which spreadeth through the far greater portion of the poem. That part of the dispute, on the ways of God, in which *he* and *they* are engaged; is the means employed by the poet to work up his discontent to its highest pitch: The other part, managed singly by Elihu, is contrived to remove the embarrassment, and to prepare him for submission. Both parts carry on the design of the poem; which is first to expose, and then to cure that discontent.

This address of Eliphaz has the appearance of friendship. But several strokes, and the tenor of the whole, too plainly shew, that he supposed the afflictions of his friend to be punishment of preceding guilt.

There is an air of majesty and authority in the eloquence of this speaker, which, I think, clearly distinguisheth his manner from that of Bildad and Zophar.

THE BOOK OF JOB.

6. Should not thy piety, beneath the rod,
Inspire a noble confidence in God?
And conscious virtue, by its glorious pow'r,
Fill thee with prospect of salvation's hour?

7. A just man perish? innocence o'erthrown?
Name the strange instance; in what climate known?
8. But sinners thus, if I these eyes believe,
Fit harvest of the crimes they sow receive.

9. A

Ver. 6. *Is not this*, &c.] The original is a period divided into two members, and may be translated thus;
Should not thy piety [a] *be thy confidence* [a]*?*
And [b] *the uprightness of thy ways, thy hope?*
The words may be construed a friendly admonition to recollect his religious principles, and to support himself by the clearness of his conscience. On the other hand, they may import that no good man would fall into *despair* under affliction, as he had done. There is an appearance of art in this ambiguity.

Ver. 7, 8. *who ever perished*, &c.] Those expressions, also, may be understood as a consolatory argument; to confirm the hope which conscious integrity should inspire. " Good men are sometimes chastised severely for their faults, but not " destroyed: calamities which end in *destruction*, are the portion of the wicked " only [c]." On the other hand, his meaning might be; " calamities like " yours being the lot of wicked men only, some wickedness of yours must needs " have brought these calamities upon you." here then we have another instance of artful ambiguity.

Ver. 8. *They that plow* [d], &c.] This general proverbial maxim is applied in particular to *oppressors*; in Prov. xxii. 8. *He that soweth iniquity shall reap vanity* (misery) *and the rod of his anger shall fail.*

---

[a] In the Hebrew, *thy fear:* which signifies the *fear of God*, or piety; chap. xv. 4.
[a] כסל. it is used for *confidence in God*, Psf. lxxviii. 7.
[b] The construction in the original is embarrassed by the dislocation of the ו, *and:* place it at the beginning of the sentence; all then becomes clear. See a like dislocation of כי *for* in Psal. cxxviii. 2.
[c] Prov. xxiv. 16. Psf. cxl. 11.
[d] Ατης αρυρα θανατοι εκκαρπιζεται, *The plowed field of sin produceth death.* Æschylus, Septem. c. Theb. v. 607.

D 2

20   THE BOOK OF JOB.   CHAP. IV.

9. A furious ftorm, th' Almighty's angry breath,
   Rufh'd down, and fmote them with enormous death.
10. At once was ftill'd the rav'ning lion's roar,
    The fierce black lion's growl was heard no more:
    One blow difarm'd the weaned lion's jaw,
11. The ftrong ftout lion mourn'd his famifh'd maw,
    And perifh'd: The mad lionefs was flain,
    Her whelps were fcatter'd o'er the fandy plain.
                                              12. But

Ver. 9. *By the blaft*, &c.] Deftruction, fudden, terrible, and vifibly from God, is here reprefented by the image of a furious tempeft.

Ver. 10. *The roaring*, &c.] His own deferts furnifhed him with thefe apt emblems of oppreffion, in its various kinds and degrees of power and rapacity. But wherefore does he fingle out this particular fpecies of wickednefs; and reprefent the vengeance it had brought on fome great tyrannical families, well known to himfelf? Is not this more than an obfcure hint, that he fufpected his friend to have committed crimes of this fort; and to be now in imminent danger of perifhing by them?

the fierce lion] *the black lion:* fo Bochart tranflates it, according to the import of the hebrew word^e. Oppian tells us, he himfelf faw lions of this colour: and Pliny affures us, there were lions of this fort in Syria.

Ver. 11. *The old lion*] *The ftout lion*. The name in the original^f denoteth a lion of extraordinary ftrength. It is the fame word that is ufed, Prov. xxx. 30. *A lion which is ftrongeft among beafts*. In one of the poems in the *Arabian Anthologia*^g it is ftyled a fierce lion: " We attacked them with the impetuofity of a " lion^h, even the fierce lion."

The ftout lion's whelps] *The whelps of the lionefs*^i. It is plainly the fame word which Ezekiel employs chap. xix. 2. *What is thy mother? a lionefs*^k: — *fhe nourifhes her whelps*, &c.

---

^e שחל for the Syriac שחר *black*. Hieroz. p. i. 718.
^f *Laifh*.
^g Publifhed by the learned Schultens, in his edition of Erpenius' *Arabic Grammar*; p. 321.
^h *Laifh*. ^i לביא.
^k לביא. The points which the Maforites have affixed to it in that paffage of Ezekiel, to make it the feminine gender, is contrary, as Bochart obferves, to grammatical analogy: for if לביא had a feminine form, it muft be, לביאה; as נביא *a prophet*, נביאה *a prophetefs*. Hieroz. p. i. 719.

CHAP. IV. THE BOOK OF JOB.

12. But hear the word divine, to me convey'd,
Than pearls more precious, in the midnight shade;
13. Amidst th' emotions which from visions rise,
When more than nature's sleep seals human eyes.
14. Fear seiz'd my soul, the hand of horror strook
My shudd'ring flesh and every member shook.
15. For a strong wind with rushing fury pass'd
So near, so loud, blast whirling after blast,
That my hair started at each stiff'ning pore,
16. And stood erect. At once the wild uproar
Was

Ver. 12—16.] This vision, or supernatural dream, is introduced with wonderful solemnity: The darkness of the night, the horror, the whirlwind, the sudden stillness, the burst of glory, and the awful voice are circumstances, which of themselves, and by the order of their succession, have a powerful effect on the imagination of the reader.

Ver. 12. *a thing*] In the hebrew, *a word*, that is a divine revelation; Jer. xviii. 18. *The law shall not perish from the priest—nor the word from the prophet.* *a little thereof*] *precious instruction*[1] *from it.*

Ver. 13. *In thoughts from the visions,* &c.] The original means such thoughts as cast the mind into astonishment [m]; produced by the awful circumstances usually attending a divine vision.

Ver. 15. *a spirit*] *a wind*; or, according to the Chaldee Interpreter, *a whirlwind.* Chap. xxx. 15. II Sam. xxii. 11. Is. xxxii. 2. This word when used absolutely as here, never means, that I can find, *a good angel*; nor yet *an evil spirit*, except in I Kings xxii. 21. II Chron. xviii. 20.

---

[1] *Shemets,* the LXX render it ἐξαίσια, *extraordinary things.* The learned Schultens hath shewn, that in Arabic it signifies *a string of pearls*; and, metaphorically, *a series of instructive sentences.*

[m] שְׂעִפִּים. Aquila translates it παραλλαγαι *abalienationes;* a state of mind wherein a man loseth the possession of himself.

Was hufh'd; a Prefence burft upon my fight
(I faw no fhape) in majefty of light:
Voice follow'd, and celeftial accents broke,
Which in thefe terms their awful dictates fpoke:

17. " Is God arraign'd? abfolv'd man's finful duft?
" Lefs pure his maker? and his judge lefs juft?
18. " Lo he difcerns, difcern'd by him alone,
" Spots in the fanctities around his throne:
" Nor

Ver. 16. *It ftood ftill,* &c.] The tranflation I apprehend fhould be; *On a fudden a glorious appearance* ⁿ *prefented itfelf* ° *before mine eyes*; but *I difcerned not the form thereof*: that is, he could not perceive that the appearance had any determinate fhape: it was, probably, *a cloud of light*.

Ver. 17. *Shall mortal man,* &c.] The important inftructions conveyed in this divine vifion are; the abfolute rectitude of God, the exceeding imperfection of human virtue, and the impiety of arraigning the juftice of his moral government.

more juft, &c.] The manifeft defign of Eliphaz, in relating this vifion, was, to fix a divine cenfure on the latter part of Job's fpeech; and to warn him againft falling into fuch querulous language any more: fince all complaint fuppofeth, that the complainant thinks himfelf injured by the party of whom he complaineth.

Ver. 18. *He put no truft,* &c.] One of the Greek interpreters turns it, *there is inftability* ᵖ *in his fervants:* his angelic minifters are not abfolutly perfect.

he

ⁿ *Temûnah.* The verb in Arabic fignifies, among other things, *to reprefent,* or act as fubftitute of, *another*; Caftell. Lex. Heptag. The noun is ufed, Numb. xii. 8. for fome glorious *vifible reprefentation* of God: we there render it, *fimilitude*; but the Septuagint, δόξα *glory.* See alfo Pf. xvii. 15.

° יִצַּב *ftetit, fuddenly prefented itfelf.* Horace ufes *ftetit* in the fame manner.
———— dexter ftetit ———— Sat. ii. 3. v. 38.

As I was about to jump into the river, to drown myfelf, the philofopher Stertinius fuddenly prefented himfelf at my right hand.

ᵖ Ἀσίξαιωτης, Symmachus.

" Nor trufts his noble minifters of flame,
" To yield him fervice unalloy'd with blame.
19. " Yet, innocent of blame fhall *man* be found?
" Tenants of clay and reptiles of the ground?
20. " Crufh'd like the moth, thefe beings of a day
" With unregarded wafte are fwept away:
21. " Their honours perifh, and themfelves defcend
" Fools to the grave and thoughtlefs of their end.

CHAP.

he chargeth, &c.] *in his angels he obferveth* ᵠ *failure*ʳ: *How much more* ˢ *in them that dwell in houfes of clay*, &c.

Ver. 19. *before the moth*] *like* ᵗ *a moth*. They are as eafily crufhed, as that feeble and contemptible infect.

Ver. 20. *From morning to evening*] They are cut off within the compafs of one day: A morning and evening are the boundaries of human life. In the firft ages of the world, as Mr. Pope obferves, there were no other diftinctions of time but by the light and darknefs; and the whole day was included in the general terms of the evening and morning. note on Il. xi. 119. fee Gen. i. 5.

they perifh for ever] they difappear ᵘ for ever from the world.

without any regarding it] The deftruction of mankind by death is not minded, or regarded, by the reft of the creation. This is only a rhetorical way of reprefenting, how infignificant a creature man is; compared with the higher orders of beings.

ᵠ *Jasim*, LXX. ισημαντι *he noticeth*. Our tranflators render it *to regard*, or notice, v. 20.

ʳ תהלה. the LXX render it σκολιον τι *fomething wrong*. Schultens proves from the Arabic, that it denoteth *flip* or *failure*. The expreffion is much too faint for the crime of the angels who finned and fell from their firft eftate. Nothing more feems to be meant than the imperfection of the moft exalted fpirits, in comparifon with the infinite perfection of the Deity.

ˢ Il.שע μαλλον, Symmachus. *quanto magis*, Vulg.

ᵗ לפני *inftar*. Vid. Noldium, p. 533.

ᵘ *Abad*. they are miffing, or loft. Deut. xxii. 3. *which he hath loft and thou heft found*. Job. vi. 18. *they* (the brooks) *go into air, and difappear*.

CHAP.
V.

Ver. 1. Be, now, complainant, the defendant fee.
Which angel will efpoufe thy daring plea?

2.   Learn, learn that mifery is the mulct of fin,
In mens own bofoms all their woes begin:
Revenge, or envy, hurries fools along,
Purfu'd by death, to cruelty and wrong.

3. Such

CHAP. V.

Ver. 1. *Call, &c.*] *call now, verily* there is one who will anfwer thee. The learned Schultens is the firft, if I miftake not, who obferved, that *call* and *anfwer* are here law-terms; the former denoting the action of the complainant, the other the part of the defendant, as in chap. ix. 16. xiii. 22.

Eliphaz confidered the complaints of his friend as an arraignment of providence. He now ironically bids him renew the charge, and referreth him to the foregoing vifion for an anfwer.

to which of the faints, &c.] *To which of the holy* beings, &c. that is, the angels*. Thofe exalted fpirits know themfelves to be fallible: which of them, therefore, will countenance thee, in juftifying thy felf and complaining againft God?

Ver. 2—7. *For wrath, &c.*] He refumes his pofition, that men *reap what they fow*: their fufferings are the fruit of their own criminal paffions *y*. He produceth another example in fupport of this principle: and traceth up the matter to its fource in a fixed law of providence, which hath ordained natural evil to be the punifhment of moral. Obferve, by what cautious gradations this fpeaker opens his uncharitable judgement of the cafe of his friend.

the foolifh man—the filly one] Thefe are terms, in fcripture, for impious and wicked men*ᶻ'* marking them as perfons of a ftupid underftanding and feduced
by

---

* ה *verily.* So this particle frequently fignifies, as Schultens hath abundantly proved. Vid. Comment. p. 1:4.
ˣ קְדֹשִׁים   See Daniel iv. 17.   ʸ Prov. i. 31, 32.
ᶻ Prov. i. 7, 32.

3. Such I have feen with rooted verdure tow'r,
I curs'd his beauty in its profp'ring hour:
4. The curfe came fudden, o'er his Eden fpread,
Crufh'd by the public hand his children bled:
5. Himfelf, a loaden fruit tree, fenc'd around
With pow'r's thick terrors in oppreffion's ground,
Was plunder'd: for the thievifh defert pour'd
Her famifh'd vagrants, and his wealth devour'd.

6. Think by their corrupt paffions. The firft, *foolifh*, is applied by the prophet Zachariah to an oppreffive ruler, chap. xi. 15, 16.

wrath—envy] Thefe paffions are fpecified, becaufe thefe are two principal fources of injuftice and cruelty [b].

Ver. 3. *I curfed [c] his habitation*] I marked it as devoted to deftruction. he defcribeth the tragical ruin of this wicked man's family and fortunes in the following fourth and fifth verfes.

Ver. 4. *They are crufhed in the gate*] The fenate-houfe, which was alfo the court of judicature, was over or near the gate of the city [d]. he glances, no doubt, at the tragical end of Job's children: though, fomewhat to cover his meaning, he fpeaks of being cut off by *human* juftice.

there is none to deliver] This phrafe denoteth a calamity which is inevitable: it is particularly applied to the judgements of God [e]; and is equivalent to that good old faying of Homer,

——Θιοθεν δ' εκ ις' αλεαθαι Odyff. π. 47.
There is no efcaping from God.

Ver. 5. *Whofe harveft*, &c.] He had compared the oppreffive man of power to *a tree*, olive or palm, *ftriking root*, ver. 3. he now takes up the image again, and extends it; reprefenting the deftruction of his wealth, by the wild Arabs pillaging

---

[b] Gen. xxxvii. 11, 20, 28. I Sam xxii. 17—19. I Kings, xxi. Pf. cvi. 16—18.
[c] אבן Ezra viii. 20. *All of them we e marked out by name.* See alfo Amos vi. 1. Mr. Heath.
[d] Job xxix. ver. 7, &c. xxxi. 21. Prov. xxii. 22.
[e] Pf. vii. 2. l. 22.

6. Think not these changes from the dust arise,
Nor seek their origin below the skies:

7. Man is to sorrow born, if man offend,
As surely as the spiry flames ascend.

8. Instead

pillaging this guarded tree of all its fruit. the harvest of a tree is its ripened fruit ᵉ. he has his eye, I suppose, on the incursions of the Sabeans and Chaldeans related chap. i. 14—17.

the thorns] the hedge of thorns representeth the means of security and defence, with which power is armed.

The robber ᶠ] The thievish inhabitants of the deserts: These pilfering Arabs not only robbed the husbandman of his seed-corn, and made depredations on the fields of ripe corn, but they likewise treated the fruit trees in the same manner; stripping the vines, for instance, of their grapes, when they are ripe. See an ingenious book, intituled, *Observations on divers passages of Scripture*, &c.

Ver. 6. *Although affliction*, &c.] *Verily affliction*, &c. Neither the afflictions of human life in general, nor the special calamities mentioned in the foregoing verse, spring from chance, or meer human agency; but from an established rule of the divine government; as it follows in the 7th verse.

Ver. 7. *Yet man*, &c.] *For man*, &c. The train of the discourse obliges us, I think, to understand his meaning to be; that men are born under a law, which subjects them to sorrow as soon as they become transgressors. Bp. Patrick's paraphrase of this verse is very concise and expressive: " Who (God) hath made it as natural to man to suffer (having offended him) as it is for the sparks to fly upward."

The sparks ᵍ] see the note ᵍ below.

ᵉ Job xiv. 9. *it will bud and bring forth an harvest* (of boughs, leaves, and fruit) *like a young plant.* קָצִיר is the bough of a fruit-tree laden with fruit. Pf. lxxx. 9, 12.

ᶠ עֲצֵי The Chaldee also renders it *robbers.* In Arabic, עצי in the 10th conj. is *expressus fuit*; the verb עצם signifies *to lay hands upon a person's whole substance.* Vid. Castell: *Lex. Hept.*

ᵍ בְּנֵי רֶשֶׁף In the other places of Scripture, where רֶשֶׁף occurs in the sense of *fire*, it denoteth *lightning:* the בְּנֵי רֶשֶׁף *the children of lightning* should, therefore, mean *its flashes.* but here they are said *to fly upward*; which cannot agree to lightning, as Mr. Peters hath observed. Most probably, therefore, the word was applied to any other flame.

CHAP. V. THE BOOK OF JOB. 27

8. Inſtead of murmur, with repenting tear
I'd leave my cauſe in God's all-gracious ear:
9. Whoſe acts are great, ſtupendous, and renown'd,
Which no thought fathoms and no numbers bound:
10. Who, pouring on the fields his genial rain,
Turns a burnt deſert into foodful plain:
11. Who lifts the lowly, from their duſt, on high,
And changes into ſong the mourner's ſigh.
12. But vaſt diſturbance on the plots he flings
Of ſhrewd ambition, and to nothing brings
13. Its deep-laid policy: He oft has caught
The wily in the wiles themſelves have wrought;

And

Ver. 8—16. *I would ſeek unto God,* &c.] Having proved, as he imagined, that the ſufferings of his friend were the juſt puniſhment of his guilt; he now recommends to him ſubmiſſive application to God for deliverance. To rouſe him out of his deſpair, and at the ſame time fix the conviction that his downfall was cauſed by his ſins, he ſets before him, in one blended view, the aſtoniſhing operations of divine providence;

  Ut redeat miſeris, abeat fortuna ſuperbis.   *Hor.*
  To raiſe the wretched, and pull down the proud.   *Roſcommon.*

Ver. 10. *Who giveth rain,* &c.] " In thoſe hot climates the ſpring is of ſhort duration : All ſummer the earth is without rain : every thing is burnt up, and the fields are turned into a deſert. But when the autumnal rains fall, a few plentiful ſhowers produce a ſudden reſurrection of vegetable nature; the paſtures are cloathed again with graſs, the trees are covered with green leaves, and all things aſſume a freſh and delightful aſpect [b]." Eliphaz here alludeth, I imagine, to ſuch a great and beautiful operation of providence; as a fitting emblem of its effecting a like wonderful tranſition, from a condition of deſpairing affliction to a ſtate of proſperity and joy.

[b] Dr. Ruſſel's *natural hiſtory of Aleppo.* p. 13, 14.

And winding craft, entangled unaware,
Is driven to stark confusion and despair:
14. They stumble in high noon, and feel their way
Through perplex'd darkness, in the blaze of day.
15. Thus innocence he saves from murd'rous wrong,
The weak thus rescues from the fierce and strong:
16. Thus hope to sorrow comes; and, dumb with shame,
Impiety no more blasphemes his name.

17. From Heav'n's rebuke what heav'nly blessings flow!
Happy who scorn not the reforming blow:
18. O scorn not thou; the same kind wounding hand
Its balm infuses, and applies its band.
19. Then ills on ills about thy path may swell;
In vain! his arm will every ill repel.
20. In famine fulness shall thy table cheer,
And war, wide-wasting, shake his harmless spear.
21. Rages the tongue of slander? undismay'd,
Walk thou in covert of Almighty shade.

22. When

Ver. 16. *Iniquity stoppeth*, &c.] Such examples of the justice and goodness of providence silence the objections of infidels, and the murmurs of all complainants.

Ver. 17—26. *Happy is the man*, &c.] As a further motive to repentance, he represents afflictions as divine remedies; and displays the blessings they procure to those who are reformed. But the description is too high for the usual course of things: The singular care of providence over the Abrahamic family seems to be the original, from which this beautiful picture of felicity was copied.

Ver. 21. *destruction*¹] ruin by calumny or false accusation; as appears from its connection with the scourge of the tongue. See Ezek. xlv. 9.

---

¹ Shod.

22. When beasts of mischief prowl, with smile behold
Thy clust'ring vineyard and thy crowded fold.
23. Thy foot shall be in covenant with the stone,
And furious dragons thy dominion own.
24. Know further; peace thy houshold reign shall bless,
And all thy councils crown thee with success.
25. Know also, that thy long-extending race
Shall multiply as grass before thy face:

26. And

Ver. 22. *destruction*[k]] *desolation*, by the incursions of lawless men and wild beasts. See Levit. xxvi. 22. Jer. v. 6. Ezek. xiv. 15. Pf. lxxx. 13.

famine[l]] extreme poverty, the effect of the incursions and depredations abovementioned. Accordingly it follows, *neither shalt thou be afraid of the beasts of the earth*. Hos. ii. 12, 18.

Ver. 23. *in league with the stones*, &c.] This sublime figure of speech may import protection in travelling. The sandals, which they wore, were a very slight guard to the feet, in the rough and stony ways of their mountains. compare Pf. xci. 11, 12.

the beasts of the field] In the foregoing verse he assures security to his vineyards, &c. from the depredations of noxious animals : here he engages for the security of his person; particularly from the various kinds of serpents, which infested the deserts of Arabia and rendered travelling dangerous. Deut. viii. 15. Pf. xci. 13. Gen. iii. 1.

Ver. 24. *shall not sin*] *shall not miscarry*[m]. The original word is a metaphor from skilful slingers, who never miss the mark : Judges xx. 16. *there were seven hundred chosen men, left-handed; every one could sling stones at an hair-breadth and not miss*[m].

---

[k] Sod.
[l] Caphan. c. xxx. 3. the word for *famine* v. 20 is רעב which signifies a *general dearth*. Gen. xii. 10.
[m] חטא, αμαρτανω. In the proverb cited from Aristotle by Erasmus (in his collection ch. 1 1. cent. 6. prov. 36.) αμαρτανω is used in this sense, τις αν ἑνος αμαρτοι; *who can miss the mark* " See Merrick on Psal. xxi. 3.

26. And thou all hoary to the grave be born,
As to its heap the mellow'd ear of corn.

27. Thus speaks our searching thought, instruction sure;
Apply, embrace it, and its good secure.

CHAP.
VI.
1, 2.   O for a balance pois'd with equal hand!
Lay all my sorrows there, 'gainst ocean's sand:

3. Light

Ver. 26. *grave* °] This is the term for the sepulchral grot in general; or else for the cells, bored in the walls of the sepulchral rooms, in which the coffins were put.

Ver. 26. *Thou shalt come*, &c.] An easy death in a good old age, worthy and respected character, and an honourable interment, are the ideas conveyed in this rural comparison.

Ver. 27. *We have searched it*, &c.] They had, it seems, conferred together on the case of their friend, agreed in their judgement of it, and concerted the plan of their discourse to him. Job, accordingly, addresseth his answer to them all.

CHAP. VI.

Job little expected so harsh a construction of his complaint; much less that his innocence would be called in question, and his very afflictions turned, by his most intimate friends, into an evidence of his guilt. This was too much to bear. His reply discovers the various turns and emotions of his mind, on this trying occasion: he apologizes, laments ᵖ, despises ᵠ, wisheth vehemently for death, protests his innocence ʳ, despairs ˢ, upbraids ᵗ, and sooths ᵘ. He apologizes again, and laments again ʷ. Then turning to God, He pleads with him ˣ, complains loudly of him ʸ, expostulates with him, and makes supplication to him ᶻ.

Ver. 2, 3. *my grief*—*and my calamity*] He means his afflictions, inclusive of

---

° קבר.   ᵖ Ver. 1—4.   ᵠ Ver. 5—7.   ʳ Ver. 8—10.
ˢ Ver. 11—13.   ᵗ Ver. 14—27.   ᵘ Ver 28, 29.
ʷ Ver. 30. and ch. vii. 1—6.   ˣ Ch. vii 7—10.   ʸ Ver. 11—16.
ᶻ Ver. 17—21.

ᵃ היתי. Bp Lowth renders it by *calamitas*, in his elevated translation of this paragraph. *Praelect.* p. 215. 8vo.

CHAP. VI.   THE BOOK OF JOB.   31

3. Light is the fand whereon the billows roll,
When weigh'd with all the forrows of my foul.
Ah! therefore, therefore, does my boiling woe
In fuch a vehemence of words o'erflow.

4. I feel, I feel th' Almighty's venom'd dart,
His arrows fire my veins, and drink my heart:
'Gainft me his terrors, fet in thick array,
War behind war, unbounded wrath difplay.

5. Brays

of their diftreffing impreffions on his mind: all thefe he would have to be put together in one fcale, and weighed againft the fand on the fea-fhore in the other fcale. This is only a poetical and pathetic manner of faying, his afflictions were infupportable; a confideration which in equitable judgement would at leaft excufe his intemperate complaint.

therefore my words are fwallowed up] *Therefore my words are vehement* [b]. Our Author's term is a metaphor from boiling water that runs over; and denotes exceffive lamentations [c].

Ver. 4. *The arrows of the Almighty—the poifon whereof*] The excruciating pains caufed by his inflammatory difeafe [d], may be fpecially intended by thefe ftrong expreffions; but not exclufive of his other calamities [e]. We may obferve, that *poifoned* arrows were ufed in war in thofe days. The metaphor in this paffage is founded on fuch a cuftom. The Chaldee Paraphraft, on Pf. lxiv. 4. alludes to this practice: For what is in the hebrew דרכו הצם (they bend *their bow to fhoot* their arrows) He renders,

כישחו גרריהון סמא
They anoint their arrows with poifon.

The terrours of God, &c.] The thick fucceffion of his paft calamities, and his apprehenfion of many more fufferings ftill to come, feem to be painted in this high colouring.

---

[b] לרע. I know of no warrant for our public verfion of this word.
[c] Schultens hath proved, from the Arabic, that this is the import of the word. See his *Commentary*.
[d] See the note on chap. ii. 7.
[e] *Like as an arrow which is fhot of a mighty archer, returneth not backward: even fo the plagues that fhall be fent upon earth fhall not return again.* II Efdras. xvi. 1(, comp. ver 13, 14.

52   THE BOOK OF JOB.   CHAP. VI.

5. Brays the full zebra? or does nature call
The beeve to bellow in his fodder'd stall?
6. Turns not the stomach from th' unfav'ry cate?
Can vapid froth a poignant gust create?
7. My soul your cordials loaths; as taste rebels
Against the viand whose corruption smells.

8, 9.   O that, indulgent to my earnest cry,
God would extend his thund'ring arm on high;
Unpitiful

Ver. 5—7. *Doth the wild ass*, &c.] The style here manifestly changes: it falls greatly below the elevation of the foregoing verses: a clear proof to me, that the poet now passeth to another subject, not capable of sublimity. I think he here lashes Eliphaz, for his harangue on the blessings of patience[f]; he characterises the whole speech as insipid, and highly offensive; wanting truth, pertinence, and charity.

Or loweth the ox, &c.] No wonder you complain not of the ways of providence, and have no feeling for me: You are in perfect ease: The very brute animals do not complain, when they are fed to the full. This seems to be the thought.

Ver. 6. *in the white of an egg*] Insipidness is plainly the idea intended. but it is not easy to fix the precise meaning of the hebrew words; which, on the authority of the Rabbis, are here rendered, *the white of an egg*[g].

Ver. 7. *The things*, &c.] *My soul*[h] *refuseth to touch: these things are like corruption' in my food.* The expressions in the first clause denote strong abhorrence: the other clause gives the reason for it. by *these things* are meant, I suppose, the things which Eliphaz had offered for his conviction and consolation.

Ver. 8—10. *O that*, &c.] The style riseth again. Reflection on the unkindness of his friends makes him break out in a vehement wish for immediate death: his wish is couched in terms of horrid grandeur.

---

[f] Chap. v. 17, &c.

[g] ריר חלמות. Schultens' interpretation is methinks too gross; *saliva somnoleutiæ, the rheum which runs out of the mouths of infants and old men in sleep.*

[h] נפשי, *my appetite*, as in Prov. xxiii. 2. *a man given to appetite*, בעל נפש.

[i] דוי. It signifies *disease* in the human body, Ps. xli. 4. *corruption* is the disease of food. Also, זדוה, in Deut. xxviii. 6c, is used for *disease*.

CHAP. VI. THE BOOK OF JOB. 33

Unpitiful his flaming trident throw,
And driving through its mark the mortal blow,
10. At once deſtroy me. In that horrid death,
Exulting hope ſhall ſpend my lateſt breath:
For never, never hath my faithful breaſt
The mandates of his holy will ſuppreſt.
11. What is my ſtrength? what beckons me to ſtay
Still ling'ring here, and hope ſome healing day?
12. Is my fleſh faſhion'd of unfeeling braſs?
My ſinews ſtubborn as the marble maſs?
13. In this weak waſted body, can I find
Recruit from one ſound vital left behind?

14. A

Ver. 10. *then ſhould I yet have comfort*] What comfort? not, ſurely, the meer ſatisfaction of deliverance from his ſufferings, and confounding calumny by his behaviour in that dreadful death. No, but a triumphing hope of felicity in a future ſtate. The ground of his hope follows, even the clear teſtimony of his conſcience: *for I have not concealed*, &c.

I would harden my ſelf] *I would exult* [k].

For I have not concealed, &c.] This is the firſt time of his juſtifying himſelf, in direct terms; and he does it with modeſty.

The great Meſſiah prophet appealeth to God for his fidelity, in ſimilar language: Pſ. xl. 10. *I have not concealed thy loving kindneſs and thy truth, from the great congregation.* Was not Job, alſo, a prophet to his countrymen and ſubjects? compare chap. xxix. 4.

Ver. 11—13. *What is*, &c.] He falls from the heroic ſtrain, into the ſoft and tender. His deſpair of recovery is oppoſed to the hopes which Eliphaz had given him.

Ver. 13. *Is not my help*, &c.] *Verily* [l] *there is no help for me within me: and vital*

---

[k] *Afulledah.* LXX. ηλομην, *I would leap.* The word occurs no more. Schultens, guided by the Arabic, makes it a metaphor from a generous horſe; who ſtrikes the ground with his foot, when he is in high ſpirits. See his *Commentary.*

[l] אם certé, omnino. See Noldius, p. 86, and Schultens' Comment. p 90, 124.

F

14. A friend the sorrow of his friend should feel,
Relieve by pity, and by counsel heal:
Else, void of bowels, and too hard for tears,
No arbiter of human woes he fears.
15. My brethren fail me, like the floods which roar,
Down the steep hills with temporary store:
16. Thick

vital vigour [m] *is driven out of me.* he had no resource of hope, in any symptoms of some strength remaining in his wasted body.

Ver. 14, &c. *To him*, &c.] He proceeds to upbraid his three friends, with having failed him in his time of greatest need.

The public translation of this 14th verse is, I think, just to the original; and yieldeth an excellent moral instruction, very proper to introduce the reproof that follows.

but he forsaketh, &c.] He that does not shew pity to his afflicted friend, stands not in awe of that Great Being, who, as Sophocles excellently says,

Is the dispenser both of smiles and tears [n].

Ver. 15—20. *brooks*] or, *torrents* [o]. This simile is exquisitely beautiful, considered as a description of a scene of nature in the deserts of Arabia. But its principal beauty lies, in the exact correspondence of all its parts to the thing it is intended to represent. The fulness, strength and noise of these temporary streams in winter, answers to the large professions made to him by these men in his prosperity: The drying up of the waters, at the approach of summer, resembles the failure of their friendship in his affliction: and the confusion of the thirsty caravans on finding the streams vanished, strongly illustrates his feelings; disappointed as he was of the relief he expected in these mens friendly counsels.

---

[m] רהושיה, *vital vigour*, Mr. Heath. it signifies, says he, *subsistentia, aliquid permanens*; somewhat that is durable and operative, *virtue* in the sense of *ability*.

[n] Sophoclis Ajax, ver. 383.

[o] The *beds* of those winter rivers are also called *torrents*: They are deep vallies between high rocks of granite marble. Bp. Pococke saw several of them perfectly dry, in his journey to mount Sinai in the month of April One, in particular, which he passed through, is a quarter of a mile broad. *Description of the East* vol. i. p. 139—142.

16. Thick with the vernal thaw their torrents grow,
And foam impetuous with diffolving fnow.
17. Anon, the fury of the fcorching beams
Drains their full channels, and imbibes their ftreams:
18. Short and more fhort the fhrinking currents run,
Steal into air, and perifh in the fun.
19. Parch'd Sheba looks, and Tema's thirfty bands
Hope the cool waters in the diftant fands:

20. They

Ver. 16. *Which are blackifh*, &c.] Thefe ftreams are firft formed by the *autumnal* rains: The warmth and rains of the *fpring*, melting the ice and fnow on the mountains, increafe them: They then rufh down into the vallies, in a large body of turbid water; and affume the appearance of deep rivers.

Wherein the fnow is hid] The *fnow rufheth violently into them* [p].

Ver. 17. *they wax warm*] *they flow* [q], like a tide.

Ver. 18. *are turned afide*] *are fhortened* [r]. They run fhorter and fhorter; as the fun continueth to beat on them, and their fupplies from the mountains fail.

They go] *they afcend*: that is, they are exhaled. Pf. cxxxv. 7. *he caufeth the vapours to afcend.*

into nothing] into empty *fpace*, chap xxvi. 7. *he ftretcheth out the north over the empty place*; that is, the air.

Ver. 19. *Tema—Sheba* [s]] Thefe were the caravans, that went from Arabia Felix with merchandife to Egypt: Their road lay through Arabia Petræa,

Job's

---

[p] יַעְלְמוּ. St. Jerom turns it, *irruet*; which is the very fignification of the word in Arabic, as Schultens hath fhown in his note on this verfe.

[q] יְזֹרְבוּ. It occurs no more. Its fignification both in Chaldee and Arabic is, *fluere, diffluere, effluere*. Michaelis renders it, from the Arabic, by the ftronger word *æftuare*. One of its derivatives in that language fignifies *a cataract*. Lowth's *Prælect.* p. 151. n. 2. Michaelis *in Prælect*. p. 75. Caftell. *Lex. Hept*.

[r] לְפַת. In Ruth iii. 8. it is ufed of a man's *drawing up* his legs in a fright, as he lay on his bed.

[s] *The troops of Tema* were a caravan of Ifhmaelites: for *Tema* was a fon of Ifhmael. The inhabitants of Mecca were Ifhmaelites. *Sheba*, the other caravan, were alfo inhabitants of Arabia Felix. The Queen of Sheba was the queen of that country.

20. They come; they view, confounded at their truſt,
Where foam'd their floods, a ſmoth'ring vale of duſt.
21. Alike my truſt in you; illuſion all!
Friends while I ſtood, but ſtarting at my fall.
22, 23. Aſk'd I or gift or ranſom? or implor'd
Your arm to ſave me from the lifted ſword?
24. Candour is all I aſk; with candour taught,
I'm mute; I never will defend a fault:
25. Whom ſhould a juſt rebuke, well-tim'd, diſpleaſe?
But what conviction in harangues like theſe?
26. Have

Job's country. The yearly caravan which goes from Grand Cairo to Mecca, in Arabia Felix, paſſeth the ſame way.

Ver. 21—29. *For now*, &c.] Our great author was maſter of the various ſorts of ſtyle: He has already given us ſpecimens of the ſublime, the pathetic, and the proverbial manner. His language now, to the end of this chapter, is plain but nervous; familiar, but not low; in no reſpect injurious to the majeſty of his poem.

Ver. 22, 23. *Bring unto me*, &c.] He ſpecifies theſe inſtances, as the ſevereſt trial of friendſhip. The Arabian Poet profeſſeth his friendſhip in much the ſame language:

I fought for you againſt your enemies:
I was bound for you, if you were in debt,
and redeemed you'.

Ver. 25. *How forcible*, &c.] *Wherefore ſhould right words be grievous*"? He replies to the introduction of Eliphaz' ſpeech, *If we eſſay to commune with thee, wilt thou be grieved? Words* here mean *reproof*"; and *right* ſignifies *juſt* and *ſeaſonable*: for in thoſe two qualities the rectitude of reproof conſiſts.

what doth your arguing, &c.] What guilt does it convict me of?

Anthologia, p. 577.

' So our tranſlators turn the verb *nimrats*, in I Kings ii. 8. *a grievous curſe*: that is, exaſperating reproaches. compare II Sam. xvi. 7, 8.

Prov. xxix. 19. *A ſervant will not be corrected by words*: that is, reproofs.

26. Have ye caball'd for this? and thou their chief?
At founds to quarrel, breath of hopeleſs grief?
27. Cruel! you wound the fatherleſs; you bend
The bow of ſatire at your bleeding friend.
28. O come, vouchſafe to view me; can you trace
Guilt's evident confuſion in my face?
29. Review my plaint, nor call rebellion mine;
Again review, its innocence will ſhine:
30. Was ſin upon my tongue? yet moral ſenſe
In me too dull to notice the offence?

CHAP.
VII.
Ver. 1. What elſe but ſorrow is the time of man;
A hireling's life his predetermin'd ſpan?

2. As

Ver. 27. *You dig a pit for your friend*] *You ſet upon your friend*[x]. You wound his reputation; and endeavour to make him odious, by inſinuating that he is wicked.

Ver. 28. *be content*, &c.] *be pleaſed to look upon me*; I *alſo look you in the face*[y]: *am I guilty*[z]? Do you perceive any ſigns of guilt in my countenance?

CHAP VII.

Ver. 1—6. *Is there not*, &c.] Theſe verſes appear to me in cloſe connection with the laſt verſe of the preceding chapter: He had there ſaid, *was there iniquity in my tongue*, &c. He could perceive nothing criminal in his wiſhing for death.. He now argues, that the common afflictions of life would juſtify ſuch a wiſh; much more his inſupportable miſery.

---

[x] ברה. In the ſecond conjugation in Arabic it ſignifies *impugnavit*, to ſet upon; alſo *to render deteſtable*. Caſtell. *Lex. Hept.*

[y] ועל פניכם LXX. ενωπιον επι προσωπα υμων.

[z] אבוב. It ſignifies *to be guilty* in Prov. xxx. 6, and *a falſe matter* in Exod. xxiii. 7. is *a bad cauſe*.

2. As the tir'd swain pants for umbrageous eve,
   To rest from labour and his hire receive;
3. So I — but I am destin'd to sustain
   Long months of woe, and tedious nights of pain:
4. Laid on my pillow, soon I wish to rise;
   O when will midnight gloom forsake the skies?
   I toss from side to side; and tossing still
   Morn eyes me, as she climbs her eastern hill;
5. A mass of putrefaction, shrowded o'er
   With ulc'rous wounds, and worms, and dirt, and gore.

6. My

Ver. 1. *an appointed time*ᵃ] that is, an appointed time of affliction ᵇ: so the word signifies in Dan. x. i. compare ver. 14.

Ver. 2. *a servant—an hireling*] The two terms are to be joined, *an hireling servant*; or labouring man. he reasons from analogy: rest and wages are the justifiable desire of the wearied labourer; ease and death equally so of the miserable. The comparison is carried no further, as the judicious Schultens hath observed.

Ver. 3. *So—*] He was going to say, *So I pant for death*: but recollecting that the comparison bore no proportion to his case, he breaks off abruptly; and expatiates on his own peculiar sufferings. *So—but alas! I am made to inherit*, &c.

Ver. 4. *and the night be gone*] *but the night*, or rather *the evening, is prolonged* ᶜ. Time seems to a person in pain and distress to move very slowly.

Ver. 5. *my flesh*, &c.] see the note on chap. ii. 7. What a tragical object is here presented to our view! a living corpse. Mr. Maundrell, in his description of the ten lepers whom he saw at Sichem in the holy land, remarks;
"The

ᵃ נצב. The verb both in Syriac and Chaldee is *voluit*; and is used of the will and appointment of God in Dan. iv. 17. Heb. 14.

ᵇ The septuagint version is, πυρατηριον *a trial*.

ᶜ *madad* it signifies in Arabic, *extendere, et augere auctione continuatâ*: "I should not have wished that my life should be prolonged," says the Arabian poet Tograi. Pocock. *Carm. Togr.* ver. 43.

CHAP. VII. THE BOOK OF JOB. 39

   6. My days, alas! how rapid they have pass'd!
     The threaded shuttle never flies so fast:

                                                   My

"The whole distemper indeed, as it there appeared, was so noisome; that it might well pass for the utmost corruption of the human body on this side the grave."

with worms ^d] Whether the *elephantiasis*, Job's disease, is attended with this dreadful symptom; I must leave to the determination of the faculty. The distemper with which Antiochus Epiphanes was smitten seems parallel, in several particulars, to that of Job: "A pain of the bowels, that was remediless, came upon him, and sore torments of the inner parts: So that the worms rose up out of the body of this wicked man, and while he lived in sorrow and pain, his flesh fell away, and the filthiness of his smell was noisome to all his army^e."

clods of dust] or *dirt*, for want of bathing; which is so necessary, and so much practised, in the east, to keep the body clean. There is, however, no authority, but that of the Talmud and some Rabbis, for rendering the hebrew word *clods*: perhaps the version should have been, *the putrefaction^f of the grave*^g.

become loathsom ^h] *is putrefied*, viz. by his ulcers.

Ver. 6. *a weaver's shuttle* ⁱ] He compares his life to a web: the days which composed it, are the threads: the work is God's; who determines the measure of every man's life. retrospection on time, that is passed away, makes it appear, to a man in misery, very swift; and past happiness as nothing. his days seemed now to him, to have gone off faster than a manufacture of the loom.

they are spent without hope] *they are consumed without a thread*; or *for want of*^k
                                                                 a thread;

---

^d *rimmah*, properly *corruption breeding worms*. Exod. xvi. 20.

^e II Maccabees ix. 5, 9. Compare Job xix. 17, 20. xxx. 17, 18, 27.

^f גוּשׁ or נגוּשׁ. The verb in Arabic signifies, *ebullivit; ebullitio* would, I think, well express the fermentation of a body that is corrupting in the grave. Vid. *Anthologia*, p. 365. ver. 3. See also Castle's criticism on this word, in his *Lex. Hept.*

^g *The dust* is used for *the grave* ver. 21. of this seventh chapter, and ch. xxi. 26. *They shall lie down alike in the dust, and the worms shall cover them*. See also ch. xvii. 16.

^h וַיִּמָּאֵס] *fut. niph. à* מאס; which, in the 5th conjug. is used, in the Arabic Psalter, of the putrefaction caused by ulcerous sores, Pf. xxxvii. 5. מאס, in Arabic, is rendered by Golius *dilatatum fuit vulnus*.

ⁱ ארג. St. Jerom renders it by *tela*, *a web*; *my days are passed away swifter quam a texente tela succiditur*, than a web is cut off the loom by the weaver.

^k באפס] *through failure*, or *want of*, Prov. xiv. 28. *Through want of people is the destruction of a prince.*

My web is finifh'd. No remaining clew
(Such hope were folly) fhall the work renew.
7. O think, my life is but a breath: its good
A flitting vifion not to be review'd:
8. Shewn to the world; ere men can look me round,
Thy glance but ftrikes me and I am not found.

9. A

a thread [1]; to carry on the work, or to begin a new web. he means, there was no hope of the continuance of his life (though Eliphaz had flattered him with fuch a hope) any more than that he fhould live his days over again.

Ver. 7—21. *O remember*, &c.] Defpairing to make impreffion on the hard hearts of his three friends, he turneth to God; with whom he pleadeth for a mitigation of his fufferings. His firft plea is the exceeding fhortnefs of life: which he expreffeth in a very ftrong and beautiful manner, in this and the following verfe. Such a brief exiftence ought not, furely, to be made fo wretched. *wind*] compare Pf. lxxviii. 39. and lxxxix. 46, 47 [m].

fhall no more fee good] In the original, *mine eyes fhall not return to fee good*. Life is fo fhort, that it fcarce allows time to take a fecond look at the few enjoyments in it. The thought is fomewhat fimilar to that of our own great Poet,

—fince life can little more fupply,
Than juft to look about us and to die.   *Effay on Man.*

Ver. 8. *fhall fee me no* more] The hebrew is, *fhall not gaze* [n] *upon*, or *contemplate me.* My ftay in the world is too fhort for men to look me over.

Thine eyes, &c.] He means not a meer look of obfervation, but an effective look: The effect is, I *am not* in the land of the living. What a fublime idea does the Pfalmift give us of fuch a look Pf. civ. 32. *He looketh on the earth, and it*

---

[1] הִקְוָה. Schultens remarks that it fignifies a *cord*, in Jof. ii. 18. I may add, that the verb in Arabic imports, *to twift a cord with divers threads*; and that the derivative noun means *a thread*: alfo, in the Targum on Ifaiah lix. 5, 6. קוֹרֵי are *the threads* in a fpider's web.

[m] רוּחַ. It might have been tranflated *a breath*, as in chap. ix. 18. *He will not fuffer me to take my breath.* Alfo chap. xix. 17.

[n] שׁוּר is to look attentively on a thing, chap. xxxvi. 21. *Remember that thou magnifie his work, which men beheld* (gaze upon) See Jer. v. 26. Hof. xiii. 7, in the original.

9. A morning-mift, foon vanifh'd out of fight,
Is man, defcending to the world of night
10. Ne'er to return: his houfe no more will own
The voice forgotten and the ftep. unknown.

11. O tort'ring thought! I will not now control
Th' intolerable anguifh of my foul:
Give, give, my tongue, th' unruly paffion vent,
In bitternefs of heart I will lament.

12. Am I a flood, or furious beaft, whofe rage
Thy mounds muft humble, and thy terrors cage?

13. Ah!

it trembleth. Whofe look (fays the Apocryphal Efdras) *drieth up the depths, and indignation maketh the mountains to melt away*°.

Ver. 9, 10. *As the cloud*, &c.] Man gone into the invifible world, never to return hither, is the fubject of the comparifon: The thing, to which he is in this regard compared, is a cloud that is vanifhed: unfubftantial in its compofition, tranfient in its duration, it difappears, and is never more feen. He alledges this as another reafon, why his exiftence here fhould not be made miferable.

to the grave] *Sheôl*, the world of death, or the invifible world: See the APPENDIX to thefe notes *Numb.* II.

He fhall return, &c.] This fentiment, and the affecting manner of expreffing it, fpreads a folemn fadnefs over the mind of every thinking reader.

Ver. 11—16. *Therefore*, &c.] The foregoing reflections caft him into an agony of impatience: he lofeth all felf command; and refolves to give his tongue full liberty to expoftulate with his maker on this ufage of him. Thus his ftriving with God gradually increafeth.

Ver. 12. *Am I a fea or a whale*, &c.] He complains, that God treated him as

° B. ii. chap. viii. 23.

13. Ah! whenfoe'er my aking eyes I clofe,
And hope the anodyne of fweet repofe;
14. Dream, on thy errand fent, dire forms uprears,
And fhakes my foul with vifionary fears:

15. Death,

as though he were fome furious tyrant; whom the moft fevere inflictions muft reftrain from breaking the bounds of juftice, and fpreading deftruction among mankind.

a fea] The hebrews called any large body of water *a fea* [p]. Their prophetical writers gave this appellation to the river *Nile* [q]; fo did the Arabians [r]. The learned Michaelis [s] thinks that by *the fea* here Job meant the *Nile*; which though it be the caufe of Egypt's fertility, by its overflowing the lands, yet when it rifes beyond a certain height becomes an inundation [t]: It then does great damage, by carrying away large portions of the banks, deftroying fometimes towns and villages near to it [u]; and by not retiring at the proper time for fowing the corn [w], threatens a famine.

a whale] rather, perhaps, *a crocodile*. The author's word is *tannin*. It muft mean here fome terrible animal, which but for the watchful care of divine providence would be very deftructive. Our tranflators render it *the dragon* in Ifaiah xxvii. 1. where the prophet gives this name to the king of Egypt: *he fhall flay the dragon, that is in the fea*. The *fea* there is the river Nile, and *the dragon* (*tannin*) is, I fhould think, *the crocodile*. Compare Ezek. xxxii. 2.

Ver. 13. *thou fcareft me with dreams*] Thefe terrifying dreams were the effects of his inflammatory difeafe [x]. If I remember right, the account of the Guardaloupe lepers, publifhed fome years ago, mentions this fymptom as one circumftance of their fufferings.

---

[p] The *dead fea, the fea of Tiberias*, &c. which are only great lakes.
[q] Ifaiah xxvii. 1. Ezek. xxxii. 2.
[r] The Nile is named *a fea*, fays Michaelis, in the Koran, Sun. vii. 12. xx. 39. xxviii. 6.
[s] *Not. in Prælect.* p. 183.
[t] Pocock. *Defcription of the Eaft*, vol. i. p. 200.
[u] Vanfleb's *Prefent State of Egypt*, p. 36.
[w] Pocock. *ubi fupr.*
[x] See the note on chap. ii. 7.

CHAP. VII. THE BOOK OF JOB. 43

15. Death, even by the ſtrangling cord, were bliſs
 To breathing in a ſkeleton like this.
16. Behold my putrid frame ; it was not caſt
 A ſubſtance through whole centuries to laſt:
 O ſtay thy hand, a dying mortal ſpare;
 The bubble life will quickly burſt in air.
17. What is this mortal? that thy lofty thought
 Beſtows ſuch honour on a thing of nought,
18. As to purſue him with a jealous eye,
 Viſit each morning, and each moment try?
19. How long ere thou refrain? awhile refrain,
 And yield me a ſhort breathing pauſe from pain.
          20. That

Ver. 15. *my life*] In the margin *my bones*. His fever, his pain, his affright-ing dreams, and the anguiſh of his mind had waſted him to a ſkeleton. See chap. xix. 20. and xxx. 17, 30.

Ver. 16. *I loath it*, &c.] I am putrifying[y], I ſhall not live always; for my days are a vapour[z]. he repreſents himſelf as a dying man : and urges this conſider-ation as another plea for the removal, at leaſt the mitigation of his pains : there was no need of theſe tortures to diſpatch him.

Ver. 17, 18. *What is man*, &c.] Here he alledgeth, that it is doing too much honour to man ; for ſo great a Being to employ ſo much time, and thought, and power, in animadverting on his failures. A perſon in diſtreſs catches at every ſhadow of an argument, to move compaſſion.

---

[y] בְמָאס, it is the ſame word which in ver. 5. is turned, *to become loathſome*. *loathſomeneſs* is the ſecondary idea : the primary one is, the ſwelling and burſting of the ſkin by a ſore when it ſuppurates. Vid. Schultens' *Orig. Heb.* v. i. 312. and *Comment.* in Job p. 193. col. 2.
[z] הֶבֶל, In ſome Greek verſions, ατμὸς. In the *Targum* on Pſ. xc. 9. it is uſed for *the breath of the mouth* : and it ought to have been rendered *a vapour* in Pro.. xxi. 6. *The get-ting of treaſures by a lying tongue, is a vapour toſſ'd to and fro of them that ſeek death*.

G 2

20. That I have sinn'd, all-watching Pow'r, I own;
But can my sins alarm th' eternal throne?
Why am I made the object to employ
Thy shafts? the nuisance, which thou must destroy?
21. Why, rather, will not gentle mercy plead,
Cancel my trespass, and my healing speed?
Lest when the morrow's dawning beams appear,
Thy mercy seek me and I am not here.

CHAP.

Ver. 20. *I have sinned*, &c.] He acknowledgeth himself a sinner: *for what man liveth, and sinneth not?* But can human infirmities affect the safety or repose of God? 'This is his argument, which none but a distracted man will think valid.

what shall I do unto thee] what can *I do against thee*[a]? Mr. Heath turns it, *what injury can I do to thee?*

O thou preserver of men] rather, *O thou observer*[b] *of men*. The character of God as *the preserver* of men hath no propriety here; where he is represented as an avenger of sin.

a burden to myself] This translation follows the printed hebrew text. But the reading seems to have been originally, *a burden to thee*[c]; which corresponds better with the foregoing clause, *why hast thou set me as a mark against thee?* For the sentiment appears to be; "I am indeed guilty of failures, inseparable from imperfection: But what *crime* have I committed; that I am become so offensive to thee, as to be singled out for a peculiar object of thy displeasure?"

Ver. 21. *why dost thou not pardon*, &c.] This is his concluding plea: it is a. pathetic address to the divine mercy.

---

[a] לך chap. viii. *If thy children have sinned against him* (לך) Olympiodorus remarks that the hebrew is, τι σοι ἐλαψα *what injury have I done thee?*

[b] נצר. LXX. ὁ ἐπισταμενος τον νουν των ἀνθρωπων *that knowest the mind of man.* The word signifies in the Ethiopic language, *intuitus est diligenter.*

[c] עליך, so it was in the copy which the Septuagint translated from, επι σοι φορτιον *a burden upon thee.*

THE BOOK OF JOB.

CHAP.
VIII.
1, 2. Then Bildad his opinion spoke: How long,
How far, will rage this tempest of thy tongue?
3. Can the Great Source of justice and of pow'r,
Who darts the lightning, and bestows the show'r,
Perverse his evil and his good apply,
And bless and punish by a rule awry?
4. What if thy children, daring to rebell,
Just victims of their own transgression fell;
5. Wouldst

CHAP. VIII.

Ver. 1. *Then answered Bildad*, &c.] Stung by Job's reproaches, but unmoved by his distress, and regardless of his protestations, this respondent calls the whole a storm of passion. With this spirit he enters upon his answer: wherein he supports the principle of Eliphaz; that all sufferings are punishments, and necessarily imply preceding guilt. He advances, in defence of that position, two arguments: the first is taken from the justice of God[d], the other from the sentiments of the ancient sages[e]. These are the outlines of his short discourse, which he fills up with amplification[f].

It is hard to say, what peculiarity distinguisheth this orator, and marks the habit of his mind. Had he spoken no more, I should have set him down for a blunt man of a middle rate genius: But it must be owned, that his second speech[g] is full of fire. However, we may venture to affirm; that he has neither the dignity of Eliphaz, nor yet the violence of Zophar.

Ver. 3. *Doth God pervert*, &c.] These men had no conception, that, in the government of an infinitely wise Being, sufferings might be made to answer many other valuable purposes besides those of justice: and therefore, that God might, without repugnance even to his goodness, lay heavy inflictions on a man of undissembled piety. But they were to learn this truth from the issue of the present affair: and to teach us this lesson, was, I apprehend, one subordinate design of the *history* of Job.

Ver. 4. *If thy children*, &c.] He instances that tragical event as an example
of

---

[d] Ver. 3.   [e] Ver. 8—13.   [f] Ver. 4—7. and ver. 14—22.
[g] Chap. xviii.

THE BOOK OF JOB. CHAP. VIII.

5. Wouldſt thou, betimes, with fervency ſincere,
   In humble ſtyle, beſeech his fav'ring ear,
6. His ear would liſten, and his arm, for thee
   If pure, ſoon rouſe its ſaving energy:
   A ſplendor round thy virtue he will caſt,
7. Twilight at firſt, but blazing noon at laſt.

8. What ſpeak our fathers? Go, I pray, inquire;
   Search hoary wiſdom, up from ſire to ſire:
9. For we the birth of yeſterday, and gone
   Like ſhades projected by the ſinking ſun,
10. Know nothing. Will not their experience teach?
    Their parables the faith of ages preach?

11. " Can

of divine juſtice. If there be any thing characteriſtical of the manners in the preſent ſpeech, it muſt be this paſſage: Eliphaz had but gently touched that tender point, in a covered hint[h]. But this man, in violation of all civility and decorum, mentions it bluntly in the moſt open terms. He has the grace, however, to qualify the cruel reflection, by putting it in the form of a ſuppoſition, *If*, &c.

Ver. 5. *If thou wouldeſt ſeek,* &c.] He thinks to ſoften the foregoing uncharitable inſinuation, by giving the afflicted father hope of his own reſtoration: but on what condition? on the condition of his ſincere repentance and humiliation. The very condition was an inſult; for it ſuppoſeth him to have continued hitherto a contumacious ſinner.

Ver. 6. *the habitation of thy righteouſneſs*] Thy reformed family. compare chap. xi. 14, 15.

Ver. 10. *Shall they not teach thee,* &c.] The ſayings of wiſe men are reſpectable. But their maxims have no authority beyond the arguments which ſupport them, in a matter of ſpeculation; or beyond the facts on which they are grounded, in a matter of experience.

---

[h] Chap. v. 4.

CHAP. VIII.   THE BOOK OF JOB.   47

11. " Can the fedge flourifh, or the paper-reed,
" When Nile forgets to overflow his mead?
12. ", Ere the feythe enter, fee their verdure fall
". Before all herbage, the contempt of all.
13. " So the ungodly perifh: change, like this,
," Shall blaft the profligate's deceiving blifs."
14. Deceiving

Ver. 11. *The rufh—the flag*] *The flag*, or *fedge*[l], is, I apprehend, the long grafs in the meadows of the Nile : *The rufh*[k], probably, means the famous *papyrus, the paper reed*; which formerly[1] grew in thofe meadows. Thefe marfh vegetables required a great deal of water: when therefore the Nile rofe not high enough for its ufual overflow, they perifhed fooner than any other plants. What a juft image of tranfient profperity is this!

can the rufh grow, &c.] We are entertained here with a fpecimen of the manner of conveying moral inftructions, in the oldeft times of the world. They couched their obfervations in pithy fentences, or wrapped them in concife fimilitudes; and caft them into metre to fix them in the memory. Bp. Lowth mentions the words of Lamech to his two wives [m] as the oldeft example of this kind on record.

Ver. 13. *So are the paths of all*, &c.] This is the moral, or application of the comparifon. It belongs to thofe only, whofe impiety and vices are notorious to all the world. Bildad, therefore, abufeth this faying of the wife, in applying it to Job; whofe life was irreproachable.

the hypocrite's] *the profligate man's*; fo Mr. Heath turns it. I cannot find that the hebrew word ever fignifies a *hypocrite*. It is here coupled with *forgetfulnefs of God*, which is a fcriptural phrafe for impiety [n]. it means evidently an oppreffive ruler, in chap. xxxiv. 30. *a profane fcoffer*, in Pf. xxxv. 16. And our tranflators render the abftract fubftantive [o] by *profanenefs*, in Jer. xxiii. 15. where it imports a contempt of the divine threatnings, and confidence in committing the moft immoral actions.

---

[l] אחו. It is wrongly tranflated *meadow* in Gen. xli. 2, 18.
[k] גבא. LXX. παπυρος.
[1] Dr. Shaw informs us, that there is fcarce any of it now to be found in the country; the inhabitants having continually rooted it up for fuel. *Travels* p. 406. 4to.
[m] *Prelect.* p. 52. 8vo.   [n] Pf. x. 4. L. 22.   [o] חנף.

14. Deceiving blifs! in bitter fhame it ends;
His prop a cobweb, which an infect rends:
15. Vain are his labours, and his leagues are vain,
Nor leagues nor labours fhall his houfe fuftain.
16, 17, To vulgar eyes a vigorous plant he feems,
Which throws out fuckers by the garden ftreams,
Verdant and gay, before the beam, awhile;
But the roots twine within a ftony foil:
18. The beam foon fwallows it: and, loft from earth,
The parent foil denies th' inglorious birth:
19. Behold

Ver. 14. *Whofe hope*, &c.] The proverbial citation ended with the foregoing verfe. Here begins his comment upon it, which he continues to the end of the 19th verfe. He enlargeth firft, in this and the next verfe, on the vain hopes of thefe wicked men to perpetuate their greatnefs by powerful alliances, or by any other means whatfoever.

Ver. 16—19. *He is green*, &c.] He expatiates on their profperity and overthrow. The metaphors are taken from a *garden plant*, perhaps a vine; which he fubftitutes in the place of the *marfh plants*, the better to reprefent the fplendour of this wicked man's fortunes and his fatal cataftrophe.

Ver. 17. *about the heap*] *about a fpring* P; fo our tranflators turn it in Canticles iv. 12. *a fpring fhut up*.

the place of ftones] In the original, *the houfe of ftones*; which is a hebrew idiom for ftony ground ⁱ. *Seeing the place of ftones* is an animated phrafe for growing in a ftony foil, as Buxtorf explains it ʳ.

Ver. 18. *If ˢ he deftroy him*, &c.] Mr. Heath juftly refers this action to the fun, mentioned ver. 16. The plant endureth the fun, fo long as the fpring, that

---

ᵖ *gal.* It fignifies in the Syriac *a wave.* Vid. Syriac Teft. James i. 6. Jude ver. 13. גלה *gullah* is a *fpring.* Jofh. xv. 19.
ⁱ Thus *the houfe of thorns*, in the Syriac Teft. Matt. xiii. 22, is *thorny ground.*
ʳ Lex. Chald. Talm. vid. עין.
ˢ אם *when;* So our tranflators render it chap. vii. 4. xvii 16.

19. Behold his fatal period. In his room,
On the fame fpot a foreign plant fhall bloom.

20. Lo, God, impartial in his frown and fmile,
Nor hates the worthy nor befriends the vile:

21. Nor thee will leave, till laughter in thy eyes
Shall fparkle, and the hymn triumphant rife;

22. While on thy foes he pours eternal fhame,
O'erthrows the wicked and uproots their name.

CHAP.

that nourifheth its roots, continueth to flow: But when that is dried by the increafing heat, his parching beams deftroy the plant.

I have not feen thee] This is a ftrong manner of expreffing utter abolition and abhorrence. The figure is a bold profopopeia; but not more daring than that of Ovid, who puts a long fpeech into the mouth of the Earth, when fhe was burnt up by the chariot of the fun [t].

Ver. 19. *others grow*] other plants fhall fucceed to his place: that is, his eftate fhall pafs into another family. Thus the period clofes with the fame metaphor that began it ver. 16.

Ver. 20—22. *God will not caft away,* &c.] This is the inference which he draws from his preceding doctrine.

Ver. 21. *Thy mouth*[u], &c.] He had begun the period, ver. 20, in the third perfon, *Behold God will not caft away a perfect man,* &c. Such a fudden turn or of the ftyle to the fecond perfon is fpirited, and catches the attention by furprize; whether this addrefs to Job was ferious or ironical: If it was ferious, it was fo on fuppofition of his becoming a righteous man: If ironical, it was a cruel infult. As if he had faid, "The effect of God's regard for the upright, and deteftation of the wicked, will be, undoubtedly, deliverance of thee from thy affliction; and reftoration of thee to thy former profperity."

---

[t] Metamorph. lib. ii.

' צחק אחר: The Septuagint read צְחֹק, αλλοι (Alex. MS. αλλω) ακαθαρτοι.

[u] *The mouth being filled with laughter* denotes that fmile of joy which is fpread over the countenance in fome happy change of condition. Pfal. cxxvi. 2.

THE BOOK OF JOB.   CHAP. IX.

CHAP.
IX.
1, 2.   I know, Job answer'd, verily I know;
         Wrong from eternal justice ne'er can flow:
    3. How should a mortal stand, in judgement stand
         Adverse to God? how answer each demand?
         Answer one charge, if he, severely just,
         Tax with a thousand faults this thing of dust?
    4. Who safely can a strife with him prolong,
         Him, wisest, strongest of the wise and strong?
    5. Rocks from their bases leap before his frown,
         He, ere they feel it, hurls the mountains down:
                                                    6. Earth

CHAP. IX.

Job was exceedingly moved at hearing his complaints and defence represented as contention with God, and an arraignment of his justice. He now purgeth himself from that crime, in a most exalted strain of piety [w].

The train of his thoughts leads him to assert an undistinguishing distribution of worldly good and evil [x]: He instances his own case, in confirmation of it; falleth insensibly into complaint of hard measure from God [y]; and, at length, has the boldness to offer, on certain conditions, to dispute his cause with God himself in person [z]. Upon this he goes into a vein of pleading exquisitely tender [a]; and concludes with prayer, for a respite from his intolerable pains the little time he had to live [b].

Ver. 2. *I know it is so*] I know and acknowledge it to be an everlasting truth, that *the Almighty doth not pervert justice* [c]. But it does not follow, that the man whom he shall please to afflict is *therefore* a wicked man.

Ver. 5. *Which removeth the mountains*, &c.] This and the following verse are manifestly a description of an earthquake. During the terrible earthquake in
                                                                    Jamaica,

---

[w] Chap. ix. 1—21.   [x] Ver. 22, 23, 24.   [y] Ver. 25—31.
[z] Ver. 32—35.   [a] Chap x. 1—19.   [b] Ver. 20, 21, 22.
[c] As Bildad had alledged, chap. viii. 3.

CHAP. IX.   THE BOOK OF JOB.   51

6. Earth staggers from her seat, her pillar'd frame
   Trembles through terror of his dreadful name.
7. Aw'd by his thund'ring voice, the prince of day
   Shuts his broad eye, and veils his golden ray:
   And night's pale queen, with her attendant fires,
   Beneath his signet in eclipse retires.

8. King

Jamaica, 1692, the mountains were split, they leaped, they moved, they fell with prodigious loud noises, they were thrown on heaps[d]. In the great earthquake in the Island of Sicily, in 1693, which destroyed above sixty thousand inhabitants, rocks were loosened and thrown down: Two very high rocks, in particular, near Ibla, with all the trees growing upon them, were by the violence of the fall quite inverted; so that their tops stood upon the ground[e].

Ver. 6. *Which shaketh the earth*, &c.] These expressions seem to describe that kind of earthquake, in which the earth vibrates alternately from right to left: whereby mountains have been sometimes brought to meet, and clash against each other[f].

Ver. 7. *Which commandeth the sun*, &c.] He may, perhaps, here refer to that thickness and darkness of the air, which sometimes precedes, or accompanies, an earthquake[g].

It riseth not] *it shineth not*[h]. II Kings iii. 22. *The sun shone upon the water.* The disappearing of the sun, moon, and stars, by reason of the thickness of the air, is a circumstance mentioned in the account of the late eruption of mount Ætna in the year 1766[i].

---

[d] *Philosophical Transactions abridged*, vol. 2. p. 411, &c.   [e] Ibid. vol. 7. p. 149.

[f] Chambers' Dict. *Article*, EARTHQUAKE.

[g] The night and day, preceding the earthquake in Sicily Jan. 11, the air was overshadowed with darkness.

On the same Jan. 11. a black cloud hung like night over the magnificent city of Catanea in that island; presently the city sunk into the earth. *Philos. Transf. abridged*, vol. 2. p. 403, 406, &c.

[h] זרח *spargere radios.*

[i] *Universal Museum* for August 1766. p. 404.

THE BOOK OF JOB.   CHAP. IX.

8. King of the flood, alone the heav'ns he bends;
And in his cloudy car upon the deep defcends:
The roaring billows threaten earth and fky,
His wheels along the wat'ry mountains fly.

9. He form'd Arcturus and his fons, to roll
In bright fucceflions round the northern pole:

The

Ver. 8. *Which fpreadeth out the heavens*] *who boweth the heavens* [k]. The hebrew poets exprefs by this phrafe the defcent of thofe black heavy clouds, charged with thunder, lightning, rain, and wind, that are the prelude of a ftorm at fea. The ftorm itfelf, and the power of the Deity in conducting it, are reprefented in the next member of the period.

alone] This word is not fuperfluous, it afferts the unity of God, in oppofition to polytheifm.

the waves] *the high places*, or *heights*. Our tranflators render it *high places* in Deut. xxxii. 13. *He made him to ride on the high places of the earth*; that is, the mountains. *The high places*, or *heights, of the fea* muft therefore mean, its billows rifing to a vaft height in a ftorm. The prodigious fwell, agitation, and tumult of the fea, during an earthquake, may be referred to here. Both the heavens and the fea were greatly affected by the earthquake in Martinico, Aug. 13. 1766. About ten at night, we are told, the whole horizon was darkened; the wind blowing fiercely from the N. W. The clouds vomited torrents mingled with flaming fulphur: the waves, intermingled with the clouds, dafhed upon the coaft, and beat to pieces all the veffels in the harbour [l].

treadeth] or, as it is rendered Habbak. iii. 15, *walketh* [m]; where it is applied to the motion of the Almighty's chariot. The magnificent image of our author is diftinctly opened by the prophet: *Thou didft walk through the fea with thy horfes (the horfes of thy chariot) through the heap of great waters.*

Ver. 9. *Which maketh Arcturus*, &c.] Shepherds feem to have been the firft Aftronomers.

---

[k] נטה *to bow*. So our public verfion turns it in Pf. xviii. 9. In that pfalm, verfes 7—15 defcribe at large the fcene which is drawn in miniature by our author in this 8th verfe.

[l] *Martinico Gazette*, Aug. 21, 1766.

[m] דרך. It may denote a very rapid progreffive motion, as well as the verb הלך in Pf. civ. 3. *who walketh upon the wings of the wind.*

The vernal Pleiades his will perform,
And stern Orion wakes his wintry storm:
While, far below, the southern heav'n proclaims
His glory sparkling in ten thousand flames.
10. Wonders by him, and mighty deeds are wrought,
Beyond all number, and above all thought.

11. He

Astronomers. The pastoral life of the Arabs led them very early to observe the rising and setting of the stars, in relation to the changes of weather that ensued ⁿ. The heat of their climate obliged them to feed their flocks by night: and the clearness and beauty of their nocturnal sky drew their attention and admiration °.

Arcturus ᵖ, *Orion* ᑫ, *and Pleiades* ʳ.] It is uncertain whether the first, *Arcturus*, was any particular constellation, or the north pole with its surrounding luminaries, or the whole northern hemisphere. The next, *Orion*, probably means, in general, the stars which rise in winter: and the last, those which usher in the spring. chap. xxxviii. 31. *Canst thou bind the sweet influences of Pleiades? or loose the bands of Orion.*

The chambers of the South] the southern hemisphere ˢ.

Ver. 10. *Which doeth great things*, &c.] Eliphaz had produced this sublime character of the supreme Being ᵗ, as a ground of trust in him in the most distressing situations. Job's view, in repeating it, is, to shew that his afflictions ought not to be laid to *the justice* of God; but to be ranked among those acts of his providence, which confound all our reasonings. He, accordingly, subjoineth his own case as an instance of that kind; as well as a further argument, that he would not dare to contend with such a power.

ⁿ Pocock. *Specim. hist. Arab.* p. 7.

° Dr. Shaw tells us, that the sky in Arabia Petræa is usually clear. *Travels*, p. 438. 4to.

ᵖ עשׁ.   ᑫ כסיל.   ʳ כימה. See *the Commentary* of the learned Schultens; and Clodii *Lex. Heb. Select.*

ˢ חדר. It signifies properly, in hebrew, the most interior and private rooms in a house, Exod. vii. 28. Judges iii. 24. II Chron. xxii. 11. Prov. xxiv. 4. In Arabic, אנדראה denotes the under part of a wheel. Golii *Gram. Arab.* p. 269.

ᵗ Chap. v. 9.

11. He smote me, like a whirlwind in his courſe;
  Himſelf unſeen, but terrible his force:
  Again he ſmote; loſt in a boundleſs maze,
  My reaſon toils in vain t' explore his ways:
12. He ſeiz'd; who wreſts the ſeizure from his hand?
  Or, " wherefore was the deed," who dares demand?
13. God's formidable wrath will ne'er ſubſide,
  Till down he tread the banded pow'rs of pride.
14. I, then, ſhall I againſt a Pow'r ſo great
  Preſume to riſe, and ſtudy bold debate?
15. My cauſe, though juſt, I never would defend
  Were he the plaintiff, but a ſuppliant bend:
  16. Or

Ver. 11, 12. *Lo, he goeth,* &c.] I think, the tranſlation of theſe two verſes ſhould have been as follows;
Ver. 11. *Lo, he fell upon*[u] *me; but I ſaw him not:*
  He ſtrook[w] *me alſo, but I underſtood him not.*
  Behold, He ſeized[x]*; who can make him reſtore*[y] *?*
  Who ſhall ſay unto him, what haſt thou done?
He referreth to the ſuddeneſs and violence of his overthrow.

Ver. 13. *the proud helpers*] In the hebrew, *the helpers of pride*[z]. The proudeſt and moſt powerful combinations againſt the ſchemes of Providence can avail nothing.

Ver. 15. *Whom though I were,* &c.] *whom, though I am righteous*[a]*, I will not anſwer.*

---

[u] עבר עלי. It ſhould have been rendred by our tranſlators *to fall upon,* in Zech. ix. 8.
[w] יחלף tranſlated *to ſtrike through,* Judges v. 26. and Job xx. 24.
[x] יחטף ſee Judges xxi. 21. where it is engliſhed, *to catch.*
[y] מי ישיבנו *who ſhall cauſe him to return?* ſc. with the ſpoil.
[z] *rahab.* Symmachus turns it by αλαζονια *inſolence.* The ſeptuagint never, I think, tranſlates this word as a proper name.
[a] צדקתי tranſlated *to be juſt* in ver. 2. See Prov. xviii. 17.

CHAP. IX.   THE BOOK OF JOB.   55

16. Or should I bring the hardy action, he
Humble his greatnefs in refponfive plea;
I never would believe my voice had found
17, 18. Audience of him; who fmote me to the ground
With tempeft unprovok'd; and urges ftill,
Not fuff'ring me to breathe, with fharpeft ill,

19. Can

anfwer. Although I have a good caufe, and know myfelf to be innocent of wickednefs; I will not put in my defence againft him.

to my judge] *to my adverfary* [b]. Mr. Heath. The hebrew word, in a different conjugation, is turned *to plead together*, in Ifaiah xliii. 26. where it means the parts both of plaintiff and defendant. *Let us plead together: declare thou, that thou mayeft be juftified.* It feems here to fignify *to go to law*, to bring an action againft another.

Ver. 16. *If I had called,* &c.] If *I fhould call* [c], *and he fhould anfwer me.* The judicial ftyle is ftill carried on. *To call* evidently importeth here the action of the plaintiff; and to *anfwer,* the part of the defendant.

that he had hearkened, &c.] that he would give a favourable hearing to my plea. To ftand on my defence would provoke that power, which hath already, without any provocation, done fuch terrible things unto me; as it follows in the next verfe.

Ver. 17. *he breaketh me,* &c.] He refers to his paft calamities, and their effect in his prefent fufferings.

without caufe] This, methinks, is juftifying himfelf in pretty ftrong terms; not very confiftently with what he had been faying juft before. But, as the judicious Michaelis obferves [d], He muft be a trifler of a poet, who would reprefent a man in the diftreffes of defpair always talking confiftently.

---

[b] מִשְׁפָּטִי *in jus eunti mecum,* as Coccieus tranflateth it. Schultens remarks, that it is in the form of the third conjugation of the Arabians; which expreffeth a reciprocal action between two perfons. See his *Commentary.*

[c] קָרָא It anfwers to the Greek law-terms προκαλεμαι and κλητευω, which fignify to *cite* an adverfary before the proper magiftrate. Vid. Potter's *Archæl.* vol. i. p. 114.

[d] Not. in Prælect. Lowthi. p. 206. 8vo.

56   THE BOOK OF JOB.   Chap. IX.

19. Can force avail? th' Almighty shakes the rod:
Can justice? who shall be the judge of God?
20. Though just my cause, ev'n innocence must wear
A blush before him, if disputing there:
With him disputing, virtue's plea is vain;
The plea itself the pleader will arraign.
21. My heart, and surely my own heart I know,
Tells me I'm upright; yet my portion 's woe:
Woe is my portion, in severe degree,
And life is made a heavy load to me.

22. From

Ver. 19. *If I speak of strength,* &c.] Here he represents the peculiar hardship of his case; in that he had to do with an adversary, against whom it was impossible to vindicate himself although ever so innocent. Even to plead his innocence, in contest with God, would be criminal; as he complains in the next verse:

Though I am righteous[e], *my own mouth would condemn me:*
Though I am upright[f], *it would prove me perverse.*

Ver. 21. *Though I were,* &c.] *I am upright: do I not know myself*[g]*?* yet *I loath*[h] *my life.* Though my own heart witnesseth to my integrity, I am, notwithstanding, made so miserable that I am weary of my life.

───────────────

[e] אצדק so in ver. 15. *though I am righteous;* and ver. 2. *how should man be just,* or *righteous, against God.* When this verb signifies *to justify,* it is in the conjugation *pihel,* or in *hiphil.*

[f] תם *upright.* it stands opposed to *wicked* ver. 22. See Prov. x. 9. *he that walketh uprightly, walketh surely.*

[g] לא אדע נפשי omission of the interrogative ה is very common. Vid. Noldium.

נפש with the affixes forms the reciprocal pronoun *self, myself, thyself, himself,* &c. in Hebrew, Syriac, and Arabic. See Job xviii. 4. Jer. li. 14. Testament. Syr. in Matt. iv. 6. Schaaf's Lex. Syr. and Pocock. Carm. Tograi p. 230.

[h] אמאס rendred chap. vii. 5. *is become loathsom.* Its primary idea, in Arabic, is, *contabescere ulceratus:* thence the secondary ideas, *loathsomness, contempt,* and *abhorrence.* Vid. Schultens' *Comm.* p. 199, 207.

CHAP. IX. THE BOOK OF JOB. 57

22. From this strange fact I argue; that he blends
Righteous and wicked when his scourge he sends:
23. War, plague, and earthquake, with insulting sweep,
Th' unguilty in the mingling carnage heap:
24. Earth to the tyrant's fury is resign'd;
To shame, the princely fathers of mankind.
Is

Ver. 22. *This is one thing,* &c.] *This is a strange thing*[f]; that I, an innocent man, am forced to abhor my life: *therefore I said,* within myself[g], *he destroyeth the upright and the wicked.* he concluded from his own case, that *all things come alike to all: there is one event to the righteous and to the wicked.* Thus he introduceth, very naturally, the doctrine of an *unequal providence,* which he afterwards supporteth at large[h].

Ver. 23. *If the scourge,* &c.] *If the scourge slay suddenly, it will laugh at the trial of the innocent.* By the *scourge* is meant public calamities, war[i], for instance, pestilence, &c. which, involving all characters in one common destruction, are said, by a noble personifying figure, to *laugh* at the sufferings of the innocent.

Ver. 24. *the judges,* &c.] These being in contrast here with the *wicked* (that is a tyrannical ruler[k]) must mean good governors; who administer justice impartially to all. Thus *a man*[l] signifies one who has the virtues proper to the male sex; *a woman*[l], one who is adorned with the qualities becoming the fair sex: And a *king*[m] is a king indeed, who acteth worthy of his royal dignity. Of these good rulers he says, God *covereth their faces*[n]; that is, God treats them as condemned malefactors, overwhelming them in calamities, disgrace, and ruin; himself being one example of this melancholy truth.

If

---

[f] אחת *unicum,* a singular thing; which is without a parallel, for difficulty of solution. Vid. Pocock. in *Carm. Tograi* p. 204.
[g] Chap. xxix. 18. and ver. 17. of this ninth chap.
[h] Chap. xii. xxi. xxiv.
[i] Isaiah xxviii. 18.
[k] רשע it signifies *a deer of wrong* in Exod. ii. 13. In the book of Job, it generally means *an oppressor,* or *tyrant.*
[l] Eccles. vii. 28. See also, Prov. xviii. 22.
[m] Prov. xvi. 10.
[n] II Sam. xv. 30. Esther vii. 8. Jer. xiv. 3. Isaiah xxii. 17. Micah iii. 7. Mark xiv. 65.

I

THE BOOK OF JOB. CHAP. IX.

Is this not providence? if not, difclofe
From whom fuch intricate confufion grows.

25. My days have fpeeded with a courier's hafte,
A glance at pleafure, not allow'd to tafte;
26. Swift as a rufh-boat down the fwelling Nile,
Swift as an eagle darts upon his fpoil.
27. If fweet hope whifper, " thy lamenting tongue
" The ftyle of forrow fhall forget ere long;
" Thy

If not, &c.] If it be not God, who doeth thefe ftrange things; where and who is the perfon who doeth them [p]?

Ver. 25. *Now my days*, &c.] His own unhappy ftate being an inftance of that inequality, in the diftribution of good and evil, which he had been afferting; he naturally falls into a defcription of his miferable fituation.

are fwifter, &c.] *my days have been fwifter*, &c. *they have fled away: they have not feen good.* Time and enjoyment that are fucceeded by great mifery, appear as an inftant that is paft. This is what he reprefents by three expreffive images of celerity, which rife one above the other in beautiful gradation.

Ver. 26. *the fwift fhips*] in the hebrew, *fhips of cane* [q]; probably thofe light veffels, made of the papyrus, which the Egyptians ufed on the Nile [r].

Ver. 27. *If I fay*, &c.] *When* [s] *I fay* (within myfelf) *I fhall leave off my countenance* (this fad countenance) *and fhall look chearful* [t]. He endeavoured fometimes to raife in himfelf a pleafing hope of deliverance from his afflictions: But the number and circumftances of them bore down his courage, and funk him in defpair; as he laments in the following verfe. Compare Jerem. viii. 18.

---

[p] LXX. וו δι μη αυτος ετι, τις ετιν; *If it is not He, who is it?*

[q] אניות אבה which Schultens tranflates *naves papyraceæ*: For אבה fignifies, in Arabic, *reeds*, and *a place where the papyrus grows*; as he proves from the Arabian Lexicographers. Vid. his *Comment*.

[r] Such, no doubt, were the *veffels of bulrufhes* in Ifaiah xviii 2. See Shaw's *Travels* p. 437. 4to.

[s] אם *when.* Vid. Noldium.

[t] אבליגה. Schultens, in his *Origines Hebrææ*, has proved, that it fignifies, in Arabic, *to fhine out again*, as the fun after it hath been clouded. It alfo means, in the 1ft conjugation, *illuxit aurora*; and in the 2d, *lætitia perfudit*. Vid Caftell. *Lex. Hept*.

" Thy brow remove its cloudy veil, like morn,
" And placid smile thy open face adorn;
28. Then all my suff'rings rife; I sink with fear,
Despairing thy absolving voice to hear.

29. Yes, I am wicked —— wherefore waste I time,
In fruitless labour to disprove my crime?
30. Unsully'd as if wash'd in melted snow,
These harmless hands I never blush'd to show:
31. Yet drown'd in mire by thee I'm so impure,
Not my own garments will my touch endure.

32. Is

Ver. 28. *Thou wilt not hold me, &c.*] *Thou wilt not declare me innocent*[t], by removing my afflictions; which have fixed upon me the imputation of guilt. He had not the least expectation that God would appear at the close of this debate to vindicate his innocence.

Ver. 29. *If I be wicked*] *If* is inserted by our translators. The hebrew is, *I am wicked*. I must pass for a wicked person: I am treated as such by God, and condemned by men. All my labour, therefore, to clear myself will be to no purpose. He uttered this sentiment with a deep sigh, and not without indignation.

Ver. 30, 31. *If I wash, &c.*] *When I had washed myself with snow water; and made my hands clean in purity*[u]*: Then thou didst plunge me in a ditch, so that mine own clothes abhor me*[w]. *By washing himself, &c.* and *making his hands clean, &c.*

---

[t] תנקק it is equivalent to הצדיק *to justify, to acquit.* Exod xxxiv. 7. *that will by no means clear* the guilty.

[u] ב *purity,* or *pureness,* as in chap. xxii. 30. *it is delivered by the pureness of thine hands.* Compare Psal. xxvi. 6.

[w] תטבלני ... תעבוני. That learned and ingenious Critic Michaelis remarks; that in the ancient state of the hebrew tongue, both the future and preterite of its verbs were, probably, aorists, and were used, like the Greek aorists, for the past, present, and future times. *Not. in Prælect.* p. 78, 79. 8vo.

Thus

32. Is he a man my fellow? can we meet,
Parties in doubtful strife, at judgement's seat?
33. Who shall, as arbiter, between us stand,
To lay on both his reprehensive hand?

34. Let

&c. he asserts the purity of his heart and innocence of his life. Thus Zophar understood him " *Thou hast said my virtue is pure, and I am clean in thine eyes.*" The Psalmist also expresseth his own integrity, in terms somewhat similar; *I have cleansed my heart in vain, and washed my hands in innocency.*

Then *thou didst plunge me,* &c.] The meaning is, that his calamities caused him to be looked upon, by his intimate friends, as an abominable wretch, smitten of God and accursed. No protestations of innocence, no appeals, no defence whatever could overcome that prejudice against him.

mine own clothes, &c.] This circumstance is added, I imagine, as a heightning of the image of impurity; to represent more strongly the infamy, with which his character was blackened by his overthrow.

Ver. 32, 33. *For he is not,* &c.] In these verses he assigns another reason, why he laboured in vain to clear his innocence: in his case there could not be a third person, to sit as judge between him and his great adversary God.

we should come together, &c.] that is, come together to a tryal ˣ of our cause.

a daysman] Our Author's word doth not signify an umpire, but an authorised judge ʸ. It has this meaning, I apprehend, in Amos v. 10. where it is englished, *him that rebuketh: They hate him that rebuketh in the gate,* that is, the court of justice. compare Prov. xxiv. 23—25.

that

Thus in Deut. xxxii. 10. the hebrew futures are turned justly in the past time, *He found, he led, he instructed,* &c. And in Job v. 7. the hebrew future is englished in the present tense, *Man is born to sorrow.*

ˣ This is what the Greeks expressed by υπαγειν τω δικρι τις το δικαστηριον *to enter the cause into the court.* Potter's *Archæl.* vol. i. p. 113, 116.

הישפט is (1) the cause to be tried, ch. xxxiv. 4. (2) the trial itself, Prov. xviii. 17. Job ix. 32. (3) the sentence passed, Job xxxvi. 17. where, and in many other passages of Scripture, it implies the execution of the sentence.

ʸ מוכיח In Prov. xxiv. 25. it is englished *to rebuke,* viz. in a court of justice, by passing a just sentence on the guilty. For it is opposed to acquitting the wicked ver. 24. *He that saith unto the wicked, thou art righteous,* &c. *But to them that rebuke him* (למוכיהים) &c.

CHAP. X.   THE BOOK OF JOB.   61

34. Let him remove his rod, nor let the blaze
Of Godhead stun me with its dreadful rays;
35. Then fearless I would plead: but thus distrest,
All is confusion in my guiltless breast.

CHAP.
X.
Ver. 1.   Sick, sick of living, my complaint I'll loose,
I will the anguish of my soul effuse;

2. Will

that might lay his hand, &c.] The laying the hand on both parties implies coercive power to inforce the execution of his decrees. This no one could have over the Almighty: it was therefore vain to contend with him. *Mr. Heath.*

Ver. 34, 35. *Let him,* &c.] He doubts not but that he should be able to prove his innocence to God himself, provided he could debate the matter with him on equal terms. But alas! how soon hath he forgotten that worthy and devout resolution which he declared ver. 15.

his rod—his fear] by the *rod* he means his present afflictions; and by *his fear*; the tremendous circumstances usually attending the appearance of the Divinity.

it is not so with me] Mr. Heath turns it, *I am not sufficient* "*master of myself*". He was all in confusion: his pains and apprehensions deprived him of self-command.

CHAP. X.

Ver. 1. *I will leave my complaint,* &c.] In a freer version it would be, *I will let my complaint have dominion over me*; that is, I will not restrain it, but give it full liberty. The sentiment is the same as in chap. vii. 11. *Therefore I will not refrain my mouth,* &c.

---

* בִּי *satis.* So Noldius understands it in Judges xxi. 14. *They found enow for them.* Crinsoz renders it, in the verse before us, *dans l'etat où je me trouve—in my present condition.*

y עָצְרִי *tenes me, in my own power,* possessed of myself. Crinsoz, *je ne suis point à moi-même.* Vid. Noldium, p. 742.

z עָלַי אֶעֶזְבָה. The verb עזב signifies, as Schultens remarks, *to let go free;* in the proverbial phrase עָצוּר וְעָזוּב *he that is shut up, and he that is let go free.* The preposition עַל importeth *dominion,* in Gen. ix. 2. xxxvii. 8. Vid. Noldium.

THE BOOK OF JOB.   CHAP. X.

2. Will fay to God, condemn not me untry'd;
Ah! why from me my accufation hide?
3. Canft thou by arbitrary will be led?
Lay guilt's demerit on the guiltlefs head?
Hate thy own workmanfhip? and dart thy ray
On daring finners, who blafpheme thy fway?
4. Is man's grofs eye, and partial vifion, thine?
Live human paffions in the mind divine?

5. Is

Ver. 2. *Shew me wherefore*, &c.] It feems evident from thefe expreffions, and from what follows, that he wifhed not to refer the difpute between him and his three friends to God; but to argue his caufe *with* God himfelf. He wanted to know, what God had to lay to his charge; that he might put in his anfwer to it.

Ver. 3. *Is it good*, &c.] He argues here from the honour and intereft of religion. To treat him as a wicked man, who had led an innocent life, was giving reputation to the principles of infidels who deny a providence.

Ver. 4—7. *Haft thou*, &c.] The origin of our knowledge is from fenfation. we judge by appearances. fenfual paffions biafs our judgement. human life is fhort. we are obliged to ftudy characters, in order to know them: and are prone to ufe violent means, to force confeffion from fufpected perfons. But none of thefe imperfections can belong to an Eternal Being. God, therefore, had no need of fuch methods to difcover, whether Job was a wicked man. This is the argument in thefe verfes.

Ver. 8. *Thine hands have made* [a] *me*, &c.] His argument now is; that it looks like caprice, to beftow great fkill and labour on a work, and then, on a fudden and without juft caufe, dafh it in pieces. This is what he meant alfo in ver. 3. *is it good* .... *that thou fhouldeft defpife* (hate) *the work of thine hands?*

---

[a] עצבוני. This verb fignifies in Syriac, *conftringere, to tie together:* which alfo is its primary notion in Arabic, in which language, Schultens informs us, it is ufed particularly of the contexture of the human body. The word *together* expreffeth the conjunction of the parts when tied: the words *round about* denote the univerfal exactnefs of the work: and the word *fafhioned* conveys the idea of a thing complicatly framed.

5. Is thy exiſtence like a mortal's ſpan?
    Are thy years bounded, as the years of man?
6. That time and torture muſt to thee reveal
    Suſpected treaſon, which my wiles conceal.
7. Thy knowledge clears me; yet thy boundleſs might,
    By none evaded or by force or flight,
8. Deſtroys my frame; which thy own matchleſs art
    Faſhion'd with curious ties of part to part.
9. Remember, O remember, that like clay
    Whoſe ſhapes the workman's plaſtic will obey,
    My form thou mouldedſt from its earthy grain;
    And thou wilt crumble me to earth again.
10. O think of thoſe kind moments, when began
    Thy hands to ſketch the rudimental man;
    Curdled the milky drop, my limbs defin'd,
11. With fleſh and ſkin my tender ſubſtance lin'd,
    With ſinews brac'd, and fenc'd with ſolid bone:
12. Compacted thus, to natal vigour grown,

Thy

Ver. 9. *Remember*, &c.] Here he pleads the common mortality. He muſt ſoon die, as all other men; what occaſion then for ſo much torture to diſpatch him?

Ver. 10, 11. *Haſt thou not poured me*, &c.] Does not this beautiful deſcription, of the origin and formation of the human body, exactly agree with anatomy? Can the modern diſcoveries in that ſcience qualify a good poet to give a more juſt account of the principles of an embryo; and of the ſeveral ſtages of its growth to a perfect fœtus? Was not our Author, and Job himſelf, indebted to the Egyptians for their anatomical knowledge?

Ver. 12. *my ſpirit*] *my breath.* ſo our tranſlators turn it, in Chap. xii. 10. xvii. 1. The argument, in this and the foregoing verſe, is taken from God's creat-

ing

Thy care educ'd me, and thy favour crown'd;
And still thy pow'r upholds on living ground.

13. Yet, well I know, the secret of thy mind
Thefe evils, in referve, for me defign'd;
14. Refolv'd to follow me with watchful eyes,
Each fin to notice, and each fin chaftife:
15. If wicked, the predeftin'd woe comes down;
Righteous, I droop beneath thy fatal frown,
Full of confufion, and o'erwhelm'd with fcorn,
By all beholders, as a wretch forlorn.

16. Chac'd ing and providential goodnefs towards him; as not being confiftent with his prefent treatment of him, which he defcribeth with too great liberty of fpeech. ver. 13—17.

Ver. 13. *And thefe things*, &c.] *Yet thefe things thou didft treafure up*[b], &c. Here he finneth with his lips and chargeth God foolishly. By *thefe things* he means his calamities: and infinuates, that God had given him being with a fecret purpofe to make him miferable; and advanced him fo high to render his fall more terrible.

this is with thee] a phrafe, which denotes the fecret decree of God chap. xxiii. 14.

Ver. 14—17. *If I fin*, &c.] This is harfh language. He accufeth the divine government of extreme rigour. He alfo complaineth, that his piety had been of no benefit to him; and that, notwithftanding his humanity and juftice, he was purfued by God to deftruction, as though he had been fome lion-like tyrant. I believe, Elihu had his eye particularly on this obnoxious paffage. chap. xxxv. 2, 3.

Ver. 15. *And if I be righteous*, &c.] *though*[c] *I am righteous I cannot lift up my head*, &c.

therefore

---

[b] צָפַנְתָּ *thou didft lay up* (or treafure up) as in chap. xxi. 19. Prov. x. 14.
[c] וְ *though*, as in Ruth ii. 13. Vid Noldium.

16. Chac'd like a lion, hotly chac'd by thee,
   Thy plagues, stupendous plagues, were heap'd on me:
17. Jav'lins, on jav'lins hurl'd, the war renew,
   And woes succeeding woes my life pursue.
                                                18. Why

therefore see thou, &c.] If, with the ingenious Mr. Peters [c], we join to this clause the word which begins the next verse (rendred *for it increaseth*) the translation will come out easy and clear, as follows;

   And the spectator [e] of my affliction also insulteth [f].

In these words he complains of the gross affronts put upon him, especially by his three friends; in treating him as a wicked man on account of his affliction.

Ver. 16. *as a fierce lion*] that is, as though I were a fierce lion. compare chap. iv. 10. The allusion, in this and the following verse, is to that manner of hunting the lion, wherein the hunters, armed with spears and javelins, formed themselves in a ring about the beast; and threw their weapons at him one after another. By this image Job represents, in lively colours, the violent and rapid succession of his calamities.

And again, &c.] Mr Heath's translation is, *thou even repeatest thy wondrous strokes upon me.*

Ver. 17. *Thou renewest thy witnesses*, &c.] What have witnesses to do in the hunting of the lion? Our Author's word may be translated *weapons*, or *attacks*, or *troops* [g]. in any of these ways of turning it, the allusion to the chace will be preferred.

                                                Changes

---

[d] *Critical Dissert.* p. 200. 4to.

[e] רְאֵה *spectator*; a noun substantive in the regimen state, from the root רָאָה *to see.*

[f] וְיִנְאֶה the ו may be redundant, or be rendred *also*. Vid. Noldium. The verb is turned by the LXX. in Jer. xlviii. 29. (*Francfort edition*) by ὕβρις contumelia afficio. Our translators there english it, *he is proud.*

[g] עֵדִים The Syriac interpreter turns it here by זַיִן *weapons of war* (see Test. Syr. Joh. xviii. 3.) and the verb, in Arabic, signifies *ornare*. This very noun is used for *ornaments* in Ezek. xvi. 7. as Schultens remarks: it there indeed means *female ornaments*. but it is a general term for whatever is called *ornament*. armour and weapons are the dress of a warrior. In Arabic the noun also signifies *attack*; and *a body of men rushing to the attack*. Vid. Castell. *Lex. Hept.*

K

18. Why did I breathe? O happy I had been,
Had I this world of forrow never feen!
19. A being, and no being; from the womb
Hurry'd in midnight filence to the tomb.
20. Ah! 'tis a little, which of life remains;
O fpare that little, O remove my pains:
21. Ere, never to return, my foot defcends
To realms where death his horrid fhade extends:
22. Realms, which in fhades of dolefome darknefs lie;
Cold denfe obfcurity, without a fky;
Without a twinkling ftar, and where the light
Is one eternal noon of difmal night.

CHAP.

Changes and war] that is, *changes of war*; or fucceffions [h] of war. he means the war of the chace carried on by repeated attacks.

Thou reneweft] The hebrew word does not feem to denote *iteration* here; but rather, as the learned Schultens remarks, the producing fomewhat new, fomewhat never done before. fee Ifaiah xliii. 19. Such were Job's calamities, taken in all their circumftances. Never before was a perfon of his exemplary life fo overthrown.

Ver. 20. *that I may take comfort*] *that I may look chearful* [i]. it is the fame word that we met with chap. ix. 27. fee the note there.

Ver. 21, 22. *Before I go*, &c.] The original of this gloomy picture, drawn in the deepeft fhades of horror, is, I fhould think, the fubterraneous chambers of the fepulchral grottos. But if thefe verfes are a defcription of *Sheól*, as the learned

---

[h] חליפות The learned Profeffor Chappelow has obferved, that it is rendred *courfes* in 1 Kings v. 14. where it is ufed of Solomon's workmen, who wrought in Lebanon by turns, or in fucceffions, ten thoufand a month.

[i] Aquila tranflates it μηδιαω *to fmile*. Vid. Trommii *Concordant*. fub voce διαιρω. See alfo Schultens' *Origines Hebr*. vol. i. p. 45.

THE BOOK OF JOB.

CHAP.
XI.
1, 2. *Zophar, inflam'd, replies: Is noise defence? Artful harangue a proof of innocence?*

3. Shall learned Windet[k] underſtands them, Job muſt have entertained as melancholy an idea of that world of ghoſts as the heathens had of the realms of Pluto.

—————————————— pigro ſedet
Nox atra mundo. Cuncta mærore horrida:
Ipſaque morte pejor eſt mortis locus.
Hercules Furens. ver. 704.

Gloomy night dwells in that motionleſs world. A melancholy horror ſpreadeth over all: and the habitation of death is worſe than death itſelf.

Ver. 22. *without any order*] Mr. Heath renders it, *where there are no conſtellations*[l].

triſtes ſine ſole domos——
diſmal habitations that have no light.

CHAP. XI.

It is too much the practice of diſputants, to paſs over, in ſilence, ſuch arguments of an adverſary as they are not able to anſwer: Inſtead of defence, they fly into a paſſion, and pour out illiberal abuſe. Zophar's reply is in that caſt. He ſeems to have been more iraſcible and vehement than the others. The ſentiment he utters in ver. 5, 6. diſcovers his ferocity: He there wiſheth, that God would indeed appear; to let this unhappy man know, that his ſufferings were not the half of what he deſerved.

He takes not the leaſt notice of Job's aſſertion of an unequal providence[m]; becauſe he could not diſprove it. He anſwers only, and with much virulence, to Job's aſſeverations of his innocence[n]; and to his queſtioning God about the reaſon of his afflictions[o]. The remainder of his diſcourſe[p] is an exhortation to repentance, with large promiſes if he obeyed; and concludes with a ſevere threatning, if he continued obſtinate.

---

[k] *De ſtatu vitâ defunctorum*, p. 12.

[l] סדרים tranſlated by the LXX. ϛεγγος *light.* It has, in Arabic, the ſignification of *dazzling.* Vid. Caſtell. *Lex. Hept.* and Schultens' *Comment.*

[m] Chap. ix. 22—24.   [n] Ver. 2, 3, 4.   [o] Ver. 5—12.   [p] Ver. 13—20.

3. Shall vain boasts silence us? no speaker rise?
   No honest tongue thy insolence chastise?
4. Thy boldness clamours to the throne divine,
   " Pure is my conscience, spotless virtue mine."
5. O would th' Almighty, to thy wish, appear!
   Expose thy guilt, and thunder in thy ear
6. Vengeance, that wisdom from our world conceals,
   Double the worst which here the sinner feels:
   Taught then, that justice hath requir'd, as yet,
   Not half the value of thy penal debt.

7. Wouldst

Ver. 3. *thy lies*] *Thy false boasts* [q]. It hath plainly this acceptation in Jeremiah xlviii. 29, 30.

Ver. 4. *my doctrine*] Job had said nothing about the purity of his doctrine. This idea, therefore, is impertinent here. Mr. Crinsoz turns it, *my conscience*; and the septuagint, *my works.* either of which versions will agree with the import of the hebrew word [r].

I am clean, &c.] He refers to these expressions; *I am righteous—I am upright—when I had washed myself in snow-water, and made my hands clean in purity—Thou knowest that I am not wicked* [s].

Ver. 5. *O that God would speak*, &c.] This is a bitter reflection on Job's presumptuous wish to debate his cause with God himself. Chap. ix. 34, 35. x. 2.

Ver. 6. *And that he would shew thee*, &c.] This is a very obscure passage, I have met with no satisfactory explanation of it. One thing however seems clear, namely, that

---

[q] ברה the verb carries in it the idea of *falshood* and *forgery*; and is englished *to feign*, in Nehem. vi. 8.

[r] לקחי In Arabic לקחה signifies *the mind*, impregnated with excellent principles and bringing forth the noble fruits of virtue. It is a metaphor from the meal of the male palm tree; which being sprinkled upon the opening clusters of the female, fecundates them, and renders the dates sweet and flavourous. Vid. Castell. *Lex. Hept.* Schultens' *Comment.* and Shaw's *Travels*, p. 141. 4to.

[s] Chap. ix. 15, 21, 30. x. 7.

CHAP. XI.   THE BOOK OF JOB.   69

7. Wouldſt thou th' Eternal with thy line explore?
   Fathom almighty thought, and find its ſhore?
8. Go, mete heav'n's height, the depth of Hades found,
9. Span the wide earth, and reach o'er ocean's bound.
10. He ſmites, impriſons, executes: what tongue
    Shall dare to mutter, " haſt thou done no wrong?"
                                              11. He

that the ſubject treated here, and to the end of verſe 12, is *divine puniſhments.* By *Wiſdom*, therefore, I underſtand the counſels of God, that fix the kind and meaſure of his puniſhments: by *the ſecrets of wiſdom*, his puniſhments in a future world, which are a ſecret to us at preſent. Thoſe future puniſhments are declared to be *double to that which is*[t]*:* that is, they are far more ſevere and terrible than any ſufferings of ſinners in the preſent ſtate. Hence he would have Job to learn, that what he now ſuffered was leſs than his iniquity deſerved.

Ver. 7. *Canſt thou*, &c.] He now takes him in hand for his preſumptuous queſtioning of God about his ways[u]. The judgements of God, he tells him, are as inſcrutable in their reaſons and the full extent of their deſigns; as they are rapid and irreſiſtable in their execution[w]. It is ſufficient for us to know, that he puniſheth men for their ſins; and that, in puniſhing, he aims to cure their pride, and to break their intractable ſpirits to his yoke[x].

Ver. 8. *It is as high*, &c.] When we cannot comprehend a thing; we ſay it is beyond our reach, or it is too high or too deep for us. But in what a noble manner does Zophar here expreſs ſuch an impoſſibility! How much ſuperior is the language of poetry to common proſe[y]!

hell] *Sheôl*, the world of the dead. If *hell* meaneth here the place of puniſhment, it is a tranſlation of *Sheôl* as inadequate, as *the grave* by which it is rendered in chap. vii. 9. See the APPENDIX. *Numb.* II.

Ver. 10. *If he cut off, and ſhut up, and gather together*] The firſt of theſe expreſſions,

---

[t] הושיה *id quod extat, that which is.* The Septuagint renders it, ται κατα τι, *thy things*; that is, thy ſufferings. See Dr. Scott's excellent *Notes on the Goſpel of St. Matthew*, p. 2.
[u] Chap. iii. 11, 12, 20, 23.   vii. 13—21.   x. 2, 18.
[w] Ver. 7—10.   [x] Ver. 11, 12.
[y] Bp. Lowth produces this paſſage as an example of the grand manner in which the hebrew poets ſpeak of the attributes of God, abſolutely conſidered, without particular mention of the operations and effects that flow from them. See his fine obſervations in the *Prælectiones*, p. 197, &c. 8vo.

11. He knows impostors: shall he not require
The sin clandestine, acted in his sight?
12. That fools may be reclaim'd, found sense supply'd
To fill the void of ignorance and pride;
And natures as the Zebra's colt untam'd,
Subdu'd by reason, into men be fram'd.

13. Thou,

pressions, *he cut off* (or rather, he smite[y]) signifies the apprehension of the criminal, by some calamity which divine justice inflicts upon him.

The next phrase, *shut up*[z], denotes the effect of the stroke; he becomes the prisoner of providence.

The last, *gather together* (or rather, gather *an assembly*[a]) expresseth the execution. It is an allusion to the custom of assembling the people, to be witnesses and assistants at the execution of a notorious offender. The meaning here is, that God makes a public example of great sinners; by the signal circumstances of their destruction. Zophar intended this stroke for Job.

who can hinder him] It may be translated, *who shall cause him to restore*[b]? who shall wrest a criminal out of his hands? Or, *who shall answer him*[c]? by cavilling at his judgements.

Ver. 11. *vain men*] *false men*[d]; that is, impostors. He glanceth at Job, as a person who, notwithstanding his character for piety, had lived in the practice of secret wickedness; particularly injustice[e].

Ver. 12. *For vain man*]

That

---

[y] יהלך See the note on chap. ix. 11.
[z] Isaiah xxiv. 22.
[a] יקהיל See Ezek. xvi. 39—41. Joshua vii. 25. Vid. Schultens' *Comment.* See also Job xxxi. 34. and the note.
[b] ישיבנו see the note on chap. ix. 12.
[c] *Shall answer him*, as in chap. xxxii. 14. xxxiii. 5.
[d] מתי שוא LXX. ανομοι *transgressours.* but שוא also signifies *falshood*, in Zech. x. 2. *and have told false dreams;* i. e. dreams which they falsely pretended to have received by inspiration. Compare also Ps. xxvi. 4, 5.
[e] See ver. 14. and chap. xxii. 5—9.

CHAP. XI. THE BOOK OF JOB.

13. Thou, therefore, quell thy haughty fpirit; bend,
Bend thy ftiff knee; thy fuppliant hands extend:
14. Shake out the bribe, th' unrighteous gain expell,
Nor fuffer rapine in thy tents to dwell.
15. Un-

That the proud [r] *may be made wife,*
And the colt of the wild afs [g] *become* [h] *a man* [i].

Thefe expreffions characterife wicked men; as void of found underftanding, opinionated, felf-willed, and intractable as the wildeft inhabitants of the defert. The intention of divine punifhments, he fays, is to recover them to folid reflection; and bring them into fubjection to reafon and the laws of God.

Ver. 13—20. *If thou prepare*, &c.] This exhortatory part of his difcourfe is, for fubftance, the fame with that of Eliphaz [k]; but diverfified by his manner of defcribing true repentance, and by the beautiful imagery in which he expreffeth its glorious reward.

Ver. 14. *iniquity—wickednefs*] he means, by thefe terms, riches acquired by fraud, or by taking bribes, or by any methods of violence and oppreffion: for this they fuppofed to have been the peculiar iniquity, which had drawn down the vengeance of God upon his head [l].

tabernacle] *Tents* having been the ancient dwellings of men, the term was retained after the invention of more durable and fixed habitations. Job, it is certain, lived in a city [m]: yet his houfe is called *a tabernacle*, or *tent* [n].

---

[r] נבוּב The verb, in Arabic, fignifies *to behave haughtily*. Vid. Clodii *Lex. Heb. Select.* and בוּב in hebrew is, in the literal fenfe, *hollow*. Exod. xxvii. 8. in metaphor, *a perfon void of underftanding, vain-glorious.*

[g] Compare Pf. xxxii. 9. Jer. xxxi. 18. Job xxxix. 5—8.

[h] יִוָּלֵד *may be born*, i. e. *may be rendred*, or *may become*. It is an Arabian phrafeology: *Let the wild affes colt be born a man,* that is, (as they explain it) Let a man who is intractable, become gentle, humane, and docile. Vid. Schultens' *Comment.* See alfo the ufe of this word in Prov. xvii. 17. and Bp. Patrick's note in his *Paraphrafe.*

[i] *A man,* i. e. one who acts according to reafon. Ifaiah xlvi. 8. We meet with a fimilar expreffion in Horace:
———Nec fi retractus erit, jam
Fiet homo——— Art. Poet. ver. 469.
Nor if you bring him off this folly, will he thereupon become a man, i e act a rational part for the future.

[k] Chap. v. 8, &c.
[m] Chap. xxix. 7.
[l] Chap. xv. 34. xx. 15, 19. xxii. 5—10.
[n] Chap. xxix. 4.

15. Unclouded then, and unconfus'd with fear,
  Thy face erect and sparkling shall appear:
16. Woe in thy memory shall leave no trace,
  Like violent waters vanish'd from their place:
17. A happier age succeeds; emerging soon
  Fair as the morn, more luminous than noon:

18, 19. For

Ver. 15. *Thou shalt lift up thy face,* &c.] He describes the happy change of his condition, by its effects in his countenance; contrasting his present dejected face, sullied and disfigured by terror, grief, and tears, with the look he shall then assume, erect, firm, and clear as the polished mirror. He refers, no doubt, to those words, *I cannot lift up my head* º.

Thou shalt be stedfast] The hebrew word is a metaphor, taken from metals fined by fusion ᵖ; and, therefore, may include *lustre* as well as *firmness*.

Ver. 16. *And remember it as waters,* &c.] That is, as Crinsoz explains it, thou shalt not remember it at all: The memory of thy afflictions will be wholly effaced; like the winter torrents, which are utterly evaporated in the beginning of summer ᑫ.

Ver. 17. *And thine age,* &c.] This period will become clearer in the following disposition ʳ and translation.

  And a happy age ˢ *shall arise* ᵗ;
  Thou shalt be as the morning,
  Thou shalt blaze out ᵘ *more than noon.*

The

º Chap. x. 15.
ᵖ כיצק see chap. xxviii. 2. xxxvii. 18. xxxviii. 38.
ᑫ Chap. vi. 15, 17.
ʳ
ויקום חלד
כבקר תהיה
מצהרים תעפה
The perspicuity of this arrangement will be, I hope, its justification.
ˢ חלד *an age or state of durable felicity;* so it signifies in Arabic. Vid. Schultens' *Comment.* and Michaelis *in Prælect. Lowthi,* p. 99.
ᵗ יקום *shall arise;* as in Dan. ii. 39. *After thee shall arise another kingdom.*
ᵘ תעפה *coruscabis.* Ezek. xxxii. 10. *When I shall cause my sword to flash in their faces.* Mr. Heath.

CHAP. XI. THE BOOK OF JOB. 73

18, 19. For thou, known favourite of celestial pow'r,
Safe in the waking and the slumb'ring hour,
Around

The meaning is, " Thy afflictions shall be succeeded by a state of durable felicity: its beginning shall be as the morning of a bright day: it shall increase as the light, until it arrive to its highest point; when it shall exceed the lustre of the sun at noon." The thought is the same, but far more nobly expressed, with that of Bildad, Chap. viii. 7. Compare Prov. iv. 18.

Ver. 18, 19. *And thou shalt be secure*, &c.] These two verses contain, if I mistake not, a pleasing rural scene; green pastures, wells of water, flocks and herds couched round them, and a little camp of Arabian Shepherds inclosing the whole.

The expression *thou shalt dig* refers most probably, as Mr. Heath remarks, to digging of wells or springs; a circumstance frequently mentioned in the patriarchal history [w]. The word translated *thou shalt lie down* [x] denoteth properly the decumbent posture of cattle, after they have well fed; and when they repose at night. As to the encampment; It was the custom, as Mr. Heath observes, of the eastern people to pitch their tents nigh wells; for the conveniency of water for their cattle. The *security* also, here promised, expresseth the protection wanted to defend them from wild beasts and from the incursions of the thievish Arabs of the desert.

because there is hope] *The hope* here mentioned as a ground of security, can be no other than hope in God: that firm dependance on divine protection, which good men are warranted to entertain.

many shall make suit, &c.] *The mighty* [y] *shall make suit*, &c. Princes and other great men shall court an alliance with thee. See Gen. xxvi. 26—29.

---

[w] Gen. xxvi. 13—22.

[x] רבצת Pf. xxiii. 2. *He maketh me to lie down in green pastures*, &c. See also Pocock. in *Carmen Tograi*. p. 95. The learned Chappelow remarks, that this word is likewise applied by the Arabians to the *shepherds*, lying down to rest in the same place with their flocks. *Comment. on Job*. The substantive, however, is used synonimous with a man's *dwelling* in Prov. xxiv. 15. where it is englished *resting place*. But in Cant. i. 7. the verb רבץ is used in the same sense as in Arabic.

[y] רבים Mr. Heath's version is, *The mighty shall intreat thy favour*.

L

Around thy wells, thy couching flocks around,
Shall range thy tents along the graſſy ground:
No terror ſhall thy peaceful camp alarm,
And princely chiefs ſhall court thy pow'rful arm.

20. But ſtubborn ſinners watch with weary'd eyes,
Help, far away, from their diſtreſſes flies,
And death's black ſhades, their laſt ſad refuge, riſe.

CHAP. XII.

1, 2. Yes, anſwer'd Job, ye are th' enlighten'd few,
Fav'rites of Wiſdom! will ſhe die with you?

3. And

Ver. 20. *Their hope ſhall be as,* &c.] The original ſays, *their hope ſhall be the giving up of the ghoſt:* that is, their diſtreſs and deſpair ſhall make them wiſh to be out of the world. He evidently reflects on Job's paſſionate wiſhes for death, which he repreſents to be the practice of *wicked men.*

CHAP. XII.

Job's reply in this chapter is in a vein of plaintive argumentation. He alledgeth facts relative partly to himſelf[a], and partly to all mankind[a]; which demonſtrate a ſtrange inequality and ſeeming confuſion in the diſtribution of good and evil: Whence it follows, that a man's worldly condition, whether proſperous or afflicted, is no criterion of his moral character. This reaſoning is in point. For his three antagoniſts had concluded him to be wicked merely from his being wretched.

Ver. 2. *Ye are the people,* &c.] He chaſtiſes them for aſſuming ſuch airs of ſuperiority over him. In the ſtyle of Arabia, *the people of riches* are rich men; and *the people of knowledge,* men of learning[b].

---

[a] Ver. 4.   [a] Ver. 11—25.
[b] Scaliger's Proverb. Arab. Cent. ii. 87. Pocock. Spec. Hiſt. Arab. p. 153.

3. And yet, my portion of the mental ray
  Is not inferior to your boasted day.
  Stale saws, and tales of tyrants overthrown,
  Those vulgar themes — to whom are those unknown?

4. The man derided by his friend, am I;
  " To God he clamours, and let God reply."
  This insult, for integrity's appeals,
  This cruel taunt, the man of justice feels.

5. Contempt pursues the fall'n; exalted ease
  With scornful eye unhappy virtue sees.

Ver. 4. *I am as one*, &c.] The original is,
  The derision of his friend am I,
  " *He calleth to God, and let him answer him :*"
  The just upright man is a derision.
The derision, or insult, is contained in the middle clause;
  " *He calleth to God, and let him answer him.*"
Thus Eliphaz had insulted him for his complaint, *call now, there is one that answereth thee* [c] : And thus Zophar had insulted him, *But O that God would speak, and open his lips against thee* [d]; deriding him for what he had said chap. ix. 35. x. 2.

Ver. 5. *He that is ready*, &c.] Adversity sinks a man into contempt with the prosperous. The literal version of the hebrew will be,
  For calamity [e] *contempt is ready,*
  In the thoughts of him who is at ease;
  For them who slip with their feet [f].

6. Peace

Calamity

---

[c] Chap. v. 1. See the note.   [d] Chap. xi. 5.

[e] לפיד a word compounded of the preposition ל *for* and the noun substantive פיד *calamity*; or *ruin*, !as it is englished Prov. xxiv. 22. It might have been rendred so in Job xxxi. 29. If I rejoiced at the *calamity*, or *ruin*, of, &c.

[f] בועדי רגל So Pſ. xviii. 36. *(heb. 37.) Thou hast enlarged my steps under me, that my feet did not slip.*

6. Peace dwells with robbers; they enjoy their spoil,
Provoke God's wrath, and revel in his smile.
7. Question the flocks and herds, whose land they feed?
Fowls, for whose riot they increase their breed?
8. Earth, to whose wealthy magazines she yields
Her flowing vintage and her cultur'd fields?
And nations of the scale, whose taste to please
Their fins in millions cut the streams and seas?
9. Dulness itself may, from these teachers, know
Th' imperial hand which governs all below;
10. The hand, which holds, as by its pow'r began,
All life, from vegetative up to man.

11. Now let a knowing ear the strain attend,
To loftier themes my tow'ring thoughts ascend.

Tastes

Calamity is here put for the *calamitous*, or afflicted; expressed in the last clause by *them who slip⁵ with their feet*, the fallen: he points particularly to himself; as he does to his three friends in the middle sentence, *him who is at ease*.

Ver. 6—10. *The tabernacles*, &c.] These verses are a contrast of the foregoing: He who had exercised himself to have always a conscience void of offence towards God and towards men, was utterly ruined; and abandoned to cruel insults: but those who had plundered his estate, and murdered his servants, enjoyed the protection and blessings of providence in abundance.

Ver. 7—10. *But ask now the beasts*, &c.] This beautiful apostrophising of the inanimate and brute creation is only a poetical way of saying, that the great author and disposer of life had given into the hands of robbers the beasts of the field, and the fowls of the heaven, &c. Such men, he complains, possess the largest property and use of the brute creation and the produce of the earth; which they abuse to the purposes of luxury and riot.

---

⁵ בְּיָדֵי *them who slip*. This word signifies *to fall into adversity*, Psal. xxvi. 1. where it is rendered to *slide*.

Tastes the found palate tries, the knowing ear,
Discourse examines and decides as clear:
12. And should not judgement be the crown of age?
And snow-white locks bespeak th' experienc'd sage?

13. Sapience and pow'r to God alone belong;
Wise are his counsels, and his arm is strong:
14. He overturns, what hand erects again?
He binds; who bursts his adamantine chain?
15. He checks the waters; all is desert round:
He sends them out; they desolate the ground.

16. Sapience

Ver. 12. *With the ancient* is, &c.] *With the ancient* should be *wisdom*, &c. As the palate distinguisheth the agreeable and disagreeable tastes in food; so the ear, or rather the mind by the ear, discerneth truth and falsehood in discourse: And we justly expect to find this discerning power, most perfect in persons of years and experience. He glances at Eliphaz, and the other two, for talking so ignorantly of the ways of providence.

Ver. 13—25. *With him*, &c.] The design of this grand discourse on the ways of God to men is, I apprehend, to establish his position, Chap. ix. 22. *He destroyeth the perfect and the wicked.* That proposition is here proved by induction : He alledgeth those great and general calamities, *drought, inundation* and *the overthrow of kingdoms*; which make no distinction between the innocent and the guilty, but involve the most respectable characters, and the noblest and most important talents, in distress, disgrace, and ruin.

Ver. 13, 14. *With him is wisdom*, &c.] These two verses seem to be an introduction to the following; being a general assertion of the supreme, absolute, and irresistable dominion of God; whenever he decreeth the destruction of some flourishing city and kingdom; or of any particular family, or man, of great eminence and power.

Ver. 15. *Behold he witholdeth*, &c.] This first sentence of the period is a concise description of a *general drought* and *famine*; such as his own country suffered

16. Sapience and pow'r are his: he rules all ill,
Misleader and misled his plan fulfill:
17. Watchmen of realms, and guardians of their rights,
He drags to bondage, he with madness smites.

18. He

fered upon the failure of the equinoctial rains : or such as Egypt was afflicted with, when the Nile did not rise high enough to overflow the lands.

Also he sendeth, &c.] This clause describes an *inundation*, such as might happen in Job's country from the torrents caused by too great an abundance of rain: Or such as does so much mischief in Egypt; when the Nile riseth beyond a certain height, and pours a body of water, on the fields, too large to be drained off by their canals.

Ver. 16. *With him is strength and wisdom*] With great judgement our admirable poet repeats *these* attributes of the Deity, to fix our attention to *these*: for he is going to describe a scene of public calamity and distraction, which is the effect of uncontrollable power directed by counsels infinitely above our comprehension.

the deceived and the deceiver are his] The terms in the original are metaphors taken from sheep [h], which through the negligence and misconduct of their shepherds go astray to their destruction.

The deceiver, therefore, or *he that causeth to err*, signifies foolish and wicked rulers; who by their male-administration bring destruction upon themselves and their country. *The deceived* or *erring* are the people so misguided and ruined. The sentence asserts, that God overrules all this madness and mischief to serve the wise ends of his own inscrutable providence.

Ver. 17—21. *He leadeth*, &c.] The sum of this whole paragraph is, that no policy, eloquence, heroism, or extent of dominion can preserve a state; which God has decreed to overturn. But the chief point in view is, that, in such a catastrophe, dignity, excellence, and the most noble talents for public utility are overwhelmed with ignominy and ruin.

Ver. 17. *Counsellors—Judges*] The former mean, I suppose, the great Statesmen,

---

[h] שגג ומשגה Ezek. xxxiv. 2—6. Ecclef. x. 5. compare Isaiah xix. 13, 14. See also the use of משגה in Deut xxvii. 18. Prov. xxviii. 10.

CHAP. XII.   THE BOOK OF JOB.   79

18. He breaks the rod of majesty, he flings
The captive's cord around the loins of kings:
19. Distracts the viceroy chiefs, and whelms them all,
Ev'n stoutest warriors, in the common fall:

21. He

men, who compose the council of the sovereign; the latter, those who preside in the administration of justice.

He leadeth away [i] *spoiled* [k]—*and maketh fools* [l]] He delivers them into the hands of their enemies to be spoiled, and carried into captivity: And by this deplorable reverse of condition, he distracts them with terror and despair.

Ver. 18. *He looseth the bond* [m] *of kings*] He destroys their binding power, their authority, by dethroning them. The expression may allude to the royal belt, one of the insignia of majesty. compare Isaiah xlv. 1.

and girdeth [n], &c.] The tenor of the discourse requires these expressions to be taken in a calamitous sense. The *girdle*, therefore, must here mean *the cord*, or *chain*, that was tied about the waist of captives. The manner of making war in our days, is very different from what it was in ancient times: We now see no such catastrophes as princes and their people led into captivity; but these were the usual effects of conquest in former ages.

Ver. 19. *princes*] Governors of provinces, viceroys. such, probably, was Potipherah, prince of On and father-in-law of Joseph [o]: and such were the sons of David [q].

and overthroweth] in battle; or, in general, he abandons them to destruction. the word is opposed to divine protection in Prov. xiii. 6.

The

---

[i] מוֹלִיךְ it is used in the sense of *carrying into captivity* II Chron. xxxvi. 6. See also II Kings xxiv. 15.

[k] שׁוֹלָל LXX. αἰχμαλώτους; *captives*.

[l] יְהוֹלֵל *he maketh mad.* LXX. ἐξίστησι, *he maketh them beside themselves.*

[m] מוּסַר Its root יסר signifies *coercive power, political discipline,* in I Kings xii. 11. where it is englished *to chastise*.

[n] אֵזֶר So Pf. cxlix. 8. *To bind their kings with chains,* &c.

[o] Gen. xli. 50.   [p] II Sam. viii. 18.

20. He ſtrikes the patriot dumb; in vex'd debate
Confounds the hoary ſages of the ſtate:

21. He

*The mighty*ᵖ] The mighty men of war.

Ver. 20. *the truſty*ᵠ] The patriotic orators; who in the general diſtraction of their country loſe poſſeſſion of their mental powers, and are no longer able to exert their eloquence.

the aged] *the elders*; that is, ſenators.

Ver. 21. *princes*ʳ] The hebrew is a different word from that which is tranſlated *princes* in ver. 19. It denotes perſons of a noble, generous temper; and is rendred *liberal* in Iſaiah xxxii. 5, 8.

Even this benevolent character cannot protect the poſſeſſor of it, in general calamities. This brings to my remembrance the unhappy fate of the good Axylus ſo movingly deſcribed by Homer.

> Next *Teuthras'* ſon diſtain'd the ſands with blood,
> *Axylus*, hoſpitable, rich, and good:
> In fair *Ariſba's* walls (his native place)
> He held his ſeat; a friend to human race.
> Faſt by the road, his ever-open door
> Oblig'd the wealthy, and reliev'd the poor.
> To ſtern *Tydides* now he falls a prey,
> No friend to guard him in the dreadful day!
> Breathleſs the good man fell, and by his ſide
> His faithful ſervant, old Caleſius dy'd ˢ.

ᵖ איתנים it is uſed as an epithet of a torrent in Amos v. 24. *Let Judgement run down as waters, and righteouſneſs as a mighty ſtream.* Homer compares the impetuoſity of his warriors to a torrent, Il. v. 87, &c.

ᵠ נאבנים Mr. Heath derives it from נאם *to ſpeak.*

ʳ נדיבים engliſhed *willing* Exod. xxxv. 5. *whoſoever is of a willing heart, let him bring it, an offering of the Lord; gold, and ſilver, and braſs.* In Prov. xix. 6, It is ſynonimous with *him that giveth gifts* (Heb. the *man of gifts*) and ought to have been rendered there *the liberal* man.

ˢ Pope's Homer's Iliad, b. vi. ver. 15, &c. in the Original, ver. 12, &c.

CHAP. XII.   THE BOOK OF JOB.   81

21. He pours contempt on every gen'rous name,
    And cloaths all mortal excellence with shame.
22. Thus, swift and sudden, from the womb of night,
    His deep designs he ushers into light;
    As though the horrors of infernal shade
    He cast abroad, and o'er the world display'd.
23. The nations with his fatal mists he blinds,
    Then sweeps, and scatters into all the winds.

24, 25. Their

Ver. 21. *the mighty*¹] It is a different word in the original from that which is thus turned in ver. 19. It signifies, in Arabia, persons eminent for any illustrious quality *knowledge, courage*ᵘ, &c. very proper therefore to close the foregoing series; as it comprehends all therein mentioned or omitted.

He weakneth the strength] rather, as the learned Schultens translates it, *He looseth the girdle*ʷ: that is, he strips these illustrious personages of their dignity and honours, and overwhelms them with disgrace in a state of captivity.

Ver. 22. *He discovereth*, &c.] This verse is a reflection on the foregoing events, and forms an easy transition to the remainder of the subject. Yet, I must own, it seems to me out of its proper situation: I think it would better have closed the whole discourse. The sentiment is, that while these terrible revolutions remain in the divine counsels; they are darkness, utter darkness to us, deep impenetrable secrets: And when they are discovered in the execution, they astonish and terrify mankind; as though sepulchral darkness covered the face of the earth. The prophet Daniel speaks in like figurative language of the counsels of God relating to the four great Empires of the world, Chap. ii. 21, 22.

Ver. 23. *He increaseth*, &c.] The calamitous fate of the illustrious personages

---

¹ אפיקים.   ᵘ Vid. the *Commentary* of Schultens.

ʷ מזיח Buxtorf in his hebrew Concordance renders it *zona, a girdle*, as our public version turns it in Psalm cix. 19. The root, says Schultens, is זוח; and זוחא in the Syriac testament, Acts xxv. 23. signifies *pomp of dress*, and other royal magnificence.

M

24, 25. Their leaders he bereaves of foul, who ftray
   In a vaft pathlefs wild without a guiding ray:
   In a vaft wild their difmal way they feel,
   Perplex'd, diftreft; from doubt to doubt they reel,
   Bewilder'd by ftrong energy divine,
   Like men who ftagger with the fumes of wine.

CHAP.

ages abovementioned, involves in it the ruin of a whole nation. There had been inftances, even before the times of Job, of a whole people carried away by the conqueror from their own country ˣ. Such a fcene is defcribed in this verfe. The verfion, if I miftake not, fhould be as follows;

   He caufeth the nations to err ʸ, and deftroyeth them:
   He fcattereth ᶻ the nations, and leadeth them away ᵃ.

God *caufeth a nation to err*, when he fuffers their rulers to miflead them by deftructive counfels. He *fcattereth them*, when he fends them captives into other countries.

Ver. 24, 25. *He taketh away*, &c.] divine infatuation of the governing Powers is here defcribed, in forcible language and ftriking refemblances. Privation of judgement and courage is expreffed by God's *taking away their heart*: In their confufion, miftakes, perplexity, and diftrefs, they refemble perfons who have loft themfelves in the Arabian folitudes; without a path, without a way-mark, without a light to guide them: and their irrefolution and unftable counfels are like the reeling motions of a drunken man.

ˣ See Gen. xiv.

ʸ I follow the feptuagint, πλανῶν *he caufeth to err*: they read מַשְׁגֶּה as in ver. 16. See Deut. xxvii. 18. in the hebrew and in the Greek.

ᶻ שׁטח It is ufed in the fenfe of *fpreading*, that is, *fcattering*; in Jer. viii. 2. The LXX. render it in the verfe before us by καταςρώνων *profternens*, *overthrowing*.

ᵃ נחה it is a metaphor from a flock of fheep driven away by an enemy: this is the acceptation of the word in II Kings xviii. 11. *And the king of Affyria did carry away Ifrael unto Affyria, and put them in (led them, as captives, into) Habor*, &c. When this word is taken in a good meaning, it denoteth leading fheep into proper places of refrefhment; as in Pf xxiii. 2. *He leadeth me in the paths of righteoufnefs*. Compare ver. 1, 2.

CHAP.
XIII.
Ver. 1. All this my eyes atteſt; and faithful fame,
Tut'ring my curious ear, atteſts the ſame:
2. Nor knowledge can you boaſt to me unknown,
Nor challenge ſenſe ſuperior to my own.

3. O how it would my longing ſoul elate,
Might I with God himſelf my cauſe debate!
4. But you, all you, are wranglers; your replies
Are pompous trifles, and defaming lies.
5, 6. Be

CHAP. XIII.

By the facts produced in the foregoing chapter, he had demoliſhed the hypo-
theſis of his antagoniſts concerning the courſe of providence. But he continues
diſſatisfied with its meaſures towards himſelf. He wants to carry his cauſe to
the bar of God: And after a ſevere reprehenſion of the futility of their diſcourſes,
and the unfairneſs of their management of the controverſy [b], declares his reſo-
lution ſo to do; let what will be the conſequence [c]. Accordingly he breaks out,
at the twentieth verſe of this chapter, in the freeſt effuſion of ſelf-defence, pleading, and complaint; which he purſues to the end of the next chapter. All this
part of his diſcourſe is the language of the paſſions.

Ver. 1, 2. *Lo mine eye*, &c.] Theſe two verſes ought not to have been disjoin-
ed from the former chapter. They authenticate the facts alleged in it.

Ver. 4. *ye are forgers of lies*] By *lies* he means their falſe accounts of the ways
of providence towards bad men and good. He calls them *forgers*, or rather
varniſhers [d], becauſe they had ſet off their untruths in the glaring colours of
rhetoric.

---

[b] Ver. 3—12. [c] Ver. 13—19.
[d] טפלי It ſignifies in the Chaldee *to plaiſter*. Vid. Caſtell. *Lex. Hept.*

5, 6, Be dumb, so prove your wisdom; dumb receive
Sharp castigation, which my lips shall give.
7. On God's behalf these methods will you dare;
Unjust in judging, in dispute unfair?
8. To him be partial, half the truth conceal;
Then sanctify the fraud and call it zeal?
9. Can you abide his test? will soothing style,
Which men deceives, th' Almighty's ear beguile?
10. If

Ver. 6. *Hear now, &c.*] *Hear now my reproof*ᵉ, *and hearken to the censures*ᶠ *of my lips.*

Ver. 7, 8. *Will you speak wickedly, &c.*] They *spoke wickedly for God*, because to justify him they were unjust to their friend; to save the honour of providence, they condemned an innocent man. *They talked deceitfully* for God; because they cunningly kept out of sight the truths that made against their own cause; namely, that many very wicked men prosper throughout life, and that many innocent persons perish with the wicked in general calamities. Thus they were partial to God; *they accepted his person,* as it is expressed in the next verse.

Ver. 8. *Will ye contend for God?*] Do you take upon you to be advocates for God? and to defend his providence in this iniquitous manner? Will this pretended zeal for his honour protect you from his resentment?

Ver. 9. *do ye so mock him*] The hebrew word signifies, among other meanings, *to flatter*ᵍ a person's humour at the expence of truth. It is the highest indignity that can be offered to God, to imagine that we gratify him by bigotry, partiality, and unjust methods of defending religion.

ᵉ תוכחת LXX ἔλεγχος *reproof*. This is the usual acceptation of the word in the book of Proverbs. The verb is englished *to reprove,* in the tenth verse of this chapter.

ᶠ רבית LXX. κρίσις *redargutio, censure.*

ᵍ הרל the derivative noun, מהתלות, is englished *deceits* in Isaiah xxx. 10. it there plainly imports untruths that flatter mens wishes.

10. If partial thoughts work secretly within,
    Tremble; be certain he will mark the sin.
11. Shall not his majesty your fears alarm?
    Nor yet the thunder of his lifted arm?
12. What are your boasted maxims? what your heap
    Of swelling promises? I hold them cheap:
    Light as the dust before the rising gale;
    Molehills of sand, as worthless and as frail.
13. Peace; unmolesting, while I pour abroad
    My honest pleadings, by no peril aw'd:

14. Befall

Ver. 12. *Your remembrances*, &c.] *Your memorable sayings* [h]. Their discourses were made up of common-place observations, maxims, and proverbs, concerning the judgements of God on wicked men; and of pompous, romantic declamations on the worldly felicity of good men. To express his contempt of them, he compares them to *dirt* and *swelling heaps of mud*; which are easily blown away or swept down.

your bodies [i], &c.] *your swelling heaps are swelling heaps of mire* [k]. he means their swelling heaps of words; their high-flown discourses, in particular, on the happy condition of pious and virtuous persons even in the present world [l].

Ver. 13. *let come on me what* will] We meet with a similar mode of speech in the Arabian *Anthologia*: " I will wipe off this dishonour with my sword, let the decree of God draw upon me what it will [m]." The meaning is, I will revenge

the

---

[h] זכרניכם Harir uses it in his first dissertation for a saying of the *Koran*. Vid. Gol. Gram. Arab. p. 218.

[i] גביכם *Your high-flown discourses*, Mr. Heath. *ves discours enflez, your bombast harangues*, Crinsoz. Buxtorf, in his Concordance, translates it *celsitates*. It properly signifies *a high building*, Ezek. xvi. 24. *Thou hast also built unto thee an eminent place*.

[k] חמר *mud*, or *mire*. Isaiah x. 6.

[l] Chap. v. 19—26. xi. 15—19.   [m] Antholog. p. 355.

THE BOOK OF JOB.

14. Befall what will; I'll put within my hand
    My trembling life, and every danger stand.
15. Yes, he will slay me (other hope were vain)
    Yet to his face I will my cause maintain,
16. And plead not guilty: his absolving voice
    With sweet salvation will my soul rejoice:
                                                    None

the affront at the hazard of my life. This manner of speaking imports desperate resolution.

Ver. 14. *Wherefore* [m], &c.] *At all events I will take my flesh in my teeth, and put my life in my hand.* These are proverbial expressions: The former is equivalent to, *I will eat my own flesh*; that is, I will be my own destroyer [n]. He means, *that he would maintain his ways before God*, though he were certain to perish in the attempt. Accordingly he resolves to expose himself to that danger; *I will put my life in my hand* [o]: What is carried in the hand may easily slip out, or be snatched away. However faulty these sentiments may be in other respects; there is yet a magnanimity in them, which discovers, in a wonderful manner, the animating force of a clear conscience.

Ver. 15. *Though he slay me*, &c.] *Lo he will slay me, I expect nothing else* [p]: *nevertheless I will maintain mine own ways before him.* He expected nothing else, but that God would cut him off by his present disease: Yet he resolves, in the face of certain death, to justify his innocence even to God himself.

Ver. 16. *He also* shall be *my salvation*] Mr. Crinsoz remarks, that *salvation* [q] here

---

[m] על מה Super quocumque tandem eventu, *notwithstanding any thing, at all events*; as the learned Schultens explains it. He proves that על signifies *non obstante* in chap. x. 7. על דעתך *notwithstanding thy knowledge that I am not wicked.* See his *Commentary*.

[n] Isaiah ix. 20. Eccles. iv. 5.

[o] Judges xii. 3. See also Mr. Merrick *on the Psalms*, p. 235. 4to.

[p] This is Mr. Heath's translation of לא איחל הן יקטלני it is agreeable to the text, whereas our Translators follow the marginal correction לו איחל *I will trust in him*.

[q] ישועה in the Psalms it signifies *temporal deliverance*; and in Ps. lxii. 6. it means particularly deliverance from false accusers: compare ver. 4. of that psalm.

None but the wicked his tribunal dread,
Guilt in his prefence dares not lift its head.

17, 18. Hear, hear, my pleading hear; the plann'd defence,
Affur'd of noble triumph, I commence:

19. Stand forth, accufer; thy inditement prove,
I'll yield to die; nor will one murmur move.

20. On two conditions (O indulge that grace).
I'll feek no fhelter from thy awful face:

21. Remove thy crufhing hand far off; and dart.
No dreadful radiance to diftract my heart:

22. Thou

here fignifies the deliverance, or *abfolution*, of an accufed perfon; whofe innocence is acknowledged by his judge. Nothing but confcious integrity, and the moft exalted fentiments of the divine equity, could give birth to this noble confidence. Our admirable poet has the art of fuftaining the pious character of his chief perfonage, in the midft of the moft daring exceffes.

for an hypocrite, &c.] *But a profligate fhall not come before him*. A wicked man, fuch as you have reprefented me, will not dare to venture on fuch an attempt; much lefs fucceed in it.

Ver. 17. *my declaration*] This is plainly a judicial term. it denotes opening his caufe, or fhewing the matter of his complaint.

Ver. 19. *Who is he*, &c.] Who will appear as plaintiff, or accufer, againft me?

for now, &c.] *for now I will be filent, and will die*; that is, as Mr. Heath explains it, if an accufer appear, and prove his charge; I will not fpeak one word more, but be content to fuffer death as a convict.

Ver. 20, 21. *Only*, &c.] See the note on Chap. ix. 34, 35.

---

¹ חנף See the note on chap. viii. 13.

22. Thou then arraign; I'll anfwer with my plea:
    Or deign thou anfwer, while I queftion thee:
23. What, and how many, are my fins? reveal
    My crimes, my treafons, which thy rolls conceal.
24. What provocation veils thy face in frown?
    Why me profcribe as rebel to thy crown?
25. Shall pow'r almighty give the whirlwind law
    To tofs a leaf, and perfecute a ftraw?
26. Decrees fevere! my youthful follies——thefe
    Now feel thy vengeance——O fevere decrees!
    27. With

Ver. 22. *Then call thou*, &c.] This is a flat contradiction to his refolution Chap. ix. 15. But no wonder; he was not mafter of himfelf. A reader who expects coolnefs and confiftency from a man under the agitation of fo many vehement paffions, can hardly be himfelf in his fober fenfes.

The expreffions clearly import, that he aimed to difpute his caufe, not meerly *before* God as a judge, but *with* God as a party. For explication of the terms, fee the note on Chap. ix. 16.

Ver. 23—25. *How many*, &c.] Here is a rapid fucceffion of interrogations, which carries an air of petulance in it. The ftyle is too fpirited to confift with reverence.

Ver. 24. *Wherefore*, &c.] He remonftrates againft the treatment he met with, as incongruous to the behaviour he had maintained: juft as if a loyal fubject were frowned upon by his prince, and punifhed as a rebel.

Ver. 25. *Wilt thou break*, &c.] Here he alleges the difproportion of the means to the end. To employ fuch numerous and fevere afflictions, to crufh fo feeble a creature, was like raifing a tempeft to blow away a leaf or a ftraw.

Ver. 26. *For thou writeft*ˢ, &c.] Now he urges the difproportion of the punifhment

---

ˢ *thou writeft*, i. e. thou decreeft. It is a law-term. Compare Ifaiah lxv. 6.

27. With bonds, and stripes, and durance hard, by thee
   The punishment of slaves is laid on me:
28. To rottenness and worms a living prey,
   Like a moth-eaten vest I waste away.

nishment to the fault. He was conscious of no other sins but the follies of his youth. He imagines he was now suffering for those inadvertencies; which he thinks extremely hard, as his youth had been in the main a course of virtue. see chap. xxxi. 18.

Ver. 27. *Thou puttest*, &c.] He complains that he was used by God as men were wont to use their fugitive slaves. that is, his afflictions had exposed him to indignity and infamy equal to what was inflicted on the vilest of mankind. Elihu chastises him for these irreverent expressions chap. xxxiii. 11.

in the stocks] Mr. Heath's translation of this verse is as follows;

*Thou puttest my feet also in a clog*¹,
Thou watchest all my paths,
Thou settest a mark ᵘ *on the soles* ʷ *of my feet.*

These expressions, he thinks, allude to the custom of putting a clog on the feet of fugitive slaves, with the owner's mark, that they might be traced and found. Some kind of ignominious punishment, either of slaves or other malefactors, is doubtless referred to. But till that can be on good authority ascertained, this verse will remain obscure.

Ver. 28. *And he as a rotten thing*, &c.] The learned Michaelis ˣ reckons this among the passages, which refer to Job's disease. It certainly answers to the description chap. vii. 5. It is equally certain, that his disease was one considerable

---

¹ סד The verb is preserved in Arabic; in which language it signifies *obstruere, to obstruct*, to put an obstacle in a person's way. See Schultens' *Comment*.

ᵘ תתחקה The verb חקה properly means to *carve*, or cut with a graving tool; I Kings vi. 35. *with gold fitted upon the carved work*.

ʷ שרשי *the roots*. a man stands upon the soles of his feet, as a tree on its roots.

ˣ *Not. in Prælect*. p. 202.

CHAP.
XIV.
Ver. 1. Frail native of the womb, his age a span
         Fill'd full with trouble, is thy creature man;
    2.   A tender flow'ret, gather'd in its prime,
         A shadow gliding o'er the plain of time.
    3.   Does this weak thing employ thy jealous eye?
         Its faults the bus'ness of thy bar supply?
                                                 4. From

able part of his sufferings, and cause of the contempt into which he was fallen. But the difficulty lies in the sudden change of the person, *He* as a rotten thing, &c. such changes, however, are very common in the sacred poems. The usage also of the third person for the first is very frequent in the tragedies of Sophocles, *This man* for *I* and *me*[y], as the learned Schultens has observed [z].

CHAP. XIV.

An air of sad solemnity is diffused over this whole chapter. It is a train of gloomy ideas, rising successively in a melancholy mind; and closing with a scene highly tragical, the deplorable condition of man in the grave.

Ver. 2. *like a flower—as a shadow*] The first of these similies beautifully represents the tender composition of man's elegant frame, which is easily destroyed by the smallest accident: The other illustrates the emptiness of his enjoyments, and the celerity with which his life is continually hasting to its period. This image in the latter comparison may be the shadow cast by the sun upon the earth: But Cocceius understands it rather of the shadow on the sun-dial. Sun-dials were probably as early as the times of Job, being an invention which would naturally occur to the Egyptians or Chaldeans; who were such great Astronomers.

Ver. 3. *dost thou open thine eyes upon*, &c.] This expression denotes in Zech.
                                                                            xii.

---

[y] Œdipus Colonus. ver. 676, 1394, 1542, 1616, 1689. See several examples of this idiom among the Greeks and Orientals in Mr. Merrick's note on Pf. xxxiv. 7.

[z] Mr. Grey, Chappelow, and Heath, are for removing this verse, and placing it next after the second verse of the following chapter.

CHAP. XIV.   THE BOOK OF JOB.

4. From a foul spring can limpid waters run?
Lives there a man from failings pure? not one.
5. His date is shorten'd, and his term assign'd,
The bound unpassable by thee defin'd:
6. Yield him some respite; turn, O turn away,
And leave this hireling to enjoy his day.

7. A

xii. 4. to look angrily at another: *In that day, saith the lord, I will open mine eyes upon the house of Judah, and will smite every house of the people with blindness.*

me[a]] Mr. Heath renders it *him*, as corresponding best to *such a one* in the former clause.

Job argues here, that it is too severe to increase the ordinary afflictions of human life; by animadverting with rigour on such a frail and short-lived creature as man. he speaks in general terms, but points in particular to his own case.

Ver. 4. *Who can bring,* &c.] He now pleads for lenity on account of the natural weakness of man's moral powers: Imperfection is entailed on man by his birth. Can such a creature be without failures?

Ver. 5, 6. *Seeing his days*[b], &c.] He alledges the contracted limits of human life, and the impossibility of extending it beyond those bounds, as a motive for the intermission of his sufferings; and for allowance of some little enjoyment to such a short existence.

---

[a] אתי *me.* Mr. Heath remarks, that all the ancient versions, except the Chaldee, read אתו *him.*

[b] *are determined*] החרוצים *are cut short.* we translate it *maimed* in Lev. xxii. 22. where it seems to mean the loss of a limb, or some part of the body, by amputation. compare the use of this word in Isaiah x. 23. with the LXX, and with Rom. ix. 28. Job probably thought of the longevity of the antediluvian men, and the present abbreviation of human life.

7. A tree which falls beneath the wounding steel,
   Hopes a new growth the cruel wound to heal:
8. Yea though its sapless bole with age decay,
   The roots half mould'ring in th' unwater'd clay;
9. Touch'd by the vital stream it buds around,
   Like a young plant, with flow'rs and fruitage crown'd:
10. But man, expir'd, what latent pow'rs restore?
    Man disappears, and who beholds him more?

11. The

Ver. 7—12. *For there is hope*, &c.] He inforceth his petition for ease (ver. 6.) by another confideration: There is no coming back from the grave into this world; to enjoy a second life, whose felicity might make amends for the misery and infamy he now suffered. That this is his meaning, appears by the illustrations which he employs. If a tree, he says, be cut down to the ground; it will spring again from its root. where? on the very spot on which it grew before. it is not so with man when he dieth. If also a pool, or lake, which feedeth some river, be by any accident dried up; the waters will indeed continue to exist somewhere, but they will run no more in their former channel: so is it with man, when he disappeareth from this world; into which he shall never return.

Ver. 9. *like a plant*] Like one newly planted; so the Septuagint translates it [c], and the sense requires.

Ver. 10. *wasteth away* [d]] The hebrew word signifies, to be so intirely subdued and weakened as not to be able to recover. Man when dead has not any strength or vigorous principle, like the root of a tree that is felled, remaining in him to renew his life.

---

[c] νεοφυτος. Vulg. quasi tum primum plantatum est, *as though it were then first planted.*

[d] יחלש See Exod. xvii. 13. Isaiah xiv. 12. In the former of these passages it is englished *to discomfit*; in the latter, *to weaken.* In Joel iv. 10. * the noun is turned by the LXX. αδυνατος *the weak*, or *impotent.* It seems to correspond exactly to the υπερθε καμοντας ανθρωπους; Homer. Il. γ. 278. compare Il. ψ. 71, 72, 444.

* LXX. iii. 10.

CHAP. XIV.   THE BOOK OF JOB.   93

11. The pool its water lofes, and the ftream
   Dries to a defert, in the fcorching beam;
12. So man is loft: in duft fupine he lies,
   Nor, till the fpheres forget to wheel, fhall rife:
   While day and night their beauteous order keep,
   Death binds him faft in ever-during fleep.
13. O hide me, fcreen me in fepulchral fhade;
   Till this fierce tempeft of thy wrath be laid:
   Set me a feafon, when, with accent mild,
   Thy voice fhall waken thy remember'd child.

14. But

Ver. 11. *the fea*] fo the orientals ftyle *a lake*, or any large body of water. fee the note on ver. 7—12, alfo the note on chap. vii. 12.

Ver. 12. *rifeth not*, &c.] that is, he rifeth not to a fecond life in this world. See the above note on ver. 7—12, and compare chap. vii. 9, 10.

Ver. 13. *O, that*, &c.] In chap. vii. 9, 10, 11. reflection on the impoffibility of coming back from the grave into this world, to enjoy a fecond and happier life, and more efpecially to clear his innocence; had caft him into a paroxyfm of defpair. The fame reflection now occurring again produceth the fame effect. This paffionate wifh fomewhat refembles that of *Io*, who in an agony of diftrefs cries out to Jupiter; " Confume me with fire, or hide me under ground, or give me to be food to the fea-monfters'".

in the grave] *in fheól*. See the APPENDIX to thefe notes. *Numb.* II.

untill thy wrath be paft] This is ftrange language. His perturbation of mind is fo great, that he fcarce knows what he fays. He thinks God is angry with him; and that his anger will continue, fo long as he is in the prefent world: but that if he were removed out of it, God's wrath would fubfide, and in time

go

* In the *Prometheus* of Æfchylus.

14. But shall a carcase, rotted in the tomb,
Quicken, and flourish with a second bloom?
Patient of life, throughout my suff'ring state,
I would that blisful renovation wait.

15. O go off; like man's resentment, when the object of it is kept a considerable while out of his sight.

appoint me a set time, &c.] He seems to suppose, that the state of death is a state of *insensibility*[f]: and begs he may remain in that condition but for a fixed term; and then recover his consciousness, and therewith the favour of God and enjoyment of felicity in a second life in the present world. This wish contradicts what he had said but a little before of the impossibility of returning from the grave to live here again. But we should remember the distracted state of his mind. He presently however recovers himself, so far as to see the absurdity of such a wish : *If a man die, shall he live again?*

Ver. 14. *If a man die shall he live again?*] He seems to correct himself for his vain request in the foregoing verse. The same thought as in ver. 12, of the impossibility of a man's returning into the world to live in it again, is here exprest in the form of an interrogation.

all the days, &c.]

All the days of my appointed time[g] I would wait,
Untill my renovation[h] come.

He means, I think, that if there were a resurrection to a new life in this world to be hoped for, he would bear his present heavy afflictions with unshaken patience. By his *appointed time* I understand his now suffering condition : and by his *renovation*, his restoration to a second life here for the vindication of his character, and the enjoyment of some happiness. The tenor of his whole discourse appears to me to suggest this interpretation.

---

[f] Compare Psal. vi. 5.

[g] צבאי *my warfare*, or appointed time of affliction. See chap. vii. 1.

[h] חליפתי *my sprouting again.* it is a metaphor from a tree springing again, after it has been cut down; ver. 7. *it will sprout again.* The septuagint turns it in the verse before us ἕως πάλιν γένωμαι *till I exist again.*

15. O hafte, arraign me, my warm pleadings hear;
And with a father's heart incline thy ear.
16. Ah! too fevere, obfervant of my ways,
Thy mem'ry numbers every ſtep that ſtrays:
17. All annall'd in thy rolls, beneath thy feal,
My fins are treafur'd, and thy wrath I feel.
18. Thy wrath lays defolate this earthy ball;
Its rocks are funder'd and its mountains fall.
19. Thy

Ver. 15. *Thou ſhalt call*, &c.] Unable to bear the thought of going out of the world under fuch a load of infamy, and having no hope of coming back into it again, to clear his innocence; He earneſtly begs of God to relent towards his creature, and to bring him to immediate trial.

Call thou, and I will anſwer;
Have thou a defire to the work of thine hands.

The terms *call* and *anſwer* ought furely to be taken in the fame judicial fenfe as in chap. v. 1. xiii. 22. the former denoting the action of bringing the complaint; the latter the part of the defendant in replying to it.

Ver. 16, 17. *For now*, &c.] as a contraſt to the tender regard he pleaded for in the foregoing verſe, and as a reaſon for his urging an immediate trial; he here fets forth, in judicial expreſſions, the feverity with which God treated him now.

Ver. 16. *For now*, &c.] His complaint here ſhews, that his difcontent with the ways of providence is ſtill increaſing: And thus the bufinefs of the poem, which is to expofe that offence, is going forward.

Ver. 17. *thou foweſt up mine iniquity.*] *Thou recordeſt*[1] *mine iniquity*. This circumſtance, though mentioned laſt, comes in order before the other: for the record muſt be made up, before it is fealed and put in a place of fecurity.

Ver. 18—22. *And furely*, &c.] Here is an abrupt tranſition to fome other matter,

---

[1] חסם *to note in a regiſter*, as Mr. Heath turns it; and fo the LXX. ιπισημηνω.

19. Thy headlong torrents through the vallies found,
Burst the stone bridges, scoop the solid ground,
Ravage

ter, after the manner of the Arabian poets[k]. He passeth, if I mistake not, from his own particular afflictions to the calamitous state of this world in general; instancing earthquakes, inundations, and the waste of mankind by death: all which he considers as effects of the wrath of God against the sins of men[l]. compare ver. 13.

Ver. 18. *The mountain falling, &c.*] by an earthquake. see the note on chap. ix. 5.

Ver. 19. *The waters, &c.*] I understand this verse to be a description of desolating land-floods, or torrents, occasioned by the falling of the autumnal or vernal rains in too great abundance.

The waters dash in pieces[m] *the stones,*
Their overflowings[n] *wash away the soil of the earth,*
And thou destroyest the hope of man.

the hope of man] that is, the hope of the husbandman; the fruits of the ground, whether in the vineyard or in the fields.

The yellow harvests of the ripen'd year,
And flatted vineyards, one sad waste appear:
When Jove descends in sluicy sheets of rain,
And all the labours of mankind are vain.

Pope's Hom. Il. v. 117, &c.

---

[k] Vid. Pocock *in carmen Tograi*, p. 50.

[l] See chap. ix. 5, 6. Homer also represents deluges as divine punishments of injustice. Il. xvi. 384, &c.

[m] שחקו it signifies not a gentle but a violent attrition and dissipation, as appears by the literal and figurative use of this word in the hebrew bible. See Exod. xxx. 36. Ps. xviii. 43.

[n] סְפִיחֶיהָ The verb signifies in Chaldee *to increase*; in Arabic, *to pour out*. Vid. Castell. *Lex Hept.* with regard to the construction, the masculine plural סְפִיחִים is the nominative to the verb תִּשְׁטֹף singular and feminine: and the affix ה refers to the dual number מַיִם as its antecedent. These are common enallages in the Arabic language. Vid. Shultens' Comment.

Ravage the fields, and with impetuous fway
Hurry the rural hope of toiling man away.

20. O'er weeping man thy legion'd ills prevail,
His face thou changeſt into ſickly pale:
Then ſudden to the nether ſhades he's hurl'd,
Cut off from all communion with the world;

21. Unknowing what befalls his children here,
Unſharing in the triumph and the tear:

22. His corſe, meanwhile, in ſorrow waſtes away,
And his loſt breath laments its mould'ring clay.

CHAP.

Ver. 20. *Thou prevaileſt*, &c.] This expreſſion referreth to the conſtant and irreſiſtable operation of the ſentence of mortality, which is paſſed upon all men.

Thou changeſt, &c.] Too often we behold, with a ſigh, this funeral preſage in the altered looks of our valuable friends and beloved relations.

Ver. 21. *His ſons*, &c.] The heart of every tender parent feels the force of this pathetic ſentiment.

Ver. 22. *But his fleſh*, &c.] As the two foregoing verſes ſpoke of man departed into another world, it is moſt natural to underſtand this verſe to relate to the ſame ſubject. According to the following tranſlation*, which the original will allow, we are preſented with a tragical picture of man's condition in the grave:

> But over ᵖ him his fleſh ſhall grieve ᑫ,
> And over him his breath ʳ ſhall mourn.

In

---

* Suggeſted in part by the learned Schultens.

ᵖ עָלָיו *over*, or *for*, *him* Amos vi. 6. *they are not grieved for the affliction of Joſeph*. Vid. Noldium.

ᑫ כאב *to be ſorrowful*, as in Prov. xiv. 13. *the heart is ſorrowful*. The adjective bears the ſame acceptation in Arabic. See the Arabic verſion of the Pſalms, Pſ. xxxiv. 17.

ʳ נפשו *his breath*. ch. xli. 21. (Heb. ver. 13.) *his breath kindleth coals*.

CHAP.
XV.
1, 2. The Temanite reply'd: What storm is this,
From our wife man, of pride and emptiness!
This, wisdom's language? is a wise man's mind
Big with the poison of an eastern wind?
3. And will he thus abuse the pow'rs of breath,
To vent opinions mischievous as death?

4. Death
In the daring spirit of oriental poetry, *the flesh*, or body, and *the breath* are made conscious beings; the former lamenting its putrefaction in the grave, the latter mourning over the mould'ring clay which it once enlivened.

CHAP. XV.

The poem is now all in a flame. Even Eliphaz has lost temper. He vents himself in bitter sarcasms and reproaches; charging Job's replies with impiety, self-sufficiency, contempt of his elders, and intolerable arrogance towards God himself. ver. 1. to the end of ver. 16.

The second part of the speech, ver. 17—30, is a citation of an old Arabian poem ', the subject whereof is the vengeance of God on some tyrannical princes: For Eliphaz and his companions supposed Job to be of that character.

He concludes, by way of application, with his own comminations on all who abuse the power intrusted to them, and make a sale of justice. The drift of the whole is to vindicate providence, to expose Job as an object of divine wrath, and to terrify him, if possible, into a confession of his guilt. ver. 31—35.

Ver. 3. *unprofitable—can do no good*] These negative expressions must here signify highly *pernicious*, by a figure of speech called meiosis. otherwise the thought in this verse will sink into flatness. for in the foregoing verse, he had characterised Job's opinions by the strong image of *the east wind*. In those climates, both in spring and summer, if the east-wind blows for some days ', all
the

' See Michaelis on *the Prælections*.
' Michaelis *in Prælect*. p. 23. n. 22.

4. Death to religion, to all virtue bane,
Thy words the lifted hand of pray'r restrain.
5. Thy mouth bewrays, spite of its glozing art,
Th' impiety close-lurking in thy heart:
6. By thy own mouth condemn'd, what need of mine?
Sufficient voucher for thy guilt is thine.

7. Born

the fields are burnt, so as that scarce any green thing remains; most of the rivers and fountains are dried up, and nature itself seems almost to die.

Ver. 4. *Yea thou casteth off fear*, &c.] He taxeth Job's doctrine of an *unequal providence* with impiety. It tended, he says, to subvert religion; by confounding all distinction of characters in the distribution of good and evil. That he refers to this doctrine, appears by his asking Job, in ver. 7, 8, whether he had been in the council of God; since he pretended to be better informed in the plan of providence than they?

Thou casteth off] The hebrew word imports *disannulling*, or *making void* [u] a moral bond or obligation. The obligation of religion is broken, he says, by Job's principle *that God destroyeth the perfect and the wicked* [w]. The wicked, then, have nothing to fear; nor the pious any thing to hope from him. In short, the providence which Job contended for, was, in this man's account, no providence at all; and nothing better than downright atheism.

Ver. 5, 6. *For thy mouth*, &c.] Behold the progress of bigotry and uncharitableness. He first falsely accuseth his friend of having vented atheistical principles; and then concludes, that there wanted no other evidence to prove him a wicked man.

Thou chusest the tongue of the crafty] He gives this invidious turn to Job's protestations of innocence, prayers, and appeals to God: which he represents as an artful address to the passions of the hearers; to blind their judgement, and deceive them into a favourable opinion of his piety.

---

[u] תפר Numb. xxx. 14, 15. *But if he* (the husband) *shall any ways make them* (the vows of the wife) *void, after that he hath heard them*, &c.

[w] Chap. ix. 22.

THE BOOK OF JOB.   CHAP. XV.

7. Born before Adam, faw thy favour'd eyes
The wood-crown'd hills from eldeſt ocean rife?
8. Haſt thou in the celeſtial fynod ſtood?
The counfels heard, th' Almighty's edicts view'd?
Doſt thou poſſefs the fecrets of his rule?
Thou only wife, and every man a fool?
9, 10. What boaſts thy knowledge above ours? Behold,
With us the head in grave experience old;
Yea th' old old man, to whofe low-bending years
Thy father's wrinkled age as youth appears.
11. Mean are divine emollients? held for vile,
Friendſhip's monitions couch'd in friendly ſtyle?
12. Whither

Ver. 7—10. *Art thou,* &c.] He now chaſtifeth him for having prefumed to underſtand the ways of God, better than they who were fo much his elders.

Art thou the firſt man, &c.] *Waſt thou born before Adam*? The farcafm in this, and in the following verfe, is fevere but noble: perfectly in the lofty manner of this fpeaker. The queſtion amounts to aſking, if he was fome fuperior being who exiſted before the world? compare Pſalm xc. 2. Prov. viii. 25.

Haſt thou heard, &c.] *Haſt thou been a hearer in the council* of God? Haſt thou been prefent, when the angelic aſſembly were in waiting before the throne of God, to give account of their miniſtry; and to receive freſh orders refpecting the affairs of providence in our world?

Ver. 11. *the confolations of God*] So he ſtyles their promifes of a fpeedy re-eſtabliſhment

---

˟ אדם הראישון אשר טרם אלהים. The Chaldee turns this clauſe, *wert thou born in the times before Adam, without father and mother?* Had the meaning been *art thou the firſt man,* the original muſt have run הראשון (Vid. Schultens' *Comment*) as אן קדם אדם the *firſt man,* in the Targum on Pſ. lxxiv. 10.

בסוד *in the council,* or *aſſembly* as our Tranſlators render it in Pſ. cxi. 1. Jer. vi. 11. It ought alfo to have been turned *council* (not *counfel*) in Jer. xxiii. 18.

12. Whither will headlong pride impell thy foul?
    How fiercely wild thy flafhing eye-balls roll,
13. Thy fpirit turning upon God again,
    And paffion raving in audacious ftrain!
14. " What, purenefs challeng'd by a child of duft?
    " By woman-born, the lofty ftyle of juft?

15. " Not

eftablifhment of his felicity, on condition of his repentance. He gives them the pompous appellation of divine confolations, on account of their pretended excellence.

Is there any, &c.] According to Schultens the tranflation fhould be;

And gentle *difcourfe*[b] *to thee?*

He means by *gentle difcourfe* their *diftant intimations* of his guilt, their warnings infinuated in the way of examples, and their exhortations to confeffion and amendment. On all which, as well as on their confolations, Job had poured contempt; particularly in chap. xiii. 12.

Ver. 12, 13. *Why doth thine heart*, &c.] This reprehenfion points in particular to thofe too high-fpirited expoftulations, in chap. xiii. 22, &c.

and what do thine eyes wink at?] *Wherefore do thine eyes look fierce*[c]? Excruciating pain, anguifh of mind, and indignation at their cruel treatment had given, perhaps, an air of wildnefs and fiercenefs to his countenance; which this inhuman cenfor attributes to paffion againft God.

---

[a] לאט *ad lenitudinem, gently*; as our englifh bible turns it, in II Sam. xviii. 5. *Deal gently for my fake with the young man*. The root is אוש *lenis fuit*, fo it fignifies in Arabic. Vid. Comment. Schultens.

[b] דבר a feries of words, or *talk* as it is rendred in ver. 3. *unprofitable talk*.

[c] ירזמון This word is no where elfe found in the hebrew bible. It is, however, happily preferved in the Arabic language: where, according to Schultens, it fignifies *to be in a rage, to fcowl, to have a wild and threatning look*; being a metaphor either from the growling of a beaft of prey, or from the afpect and rumbling of a thunder-cloud.

15. " Not pure, not juſt, before his piercing ſight,
" Are ev'n his holy miniſters of light:
16. " How then, that foul abominable thing,
" Who ſins as eager as he quaffs his ſpring!"

17. Hear thou my doctrine, what theſe eyes atteſt,
18. By ancient bards in living verſe expreſt:
A line of worthies, in ſucceſſion long,
With faithful voice roll'd down th' immortal ſong;
19. For

Ver. 14, 15. *What is man*, &c.] His citation of the oracle (chap. iv. 17, &c.) a ſecond time, is intended as a reproach of Job's diſobedience to it by perſiſting to juſtify himſelf to God.

How much more abominable, &c.] In the firſt recital of the oracle, the application was addreſſed to mankind in general (chap. iv. 19.) But the words *abominable*ᵈ and *filthy*ᵉ, which he now uſeth, are, in ſcripture, epithets of the vileſt ſins and ſinners: And the ſtrong phraſe *which drinketh iniquity like water*ᶠ implies committing crimes without reluctance, yea with eagerneſs and guſt; which is an effect of *inveterate habits* only. All this perfectly agrees with their injurious idea of Job; to whom the application is now perſonally made.

*How much leſs*ᵍ *(clean in his ſight*, ver. 15.) is the *abominable and filthy man*ʰ, *who drinketh iniquity like water?*

Ver. 17—19. *I will ſhew thee*, &c.] Bildad had quoted half a dozen lines of
the

ᵈ נתעב

ᵉ נאלח See Levit. xviii. 30. Pſalm xiv. 1, 3. 1 Pet. iv. 3.

ᶠ Prov. xix. 28. *The mouth of the wicked devoureth iniquity.*

ᵍ אף כי Chap. ix. 14. *How much leſs ſhall I anſwer him?*

ʰ איש *the man.* Pſ. cxii. 1. אשרי איש ירא את יהוה *Bleſſed is the man that feareth the Lord.*

19. For wisdom fam'd, on whose high-favour'd land
    Invasion's foot was never known to stand.

20. " The tyrant, all his days of dreaded pow'r,
    " In dark suspicion of its fatal hour,
                                                        " His

the ancient poetry, that were in the *proverbial* style [1]. Eliphaz is going to cite a much larger number; of *the descriptive* kind, and in a sublimer strain. He prefaceth the citation with observing; first, that the facts alledged in these verses were verified by his own experience; *that which I have seen, I will declare.* Secondly, that these verses contain the observations of the wise in very ancient ages; and had been carefully conveyed down by oral tradition to the present times; *which wise men have told from their fathers, and have not hid it*: and thirdly, that these traditional verses had been preserved pure and perfect, by means of the peculiar circumstances of the persons through whose hands they had passed: for no foreign colony had intermixed with them; *unto whom alone the land was given.* Neither had their country ever been conquered, *and no stranger came upon them* [k]; characters, which determine the country, spoken of, to be *Arabia Felix* [l]; and consequently the cited poem to be an *Arabian* poem.

Ver. 18. *have told*] that is, have expressed in memorial verses: for this was the ancient mode of conveying instruction [m]. Poetry was the favourite study of the Arabs in the earliest times, and was used as the vehicle of all their knowledge [n]. 'Tis further observable, that Eliphaz says, *have told*, not *have written*: He speaks therefore of times anterior to the invention of letters.

Ver. 20, &c. *The wicked man*, &c.] We have here the pleasure of reading a
                                                                    piece

---

[1] Chap. viii. 11, 12, 13.

[k] לא עבר זר בתוכם LXX. ωκ ιπηλθεν αλλογενης επ' αυτες, *no stranger came upon them*. See Joel iii. 17. Heb. iv. 17.

[l] Mr. Le Clerc supposes, with great probability, that *the wise men*, whom Eliphaz speaks of, were the *Joctanidæ*, the pure original Arabs, descendants of Jocktan the son of Eber; who settled in *Arabia Felix*, which they enjoyed *alone:* They became famous for their wisdom, that is, philosophy. Vid. Pocock. *Specim. hist. Arab.* p. 3, 6, and 1 Kings iv. 30. The Queen of Sheba was of this country.

[m] See the note on chap. viii. 10.

[n] Pocock. *Specim. hist. Arab.* p. 158, 159.

"His own soul tortures with divining fears:
21. "He starts, dire noises eccho in his ears;
"He hears the ruffian's step, in peace profound,
"He trembles at th' imaginary wound;
22. "His conscious heart despairing to evade
"The midnight vengeance of the watching blade:
23. "An exile now, unfriended, hard bested,
"Wand'ring, inquiring, crouching low for bread;
"He

piece of poetry, that was the production of Arabia Felix; more ancient, perhaps, than the old Caananitish song quoted by Moses°, and no less admirable for its sublimity than venerable for its age. The citation ends with the thirtieth verse: For that verse closeth the description which begins at this twentieth verse.

travelleth with pain] *tormenteth himself*ᵖ. He is in perpetual dread of some tragical catastrophe.

Ver. 21. *A dreadful sound*, &c.] *A dreadful sound is in his ears, that in peace*ᵈ *the destroyer will come upon him*. When there are no signs of invasions, insurrections, or plots against him, his disturbed imagination is continually presenting destruction to him. This is strong painting.

Ver. 22. *He believeth not*, &c.] His despair of escaping some unhappy end, assassination for instance, is described here:

He believeth not that he shall return out of darkness,
But (believeth) that *he is watched for*ʳ *of the sword*.

Ver. 23. *He wandereth*, &c.] This abrupt transition, to *the punishment* of the wicked

---

° Numb. xxi. 27, 23.

ᵖ מתהולל ἑαυτὸν τιμωρουμενος *tormenting himself*, as Grotius explains it. Buxtorf, in his hebrew concordance, renders it, *dolore se conficit*. It is englished *was exceedingly grieved*, in Esther iv. 4.

ᵈ בשלום St. Jerom's version is free and clear; *et cum pax sit, ille semper insidias suspicatur*, *and when there is peace, he is always suspicious of plots*.

ʳ צפו Ps. xxvii. 32. *The wicked watcheth the righteous, and seeketh to slay him*.

" He knows, he knows his predetermin'd doom,
" Sees it arriv'd, the day of direful gloom:

24. " Gigantic wicked oppreffor, admirably expreffeth the fuddenneſs of the event; and prefents him to our very fight in a moſt deplorable ſtate of calamity. It was no uncommon thing, in ancient times, to fee bad princes expelled their dominions, and reduced to beggary in a foreign land. Homer alludes to fuch examples, in thoſe beautiful lines where Achilles fays to king Priam;

>   Two urns by *Jove*'s high throne have ever ſtood,
>   The fource of Evil one, and one of Good;
>   From thence the cup of mortal man he fills,
>   Bleſſings to théſe, to thoſe diſtributes ills;
>   To moſt he mingles both: The wretch decreed
>   To taſte the bad, unmix'd, is curſt indeed;
>   Purfu'd by wrongs, by meagre famine driv'n,
>   He wanders, outcaſt both of earth and heav'n.
>   Mr. Pope's Iliad, B. xxiv. 663ᵗ, &c.

He knoweth, &c.] *He knoweth* by experience', *that a day of darkneſs was decreed*ᵘ; *it is preſent to him* ʷ. He had lived in terrible apprehenſions of this *day of darkneſs*, or time of vengeance ˣ. He now finds by experience, that fuch a fatal day was preordained to his crimes. *The day* of the wicked means the time appointed in the counſels of God for the puniſhment of his wickedneſs. Pſ. xxxvii. 13.

ᵗ In the original, ver. 527, &c.

ᵘ ידע *He knoweth by experience:* fo it fignifies chap. v. 25. *Thou ſhalt know alſo that thy feed ſhall be great*, &c.

ʷ נכון *decreed*, eſtabliſhed by the decree of God, Gen. xli. 32. *the thing is eſtabliſhed by God*.

ʷ בידו *it is in his hand*, i. e. before him, in his preſence. Thus in the apocryphal book of Eſther, chap. xiv. 4. the queen fays to God, *my danger is in mine hand.* In Arabic the phraſe בין ידיו is frequently uſed for *coram eo*, in his preſence. See the Arabic verſion of the Pſalms, Pſ. v. 5. ix. 3.

ˣ Ver. 22. *He believeth not that he ſhall return out of darkneſs.*

24. " Gigantic Woe and desperate Remorse
" Assail, distract, o'erpow'r him; like the force
" Of some great sultan, when he pours his might
" On the bold satrap who provokes the fight.
25. " This is the daring criminal, whose pride
" With lofty arm the thunderer defy'd:

26. " Who

Ver. 24. *Trouble and anguish,* &c.] One of these terms meaneth, I suppose, his *outward calamities*; the other, his *despair*. To express both in the language of sublimity, and withal to give a strong idea of the number and irresistible violence of his distresses, the Poet represents *trouble* and *anguish* as persons, and leaders of a formidable army of evils; attacking and overpowering this high delinquent. He illustrates this thought by the simile of a monarch, who with his whole force falls upon one of his great lords that is in open rebellion against him; as Grotius explains the comparison: *as a king ready to the battle.*

Ver. 25—28. *For he stretcheth out,* &c.] The poet breaks the thread of his description of this wicked man's *punishment,* to delineate his *crimes*; which are impiety ʸ, luxury ᶻ, and rapacity ᵃ.

He stretcheth out, &c.] These images are borrowed from the single combat, which was much in practice in the ancient wars. *Stretching out the hand* is the attitude of defiance: *strengthening himself,* or *behaving himself insolently,* may denote the haughty terms of the challenge; and *running,* &c. the intrepidity and fury of his attack. These bold metaphors are intended to express the most daring impiety, atrocious violation of the laws of God with contempt of his vindictive justice. The whole may be thus translated,

For he stretched out his hand against God,
And bade defiance ᵇ to the Almighty.

He

ʸ Ver. 25, 26.   ᶻ Ver. 27.   ᵃ Ver. 28.

ᵇ So Mr. Heath turns יִתְגַּבָּר. The LXX. render it by ηγαγκλακε, which signifies, says Drusius, *collum attollo, superbio, ferocio.* The hebrew word in this conjugation imports literally, *to make himself a mighty man.* The idea, which it contains, is opened and extended in Ps. xii. 3, 4, 5.

26. " Who stretching out his neck, in open field,
   " Rush'd on the terrors of the blazing shield.
27. " His heav'n was riot, and his god was wine,
   " Fat cloath'd his ample face, and fat his spreading loin:
28. " By rapines rich, by desolations great,
   " The ruin'd city and the pillag'd state.
29. " 'Tis wealth accurs'd, pow'r for a season tall,
   " On canker'd root, aspiring but to fall:

30. " Dark

He ran upon him with his neck[c],
Upon the thick boss of his buckler.

Homer gives to Jupiter a spear and a shield. The scripture poets arm the Almighty with a shield, a sword, and a bow.

Ver. 27. *he covereth—and maketh*, &c.] *he covered—and made*, &c. This verse is a graphical description of luxury. compare Pf. lxxiii. 7, 8.

Ver. 28. *And he dwelleth*, &c.] *And he dwelled*, &c. The foregoing verse marked the *sensuality* of this wicked man. The character would have been left unfinished, had the poet added nothing concerning the *oppressions* by which that luxury was supported. I think therefore, that by *dwelling in desolate cities*, &c. must be understood his getting possession of them by conquest; and depopulating them partly by his sword, and partly by severe contributions and taxations.

Ver. 29. *He shall not*, &c.] The poem here returns to the description of this man's *catastrophe*.

He shall not continue to be rich[d],

Neither

---

[c] בצואר *cum prono collo*, with his neck stooping and stretched out; the very attitude of a combatant running upon his adversary, as Mr. Le Clerc, I think, has remarked.

[d] לא יעשר *He shall not continue to be rich*. A verb is sometimes to be understood of the continuation of the action expressed by that verb. Vid. Guarin's *Grammat. Heb.* vol. i. p. 518.

108   THE BOOK OF JOB.   CHAP. XV.

30. " Dark clouds involve him, on his branching head
" Devouring flames fierce devaftation fpread:
" Uprooted by the furious breath of heav'n,
" Impetuous down his mountain's fteep he's driv'n."

31. Woe to the man who by oppreffion climbs,
Drunk with fucceffes, and fecure in crimes:

32. For

Neither fhall his power ᵉ *endure,*
Neither fhall their profperity ᶠ *ftrike root* ᵍ *upon the earth.*

This is a negative manner of expreffing the total overthrow of fuch men's greatnefs and felicity.

Ver. 30. *He fhall not depart,* &c.] he fhall not come out of his calamities. The deftruction of the tyrant, with his whole family and fortunes, is here reprefented by that of a lofty tree; which on fome dark tempeftuous day is fired by lightning, torn up by the wind, and hurled down the precipice on which it grew.

Ver. 31. *Let not him,* &c.] Eliphaz now fpeaks in his own perfon, and denounceth a commination, grounded on the example in the lines juft cited, againft all who raife themfelves to wealth and power by iniquitous means; pointing in particular to Job.

Let him not truft in profperity ʰ, who *is intoxicated* ⁱ therewith:

For

ᵉ חיל fignifies *power* very frequently.

ᶠ מנלם *their profperity,* as Mr. Heath turns it. The root נלה is in Arabic, *affecutus eft, obtinuit votum fcopumque.* מנלה therefore is *fuccefs,* or a ftate in which all things go according to a man's wifhes and endeavours. Schultens.

ᵍ לא יטה *fhall not extend,* viz. its roots; *non radices aget in terram,* Schultens: more arborum quæ radices fuas longé latéque extendunt. Drufius.

ʰ בשו it fignifies in Arabic, an *equilibrium,* and is applied to the fun in his meridian altitude; and in metaphor denotes *the height of profperity.* Schultens.

ⁱ נתעה *qui eâ inebriatus infanit.* Ifaiah xxviii. 7. xix. 13, 14. Hof. iv. 12. Schultens.

CHAP. XV. THE BOOK OF JOB.

32. For bitter change shall come: untimely blast
    His boughs shall wither, and his fruit shall cast;
33. As when the vine her half-grown berries show'rs,
    Or poison'd olive her unfolding flow'rs.
34. Know all the wicked, all the venal crew,
    Their splendid tents the skulking bribe shall rue:
    A fire it kindles, and the flame supplies,
    Till the gay scene a dismal desert lies.
                                          35. See

For his change [k] shall be misery [l].

Ver. 32. *It shall be*, &c.] *It*, the calamitous change before mentioned *shall be accomplished before his time*; that is, before his days are fulfilled: He shall perish by an untimely death.

His branch shall not be green] *shall not continue green* [m]. His fate shall be like that of a vine, or olive, that is withered by drought, or by a poisonous east-wind; as it follows in the next verse.

Ver. 33. *He shall shake off*, &c.] The green grapes shew themselves early in the spring [n], in those hot climates; and the olive blossoms in June and July [o]; in which months a burning pestilential east-wind bloweth there [p].

Ver. 34. *Hypocrites*] *Profligates*. it is clear, that *the congregation of hypocrites* and *the tabernacles of bribery* mean one and the same character; such impious
                                                                    oppressors

---

[k] תמורתו it is englished *exchange* chap. xxviii. 17. *and the exchange of it shall not be for jewels of fine gold.* A change of condition, from good to bad, is like an exchange of a valuable commodity for another that is nothing worth.

[l] שוא *vanity*, that is, *misery*. So it is used chap vii. 3. *I am made to possess months of misery.*

[m] So in ver. 29. *He shall not continue to be rich.* See the note.

[n] Cantic. ii. 11, 13. vii. 12.

[o] See Johnson's *Herbal*.

[p] Chap xxvii. 21. Ezek. xvii. 10. Jonah iv. 7, 8. Vid. Michaelis *in Prælect.* p. 39, p. 41. Schultens in Job xxvii. 22.

35. See now oppreffion, (and its boafted gain)
Conceiv'd and ufher'd into birth in vain:
The flatt'ring crime, with fo much anguifh bred,
Turns all its plagues on its own parent's head.

CHAP.
XVI.
1, 2. Dull ecchos of dull things too long, reply'd
The fuff'ring man, my patient ear have try'd.
                                                    Officious

oppreffors as are defcribed in the Arabian poem, which he had been reciting.
See the note on chap. viii. 13.

Ver. 35. *They conceive*, &c.]

> *They conceive mifchief* ⁿ, *and bring forth iniquity* ʳ :
> *But their belly prepared a cheat* ˢ *to themfelves.*

Mifchief and iniquity, that is, mifchievous iniquity, undoubtedly mean the fchemes of injuftice which they *conceive:* and they are laid *to bring forth* thofe fchemes, when they carry them into execution. But it turns out, that the wrong, which they defign and do to others, proves *a cheat* ; that is, the caufe of their own deftruction. That this is a true explication of the words, appears from the parallel paffage; Pf. vii. 14, 16. (Heb. ver. 15, 17.) *Behold he travaileth* ᵗ *with iniquity* ᵘ, *and hath conceived* ʷ *mifchief* ˣ, *and brought forth a falfhood* ʸ. *His mifchief fhall return upon his own head, and his violent dealing* ᶻ *fhall come down upon his own pate.*

C H A P. XVI.

Such a fpeech as the foregoing was admirably fitted to carry on the defign of the poem, by irritating the paffions of Job, and inflaming his difcontent with the ways of providence. In this part of his reply, he expreffeth his refentment in a
                                                                                                moving

---

| עמל ʳ | און ⁿ | מרמה ˢ | יחבל ᵗ |
| און ᵘ | הרה ʷ | עמל ˣ | שקר ʸ | חמסו ᶻ |

Officious to torment I find you all,
Your documents are stings, your comforts gall.

3. With endless brawl shall declamation roar?
What rous'd thy passion to one tempest more?

4. Would I thus pour rough answers in your ear,
Hard as your hearts, and as your style severe,
Or shake the scornful head, should Heav'n assign
Your souls the miserable place of mine?

5. Ah! no —— soft pity should inspire my phrase,
I'd sooth your sorrows and your courage raise.

6. For me —— O what shall mollify my grief?
Nor plaining yields, nor silence yields relief:

7. And now, I faint beneath its swelling load,
Thy sland'rous tongue unpeoples my abode:

8. I'm

moving representation of their inhumanity [z]; in vehement description of their brutal usage [a]; and in affecting remonstrances to God, for delivering him into the hands of these unmerciful men [b]. He concludes with renewed and most solemn asseverations of his innocence [c], and an earnest petition to be brought to immediate trial before God.

Ver. 4, 5. *I also could speak*, &c.] This reproof is inimitably tender, and at the same time exquisitely keen.

Ver. 7. *But now he hath*, &c.] *But now it* (my grief [e] ver. 6.) *hath made me weary*. My affliction is become insupportable, since I can find no relief either

from

---

[z] Ver. 1—6. [a] Ver. 7—10. [b] Ver. 11—16.
[c] Ver. 17, 18, 19, 20. [d] Ver. 21, 22.

[e] The latin vulgate justly supplies the word *grief* from the foregoing verse; *nunc autem oppressit me dolor meus*.

8. I'm feiz'd, as though a homicide, by thee;
Then blacken'd with thy daring calumny:

Fierce from filence or lamentation. Moreover, I am, by this man's calumnies, deprived even of the comfort of a friend to pity me.

Thou haſt made defolate[f], &c.] Thou Eliphaz (fo the tenor of the difcourfe requires us to underſtand the addreſs) by thy ſlanders, fanctified by thy years and character, driveſt away the few friends my adverfity had left to me. It is ſuppofed, he alludes to the words in chap. xv. 34. *The congregation of profligates ſhall be defolate.*

Ver. 8. *And thou haſt*, &c.] This obfcure verfe will become clearer, I think, in the following verſion;

Thou alfo haſt apprehended me[g], *as a malefactor.*
He is become a witneſs againſt me:
Yea he that belieth me[h], *rifeth up againſt me;*
He accuſeth me to my face.

Thou haſt apprehended me, &c.] He ſtill directs his speech to Eliphaz; who had fet him forth as a cruel tyrant, and an example of divine vengeance. This treatment he compares to feizing and binding a notorious offender.

He is become, &c.] By a ſudden change of the perfon, expreſſive of great emotion, he turneth from Eliphaz to the audience; and inſtead of continuing his addreſs to him, complaineth bitterly of him. *He*, this man, my profeſſed friend, is become my falſe accuſer.

---

[f] השמות If the root, שמם, properly fignifies, as Schultens affirms, *to be blaſted by lightning*, or *by a fcorching wind*; it affords a ſtrong and beautiful metaphor to expreſs the effect of the breath of ſlander.

[g] תקמטני LXX. ἐπέλαβέυ μυ, *Thou haſt laid hold on me.* Grotius remarks, that it is a judicial term, denoting the feizure of a ſuppofed criminal; in order to bring him to a trial. It ſignifies in Chaldee and Syriac *to bind* (Caſtell. Lex.) and in Arabic, *to tie the hands and feet*, alfo *to bind a captive*; Schultens. We tranſlate it *to be cut down* chap. xxii. 16. But I know of no authority for that verſion; any more than for rendering it here, *thou haſt filled me with wrinkles*. Theſe are the only places where קמט occurs in the hebrew bible.

[h] כחש׳ Symmachus reads it as a participle of the preſent tenſe in *Kal.* for he turns it καταψευδόμενος *belying me*. It is engliſhed *to lye*, Hof. iv. 2. The ſubſtantive denotes *a lye* told by informers and falſe accuſers, Hof. vii. 3. Nahum iii. 1. See alfo Pf. lix. 13.

CHAP. XVI.   THE BOOK OF JOB.

Fierce in my face this lying witnefs flies,
9. He grinds his teeth, rage lightens from his eyes:
10. All rufh with open jaws, all tear my name,
And glut their fury on my murder'd fame.

11. Ah! fo it pleas'd th' Almighty to ordain,
Ev'n to expofe me, in his fhaming chain,
To fons of Belial, to licentious throngs,
And the rude infult of reviling tongues.

12. I

Ver. 9. *He teareth me,* &c.] This is a lively piece of painting: He reprefents thefe men as fo many beafts of prey, greedily worrying him to death with their flanders and comminations [b].

Ver. 10. *They have fmitten,* &c.] A proverbial form of fpeech for *atrocious defamation.* Lam. iii. 30.

They have gathered themfelves together, &c.] This is flat. The original denotes exceffive greedinefs 'in devouring; and, in the metaphor, a malignant fatisfaction. *They have glutted, or gorged, themfelves* [i] *upon me.*

Ver. 11. *God,* &c.] He now complains of God, for having by means of his affliction expofed him to this barbarous ufage.

The ungodly—the wicked] They had painted *him* in thefe black colours. He might, with much more juftice, retort the charge upon *them*; if uttering the fouleft calumnies will denominate a perfon wicked.

delivered

---

[b] The royal poet defcribes the abufe and flanders with which he was worried in fimilar language; Pf. xxxv. 15, 16. But what our Bible there renders, *with hypocritical mockers at feafts,* is perhaps more juftly turned by Caftellio, *impurorum heluonum ritu, after the manner of profligate gluttons.*

[i] It bears this ftrong meaning in Exod. xv. 9. *my luft fhall be fatisfied* (fatiated) *upon them.* נפשי, here rendred *my luft,* fhould, I think, have been turned, *my appetite;* as in Prov. xxiii. 2.

Q

THE BOOK OF JOB. CHAP. XVI.

12. I once was happy——but his forceful hand
Seiz'd, shook me, hurl'd me from my lofty stand:
Then, bruis'd and dash'd to pieces, still on me,
Fix'd for his mark, he wreaks his stern decree:
13. His unrelenting bowmen hem me round,
Pierce, cleave me, shed my vitals on the ground.
                                                14. 'Tis

delivered me—turned me over] The terms in the original are expressive of the most ignominious usage. They are metaphors taken from the punishment of a malefactor: The former [k] is supposed to denote *the putting an iron collar about his neck*, the other [l] *casting him down into a deep and miry dungeon*.

Ver. 12. *I was at ease* [m]] It is observable, that he does but just mention his former prosperity. He expresseth it by a single word, as though it were nothing. whereas he dwells upon his calamities, and describes them in the strongest terms that language could supply. This is perfectly agreeable to the nature of distress.

He hath broken me asunder, &c.] He describeth the ruin of his fortunes and family, the disease inflicted on his person, and the cruel attack of his character by his three friends. He compares his case to that of a man who is seized by the hair of his head, and thrown down a precipice; then, with his limbs all broken, and scarce able to breathe, is set up for a mark to be shot to death with arrows. Whether these highly tragical images existed only in the poet's fancy,
                                                                                                        or

---

[k] יסרני See the note on chap xi. 10. in the *Commentary* of the learned Schultens.

[l] ירטני In the Arabic language טרי for ירט signifies *to sink in a bog* so as not to be able to get out, as Schultens informs us; who turns it here *in barathrum me dejecit, he hath thrown me down into a dungeon*; such for instance as Jeremiah was cast into Jer. xxxviii. 6. Vid. Comment. Schultens and the note of the learned Dr. Hunt in *Prælect.* p. 213. The LXX. render it by a very strong word ηδαφισεν *he hath hurled me*.

[m] שלוי the word שלו is that by which Nebuchadnezzar expresseth his untroubled prosperity. Dan. iv. 4. Heb. ver. 1.   5

14. 'Tis he——ev'n he, th' Almighty, is my foe,
His strong arm hews me, thund'ring blow on blow.

15. Grief's sable weed to my flay'd body grows,
Grief on my honour'd head foul ashes throws:

16. Grief marrs my face with scalding tears, and night
Black as the grave sits heavy on my sight.

17. Yet

or whether they allude to a real mode of punishment, practised in that country and in those times; I leave to the decision of abler judges.

Ver. 14. *He breaketh*[n], &c.] He represents the rapid succession of his calamities, and God as the supreme author of them; whom he compareth to a mighty warrior attacking a city, or fortress, with a powerful army.

Ver. 15. *I have sowed sackcloth*, &c.] He had put on this habit of mourners, we may suppose, upon receiving the news of his children's death. He had worn it ever since. he had worn it so long, that by means of his ulcers it stuck fast to his skin.

I have defiled my horn[p], &c.] Or, *I have defiled my head with dust*. This was another rite of mourning among the Arabians, chap. ii. 12. who derived it, perhaps, from the Egyptians. It was in use also among the ancient Greeks. Priam lamented the death of Hector by covering his head with dust, and also rolling himself in the dust. Achilles, in the extravagance of his grief for Patroclus, sprinkled embers, instead of ashes, upon his head.

Ver. 16. *on my eye lids*, &c.] His eyes had the appearance of a dying man: He thought himself to be near his end. See the first verse of the next chapter.

---

[n] יפרץ Prov. xxv. 28. *a city that is broken down*, (פרוצה) *and without walls*.

[p] The Syriac renders it, as Mr. Heath observes, *my head*. The Chaldee interpreter turns it, *my glory*. His head which of late was so highly exalted, and adorned perhaps with the tiara, now hung down; covered with sordid dust, or ashes. Compare Psalm lxxv. 6. cxii. 9.

17. Yet are thefe hands with no injuftice ftain'd,
 Pure from thefe lips ftill flows the pray'r unfeign'd:
18. O earth, the blood accufing me reveal;
 Its piercing voice in no recefs conceal:
19. My witnefs lives in heav'n, whofe confcious view
 Does all my goings and my thoughts purfue.

20. The

Ver. 17. *Nor for my injuftice*, &c.] He exculpates himfelf from the charge of *oppreffion*, in this firft claufe; and from *impiety*, in the latter claufe. Eliphaz had accufed him in open terms of *impiety* chap. xv. 4—6. and of *oppreffion*, by infinuation ver. 20, &c.

Ver. 18. *O earth*, &c.] He confirms the foregoing proteftation, by a folemn imprecation delivered in noble and accumulated figures of fpeech. The earth is made a perfon, then addreffed in vehement apoftrophe. The blood of the murdered is imagined lying and reeking on the ground, and a loud voice is given to it which pierceth into heaven. This is the ftyle of the grand poetry: this is the language of the higher paffions.

my blood!—my cry] The blood fhed by me, and its cry againft me for vengeance. Ezek. xxiv. 6, 7, 8. Gen. xviii. 20, 21. iv. 10.

cover not, &c.] This is equivalent to faying, let not the blood which I have fpilled be unrevenged. When the Arabian poets would fay, a murder has been unrevenged; their expreffion is, the blood of the murdered perfon moiftens the ground like dew: that is, it lies uncovered, and being exhaled by the fun falls down in dew. Vid. the Arabian *Anthologia*, intituled *Hamafa*, p. 417. n. ad ver. 1.

But why does Job exculpate himfelf from the crime of murder? Who had accufed him of it? Eliphaz had done fo virtually, by reprefenting him as a tyrant: for whoever heard of an unbloody tyrant?

Ver. 19. *my record*, &c.] rather, *He who is privy to my actions* is *on high*, as Mr. Heath tranflates it.

---

⁹ שָׂרִי The LXX. render it by Συνίστωρ *he that is confcious to my actions*. It fignifies in Arabic, fays Schultens, *teftis oculatus, an eye-witnefs*.

CHAP. XVI.   THE BOOK OF JOB.   117

20. The paſtime of my friends, my ſtreaming eye
    Looks up for pity to the Pow'r on high:
21. O might I argue in his ear, and free
    As in a mortal court maintain my plea!
22. For my ſhort life's ſhort remnant ſoon muſt end,
    And I th' irremeable way deſcend.
                                                    CHAP.

Ver. 21. *O that*, &c.] He earneſtly wiſheth he might plead his cauſe with God, with the ſame freedom that a man defends himſelf in a court of human judicature.

*O that a man might plead*ᵍ *with God,*
As a man pleadeth with his fellow man.

By *a man*, in the firſt clauſe, he means himſelf. The ſentiment coincides with what he had expreſt before, chap. ix. 32. *For he is not a man*, &c. and chap. xiii. 3. *ſurely I deſire to reaſon with God.*

Ver. 22. *When a few years are come*, &c] He did not expect to live a few years longer, nor even a few days. ver. 16. and ver 1. of the next chapter. ſee alſo chap. vii. 21. This verſion therefore cannot be right. The tranſlation ſhould be, I think;

*For*ʳ *my few years are come*ˢ *to an end,*
And I go the way whence *I ſhall not return.*

He urgeth this conſideration as a motive for haſtening his trial before God.

ᵠ ויוכיח לגבר In the oriental tongues, when an imperſonal verb (as יוכיח here) is followed by a dative of the noun (as לגבר here) that dative is often the nominative caſe to the verb. thus Prov. xiii. 13. יחבל לו *he ſhall be deſtroyed.* Exod. xviii. 27. וילך לו *and he went.* ſo in the ſyriac teſtament, *ve-lo timan le-hun, and that they ſhould not faint.* Luke xviii. 1. ſee alſo Luke x. 34.

ʳ בן אדם *man*, indefinitely; as ברנשא in Syriac.

ˢ כי It is frequently a particle of ratiocination, *for.* Vid. Noldium.

ᵗ יאתיו *are come.* אהלך *I go.* 'The learned reader may recollect the obſervation of Michaelis, that in the ancient ſtate of the language the futures were aoriſts. The LXX. tranſlate the firſt member of the verſe, ετη αριθμητα ηκασι *my numbered years are come*, i. e. to the end of their number. The vulgate turns the whole verſe, *ecce enim breves anni tranſierunt; et ſemitam, per quam non revertar, ambulo.*

CHAP.
XVII.

Ver. 1. My breath is almost spent——my vital date
 Expires——for me the burial chambers wait.

2. Sarcastic tongues my dying couch surround,
 Vex my last hours, and scoff me into ground.

3. Fix,

CHAP. XVII.

An attentive reader will observe, that the style in the first ten verses of this chapter expresseth great discompofure. There are frequent and sudden changes of the person. The transitions are abrupt, without the joining particles: and the sentiments follow one another in a hurry, with little or no connection, just as the tumultuous and shifting emotions of his mind suggested them.

From the eleventh verse to the end of the discourse, all is in the moving strain of elegy. With a melancholy calmness he resigns himself to despair and the grave.

Ver. 1. *My breath*, &c.] He feels the powers of his body failing, and apprehends himself to be drawing near his end. The sentences are very short and broken, like the speech of a man who panteth for breath. This verse ought not to have been separated from the last verse of the foregoing chapter, with which it is closely connected in sense.

is corrupt] *is destroyed*[u]. it is on the point of being exhausted. Mr. Heath's version is, *My life draweth near to destruction.*

The graves[v]] The cells or holes in the sepulchral chambers for the coffins. The walls of these subterraneous rooms hewn in the rock were sometimes scooped into rows of cells, like the holes in a pigeon-house, wide and deep enough to receive a coffin of seven or eight feet long[x].

Ver. 2. *Are there not mockers*, &c.] The thought of their injurious usage of
 him

---

[u] הבלה Prov. xiii. 13. *He that despiseth the word shall be destroyed.*

[v] קברים *The cells* in the sides of the sepulchral chambers. So this word plainly signifies in Ezek. xxxii. 22, 23. though it be there also translated *graves*.

[x] Maundrell's *journey to Aleppo*, p. 21, 22. Sandy's *travels*, p. 175. Shaw's *travels*, p. 263, &c. 4to.

CHAP. XVII.   THE BOOK OF JOB.

3. Fix, fix my trial; cheerful I'll appear
Before thy face, my injur'd fame to clear.
Who shall arise, who give his plighting hand,
As adverse party, in this strife to stand?
4. Not these; for these thou leavest to a mind
Bemaz'd in error and with passion blind:
These thou wilt ne'er exalt, nor such ordain
Thy cause to argue and thy ways explain.
                                    5. Whoe'er

him rouseth his indignation; and causeth him to collect all the breath he had, to utter this and the following sentiments, to the end of the tenth verse, with spirit and vehemence.

doth not mine eye, &c.] His eye had been for a long time, and still was vexed with their insulting gestures; as his ear had been with their provoking speeches. See chap. xvi. 4, 5.

Ver. 3. *Lay down now*, &c.] *Appoint*[y], *I pray, my surety*[z] *with thee.* These are law-terms, and allude to the custom of a person's giving bail for his appearance in court on the day of trial. The thought of the injury done to his character, by these censors, makes him break out on a sudden in this passionate request; that God would fix a time for his trial before him speedily.

Who is he that will strike hands[a], &c.] In the days of ancient simplicity, *striking hands* was thought a sufficient ratification of the most solemn engagements[b]. The meaning is, Who shall undertake the part of plaintiff in this cause; or be advocate for God, to justify the ways of his providence towards me?

Ver. 4. *For thou hast hid*, &c.] He excepts to the appointment of any one
of

---

[y] שִׂימָה *appoint thou.* Exod. xxi. 13. *I will appoint thee a place whither thou shalt flee.*

[z] עָרְבֵנִי It may be read as a participial noun from עָרַב *spospondit, to be bound for another, to be surety.*

[a] Prov. vi. 1.

[b] We learn from *Oedipus Colonus*, ver. 646, that a treaty of peace was ratified by the contracting powers giving the right hand to one another.

5. Whoe'er with libel stabs his weeping friend,
   His race shall friendless to the grave descend:
                                            6. This

of his three antagonists to plead the cause of God. They had proved themselves unqualified for that honour, by their ignorance in the course of providence; and by their prejudice against him.

thou shalt not exalt them] If we add the word which in the hebrew begins the next verse[c], as the Syriac interpreter has done, the sense will be compleat[d]:

For thou hast hid their heart from understanding,
Therefore thou wilt not exalt them to a part.

He means, they were not worthy of the honour of *a part* in this cause; that is, of being parties, or advocates, in behalf of God. So Elihu useth the very same word chap. xxxii. 17. *I will also answer my part.*

Ver. 5. *He that speaketh*, &c.] The word which, in the hebrew, begins this verse, being removed to the end of the foregoing verse; there will come out the following clear translation,

He uttereth malicious things[e],
And the eyes of his children shall fail.

In this abrupt manner he points particularly at Eliphaz, as likewise in the next verse. Eliphaz was uppermost in his thoughts, not only as the last who spoke against him; but as the ringleader in these malicious aspersions.

                                                                    The

---

[c] לחלק *to a part.* Our Translators render it *flattery.* The Syriac interpreter also, though he hath restored it to its right place, mistook its meaning: for he turns it, *by division.* The LXX. rightly render it τη μηριδι *to a part.*

[d] The distich also will be compleat: for as the first verse is an iambic of nine syllables, by this means the second will be so too:

כי לבם צפנת משכל
על כן לא תרמם לחלק

[e] רעים LXX. κακιας. They read רָעִים *evil things.* It signifies *malicious aspersions* in Psalm lii. 3, 4. *Thou lov'st? evil* (רָע) *more than good, and lying rather than to speak righteousness: Thou lov'st all devouring words, O thou deceitful tongue.*

CHAP. XVII.   THE BOOK OF JOB.

6. This bold defamer shews me for a sign,
A dire example of the wrath divine:
7. Hence my wan look, and eye with sorrow dim,
Hence like a shadow seems each wasted limb.
8. Doubtless the just, astonish'd at the sight,
'Gainst the proud scorner will their zeal excite:

9. The

The eyes [f], &c.] This denunciation appears to me, founded only in Job's observation of what frequently happens in the world. The infamy which a parent draws upon himself by some flagrant crime, usually involveth his children in its unhappy consequences.

Ver. 6. *He hath made me also a by-word*] His invectives have marked me out for a proverbial example of divine vengeance.   compare Jerem. xxix. 22.

And afore time I was as a tabret, &c.] *And I am become a gazing stock* [g] *in their sight* [h]. He means, that in consequence of the slanderous speeches of this venerated man, Eliphaz, he should be looked upon by all mankind as an object of horror.

Ver. 8, 9. *Upright men*, &c.] The scandal which his sufferings would bring upon

───────────────────────────────

[f] There seems to me some word wanting in the first verse of this distich, to fill up the metre; perhaps לרעהו (*against his friend*) was originally inserted.

יגיד רעים (לרעהו)
עני בניו תכלנה

Thus each sentence of the period will be an iambic verse of seven syllables. The Syriac version supplies חביבה (i. e. לרעהו) in the first sentence, and in general has hit the meaning, *A friend insulteth his friend*.

[g] תפת   The LXX. render it γιλως *a laughing-stock*. But it rather denotes an object that causeth astonishment and horror, *a prodigy* (or portent) as Mr. Heath turns it; who derives it from פי, which in Chaldee signifies, according to Castell. *demonstravit*. It seems to be synonimous with מופת, which we english *a wonder* in Deut. xxviii. 46. *and they* (the fearful curses aforementioned) *shall be upon thee for a sign and a wonder*, &c.   In short, תפת seems to answer exactly to υποδειγμα in St. Peter, II Pet. ii. 6.   St. Jerom had this idea of תפת, for he translates it *exemplum, an example*; namely, of divine vengeance.

[h] לפנים   Vulg. *coram eis*. Mr. Heath supposes it to be a contraction of לפניהם   LXX. αυτοις.

R

THE BOOK OF JOB. CHAP. XVII.

9. The friends of virtue will their way pursue,
   And fearless innocence its force renew.

10. But you, all you, repent; your thoughts revise:
    Shall I not find ev'n one among you wise?

11. 'Tis past—O life, farewell—my blisful schemes
    Are broken off—ah too, too pleasing dreams!

12. All-

upon religion, now occurs to his thoughts. Good men, no doubt, would be shocked, to see so good a man abandoned by God to these afflictions and cruel usage. *Upright men will be astonished at this.* But when he adds, *and the innocent shall stir up himself against the profligate,* &c. he must be understood to speak ironically, as Castalio and Mr. Heath have remarked. The irony strongly marks the indignation of the speaker; and is a keen rebuke of his antagonists, for occasioning such prejudice to the interests of religion by their injurious usage of him.

shall stir up himself[i], &c.] Doubtless they will triumph in their advantage, over impious men, from the blessings of religion.

the hypocrite[k]] *the profligate.* It stands opposed here to the *upright, the innocent,* and *the righteous;* and must therefore denote men of no religion. See the note on chap. viii. 13.

Ver. 11—16. *My days are past*, &c.] Whether he meant to shew the vanity of the hopes which these men had set before him; or to paint more strongly the cruel disappointment of his own expectations of the divine benediction on his virtue,

---

[i] יתערר It is used in the sense of *exulting over an opponent* in chap. xxxi. 29. where it is translated *lift up myself; If I rejoiced at the destruction of him that hated me, or lift up myself when evil found him.*

[k] חנף, LXX. παρανομος a *transgressor.* They often turn it ασεβης, *an impious man;* and twice only υποκριτης, *an hypocrite.*

[l] Oedipus, being about to die, bids farewell to life in much the same strain; ολωλε γαρ δη παντα τα εμα, &c. *all my affairs and connections with the world are perished,* &c. Oedipus Colon. 1684.

CHAP. XVII.   THE BOOK OF JOB.   123

 12. All-cheering fun, adieu. Sepulchral night,
   Blot the bright vifion ; and be thou my light;
 13. My hope another bed, another home,
   A bed in darknefs, and my houfe the tomb.
                 14. Thou

virtue, he now moft pathetically takes his leave of the world, and embraces death in a ftrain of elegy full of defpairing grief and horror.

 my purpofes ᵐ, &c.] He means, I fuppofe, his pious and virtuous defigns; from which he had promifed himfelf high enjoyment and a long train of divine bleffings : For he calls thefe *purpofes*, in the next fentence, *the poffeffors* ⁿ *of his heart*, to exprefs how much he had fet his mind upon them.

 Ver. 12. *They change*, &c.] The obfcurity of this period will, I imagine, be cleared away by the following tranflation;

   Night is appointed ᵒ *to me for day*,
   Light is near from the face of darknefs ᵖ.

That is, Henceforth *the day* which I am to enjoy is the *night* of death: and *the light* which is ordained for me, is *the darknefs* of the tomb. The expreffion is in the lofty ftyle of Æfchylus and Sophocles. In common profe he would have faid, The only comfort left me, and the only thing I have to hope for, is death and a grave.

 Ver. 13. *The grave*, &c.] There is a mixture of horror in the folemnity of thefe images.

 the grave] *Sheôl*. See the APPENDIX, *Numb*. II I think, *Sheôl* muft fignify here

---

 ᵐ זמותי It often means *wicked defigns*, but is evidently ufed here in a good fenfe. It fignifies *wife thought* or *intention*, as appears from chap. xlii. 2. *no thought of thine can be hindered:* and from Prov. xxxi. 16. where we render the verb זמם *to confider*.

 ⁿ כיורשי *the thoughts*, as our public verfion turns it. But this is too faint. It fignifies *the poffeffors*, thoughts which had gotten poffeffion of his heart; from ירש *to inherit*.

 ᵒ ישימו it feems to be ufed here imperfonally; as יהדפהו and ינדהון ch. xviii. 18. *He fhall be driven — and chafed*, &c.

 ᵖ This is Schultens' verfion, and is literal.

THE BOOK OF JOB. Chap. XVII.

14. Thou art my father, Grave: my mother's claim
Be thine, O Worm, and thine a sister's name:
15, 16. My hope! where is it? who my hope shall see?
It shall descend the winding grots with me:
                                                    Behold

here the *sepulchral grot*, or tomb. For where his bed was to be, there his house also was. but his bed was to be *in darkness*, that is, the sepulchral chamber. See chap. x. 21, 22. and Psalm. lxxxviii. 12, 13. where *destruction, darkness,* and *the land of forgetfulness* are but various terms for the *grave*.

Ver. 14. *I have said*, &c.] He transferreth all his filial and fraternal affections to *the grave* and *worm*; shewing, by this strong and beautiful mode of expression, how welcome death and dissolution would be to him. Solomon has exprest a high degree of affection in much the same manner, Prov. vii. 4. A greater than Solomon has given his sanction to this phraseology, Matt. xii. 50. I may add, the Roman Tragedian has marked the mighty power of another passion, *hatred*, by the same images; " One thing is left me, dearer than brother, father, and mother, &c. even hatred of thee ⁹."

to corruption'] *to the pit*, as our translators turn it in chap. xxxiii. 18, 24. 28, 30. but in ver. 22. of that chapter *the grave*. The sepulchral grot is thus denominated as being the place of corruption.

Ver. 15. *where is now my hope*, &c.] By his *hope* he here means, I apprehend, the durable blessings and honours, which he had expected as a reward of his exemplary virtue'. These lively interrogations express with great force the severity of his disappointment. But the figurative language riseth much higher in the next verse; where he gives personality to his *hope*, and represents this imaginary being as lying down with him in the sleep of death. This is saying in a poetical manner, that all his expectations ended in misery, death, and putrefaction.

---

⁹ ———————— una res superest mihi,
Fratre ac parente carior, regno ac lare.
Odium tui.   *Hercules Furens*. 380.

' שחת we render it a ditch chap. ix. 31. It there means a deep pit of filthy mire. It signifies *the sepulchre* in Psalm xxx. 9. and in many other places.

' Chap. xxix. 18, &c.

CHAP. XVII.   THE BOOK OF JOB.

Behold and wonder! there my hope and I
On the fame couch of duſt repoſing lie.

CHAP.
XVIII.
1, 2.   The Shuhite anfwer'd: Thou and thy clan, how long
Shall words evaſive lurk beneath your tongue?

Affirm

Ver. 16. *They ſhall go down*[t], &c.] *It (my hope*, ver. 15.) *ſhall go down*, &c.

to the bars of the pit] The word tranſlated *the pit* is *Sheôl*, which here alfo muſt ſignify furely *the grave:* for he fays, That his hope by going down to *ſheôl* ſhall reſt together with him in the *duſt*. *The bars* ſhould, I think, be rather turned *the branches*. Our Author's word feems to denote literally *the branches of a tree*[u]; and thence is applied to other things which have a ſimilar relation of parts to their refpective whole, the members of an animal body[v] for inſtance, and here the *ſepulchral chambers*; which open in the ſide of the ſubterraneous grot, and go off from it as branches from the trunk of a tree.

When, &c.] *Verily*[x] our *reſt together* will be *in the duſt*.

CHAP. XVIII.

I cannot call this ſpeech *oratio morata*, a ſpeech that marks the peculiar temper of the ſpeaker. It might, for all I can fee, have come with equal propriety from the mouth of Zophar. It expreſſeth, however, very ſtrongly the progreſs and effect of *anger*. The courfe of the difpute has heated this phlegmatic man: His introduction ver. 1 — 4. is full of high refentment; And the reſt of his difcourfe ſhews that his paſſion greatly elevates his poetry.

In

---

[t] תרדנה If this were the third perfon plural feminine of the future tenfe, *they ſhall go down*, it would require a nominative plural, or two ſingular nouns, in the fame gender: But no fuch nominative is found either in this or the preceding verfe. I take it therefore to be the third perſon *ſingular* feminine, with the paragogical ſyllable נה like תישלהנה *ſhe put forth*, Judges v. 26. The nominative to the verb תרדנה is תקותי *my hope*, ver. 15.

[u] Ezek. xvii. 6. *It became a vine, and brought forth branches*, בדים

[v] Chap. xli. 12. (ver. 4. in the hebrew) *I will not conceal his parts*, i. e. his limbs בדיו

[x] אם We engliſh it *furely* in Pſalm cxxxix. 19. Vid. Noldium.

Affirm *the righteous punish'd*, we'll oppose.

3. What, merit we the scorn thy mouth bestows;

Despis'd.

In ver. 5, 6. he lays down his general position, the common and favourite principle of all the three, that *destructive* calamities are the portion of the *wicked*, great oppressors in particular, and of such only.

He confirms and illustrates his point by a new example, after the manner of Eliphaz, ver. 7—21.

But he hath so varied his choice of images, so heightened his colouring, adapted some particulars so closely to the case of Job, and wrought up the whole scene to such a pitch of tragical terror, that no reader of taste will, I imagine, be tired with his speech.

Ver. 2. *How long*, &c.] *How long will ye put insnaring words* [z] ? By *insnaring words* he means artful harangues to catch the passions, and divert the attention of the hearer from the main point in dispute. In this view he considered Job's declamations on his innocence and sufferings. It is remarkable that Bildad addresseth himself to a plurality of persons, *how long will ye put*, &c. either because he had observed some of the audience giving signs of favouring the part of Job; or intending, as Schultens thinks, to represent him as the leader of an *infidel sect*: If so, by *insnaring words* must be meant sophistical evasions.

mark [a], &c.] Mr Heath turns it, *speak your meaning plainly, and afterwards we will reply*. " Give a direct and clear answer to the question, *who ever perished being innocent* [b], &c." If you affirm it, we are ready to argue the point with you.

Ver. 3. *Wherefore are we counted*, &c.] He refers to that contemptuous reflection on their understandings in chap. xvii. 4, 10.

---

[z] תשמון קנצי לבלין *ponetis laqueos (aucupia) verborum*. The word קנצי is found no where else in the Hebrew bible. But the verb in Arabic signifies *to hunt, to lay nets and snares*; and is applied, as Schultens shews, to *the using of deceitful arts*. See his *Commentary*. The noun קואנץ is a *snare*. Vid. Castell. *Lex. Hept.*

[a] תבינו *claré at diserté loquamini, speak clearly and to the point*, Explain yourselves. This is Schultens' interpretation, who refers us to ch. vi. 24. and Dan. viii. 16. as examples of this signification. we english it there *to cause to understand, to make to understand*.

[b] Chap. iv. 7.

Despis'd, and vilify'd as void of mind,
Dull as the dullest of the grazing kind?

4. O thou whose passion at the ways of God
Rends thy own soul, shall he renounce his rod,
Desert our world; or change his fix'd decrees,
As the rock fix'd, thy murmurs to appease?

5, 6. Know thou, one dreadful moment shall destroy
The wicked in his glitt'ring scenes of joy:

His

Ver. 4. *He teareth himself in his anger*] He retorts the expression which Job directed to Eliphaz, chap. xvi. 9. *He teareth me in his wrath who hateth me.*

shall the earth, &c.] These are proverbial forms of speech, for altering what is fixed and unchangeable. The meaning is, if I mistake not, that God must give up his moral kingdom among men, or violate the immutable laws of justice by which it is administred; if such a man as Job escaped punishment. This interpretation makes an easy transition to the other part of the discourse, which is designed to prove, that by an unchangeable rule of providence the signally wicked shall signally perish.

Ver. 5, 6. *Yea, the light,* &c.] These metaphors denote, in general, the splendor and festivity in which such men live. There is however an allusion I think, in the fifth verse, to what the Arabian poet calls *the fires of hospitality:* These were beacons lighted upon the tops of hills by persons of distinction among the Arabs; to direct and invite travellers to their houses and table. Hospitality was their national glory: And the loftier and larger these fires were, the greater was the magnificence thought to be [c]. A wicked rich man therefore would affect this piece of state, from vanity and ostentation.

Another Arabian poet expresseth the permanent prosperity of his family almost

---

[c] Vid. Pocock. in Carm. Tograi, p. 111.

His feftal fire, his lamp's high-fparkling light,
Shall be extinguifh'd in eternal night.

7. Strong like a lion, and as proud his gait,
The tyrant is pufh'd headlong on his fate

8, 9, 10. By moft in the very words of our author: " Neither is our fire, lighted for the benefit of the night-ftranger, extinguifhed [d]."

Ver. 6. *and his candle*, &c.] *And his lamp over him* *fhall be put out* [f]. He refers to the lamps which hung from the ceiling of the banqueting room, in their nocturnal revels: for the Arabian entertainments were in the night.

Ver. 7—15. *The fteps*, &c.] If the defcription contained in thefe verfes, were copied by the pencil; it would form a picture of terror in three parts.

In the firft piece, this wicked man of opulence appears in the midft of his beautiful gardens and ftately walks; caught by the foot in one of the innumerable fnares which furround him. He is in the attitude of ftruggling to get loofe. This reprefents the numberlefs evils to which men of his character are expofed, and points at the overthrow of Job. ver. 7—10.

In the fecond piece, He is feen again in the fame fituation. A groupe of *Furies* are in purfuit of him; He is feized by a *Fury* of enormous fize and ftrength who is devouring him. His countenance is diftorted with pain, and his features wild with horror. This reprefents Job's dreadful difeafe. ver. 11, 12, 13.

In the third, an army of *Furies* are deftroying his vineyards and corn-fields, his flocks and herds. A party of them have poffeffed themfelves of his fuperb manfion, which is fet on fire by a fhower of flaming fulphur. This reprefents the various calamities by which Job's fortunes and family were deftroyed. ver. 14, 15.

Ver. 7. *The fteps of his ftrength*, &c.] In regard to his power and pride, he is compared to a lion; which is remarkable for its ftrong and ftately walk.

are

---

[d] Hamafa, p. 473. [e] עליו LXX. ἐπ᾽ αὐτῷ. Vulg. *fuper ipfum*.
[f] Compare Prov. xx. 20.

CHAP. XVIII. THE BOOK OF JOB. 129

8, 9, 10. By his own counsels. Where aloft he stalks,
The toils steal on and circumscribe his walks:
Close-lurking gins and cover'd pits around
Beset his paths, o'er all his guilty ground.
He rusheth to his prey: but unaware
Treads on the meshes of the ambush'd snare:
His foot is caught in the tough tangling fold,
He struggles hard to burst its stubborn hold.
11. Fell furies then, who hung upon his rear,
·Surround and shake him with distracting fear:
12. One

are straitened] According to the greek version, *are hunted*ᵍ. This idea agreeth best to the others that follow, being all of them allusions to the chace.

His own counsel, &c.] His oppressions bring the vengeance of God and men upon him; as a lion is taken in a net while he is in pursuit of his prey. See Ezek. xix. 6, 7, 8.

Ver. 9. *the robber*ʰ, &c.] What have robbers to do here? The translation should be, *and the entangling cord holdeth him fast.* He is now caught. This verse therefore, as Mr. Heath remarks, should be placed after the next. It finisheth this branch of the description.

Ver. 11. *Terrors*] Terrible calamities. The poet here makes them allegorical persons. Homer calls them *the Furies,* the ministers of divine vengeanceⁱ.

and shall drive him, &c.] *and shall shake*ᵏ *him at his feet.* He is pursued by these

---

ᵍ Θηρευσωσιν. They read יצדו for יצרו Compare Psal. cxl. 5, 11, 12.

ʰ צמים *funis implexus,* from the root צמם *plectere,* as Schultens shews from the Arabic. See his *Commentary.*

ⁱ Il. ix. 454. xv. 204.

ᵏ הפיץ It is synonimous with נפץ, which signifies in Arabic, among other senses, *to be shaken with an ague.* Castell. *Lex. Hept.*

S

12. One fastens on his side, voracious ill,
   It gnaws his flesh, commission'd slow to kill:
13. It rends his brawny limbs, it sucks his blood,
   Death's eldest born and fiercest of his brood.

14. Furies, these *Terrors*, or *Furies*. They are close at his heels. He trembles with horror.

Ver. 12, 13. *His strength*, &c.] *His pain*¹, or *painful disease*. The poet thus styles one of the *Furies.* to raise the idea, he adds, it *shall be hunger-bitten*, furious as a beast of prey in the rage of hunger. He next names it *destruction*; and says, *it was decreed to his side*; to signify that it was of an extraordinary kind, sent by the immediate hand of God, and would prove mortal: And to compleat the climax, he styles it *the first-born of death*, an expression that denotes the exceeding terribleness of the death in which this disease will end. That *a bodily affliction*, some terrible and mortal disease, is intended, appears from its being represented *devouring the strength of his skin*.

Ver. 12. shall be *ready at his side*] is *decreed* ᵐ, or *appointed, to his side* ⁿ, that is, to his body. This expression is another proof that *a destructive disease* is the thing intended.

Ver. 13. *It shall devour*, &c.]
   The members ᵒ *of his body it devours,*
   Death's eldest-born devoureth his members.

his body] In the hebrew, *his skin*; which by a metonymy is here put for the whole body, as in Chap. ii. 4. *skin for skin,* i. e. body for body, and in Exod. xxii.

---

¹ אנן it is the same with און, which we english *affliction*, chap. v. 6. The Arabic interpreter renders it, in the verse before us, רי *disease*; The Syriac, כאב which signifies any *painful disease*, in the bowels, the loins, the head, &c. also *the leprosy*. Vid. Castell. *Lex. Hept.* כאב

ᵐ נכון See the note on chap. xv. 23.

ⁿ Thus Sophocles useth πλευρα for Σωμα, ποσες πλευραν μαρανων *an affliction that emaciates the side.*

ᵒ בדי *the members,* and in the next clause בדיו *his members.* See the note on chap. xvii. 16.

14. Furies, in numbers like a black'ning hoſt
   Led by their ſcepter'd chief, invade his boaſt;
15. Dwell in his dwelling, and with raging haſte
   Lay all the beauty of his Eden waſte:

Accurs'd

xxii. 27. *it is his raiment for his ſkin*, that is, his body. But *the ſkin* is particularly mentioned, as being the ſeat of the leproſy, Job's diſeaſe [p]. Æſchylus [q] deſcribes the ſame diſeaſe in almoſt the ſame highly figurative language; " Leproſies, making progreſs over the fleſh and devouring with ſavage jaws the former habit of the body."

the firſt-born of death] The ſentence of death, pronounced on all mankind, gave birth to diſeaſes; which therefore by a ſublime allegory are ſtyled the offſpring of death; and the moſt horrible diſeaſe, that which hath the preheminence in cruelty, his *firſt-born*, his might, and the beginning of his ſtrength.

Ver. 14. *His confidence*] All that he gloried in, and truſted to; his numerous family and great poſſeſſions.

It ſhall bring him, &c.] *Terrors ſhall march againſt him* like a king [r]; that is, like a king at the head of his army, laying waſte an enemy's country with fire and ſword. He borrows this compariſon from Eliphaz. See chap. xv. 24.

Ver. 15. *It ſhall dwell*, &c.] *They* (the *Terrors*. ver. 14.) *ſhall dwell* in his tabernacle,

---

[p] See the note on chap. ii. 7.

[q] In his *Chœphoræ*.

[r] תצעידהו *gradientur in eum*, Schultens. Its nominative is בלהות (for there is no other) which is in the plural number; whereas the verb is in the ſingular. But, as he remarks, we have an example of the ſame conſtruction chap. xxvii. 20. בלהות .... תשיגהו *Terrors take hold on him.*

[s] למלך *like a king*. So Levit. xiii. 2. *like the plague* (לנגע) *of leproſy.* Vid. Nold.

[t] תשכון here again we have a verb ſingular to בלהות a nominative plural. Nothing is more common than this conſtruction in the Arabic language; to mention one inſtance out of the Koran, Sur. ii. (9. *Kaſat koloubo-com, indurata eſt corda veſtra*, your hearts is (are) hardened. where the nominative is maſculine and plural; but the verb, ſingular and even feminine.

Accurs'd it lies, a dire example shown,
Like Sodom's field with barren sulphur strown.
16. As a tall oak, which fire ethereal burns,
Sinks down, and to a smoking ruin turns,
17. He perisheth. Him no memorial pile
Saves from oblivion, with inscriptive style:
18. Pursu'd

bernacle, because nothing shall be left *for him*[u]. These Furies are commissioned to make an utter destruction.

brimstone, &c.] This is supposed to allude to the overthrow of Sodom and Gomorrah; which the hebrew poets and prophets, Bp. Lowth remarks [w], used as an image of all other desolating judgements of God.

Ver. 16—20. *His roots*, &c.] He had represented the punishment of this wicked man to be *extermination*. He dwells upon that horrible idea, and opens the particulars contained in it. In the 16th verse he describes it by an image taken from the vegetable world, a lofty tree suddenly killed[x] by lightning, as I suppose. Silius Italicus, quoted here by Schultens, has drawn the image at large:

> Tandem cum toto cecidit, &c.
>
> At last he fell, with all his kindred band;
> A name so long renown'd in Umbrian land.
> So falls an oak, beneath whose lofty shade
> Our ancestors their mighty limbs desplay'd:
> Struck by Jove's bolt it smokes, the sulph'rous flame
> Rages with crackling havock o'er its frame:
> Subdu'd by heav'n it sinks, and spreads the ground
> With its fear'd trunk and arms a spacious ruin round.
>
> L. x. 164.

---

[u] מבלי לו the phrase is elliptical. Schultens has produced the entire form, from Deut. xxviii. 55. בבלי חישאיר לו כל *because he hath nothing left him*.

[w] *Prælect.* p. 106.

[x] Amos ii 9.

CHAP. XVIII.   THE BOOK OF JOB.   133

18. Purfu'd with hiffings and reproach he's hurl'd
   To fhades below, vile eject of the world:
19. Nor fon to him, nor grandfon fhall remain,
   Nor one poor vaffal of his cringing train.
20. Our fires the vengeance faw with facred fear,
   And rifing ages tremble while they hear.

21. Such

Ver. 18. *He fhall be driven*, &c.] He fhall not be conducted out of life, as Plato expreffeth it [y], with funeral pomp, by a numerous train of mourning citizens and relations; but fhall be caft out of human fociety like a malefactor, and thrown under ground with infamy and execration.

Ver. 19. *nephew*] Or *fon's fon*, as in Gen. xxi. 23.

Nor any remaining, &c.] All his dependents will be involved in his destruction. The original word for *dwellings* [z] fignifies, fays the learned Schultens, *a territory of refuge for ftrangers*. The great men among the Arabs called their refpective diftricts by this name; becaufe they took under their protection all defencelefs and neceffitous perfons who fled thither. They prided themfelves in having a great number of thefe clients, or dependents. This was an ancient cuftom in Arabia, and continues to the prefent day [a].

Ver. 20. *they that went before* [b], &c.] *the ancients*; who were eye-witneffes of this dreadful cataftrophe. Hence it appears that Bildad had been fpeaking of things which happened long before his own times. Why then does he exprefs himfelf in the future tenfe? Becaufe he and his companions eftablifhed thefe paft cafes into precedents; and inferred from them that general maxim which he lays down in the laft verfe, *Surely fuch are the dwellings*, &c.

On comparing this oration of Bildad with his former, in chap. viii. I am
ready

---

[y] Quoted by Longinus, cap. 28.

[z] בגוריו

[a] The Arabian Poets frequently refer to this cuftom. See the *Arabian Anthologia*, p. 424. n.

[b] קדמנים *They of old*. Thus קדמניות things of old. Ifaiah xliii. 18.

21. Such is the portion to the wretch aſſign'd,
Alien from God and foe of human kind.

CHAP.
XIX.
1, 2. Job anſwer'd quick: Unfeeling men, how long
Mean you to cut and cruſh me with the tongue?

3. Inſults enow I've born: ſtill, loſt to ſhame,
Stubborn defiance do your looks proclaim?

4. Be
ready to apply to him what Longinus[c] ſays of Euripides; " He was not formed by nature for the ſublime : yet by mighty efforts and ſtraining his powers, when his ſubject required grandeur, he had reached that noble elevation." What ambition effected in Euripides, paſſion ſeems to have produced in Bildad.

CHAP. XIX.

Is it poſſible to read from the firſt to the twenty-ſecond verſe of this chapter, without feeling the moſt tender emotions of compaſſion for this good unhappy man? we may thence infer, that the deſign of this portion of his reply was to melt, if poſſible, his hard-hearted friends; by a moſt pathetic repreſentation of their inhumanity and his own deplorable condition.

Deſpairing, however, to make any impreſſion on them, he on a ſudden elevates his voice; and, with a wonderful erection of ſpirit, conſoles himſelf in the faith and expectation of a future judgement, which will do juſtice to his innocence and reward his virtue. ver. 23.—27. He concludes with warning them of the puniſhment which calumny will receive, in that day of righteous retribution; ver. 28, 29.

Ver. 3. *Theſe ten times*] that is, over and over. Men who are greatly moved are not wont to ſpeak with preciſion. The upbraiding ſtyle is always exaggerating.

---

[c] De ſublim. chap. xv.

CHAP. XIX.   THE BOOK OF JOB.   135

4. Be it, some error, incident to all,
   Is mine; my error on myself must fall.
5. What, still abuse me? and, with cruel strife,
   Urge my affliction to condemn my life?

6. Learn then; that God, the fatal cause unknown,
   Hath me pursu'd, and in his toils o'erthrown.
7. I cry aloud of wrong, no answer gain;
   For justice call, no justice can obtain:

8. But

Ver. 4. *mine error remaineth* [d], &c.] The sentiment is like that in the Roman poet,

Mihi dolebit, non tibi, si quid ego stulté fecero [e].

" If I do a foolish action, it is I who shall suffer for it, not you."

Ver. 5. *magnify yourselves against*, &c.] The expression signifies to treat a person with insolence. Psalm xxxv. 26. Zeph. ii. 10.

my reproach] my ignominious calamities.

Ver. 6, 7. *Know now*, &c.] He freely owns that his overthrow was by the hand of God: but insisteth that he had done nothing to deserve it; and that he had often begged to be brought to his trial; though hitherto without effect.

of wrong] he certainly means wrong, or violence, done to him by God. This language is extremely harsh, and utterly inexcusable. It is however nothing more than what he had already said in effect chap. ix. 17. x. 3. xvi. 17.

Indeed

[d] הלין Zech. v. 4. *It (the curse) shall remain in the midst of his house, and shall consume it.*

Ver. 5. *that ye make yourselves strange*, &c.] *Are ye not ashamed to be so very obstinate against me?* Mr. Heath. תהכרו *to be so very obstinate.* the root is supposed to be הכר; one of whose derivative nouns in Arabic signifies *vehemence,* another of them *impudence.* Vid. Castell. *Lex.*

[e] Plautus in *Menæchmi* Act. ii. sc. iii.

8. But in dark dungeon he confines me faſt,
   With bolts and walls that never can be paſs'd.
9, 10. O bitter change! how happy I and great!
   Till he in ruins laid my glorious ſtate,
   Rent the tiara from my princely head,
   And ſwept my all——now hurls me to the dead:

I leave

Indeed if ſuch raſh ſpeeches as theſe had not come out of his lips, what ground would there have been for thoſe cutting reproaches chap. xl. 8. *Wilt thou alſo diſannull my judgement? Wilt thou condemn me, that thou mayeſt be righteous?*

Ver. 8—20. *He hath fenced*, &c.] This paragraph is a mournful amplification of the ſuppoſed *wrong* ver. 7. He repreſents his hopeleſs condition, ver. 8.—the utter ruin God had brought upon him, ver. 9, 10.—the unprovoked violence with which it was executed, ver. 11, 12.—the effect it had in cauſing his relations, acquaintance, the partner of his bed, and his moſt intimate friends to deſert him; yea his dependents, ſervants, ſlaves, to deſpiſe him, ver. 13. to the end of ver. 19.—And laſtly, the deplorable ſtate to which all theſe afflictions, his diſeaſe in particular, had reduced his body, ver. 20.

Ver. 8. *He hath fenced up*, &c.] He compares his ſituation to that of a condemned malefactor, who is thruſt down into a dark dungeon; and there bolted in, ſo as that it is impoſſible for him to eſcape. The mournful prophet, perſonating his country, deſcribes its deſperate condition by the ſame image [f].

Ver. 9. *the crown*] This may mean the richer kind of *turbant*, which is worn by perſons of diſtinction among the Arabs at this day. The *turbant* appears from medals and ſtatues to have been the ſame with the *tiara*, or diadem [g]. Or the expreſſion may be metaphorical; and *the glory* and *the crown* may denote his dignity, and the honours paid to his authority, juſtice, and beneficence.

Ver. 10. *I am gone*] *I am going*, to the grave. So the word is uſed chap. x. 21. xvi. 22.

mine

---

[f] *Lamentations* iii. 7—9.
[g] Shaw's *Travels*, p. 226. 4to.

> I leave my hope behind, like some fair tree
> Uptorn by tempest, when its boughs you see
> Rich laden with a blooming progeny.

11, 12. Me hapless object of his hate he chose,
> Me (so he will'd) he numb'red with his foes:
> His ire he kindled, and his armies sent
> On rapid march to my devoted tent:
> His legions round my harmless dwelling form'd
> Dreadful encampment, and with fury storm'd.

13. My brethren and acquaintance fled afar,
> With horror fled, from this stupendous war:

14. My kindred shunn'd me, of my boasting friends
> Who now my unremember'd grief attends?

15. The

---

mine hope] all his expectations, as to this world, from the divine benediction on his virtue. See the note on chap. xvii. 15.

like a tree] which, when full of blossoms, is uprooted by a storm; or destroyed by lightning. Chap. xv. 30. xviii. 16. This is one of those abrupt similes, which leave to the reader's imagination the pleasure of discovering the point of likeness. We meet with a few instances of this kind in Homer: Speaking, for instance, of the appearance of the white plumes on Hector's helmet, and alluding also to his lofty stature, he says; " he rushed on, like a mountain covered with snow [b]."

Ver. 12. *his troops*] of evils. The metaphors which follow, are borrowed from the works cast up by a besieging army; for the annoyance of a city with their

---

[b] Il. xiii. 754.

15. The strangers whom I shelter'd in my shade,
The maidens who my awful nod obey'd,
Pass me as though unknown, or gaze me o'er
As some strange thing from some strange distant shore:
16. My meanest slave with stupid insult stares,
Deaf to my calls, regardless of my pray'rs.
17. Ev'n she whom wedlock's charities should move,
Nauseates my breath; the tend'rest notes of love
Unheeding, though conjur'd, in mournful strain,
By the dear mem'ry of our children slain.

18. Yea

their arrows and engines of war. Isaiah xxxvii. 33. The art of war must surely have made a considerable progress in those early days.

Ver. 15. *They that dwell*] *The clients* of *my house.* Our author's word, as the learned Schultens hath shown, is that by which the Arabs denote such as put themselves under a great man's protection, are adopted into his family, and become dependent on him for their maintenance and security. See the note on chap. xviii. 19.

Ver. 17. *is strange*] " *is become loathsome* ." This way of translating the expression turns the complaint into a tender apology, by imputing her avoidance of him to the excessive nauseousness of his disease. The married ladies are indebted to the learned Schultens for this candid and polite remark.

I intreated] The hebrew word implies in it the most tender emotions of parental affection.

It

---

¹ נֻרִי Vid. *Hamasa*, p. 423. n. " Fortune has deprived me of a brave man whose *client* (נָאַר) was not contemptible."

ᵏ זָרָה in Arabic *fastiditus est, computruit spiritus meus.* Schultens *in Comment.*

ˡ הִנְתִי the root הבן signifies, in Arabic, *to be moved with natural affection*; being a metaphor from the tender modulation of the voice by which the camel expresseth fondness to her young one. Castell. *Lex.* Pocock. *in Carmen Tegr.* p. 29. *Commentarium* Schultens.

18. Yea flav'ry's fpawn, beneath my table fed,
Pufh me afide, and flout me to my head.

19. All who the fecrets of my foul poffefs'd,
All whom affection cherifh'd in my breaft,
Are turn'd againft me ; as a wretch impure
Whom God abominates, and men abjure.

20. Thus left, my bone juft ftarting from within
Through the poor remnant of my tatter'd fkin,

21. Pity

It is obfervable that he never makes mention of his children except here and chap. xxix. 5. The thought of their tragical death was too painful to be dwelt upon, or often fpoken of.

Ver. 18. *Yea, young*^m *children defpifed me*] Thefe were, I imagine, the children of his flaves, born in his family. Nothing could fo touchingly reprefent the contempt into which he was fallen, as this circumftance.

I arofe] " I am prefentⁿ." *The moment I appear* (as Crinfoz turns it) *they give me abufive language.*

Ver. 20. *My bone cleaveth*, &c.] The learned Michaelis obferves °, that his offenfive breath ver. 17. the loathfomenefs and infection of his whole body ver. 19. his atrophy mentioned in this twentieth verfe, and the torn condition of his fkin ver. 26. are all circumftances attending the *elephantiafis*, Job's difeafe.

I am efcaped, &c.] The learned Profeffor Chappelow tranflates, *I am efcaped with*

---

^m עוילים The verb in Arabic fignifies to *maintain a numerous family*. The noun therefore muft denote in general *thofe who were fed from his table*; but as his *fervants*, or flaves, were mentioned ver. 16. he may be fuppofed to mean here *the young children of his fervants*, or flaves. Vid. *Comment*. Schultens.

ⁿ אקומה *adfto*. The LXX. turn it παρίτημι in Dan. vii. 10.

° *Not. in Prælect.* p. 202.

140   THE BOOK OF JOB.   CHAP. XIX.

21. Pity me, pity; let my urgent need,
    Let ancient friendship for compassion plead,
    For smitten by th' immortal arm I bleed.
22. Will you (ah why?) your persecutions join
    To those I suffer by a hand divine;
    Insatiate still, still eager to defame
    And glut your rancour with my worry'd name?
23.   O that, fair written in a faithful scroll
       Time in his archives would my words enroll!
                                                24. O

with a torn skin. Job describes the effect of his disease on his skin in much the same manner in ver. 26. *my skin which is thus torn*, &c. See the *note*.

Ver. 22. *and are not satisfied with my flesh*] that is, why are ye not satisfied with the reproaches and slanders, with which ye have already worried me? The learned Schultens remarks ⁿ that *to eat the flesh* of another is an Arabian phrase for *calumniating* him. " I am not addicted to slander, or one who devoureth the flesh of his friend." So one of their poets sings. Another, speaking of his calumniator, says; *who worries my flesh, and yet has not satisfied his avidity*. The phraseology is taken from a wild beast rending his prey. This image of a furious defamer is drawn at full length chap. xvi. 9, 10. where the expression *They have filled* (or *satiated*) *themselves upon me* is plainly similar to *why are ye not satisfied with my flesh*. See the note there.

This interpretation of the words of Job makes a natural transition to the following declaration of his faith in a future judgement, for the vindication of his character.

Ver. 23. *O that my words*, &c.] He means, surely, such of his words as
                                                                    would

---

ᵖ עוֹר שְׁנִי *a torn skin*. Mr. Chappelow derives שְׁנִי from the Arabic שָׁנַן; which signifies in its seventh conjugation according to Castell. *vetustus, tritus fuit uter, corrugata fuit cutis senis.*

ᵠ In his *Commentary*.

ʳ *Hamasa*, or the *Arabian Anthologia*, p. 591. and *the note* of Schultens.

24. O furrow them in lead; their letters give
Through endlefs ages in the rock to live.

25. *I*

would come within the compafs of an infcription upon a rock; the words, therefore, which he delivers in ver. 25, 26, 27.

were now written] Sir Ifaac Newton[t] fuppofes, If I remember right, that letters were invented by the Edomites; from whom Mofes learned them, when he fled into Arabia from the wrath of Pharaoh.

O that they were printed in a book!] *O that they were noted*[u] *in a regifter*[v]! He wifheth that his memorable words might be tranfmitted to pofterity; firft, by writing, the ufual method of preferving paft tranfactions: fecondly, by the ftill fafer method of lodging this writing in the public archives: thirdly, by infcribing them on lead, as more durable than linen or paper; and laftly, by engraving them in the natural rock as the moft durable of all.

were written] on linen perhaps. *Painting* upon linen was very ancient among the Egyptians. Their paper, made of the papyrus, was a later invention[w].

Ver. 24. *and lead*] to grave upon with the iron pen, or ftyle[x]. The learned Gottingen Profeffor[y] fays, he does not underftand what the hebrew word means which we englifh *lead*. We are certain, however, that it is claffed with metals; gold, filver, iron, and tin[z]: Alfo that it fignifies a fubftance ponderous[a] and fufible[b]. It muft therefore denote fome heavy metal or mineral. We learn,

---

[t] In his *Chronology.*

[u] יחקו *were infcribed*, or *noted* as in Ifaiah xxx. 8. *note it in a book, that it may be for the time to come, for ever and ever.*

[v] ספר *a regifter.* In Ezra iv. 15. *the book of records* (ספר דכרניא) means the archives of the kingdom, *the roll,* or *book, of the chronicles,* as it is called Efther ii. 23.

[w] Greaves *on the pyramids*, p. 50. Plinii *Hift. Nat.* lib. xiii. c. 11.

[x] See Gale's account of the *ftyli* and *forts of paper* ufed by the ancients, in *Philofoph. Tranfactions abridged.* vol. vii. part iv. p. 18.

[y] Michaelis, *in Epimet. Prælect. Lowthi* xxxii. p. 211. 8vo.

[z] Numb. xxxi. 22.   [a] Exod. xv. 10.   [b] Jer. vi. 29.

25. *I know, that He whose years can ne'er decay*
Will from the grave redeem my sleeping clay.
When the last rolling sun shall leave the skies,
He will survive, and o'er the dust arise:
26, 27. *Then shall this mangled skin new form assume,*
This flesh then flourish in immortal bloom:
My raptur'd eyes the judging God shall see,
Estrang'd no more, but friendly then to me.

How

learn, further, from Dr. Shaw [c], that very probably there are lead-mines in the mountains of Arabia Petræa: For he found among those rocks plenty of *Selenites*, or moon-stone, which is said to be a certain sign of lead-ore underneath. Add to all this, Pliny [d] informs us that writing on *lead* was of high antiquity, and came in practice next after writing on the bark and leaves of trees, and was used in recording public transactions.

in the rock] Dr. Pocock met with hieroglyphic characters cut in the rock, in the sepulchres of the kings of Thebes [e]. Greaves [f] also makes mention of an inscription of one line in those sacred Egyptian characters, which he observed in the second pyramid. As to the *Written Mountains*, in the desert of Sinai, which are covered with unknown characters; that accurate traveller the Honourable Edward Wortley Mountagu [g], who nicely examined them, has offered good arguments to prove they were the work of christian pilgrims in the first ages of christianity.

Ver. 25, 26, 27. *For I know*, &c.] I would beg leave to offer the following
literal

---

[c] *Travels*, p. 442. 4to.
[d] *Hist. Nat.* lib. xiii. c. 11.
[e] *Description of the East*, vol. i. p. 98, 99.
[f] *Description of the Pyramids*, p. 106, 107.
[g] See his *Journey to the Written Mountains*.

> *How does the lofty hope my foul infpire!*
> *I burn, I faint with vehement defire.*

28. Be warn'd; no more my innocence purfue:
 Its caufe fhall triumph in that juft review.
29. Tremble; thefe wrongs th' avenging fword demand,
 The fword which arms th' almighty ruler's hand:
 You then fhall know, that injur'd virtue's figh
 Found audience with an equal judge on high.

CHAP.

literal tranflation of this famous paffage; and refer the reader to the APPENDIX, *Numb.* III. for explication of it.

Ver. 25. *For I know, my redeemer* is *the living* one,
 And he, the Laft, will o'er the duft ftand up:

Ver. 26. *And my fkin* which *is thus torn,* fhall be *another; and in my flefh I fhall fee God.*

Ver. 27. *Whom I fhall fee, even mine eyes fhall behold, on my fide, and not eftranged: my reins are confumed within me.*

Ver. 28. *But ye fhould fay, &c.*] *Wherefore ye fhould fay, why fhall we perfecute him?* that is, why fhall we continue in our perfecution of him? *feeing the root of the matter*[h] *will be found in me:* that is, when the matter, or caufe between you and me, fhall come into judgement before God; its root, its bafis and fupport, which is truth, will be found on my fide of the queftion.

Ver. 29. *Be ye afraid of the fword*] The fword in the hand of earthly magiftrates is the emblem of punitive juftice. The fcripture, accordingly, puts a fword into the hand of God, the fupreme magiftrate, to fignify his vindictive juftice[i]. And the greateft of all teachers reprefents the *future punifhments* of

wicked

---

[h] דבר *the matter,* in difpute. It fignifies *a caufe,* or matter for judicial inquiry, Exod. xviii. 16. *when they have a matter they come unto me, and I judge between one and another.*

[i] Pf. vii. 12, 13. Ifaiah xxvii. 1.

CHAP.
XX.
1, 2.   Therefore, the fierce Naamathite reply'd,
My thoughts, returning with impetuous tide,

3. Impell

wicked men, in terms of allusion to the punishments inflicted by the courts of human judicature. Matt. v. 22.

for wrath bringeth, &c.] Mr. Heath's version is, *for these are crimes punishable by the sword*[x]. that is, your inhumanity, uncharitableness, and calumnies are capital crimes before God; and will meet with severe punishment in the day of the revelation of his righteous judgement.

CHAP. XX.

Some readers perhaps, of an over delicate taste, may grow tired with these repeated declamations on the transient prosperity and fearful catastrophe of great oppressors. But these three men having the same ideas of the course of providence, and of the case of their unhappy friend, must of necessity speak with a general uniformity on the subject. In the mean while these very repetitions promote the design of the poem. They teaze and exasperate the good man's spirit, and carry him further in those excesses of complaint and self-justification; which excesses, being afterwards properly represented to him, prove the very means of his conviction and repentance.

The subject, however, in this second speech of Zophar is placed in so many different views, and represented by emblems and metaphors so intirely his own, that these at least have the charms of novelty.

Upon the whole, there is great poetical merit in this speech. It is a torrent of oriental eloquence, rushing on with the vehemence of a fiery temper inflamed by resentment and mistaken zeal.

---

[x] He reads הֵמָּה *hæc, these*; (the pronoun of the third person plural masculine with a paragogic ה) instead of חֵמָה *wrath.*

כי המה עונות חרב
Hæc enim sunt crimina gladii. sc. *digna gladio.*

In Psal. xvii. 13. רשע חרבך (*impius gladii tui*) is turned by the Chaldee קְטוֹל בְּסַיְפָךְ דְּאִתְחַיָּב *qui reus est occisionis* (*ut occidatur*) *gladio tuo, who is worthy to be slain by thy sword.*

CHAP. XX.   THE BOOK OF JOB.   145

3. Impell one anfwer more: Nor heeds my ear
Thy warning, nor thy menace will I fear.

4. Art thou unknowing, that the voice of Time,
Since man was planted in this earthly clime,

5. Proclaims; The fong of profligates is fhort,
Th' oppreffor's feftal but a moment's fport?
                                6. Advancing

Ver. 2. *Therefore*, &c.] namely, becaufe we *know there is a judgement*, with which you threaten us.

my thoughts, &c.] a multitude of agitating thoughts impell me to make a reply. The word which we render *I make hafte*[k], imports great eagernefs and impetuofity in Habak. i. 8.

Ver. 3. *the check of my reproach*] *my reproachful correction*[l]. He refers to the commination in the laft verfe of the foregoing chapter.

the fpirit of my underftanding] *The fpirit* which *is within me*[m]. Mr. Heath.

The meaning is, that he has the courage[n] to anfwer him, in defiance of his minatory warning. Chap. xix. 29.

Ver. 4—11. He comprifeth (ver. 4, 5.) the fubject of his difcourfe in a fententious aphorifm, founded on a feries of facts deduced from the earlieft times of the world. He then opens the contents of that aphorifm, viz. the gradual increafe of the oppreffor's greatnefs to its acme, ver. 6. its ignominious period, ver. 7. a reflection on the emptinefs and tranfient duration of his felicity, ver. 8, 9. the calamities of his family, ver. 10. and his untimely death ver. 11.

Ver. 5. *the hypocrite*] *the profligate*. It is a variation of the *wicked* in the former

---

[k] חוּשִׁי בִּי

[l] מוּסַר כְּלִמָּתִי The latter of two fubftantives in this conftruction is convertible into an adjective. Vid. Guarin Gram. Heb. lib. ii. cap. 2. can. 3.

[m] מִבִּינָתִי It is a prepofition compounded of מִ *from* and the chaldee בִּינַת *inter, intra, among, within*.

[n] רוּחַ We tranflate it *courage* in Jofhua ii. 11. but *fpirit* (in the fenfe of *courage*) in chap. v. 1. of that book. Mr. Heath refers us to both thofe paffages.

U

6. Advancing and advancing let him rife,
   Till his proud climax touch the ftarry fkies:
7. Behold his fall! like his own ordure toft
   Into oblivion, from the world he's loft:
   And wond'ring throngs, who faw his envy'd height,
   Afk, " whither has the meteor wing'd its flight?
8. He's vanifh'd, as a dream; he's chas'd away,
   Like a night-vifion by the waking day.
9. No eye that glanc'd him fhall the glance renew,
   His place no more its haughty mafter view.
10, 11. For full of manhood's fap his bones robuft
   Lie in the grave, and with him rot in duft:

mer claufe; another term to exprefs the fame idea. See the note on chap. viii. 13.

Ver. 7. *like his own dung* °] This fimile may perhaps be thought too indelicate. There cannot however be a ftronger image of the odioufnefs, contempt, and infamy of a wicked and mifchievous character. exact refemblance is the principal beauty in all comparifons ᵖ.

Ver. 9. *The eye which faw ᑫ him*] *The eye which hath caught a glance of him.* Mr. Heath.

This is a beautiful paraphrafe of the *moment* in ver. 5. The latter claufe, *neither fhall his place any more behold him*, is an explication of the phrafe in ver. 7. *He fhall perifh for ever.*

Ver. 10. *His children fhall feek to pleafe ʳ the poor*] This is much ftronger than

---

° Compare I Kings xiv. 10. Zeph. i. 17. Pfal. lxxxiii. 10.
ᵖ See Mr. Pope's note on Il. xi. ver. 669. of his tranflation.
ᑫ שׁוּף LXX. παμβλιψι.
ʳ ירצו So in II Chron. x. 7. *If thou be kind to this people, and pleafe them* (וְרָצִיתָם) *and conciliate their affection, and fpeak good words unto them,* &c.

Heirs of his woes, his helpless orphans flee
For shelter to the huts of poverty.

12, 13. Sweet was his sin, the greedy lust of wrong,
A luscious viand, roll'd beneath the tongue;
The

if he had said, *they shall become poor*. It is placing them below poverty itself. They shall court the good-will and assistance of the most destitute and abject.

his hands] *his own hands shall recompense' his iniquity'*. He shall by his oppressions be the cause of ruin to himself and family.

Ver. 11. *his bones*, &c.]

His bones are full of his youth",
And It shall lie down " *with him in the grave.*

This is saying, in the language of animated poetry, He shall be cut off in his youth and the fulness of his strength.

Ver. 12—28. *Though wickedness*, &c.] The *crime* of this delinquent having not been *specified*, and his *punishment* but lightly touched; it was necessary to resume those topics, and enlarge upon them, in order to make a deeper impression of terror. This amplification begins with the twelfth verse, and ends with the twenty-eighth verse.

Ver. 12. *Though wickedness*, &c.] *The wickedness*, in which he takes so much pleasure, is *a rapacious avarice*; *he hath swallowed down riches* ver. 15. This is *the crime* which they suppose Job to have lived in the practice of. The great force of a vicious habit is strongly marked in this and the following verse: The pleasure which a corrupt mind feels in the indulgence of its criminal inclination, is compared to an epicure's high enjoyment of some delicious morsel.

' תשבנה *shall recompense*; or *requite*, as in Gen. l. 15. *He will certainly requite us all the evil which we did to him.*

' אונו *his iniquity*, as in chap. xxi. 19. and Psalm xciv. 23. *He shall bring* (וישב *he shall requite*) *upon them their own iniquity*, &c.

" עלומיו *his youth*, chap. xxxiii. 25. נעורים *childhood*, עלומים *youth*, and זקנים *old age*, are singular nouns; with a plural termination, and probably of the common gender.

* תשכב Its nominative must be עלומים There is no other nominative, singular and feminine, to agree with this verb.

The cud of pleasure, and tenacious chew'd,
Spar'd in the mouth, its flavour oft renew'd:
14. But, soon as swallow'd, it to poison turns;
And darting through his veins with fury burns:
15. The wealth his vast avidity devour'd
He shall disgorge; from out his entrails pour'd
With tort'ring violence by the force of God,
The wicked plunder shall be cast abroad.
16. A deadly potion he shall drain; the wine
Of vipers gall, the cup of wrath divine.
17. Forbid, just Heav'n, that e'er his eye behold
Thy cheerful blessings round his mansion roll'd;

That

Ver. 14. *his meat*] *his meat* is riches acquired by oppression. but his meat is poisoned. A curse is mixed with iniquitous acquisitions. This is *the gall of asps within him*, even the divine vengeance. Deut. xxxii. 33, 34.

Ver. 15. *he hath swallowed down*] The original word is very forcible: it denotes vast avidity and rapacity, being a metaphor from a ravenous beast devouring his prey. compare Jerem. li. 34.

and he shall vomit them up again] as an epicure his poisoned draught, or morsel. The sudden loss of his wicked wealth and intolerable anguish of mind in suffering such loss, are involved in this powerful metaphor. The curse, or vengeance, of God will bring this punishment; *God shall cast them out of his belly*.

Ver. 16. *He shall suck the poison*, &c.] *The poison of asps* and *the viper's tongue* are only variations of *the gall of asps* ver. 14. all mean the curse and vengeance of God that mingle with his riches; and which in time will work the destruction of them and of his person. he dwells upon *the punishment* of this criminal, and on its causes.

Ver. 17. *He shall not see the rivers*, &c.] that is, *he shall not continue to see the rivers*, &c.] These figurative expressions undoubtedly represent some part of

his

CHAP. XX.   THE BOOK OF JOB.

That fountains flow for him, and rivers foam
From the fweet dairy and the fweeter comb.

18.   Yea, ev'n his *guiltlefs treafures*, won with toil,
(No weeping widow's wrong, no orphan fpoil)
Shall fwell his forfeit: in that humbling hour,
He fhall not boaft his opulence and pow'r:

19. For
his punifhment. Rivers, honey, and milk are oriental emblems of felicity [x]:
And it is poffible, that the utter lofs of all his former abundance and enjoyments
may be intended. But I very much fufpect, that a worfe punifhment is here
threatened; even exclufion from *the feats of the bleffed*. The bleffings of religion and the future happinefs of good men are reprefented in fcripture by thefe
pleafant images [y]. Similar to thefe is the defcription of paradife in the Koran [z],
" Therein are rivers of incorruptible water, and rivers of milk, the tafte whereof
changeth not; and rivers of wine, pleafant unto thofe who drink; and rivers of
clarified honey [a]." If this 17th verfe be underftood of happinefs in a *future* world,
it is certainly out of its place; and will enter more properly next after ver. 25.
The laft fentence of that verfe, I think, relates to *future punifhments: Terrors
are upon him.* The tranflation will then be,

And terrors apprehend his flitting foul.
For never never fhall his eyes behold
The happy fields, where brooks of liquid gold
Gufh from the comb, and where on milky ftreams
The purple light expands its pureft beams.

Ver. 18. *That which he laboured for*, &c.] He *fhall reftore the labour which* [b]
he

---

[x] Chap. xxix. 6. Ifaiah vii. 22.

[y] Ifaiah lv. 1, 2. Joel iii. 18. Revel. vii. 17. xxii. 1, 2.

[z] Surat. xlvii. 16, 17.

[a] Mr. Sale's *Tranflation*.

[b] ולא יבלע The ו converts the future into a preterite; and at the fame time does the office of the relative *which*, as in chap. xv. 9 *what knewefl thou that* (which) *we have not known? what underflandefl thou, which is not in us?* Vid. Noldium.

19. For on the weak his iron hands he threw,
  By cruel wrongs his wicked rent-roll grew;

                                    20. Yet,

he did not swallow down. To *swallow down* is the phrase in ver. 15. for possessing by rapacity. *The labour* therefore, or fruit of industry, must mean that part of his fortunes which was not acquired by iniquitous measures. He shall, however, be plundered even of this innocent part of his wealth, as an aggravation of his punishment.

According to his substance, &c.] *In the riches* [c] *of his exchange* [d] *he shall not rejoice* [e]. This is a literal version of the hebrew, and makes a sarcastic *meiosis*. He shall have no cause to boast of his wealth, or power; when he comes to exchange his prosperity for that terrible reverse, which divine vengeance has prepared for him.

There is a fine passage in *Oedipus Tyrannus,* where old Tiresias useth this stinging figure of speech to that unhappy prince: " I say, that the very man whom thou art seeking, and whom thou hast threatened with public malediction for the murder of Laius, is here present. He is called indeed a foreigner, but he shall be known hereafter to be a native of Thebes; neither shall he rejoice in the discovery." The discovery of the birth of Oedipus plunged him immediately in the depth of misery.

Ver. 19—21. *Because he hath oppressed,* &c.] In these verses he speaks, with more particularity, both of the *crime* and the utter impoverishment with which *it is punished.* the circumstances of the one are contrasted with corresponding circumstances of the other.

Ver. 19. *he hath oppressed* and *hath forsaken*] *He hath oppressed, he hath*
                                                                           grievously

---

[c] I follow the Syriac interpreter in reading בְּחֵיל *in the riches,* or *power.*

[d] תְּמוּרָה *a change,* or *exchange.* see the note on chap xv. 31. The Syriac version, If I mistake not, is, *And by the riches of his change he shall not be profited.*

[e] וְלֹא יַעֲלֹם The copulative ו is here either redundant as in chap. xxi. 6. וּנְכֹחַלַת *I am afraid;* or it is transposed, and ought to have begun the sentence; *and in the riches of his exchange he shall not rejoice.* There is a like transposition in chap. iv. 6. *Thy hope and the uprightness of thy ways,* for *And thy hope the uprightness of thy ways.*

20. Yet, reftlefs, greedy, ftill he crav'd for more:
See now the balance of his boundlefs ftore,
21. A cypher! Not a prey unfeiz'd remains;
Therefore no heir fhall feek his blafted gains:
27.* His crime is witnefs'd by the ftormy fkies,
The hoftile earth againft his crime will rife;
28. And

grievoufly afflicted ᶠ, &c. This is an epitome of tyrannical government. Compare I Sam. xii. 3. Zech. xi. 17.

the poor] *The weak.* They are not abfolutely poor; for they are fuppofed to poffefs *houfes*, which the oppreffor taketh violently away.

Ver. 20. *He fhall not feel quietnefs in his belly*] *Neither is his belly fatisfied*, as the Vulgar Latin turns it ᵍ. his *vice* is defcribed: 'Tis an infatiable appetite of rapine.

He fhall not fave, &c.} *By his covetoufnefs* ʰ *he fhall bring forth nothing* ⁱ. This expreffeth the *punifhment* of his rapacious avarice. All the wealth which he fo greedily amaffed, by every method of violence, fhall come to nothing.

Ver. 21. *There fhall none of his meat be left*] The hebrew is, *There is none left for his prey* ᵏ. Mr. Heath's freer verfion expreffeth the fenfe, *Nothing could efcape his rapacity.* His *vice* is here marked, in language more forcible than in the foregoing verfe.

therefore fhall no man look for his goods] His punifhment fhall tally with his crime: He plundered every one, and left nothing to any; therefore nothing. fhall be left to him, no eftate, or effects, for any heir to expect.

* See the note on thefe verfes, 27, 28.

ᶠ עוֹב In Arabic עָרָב, which anfwers to עוֹב, fignifies *to torment.* This idea rifes above the foregoing *he hath oppreffed:* whereas *he hath forfaken* is flat, and finks below the other.

ᵍ *Nec fatiatus eft venter ejus.*

ʰ בחמודו *by his covetoufnefs.* חמד fignifies, in Hebrew and Chaldee, *to covet.* Thus the Targum of Onkelos, in Exod. xx. 17. *thou fhalt not covet* (לא תחמיר) *thy neighbour's houfe.*

ⁱ לא ימלט *he fhall bring forth a nothing.* לא *nothing*, as in chap. vi. 21. מלט fignifies *to bring forth*, Ifaiah xxxiv. 15. *There fhall the great owl make her neft, and lay* (תמלט) *and hatch.*

ᵏ לאכלו *his prey.* Chap. ix. 26. *as the eagle hafteth to the prey.*

28. And his whole fortunes, that avenging day,
Like torrents rattling down the rocks shall rush away.

22. In the full season of exulting pride,
Distress shall straiten him on every side:

23. Ev'n while he gluts his avarice, when its feast
Is to the height of luxury increas'd;
All ills shall burst upon him, like the show'rs
Of flaming sulphur on Gomorrah's tow'rs:

24. Flight

Ver. 22—25. *In the fulness,* &c.] Here the description marks the *season,* in which this dreadful ruin of all his fortunes will come upon him; namely in the very height of his prosperity. to this is added the destruction of his person by some fearful judgement of God.

Ver. 22. *In the fulness of his sufficiency*] *In the fulness of his exultation*¹.

every hand of the wicked, &c.] *every hand of the miserable*ᵐ *shall come upon him;* That is, all whom his oppressions have made miserable, shall suddenly combine to strip him of his plunder.

Ver. 23. *When he is about to fill his belly*] *He shall be filling his belly*ⁿ; that is, swallowing down riches; committing new depredations; when the divine vengeance shall surprise him, a vengeance terrible and exterminating like that on Sodom and Gomorrah. God *shall cast the fury of his wrath upon him, and shall rain it upon him,* &c. compare Psalm xi. 6. *upon the wicked he shall rain . . . fire and brimstone, and an horrible tempest.*

while he is eating] glutting his rapacious avarice, and enjoying new plunder.

---

¹ ספקו *his exultation.* Its root signifies *to clap the hands,* which is an act of applause and triumph: Chap. xxxiv. 37. *He clappeth* his hands *amongst us.*

ᵐ עמל *the miserable.* Chap. iii. 20. *to him that is in misery.* The Septuagint however render it by αδικα, *every kind of distress* πασα α. γκι. They read עָמָל *misery, sorrow, trouble.* Chap. v. 6. *neither doth trouble spring out of the ground.*

ⁿ יהי למלא בטנו It is a periphrasis of the future tense ימלא *he shall fill* Thus II Sam. xviii. 3. *Thou shalt succour us* תהיה לנו לעזור. This criticism belongs to Cocceius.

24. Flight unavails, immortal arms purfue,
    The brazen bow fhall ftrike his vitals through:
25. The fhaft of God from out his body gleams,
    And glowing with his boiling liver fteams;
    In fhades of night his dying eye-balls roll,
    And Terrors apprehend his flitting foul.

26. Woes,

Ver. 24. *He fhall flee*, &c.] *He would flee° from the weapons*ᵖ, *but the brazen*ᵠ *bow fhall ftrike him through.* God is at war with him. The fcripture arms the divine being with a fword, a bow, and arrows, to reprefent his vengeance. Pfalm vii. 12, 13. (compare chap. vi. 4. xv. 24. fee alfo the note on chap. xviii. 14.) all his efforts to ward off the calamities which fall upon him will be ineffectual. The Arabian writers are very fond of the idea of *a bow*, and frequently ufe it to image extraordinary, inevitable, and deftructive calamities from the hand of God. The learned Schultens hath favoured us with feveral examples from their poets, in his note on this verfe.

Ver. 25. *It is drawn*, &c.] This lively piece of poetical painting is an extenfion of the laft claufe of the foregoing verfe, *the brazen bow fhall ftrike him through.* The ftroke is mortal, and brings on a terrible death.

It is drawn] *He draweth*ʳ, *and it cometh out of his body; even the glittering arrow*ˢ *out of his gall. he goeth*ᵗ, that is, expireth.

Terrors are upon him] A Greek or Roman poet would have faid, The Furies
feize

° יברח *he would flee*, as in chap. xxvii. 22. *he would fain flee out of his hands.*

ᵖ נשק It fignifies *arms*, or weapons of every fort, as the bow, fhield, arrows, fpears, &c. (Ezek. xxxix. 9.) and is here put for the armed hoft, viz. of evils.

ᵠ נחושה *brafs.* Gen. iv. 22. II Kings xxv. 13, 14. Anciently all armour was made of brafs. The Pfalmift mentions *a bow of brafs*, Pfal. xviii. 35. קשת נחושה

ʳ שלף *he draweth*, the arrow fhot into him by the brazen bow.

ˢ ברק *the lightning*, the arrow which glitters like lightning.

ᵗ הלך *he goeth*, that is, dieth. Chap. xiv. 20. *Thou prevaileft for ever againft him, and he geeth,* &c.

26. Woes, horrid woes, as yet of unknown name,
For him are treafur'd; a devouring flame,
                               Prepar'd

feize him. But what can thefe *Terrors* be, which are upon him the moment his breath is out of his body? Surely the punifhments of a future world[u]. Immediately after thefe words, and before the following verfe, we may introduce ver. 17. *He fhall not fee the rivers*, &c. provided that verfe is to be underftood of his exclufion from the manfions of the bleffed.

Ver. 26. This verfe is an amplification of the *terrors* ver. 25.

all darknefs, &c.] every kind of mifery.

is hidden] The nature and circumftances of future punifhments are concealed[w] from us in this world.

in his fecret places] *for his treafures*[x]; fo our tranflators turn the fame word in Pfalm xvii. 14. where the facred poet is fpeaking of the punifhment which God referves for the wicked; *whofe belly thou filleft with thy hid treafure.* The apoftle alfo adopts this metaphor Rom. ii. 5. *But . . . treafureft up unto thyfelf wrath againft the day of wrath*, &c.

A fire] This is one of thofe terrible images, by which the fcripture reprefents the future punifhments of the wicked.

not blown[y]] it is unquenchable fire: for it is not kindled by the breath of man, but of God.

it fhall go ill with him that is left, &c.] While he himfelf is fuffering the wrath of God in another world, vengeance purfues the family he left in this world, to utter extermination.

---

[u] The Greeks affigned to the Ερινυες *the Furies* the offices of driving wicked fouls down to Erebus the place of punifhment. See Windet *de vita functorum ftatu*. p. 118. בלהות feems to mean future punifhments in Pfal. lxxiii. 19. Vid. Targum on ver. 20. of that Pfalm.

[w] See the note on chap. xi. 6.

[x] צפוניו Its root fignifies *to lay up in ftore*. Chap. xxi. 19. *God layeth up his iniquity for his children*. See alfo Cant. vii. 14.

[y] לא נפח ασβεςον *unquenchable*, as the Alexandrian Septuagint turns it. Symmachus renders it μη ζωπυρω; Theodotion ανευ φυσηματος, *not kindled by the breath*, or *wind*.

CHAP. XX.   THE BOOK OF JOB.   155

Prepar'd of old in secret cells beneath,
A flame not kindled by a mortal breath,
Shall feed upon him; and a curse be sent
To the poor lone survivor in his tent.

29. Such heritage, by just decree, must fall
To such delinquents, from the judge of all.

CHAP.

Ver. 27, 28. *The heaven,* &c.] The description of his *punishment* was compleated in the foregoing verse, with solemnity and terror. But these two verses, in their present situation, are an inelegant, disorderly, and frivolous return to the loss of his temporal possessions. I think they will come in next after ver. 21. with propriety, as explanatory of the means by which the dissipation of his fortunes shall be accomplished: The means are the operations both of the heavens and the earth.

Ver. 27. *The heaven shall reveal,* &c.] The heavens shall publish his guilt, by lightning, for instance; such as destroyed Job's sheep: and by storms of wind, such as destroyed his children.

And the earth, &c.] The earth will rise up against him, when those whom he hath plundered shall in their turn plunder him: or when, as in the case of Job, the thieves of the desert shall make incursions and carry off his cattle.

Ver. 28. *The increase,* &c.] The effect of the combined operations of the heavens and the earth against him, is the swift and violent dissipation of his whole estate.

The increase of his house shall roll away [z],
like *torrents* [a], *in the day of his wrath.*

---

[z] יגל If we read *jagel* instead of *jigel*, the root will be גלל *devolvit.* Accordingly Mr. Heath turns it, *shall roll away.* Thus we gain a powerful metaphor, which suggested the still more powerful idea of *torrents.*

[a] נגרות ut *aquæ fluentes*, as Grotius renders it; or according to Mr. Heath, like *the torrents*; the particle of comparison כ *(like, as)* is understood: so chap. xi. 12. like *a wild asses colt.* xxiv. 5. as *wild asses in the desart.* If we read *nigrath*, it is a substantive, the plural of *nigrah*; which in the Chaldee, as Mr. Heath observes, signifies *a torrent.* Vid. Buxtorf.

CHAP.
XXI.
1, 2.   Then Job: Give audience, audience I implore,
         Be that your charity; I ask no more:
3. Indulge me utt'rance——then insult again.
4. Shall I of man, censorious man, complain?

The

C H A P. XXI.

This chapter is argumentative. The three antagonists still insisted, that, by a constant rule of providence, great and destructive calamities are the portion of wicked men; and of them only. He overthrows that position, by adducing many instances of atheistical men, who pass their lives in affluence and ease, are favoured with a gentle death, and have all the honours of sepulture paid to their remains. This is a solid confutation of their false idea of the divine government, and, at the same time, of their unjust censures of him founded on that mistaken notion.

We are not to imagine, however, that his reasoning is calm and cool. It is the reasoning of a man in great emotions of mind. It is mixed with a sort of indignation at his own miserable lot. Thus the great design of the poem is going forward; His discontent with the ways of providence is inflamed, by the very arguments which prove the usual and established order of its dispensations.

Ver. 4. *is my complaint to*[b] *man*] *is my complaint of man?* This is an intimation,

---

Buxtorf. *Lex. Talmud.* נגרא. By this reading also the latter sentence of the period will consist exactly of six syllables, and will tally with the former; according to the manner of the hebrew poetry.

Jigel | jebul | Bet-o |
Nigroth | be-jom | app-o |

But our Translators have followed the Masoretic pointing *niggaroth*; which is the feminine plural of the participle in *niphal.* They turn it, *shall flow away.* The construction however is imperfect, and they are forced to insert the supplemental words *and his goods,* to compleat the sense. The root is נגר (as it also is of *nigrah*) which is used of water rushing down a precipice; Micah i. 4. *as the waters that are poured down* (מגרים) *a steep place.*

[b] לאדם   The preposition ל signifies *of* or *concerning* in Gen. xx. 13. *Say of me* (לי) *he is my brother.* Vid. Noldium.

The cruel slanders which my fame defile,
Would justify resentment's sharpest style.

5. Observe me, wonder, and in silent fear
The mystic ways of Providence revere.

6. Astonish'd, trembling, I the scene review;
Which truth displays and mem'ry wakes anew.

7. Why live the wicked, and wax old in pow'r,
Their wealth augmenting to the mortal hour;

8. Live,

tion, that the discourse he was entring upon was a complaint against God. It is indeed partly an expostulation with God for treating so many wicked men with such favour, and him with so much rigour.

why should not my spirit, &c.] *why should I not be angry*[c]? If his subject were the usage he met with from man, he should be justified, he says, in expressing the strongest resentment.

Ver. 5. *be astonished*, &c.] Silent astonishment, he tells them, instead of censure, should be the effect of their reflections on his case; a man of piety and virtue made miserable, while so many profligate wretches are made happy. These measures of providence, he adds in the next verse, filled his own mind with the utmost consternation.

Ver. 7—13. *Wherefore*, &c.] We have here a lively description of worldly felicity, drawn from the manners of Arabia; and adapted to the mode of wealth and sensual gratification in ancient times.

Ver. 7. *Wherefore do the wicked live*, &c.] Schultens has remarked the climax of sentiments in this verse: The wicked are happy[d], they grow old in happiness, their happiness is continually advancing.

---

[c] תקצר רוחי *why should I not be angry?* This is Mr. Heath's version. He follows the LXX. ... ; it is justified by Prov. xiv. 29. *He that is hasty of spirit* (רוח קצר) *exalteth folly*.

[d] יחיו *why do the wicked live, grow old, you increase in wealth?*

גברו *they increase*. This verb denotes continual augmentation, Gen. vii. 19, 20. where we english it *to prevail*.

חיל *power*, or *wealth*.

8. Live, while the children of their children rife,
    And the ſtrong nurſlings ſhoot before their eyes?
9. They dwell ſecurely, all is peace ſincere,
    The rod of heav'n knows no commiſſion there:
10. Whoſe truſty bull, ne'er butts his amorous ſpouſe,
    But, full of genial fire, abſolves his vows:
    Whoſe heifer calves, with no untimely throe,
    And lively births in all their paſtures low:
                                    11. Fruitful

Ver. 8. *Their ſeed is eſtabliſhed*, &c.] This ingredient in their felicity, ſo ſweet to every tender parent, ſtands oppoſed to Bildad's aſſertion chap. xviii. 19. and to Zophar's chap. xx. 10. Eliphaz had repreſented this as the peculiar bleſſing of good men, chap. v. 25.

Ver. 9. *Their houſes*, &c.] They and their families live in perfect peace and ſecurity, and enjoy firm and permanent health. By *fear*, I apprehend, is meant, alarms from the incurſions of the Arabs of the deſert and from the ravages of wild beaſts. By *the rod of God* is principally intended diſeaſes: For Job expreſſeth his own grievous diſtemper by this ſignificant phraſe ᵉ. Other calamities however, which come immediately from heaven, are not excluded; the miſchiefs, for inſtance, done by lightning, by ſtorms of wind, and by inundations. Eliphaz had repreſented this protection to be the peculiar privilege of good men ᶠ.

Ver. 10. *Their bull*ᵍ *gendereth*ʰ *and faileth not*] This verſe deſcribes the proſperous increaſe of their wealth, which in thoſe countries conſiſted chiefly of cattle.

ᵉ Chap. ix. 34.   ᶠ Chap. v. 19—24.

ᵍ שׁוֹר This word ſignifies *a beeve*, whether male or female; but when it is put along with the female, as here, it conſtantly, if I miſtake not, means *the bull*.

ʰ עִבַּר *tranſivit*. This moſt naturally expreſſeth the act of the male in propagation. The next term גָעַל (*faileth not*) *faſtidivit*, may be well underſtood de languore quadrupedum venerem averſantium, as Codurcus explains it. The Chaldee paraphraſe is ſomewhat obſcure, תוריה מבטין ולא יפלט *bes ejus gravidat* (concipere fecit) *nec eripiet* (*nec in irritum jacit ſemen*, as the latin verſion in the *Polyglet* turns it).

CHAP. XXI. THE BOOK OF JOB. 159

11. Fruitful their fold; alike in fruitful pains,
Their wives with young fucceffion fill their plains;
A fry undifciplin'd, that fkip around,
Like wanton kids, upon the houfhold ground:
12. Mean while the fires, with mufic's lighteft airs,
Flute, harp, and timbrel, laugh at human cares;

13. A

Ver. 11. *They fend forth*] The word which our author ufes is a metaphor, I think, from thriving trees, which throw out plentiful fhoots [1]. But this idea being not fufficient to exprefs the increafe of their families, he fuddenly changes the image; and compares their multiplication to that of fheep, *like a flock*. By this management we alfo gain another circumftance of their profperity, the fruitfulnefs of their fheep and goats; *They fend forth their little ones*, as their *flock*.

Their children dance] *Their children fkip* [k], like lambs. This is a very natural and pleafing domeftic picture.

Ver. 12. *They take the timbrel*, &c.] This muft, I imagine, be underftood of the gay feftival life led by the Parents: for they are the principal fubjects of the difcourfe. The timbrel, tabret, or tabour was an inftrument of mufic as old as the days of Jacob and Laban [l]. It was portable, and of a foft tone: for it was carried and ufed by women of quality [m]. It was played upon with the the hand [n], and feems to have been a kind of fmall drum. They ufed it both in their religious and civil feftivals. Exod. xv. 20. Pf. cl. 4. If. xxiv. 8, 9.

rejoice] The character of the perfons obliges us to underftand this to mean riotous and diffolute mirth. Compare Ifaiah v. 11, 12. xxiv. 8.

the

---

[1] ישלחו See Pfal. lxxx. 11. (Heb. ver. 12.) Jerem. xvii. 8. In Prov. xxix. 15. מִשְׁלָח is rendered *left* to himfelf, i. e. not corrected.

[k] The word is fo tranflated in Pfal. cxiv. 4.

[l] Gen. xxxi. 27.   [m] Exod. xv. 20.

[n] The prophet defcribing the women in their public lamentations fmiting on their breafts, and keeping time perhaps in that action, calls it *tabering upon their breafts*. Nahum ii. 7. (Heb. ver. 8.)

13. A long, long life in senſual bliſs conſume,
   Then inſtant drop, full mellow'd for the tomb.
14, 15. Bold therefore to blaſpheme, " Away (they cry)
   " Thou phantom of weak fear, call'd Deity ;
   " Our necks the burden of thy yoke diſdain,
   " Vain is our incenſe, and our vows are vain."
16. Not their own hand their bleſſings could beſtow,
   Their bleſſings from a higher fount muſt flow :

But,

the organ °] *the pipe.* The organ is a compound of pipes, and of later invention, as Mr. Heath remarks.

Ver. 13. *in wealth*] *in good* ᵖ, that is, worldly felicity.

in a moment, &c.] This aſſertion is oppoſed to Zophar's repreſentation of the terrible death of ſuch men chap. xx. 24, 25. See alſo chap. xviii. 12, 13. This is that ſudden and eaſy death, in a green old age, without pain, without lingering ſickneſs, and while their families are flouriſhing around them, which Tireſias predicts to Ulyſſes in the ſhades : " Death ſhall come to thee from the ſea : It ſhall be a gentle death. It ſhall come, when thou art ſubdued by a happy old age, and thy people about thee are happy ᑫ."

Ver. 14, 15. *Therefore*, &c.] It was to the advantage of his argument, and agreeable to the diſcontented temper he was in, to ſpecify more circumſtantially the *character* of theſe proſperous men.

Ver. 16. *Lo, their good*, &c.] They could not be the authors of their own felicity : It is intirely the work of providence. The ſentiment appears to me the ſame as in chap. xii. 9. *Who knoweth not in all theſe, that the hand of the Lord hath wrought this?* This interpretation is confirmed by chap. xxii. 18.

where

° עוגב The Chaldee interpreter renders it *abuba, a pipe,* or *flute:* whence, as Buxtorf obſerves, the Romans by inſerting *m* formed their *ambubaia.* The *ambubaiæ* in Horace were Syrian courtezans, who played on flutes. Buxtorf. *Lex. Talmud.* Dacier's *Horace*, ſat. ii. lib. 1.

ᵖ טוב *good*, as in chap. ix. 25. *My days . . . . they flee away, they ſee no good.*

ᑫ *Odyſſ.* xi. ver. 133. &c.

But, O my foul, from their affembly flee,
Far be their counfels and their lot from me.

17. Oft mourn thefe mifcreants their high-fparkling light
Extinguifh'd? Often in tempeftuous night
Are they involv'd? For them hath vengeance ftor'd,
Of plagues enormous a peculiar hoard?

18. Are

where Eliphaz fneeringly retorts thefe words; *Yet be filled their houfes with good things: but the counfel of the wicked is far from me.*

the counfel, &c.] He declares his abhorrence of their principles and practices. This fentiment is thrown in, to prevent an ill conftruction of his difcourfe; as though he was arguing againft a providence, by giving a true account of its adminiftrations.

Ver. 17—21. *How oft is the candle of the wicked,* &c.] He feems, in this branch of his difcourfe, to contraft with the great majority of wicked men who are happy in the world, the *few* examples of other wicked men who are calamitous.

Ver. 17. *How oft*[1]] The fenfe of this verfe and the next depends much on the right explication of this particle *how oft*; which muft be underftood to be repeated at the beginning of every fentence, How oft *cometh,* &c. how oft *doth God diftribute,* &c. how oft *are they as ftubble,* &c.

If we take it for a particle of *exaggeration,* and lay the ftrefs of the pronunciation upon *oft, how óft is the candle of the wicked put out!* The meaning will be, it is put out very often; Inftances of the fad cataftrophes of fuch men are very frequent and common. But this explication cannot be right: becaufe it puts into the mouth of Job an affertion, which flatly contradicts what he had been juft faying in the former part of the fpeech. It is the very doctrine of his antagonifts, and the ground of their condemnation of him.

Whereas

---

[1] The hebrew particle is כמה, which admits of the fame variation of the accent and the fenfe as the englifh *how oft*; *cámmah* hów oft, *cammáh* how óft.

18. Are they like stubble, when the tempest roars?
Like chaff, when sweepy whirlwinds cleanse the floors?

19, 20. You'll urge " God treasures vengeance for their seed."
But he, the criminal, himself, should bleed:
Living,

Whereas if we understand this to be a particle of *interrogation*, and lay the accent upon *how*, hów *oft*, or hów *many times*, the answer will be *not often, seldom*. as in chap. xiii. 23. when Job asks, *how many are my sins?* he means, they were not many. Mr. Heath therefore did well in translating hów oft, *how seldom*. This interpretation agrees with fact, and with Job's sentiments, overthrows the position of his adversaries, and subverts the foundation of their censures.

The first sentence, *hów oft is the candle of the wicked put out?* is a reply in particular to Bildad's assertion chap. xviii. 5, 6. see the note. The next sentence, hów oft *cometh their destruction*, &c. points to another proposition in that speech of Bildad, ver. 12. *destruction* shall be *ready at his side*.

God *distributeth*, &c.] Hów oft *doth he distribute sorrows*, &c. The original word for *sorrows* signifies *snares*, that is, mischiefs, calamities. This metaphor had been used by Bildad chap. xviii. 8. &c.

Ver. 18. *They are*, &c.] Hów oft *are they as stubble before the wind, and as chaff that the storm carrieth away?* Or, *are they as stubble*, &c. We cannot enter into the propriety and beauty of these images, unless we recollect the practice in the east of threshing their corn in the open field; so that if the wind happen to rise, the shattered straw and chaff are easily carried away'.

Ver. 19—21. *God layeth up*, &c.] These verses are not without their difficulty. But the difficulty, I think, will vanish, if we allow the ingenious conjecture of Cocceius; that the first sentence is the evasion of his antagonists. They are supposed to alledge, that when God doth not punish the *persons* of the wicked, he punisheth them in their *posterity*.

" God layeth up his iniquity (*his punishment*) *for his children*."

The answer of Job is, The transgressor himself ought to be the sufferer, according

---

' Shaw' *Travels*, p. 138, &c. 4to.

Living, himself should his own treason rue,
And his own eyes his tragedy should view;
While at his lips the wrathful cup he fees,
Compell'd to drain it with its bitter lees:

21. For when his number'd months their tale have spent,
When to oblivion's land himself is sent;
Are then the fortunes of his house his care?
Feels he its triumph or its sorrow there?

22. Shall man instruct, in his presuming school,
The Lord of heav'n this petty orb to rule?

23. Here

ing to your own principles. What punishment is it to him, that his children suffer? He has no concern about them, when he himself is gone into another world[t].

Ver. 19. *"God layeth up his punishment for his children."*
He (God) *should recompense him* (the criminal himself)
And he (the criminal) *should know it* (should feel punishment).

20. *His eyes should see his own destruction,*
And he (himself) *should drink of the wrath of the Almighty.*

21. *For what careth he for his family, when the number of his months is fulfilled*[u]*?*

What careth he for his family] This is Mr. Heath's version.

is fulfilled[u]] Our Translators turn it, *is cut off in the midst.* But the original signifies, *is reckoned in full tale.* The whole expression denotes the living out the full term of human life: *When the number of his months is reckoned out.*

Ver. 22—26. *Shall any teach God, &c.*] In these verses he takes notice of the
strange

---

[t] See the *Commentary* of Schultens, and Mr. Heath's translation of these verses.

[u] הִצֵּצוּ It is an allusion (says Cocceius) to the ancient way of computing, by *pebbles*
(חִצָּץ) or by *arrows* (חֵץ)

23. Here one prolongs voluptuous life in eafe,
   Deflow'r'd by no misfortune or difeafe:
24. Sweet in his veins his fatt'ning dairy flows,
   And death's foft dews his flumb'ring eyelids clofe.

25. Another,

ftrange inequality in thefe meafures of God towards perfons of the fame demerit; in profpering fo many of them, and making examples of fo few. It confounds all our notions of juftice. Yet it muft needs be right.

Ver. 22. *Shall any teach God*] Who will prefume to amend his difpenfations? Or as Mr. Pope ftrongly expreffes it,

> Snatch from his hand the balance and the rod,
> Rejudge his juftice, be the judge of God.
>   *Effay on Man.*

Seeing he judgeth, &c.] To *judge* often fignifies in fcripture to *govern*. It comprehends the whole office of a fupreme magiftrate [v]. The argument here is from the greater to the lefs: He that ruleth the higher world of intellectual beings, knows furely how to manage the little affairs of human kind. This is a noble fentiment, and ought to have filenced his own murmurings. But his mind was too much difcompofed by his paffions, to be conftantly influenced by his better principles.

Ver. 23, 24. *One dieth*, &c.] He here fummeth up in few words, the happy circumftances of the major part of wicked men; which he had defcribed at large ver. 7—13.

In his full ftrength, &c.] *In his very perfection* [x]; that is, in full poffeffion of all worldly felicity.

his

---

[v] I Sam. viii. 5, 6. I Kings iii. 9.

[x] בְּעֶצֶם תֻּמּוֹ. עֶצֶם anfwers to the englifh emphatical particle *very* Gen. vii. 13. *in the felf-fame day (in that very day) entered Noah*, &c.

תֻּם denotes the intirenefs of fome whole, integrity of parts, the compleat condition of a perfon or thing: Thus in the title of the Arabic verfion of the *Table of Cebes*, תַּמָּה fignifies *compleat*: That title is, " What a wife man is to do that he may be happy with a compleat (or perfect) happinefs."

25. Another, comfortlefs, and hard befted,
   With forrow worn, with fighing eats his bread;
   Long while in pain and pining ficknefs lies,
   Then with deep groans and violent ftruggle dies:
26. Both equal in the grave; on both is fpread
   The worm for covering, and the clay their bed.
27. I penetrate your thoughts; refolv'd in wrong,
   Harfh anfwer ftill fprings forward on your tongue;
                                          28. "His

his breafts, &c.] There is no authority for this tranflation, and the fenfe it yields is abfurd. It ought to be turned, *His paftures^r are full of milk*; that is, of flocks and herds. He dies in opulence.

his bones, &c.] This claufe reprefents the hale and vigorous ftate of his body to the laft moment of his life.

Ver. 25. *another dieth*, &c.] that is, another wicked man. For he fpeaks of fuch throughout the whole difcourfe, and plainly, I think, points in this verfe to fome few examples of wicked men made miferable. This was fufficient to fhew the perplexing inequality of the ways of God to men.

Ver. 26. *They fhall lie down alike*, &c.] Our obfervation can reach no further than to the grave. But there we behold him who had lived happily and him who had lived in mifery (though both alike wicked) in the fame deplorable ftate of corruption. So that this feeming diforder in the adminiftrations of providence is not rectified in the compafs of our view.

Ver. 27, 28. *Behold*, &c.] It feems to me, that he intended to have ended his difcourfe, of the profperity of the wicked, with the foregoing verfe. But,
                                                                    I imagine,

---

r עטיניו This word is no where elfe found in the hebrew bible. It is however preferved in the Arabic language: in which it fignifies, as the learned Schultens has proved, *the places about ponds where camels and fheep go to drink:* thence it came to be ufed for a large abundance of thofe things which are accounted riches in Arabia, fuch as *extenfive paftures well ftocked with cattle.* Mr. Heath therefore was not out of the way in tranflating it *his granges*, that is, his farms.

28. " His own sad story will his cause disgrace,
 " Why mourns our Emir his extinguish'd race?
 " Where is th' encampment of the wicked Great,
 " The circling clan, and roomy tent of state?"
29, 30. Hath trav'lling wisdom never won your ear,
 With foreign histories imported here?

Scorn

I imagine, he perceived, by their looks and gestures, that they gave no credit to what he had been saying; and that they still insisted on his overthrow as an evidence of his guilt. Whereupon he turns short upon them with indignation, and refers them to the testimony of sensible travellers; which confirmed his assertions by what happened in other countries.

Ver. 27. *I know your thoughts*, &c.] *your reasonings, and the harsh sentiments*[z] *which you unjustly conceive against me.*

Ver. 28. *For ye say, where is,* &c.] Although these questions relate to tyrannical princes in general, and to other wicked men in high stations; they are intended to be applied to Job's overthrow in particular. His adversaries still insisted, that destructive calamities are the usual portion of the wicked; and that such calamities being his portion, there wanted no other evidence of his guilt. But the testimony of travellers, he tells them, shews the falsity of their premisses, and, therefore, of the conclusion drawn from them.

where are the dwelling places, &c.] The hebrew is, *where is the tent of the tabernacles of wicked men.* The mode of expression alludes to an Arabian encampment, in which the pavilion of the *Emir,* or chief, was surrounded by the tents of his clan. Job did not live in tents. But his situation answered literally to these expressions, when he went upon any military expedition.

Ver. 29. *Their tokens*] their arguments[a], or allegations. By the phrase *them that*

---

[z] מְזִמּוֹת the harsh sentiments, *cruda,* as Schultens turns it. He observes that it is a metaphor from unripe fruit. Symmachus translates the whole verse, οιδα τας ενθυμησεις υμων, και τας ἀδικας καθ' ἡμων, *I know your reasonings, and your unjust thoughts against me.*

[a] אתת This word is generally translated σημεια by the LXX under which term Aristotle

CHAP. XXI. THE BOOK OF JOB. 167

 Scorn you their allegations? " That the day
 " Whose vengeance sweeps the sick'ning tribes away,
 " Spares the lewd tyrant? With carousal high,
 " His riots the destroying scourge defy.
31. " Who dares reprove his crimes? what hand presume
 " To sign the mighty malefactor's doom?
32. " With pomp he's carry'd to the grave; his name
 " There lives afresh, in monumental fame:

33. " There

that go by the way is meant travellers, Prov. vii. 19. *he is gone a journey*; in the original, *he is gone by the way.* The travellers to whom Job appeals, were probably the caravans of Tema and Sheba trafficking to Egypt. See chap. vi. 19. and the note.

 Ver. 30. *the wicked is reserved to the day*, &c.] The original will admit, and his argument requires the translation to be,

 The wicked is preserved[b] *in* [c] *the day of destruction.*

 They shall be brought forth, &c.] *They are feasted,* or *they feast in the day of wrath.* The hebrew will, I think, bear this sense, perfectly agreeing with the tenor of the whole discourse; which is intended to shew, that multitudes of wicked men live in splendor and festivity even in the most calamitous times.

 Ver. 32. *Yet shall he be brought,* &c.] Mr. Heath's version expresseth the whole
force

---

stotle (in his Rhetoric, lib. i. cap. 2.) comprehends all kinds of evidence. Sophocles also (in Oedipus Tyrannus ver. 725.) uses σημα for *convincing proofs.* The Psalmist means by אות *evidence* in general, Psal. lxxxvi. 17.

[b] וחשך *is preserved, is spared, is withdrawn.* It is used in the sense of *sparing,* or *preserving,* in chap. xxxiii. 18. where it is englished to *keep back,* He *keepeth back (spareth) his soul from the pit.* So in Psal. lxxviii. 50. *he spared not their soul from death.* In the Syriac Testament אתחשׁך signifies *to escape, to be preserved,* Acts xxvii. 21. *we should have been preserved from this loss and this distress.* Symmachus turns it in this verse of Job ὑπεξῃρέθη, *is kept;* Aquila, ὑπεξαιρεθήσεται *shall be withdrawn,* drawn out of the way of danger.

[c] ליום Psal. lxxxi. 4. *in,* or *on, the day,* Prov. vii. 20. *he will come home at the day (or*

33. " There he enjoys, in some delicious vale,
    " Turf ever green and springs that never fail ;
                                                    " Preceded,

force of the original, *Even this very man shall be carried*[d] *in pomp to the sepulchre,* &c. he is too powerful to be called to account by man, and not meeting with chastisement from God, he goes to the grave with all the honours of interment paid to personages of the highest rank.

and shall remain[e] *in the tomb*] Mr. Heath's version is, *and shall rest undisturbed in the tomb*. But our author's word never signifies *to remain*, or *to rest undisturbed*; either in the hebrew bible or in the dialects. I think the translation might be *and he flourisheth in the tomb*. He enjoys as it were a second life, in the tomb: he lives in fame, by means of his superb sepulchre and its delightful situation.

                                                                                in

---

on the day) appointed. Exod. xxiii. 15. *in the time appointed of the month Abib.* See also II Chron. viii. 13. and Psal. lix. 15, 17. לערב *in the evening*, לבקר *in the morning.* Also Psal. lxxi. 9. לעת *in the time*; and in the Chaldee, לעדן *in the time*, &c. of old age. The Chaldee again, in Ps. xcix. 5, 9. לבית *in the house*, לטור *in the mountain.* The learned Schultens therefore is justified in turning this clause, *Profectò in die exitii subducitur malus, verily the wicked is withdrawn in the day of destruction.* See also Isaiah x. 3. *in the day of visitation*, and Habak. iii. 16. *in the day of trouble*.

they are feasted] יובלו if we read *juballu* the root will be בלל *to anoint*, Psal. xcii. 10. *I shall be anointed with fresh oil:* And as perfumes made a distinguished part in the eastern banquets, hence the word might naturally come to signify *feasting*. Accordingly, in Arabic, the substantive noun בלל is *convivium*, a banquet. Vid. Castell. *Lex*.

[d] יובל *is carried in pomp*. The future is often used for the present tense. So ver. 30. יהשך *is reserved*.

[e] ישקוד The noun substantive שקד signifies *the almond tree*. Why may not the verb be derived from that root, and mean *to flourish* as the almond tree, and in general *to flourish?* If this be not admitted, let the verb be translated *he is awake*, or *watcheth* (Psal. cii. 7.) *in the tomb*. It will then be a metaphor denoting *life*, in opposition to *sleeping* the common metaphor for the state of death. The meaning, according to this interpretation, comes out the same as before: *he is awake in the tomb*; he liveth still, he liveth in the splendid memorial of him, his magnificent tomb. See the note of the learned Schultens on one of the poems in the *Arabian Anthologia*, intituled *Hamasja*, p. 560. Mr. Heath's version is taken from Le Clerc, and is founded on the change of שקוד into ישקוט *quiescet*.

CHAP. XXI.   THE BOOK OF JOB.

" Preceded, follow'd, to his dusty bed,
" By all the former, all the future dead."

34. Cease

in the tomb ᵗ] The hebrew word signifies first *a heap of corn* that is cut down; and thence in metaphor the heap of *dead bodies*, and the *sepulchre* or place where they are deposited. It is used here in the last acceptation; and in the first, chap. v. 26. where it is englished *a shock of corn*.

Ver. 33. *The clods of the valley shall be sweet to him*] *The soft clods* ᵇ *of the valley* (made soft and tender by gentle showers) *are sweet to him*. Their sepulchral grots were frequently in vallies, cut in the bottom of rocky hills. Such a situation of a tomb, together with springs of water or moderate rains to keep the turf perpetually green, was accounted a happy sepulture among the Arabians; as being a means of preserving the remembrance of the deceased in honour. Schultens, in his notes on this verse, cites the beginning of an Arabian poem ᶦ to this purpose. 'Tis an elegy on a person celebrated for his beneficence and liberality: and if we except one epigrammatic conceit, it is a beautiful composition. As it is short, the reader will not perhaps be displeased with the following faithful translation of the whole.

> Come, let us visit Maan's lov'd remains;
> Say to his tomb, may mollifying rains
> Water thy hallow'd turf! O narrow bound,
> Bounty her grave in thee, thee only, found.
> Bounty, which fill'd the spacious earth and sea,
> O tomb of Maan, how inclos'd in thee!
> Yes, Bounty thou dost hold, but Bounty dead;
> Which living would despise thy scanty bed.
> Maan's a name whose generous gifts survive
> The noble giver, and immortal live;

As

ᵗ גדיש *the tomb*, as in the Arabian poem;
   " Let ever-dropping showers water
        The tomb (גדיש) of Aryb."
Vid. *Hamasa*, p. 567.

ᵇ רגבי *the soft clods*, Mr. Heath; *glebæ molles*, Schultens. It signifies, in Arabic, earth that is made soft and tender by rain. Vid. *Comment.* Schultens.

ᶦ In Hamasa, p. 555.

34. Cease then; nor falsities for comforts vend,
Alike to truth unfaithful and your friend.

CHAP.
XXII.
1, 2. When man is wise, the Teman Sage reply'd,
'Tis for himself: does Heav'n the gain divide?

3. Must

As when some rich o'erflowing stream recedes,
It leaves behind a verdant wealth of meads.
But ah! with Maan Bounty sunk in dust;
The glory of munificence is lost.

every man shall draw[k] *after him*] I take the meaning to be, that in going down to the grave he does but share the common lot of mortals. Innumerable multitudes have gone thither before him, and the succeeding generations of men shall follow him to the same house of all living.

in your answers there remaineth falshood] Their exhortations to repentance were founded on a false supposition of his guilt. The hopes they gave him of restoration, were on condition of his repentance. The blessings they promised him, on that condition, were romantic: and in short, the whole of their answers proceeded on false ideas of the administrations of Providence.

CHAP. XXII.

This last speech of Eliphaz puts an end to the controversy on the part of Job's antagonists. It is in the true spirit of a baffled disputant. Unable to invalidate

Job's

---

[k] ימשׁך *shall draw*; rather, *he shall draw every man*, &c. It is a transitive verb, and is used of a number of persons following one another in long and close succession (Judges xx. 37.) as Cocceius remarketh. Seneca useth *traho* in much the same sense as משׁך here. Megara apostrophising her husband Hercules, who was gone down to the realms of Pluto, says;

————————aut omnes tuos
Defende reditu sospes, aut omnes trahe. *Hercules Furens,* ver. 306.

Either come back safe from the realms of death, *and protect all your family; or draw us all* thither after you.

CHAP. XXII.   THE BOOK OF JOB.   171

3. Muſt God high value on thy virtue ſet?
If thou art juſt, is Providence in debt?
4. And will he, trembling, from his throne deſcend,
To ſtill thy cavils and his ways defend?

5. Art

Job's defence, he flies out in abuſive language and the moſt atrocious calumnies. ver. 2. to the end of ver. 11.

Unable alſo to refute the reaſoning in Job's laſt diſcourſe, he endeavours to render it invidious. he taxes it with atheiſm, and warns him, by the example of the old world, of the vengeance men of his principles are to expect. ver. 12. to the end of ver. 20.

However, that he might quit the field with the air of a victor, and a reputation for charity, he once more exhorts him to repent; and in magnificent terms aſſures him he ſhould become happy and great on that condition. ver. 21. to the end of the chapter.

Ver. 2. *Can a man be profitable*[l], &c.] This verſion yields a very juſt ſentiment, which perfectly agrees with what Elihu ſays chap. xxxv. 7. *If thou be righteous, what giveſt thou him*, &c. compare Pſalm xvi. 2. Rom. xi. 35.

as he that is wiſe may be profitable, &c.] Sophocles puts the like ſentiment into the mouth of Oedipus [m],

" What good man is not a friend to himſelf?"

Ver. 3. *Is it any pleaſure to the Almighty*, &c.] *Is it a matter of care*[n] *to the Almighty that thou ſhouldſt be righteous*, &c. Is it a thing which he ſets his heart upon as an affair in which his intereſt and happineſs are deeply concerned? Eliphaz intends to expoſe to ridicule Job's complaints and juſtification of himſelf, as arrogant claims upon God.

---

[l] יסכן *can he be profitable?* It evidently has this meaning chap. xxxiv. 9. *For he hath ſaid, it profit.th a man nothing, that he ſhould delight himſelf in God.*

[m] *Oedipus Colonus*, ver. 313.

[n] חפץ *a matter of care.* In chap. xxi. 21. it ſignifies *care, anxiety.* So the LXX. underſtood it here, τι γαρ μελει τω κυριω, &c. *what careth the Lord, if thou wert blameleſs in thy works?*

Z 2

172   THE BOOK OF JOB.   CHAP. XXII.

5. Art thou unconscious of thy vast offence?
    Is not the number of thy sins immense?
6. Extortions from thy kin defile thy hands,
    The shivering loin its rag from thee demands.

7. To

Ver. 4. *Will he reprove thee*, &c.] *Will he reason° with thee for fear of thee? will he enter with thee into judgement?* Is he afraid his character will suffer by thy complaints, unless, in obedience to thy citation, he submit to a trial and argue his own cause? This is strong irony, and manifestly designed to ridicule those rash expressions in chap. ix. 32—35. xiii. 22, &c.

Ver. 5—11. *Is not thy wickedness*, &c.] There is no occasion for God to vindicate the measures of his providence towards thee. Thy own wickedness is manifestly the cause of all thy sufferings. Hitherto this magisterial censor had dealt in distant hints and general insinuations: But being now reduced to his last shifts, he has the temerity to charge his friend openly with particular crimes. This violent proceeding admirably serves the purpose of the poem: for it gives a fair occasion for that circumstantial defence (chap. xxxi.) in the close whereof dissatisfaction with the ways of God and self-justification are carried to the highest pitch that the poet intended.

Ver. 6. *Thou hast taken a pledge*, &c.] He is here charged with such rapacity, as to force even his relations to give security to him for debts which they did not owe; and with seizing the upper garment of the poor for pawn, which answers to a creditor among us taking a poor man's bed from under him for payment; for the poor in those countries had no other covering at night, when they slept, than their outward garment ᵖ which they wore in the day ᑫ.

naked]

° יוכיח. It signifies *to plead one's cause*, chap. xiii. 3. *I desire to reason with God.* The other phrase, *enter into judgement*, is also judicial; and means *to come to a trial.* Chap ix. 32. *He is not a man as I am that . . . we should come together in judgement.*

ᵖ The Arabs call their upper garment *a hyke*; which is a blanket, or gown, five or six yards long, and five or six yards broad. This is wrapped over the tunic, or close-bodied frock, (which is the inner garment) and girded about their waist in time of work or action. Shaw's *Travels*, p. 226, &c. 4to.

ᑫ Deut. xxiv. 13.

7. To thee the thirsty su'd, the famish'd sigh'd,
Seal'd was thy fountain, and thy crust deny'd.
8. A fav'rite name enjoy'd his spoil secure,
The strongest arm still made the title sure;
9. While the wrong'd widow pour'd her fruitless moan,
And orphans crush'd by thy injustice groan.
10. Hence ambush'd ills about thy path were set,
Hence the dire sweep of desolation's net:

11. Hence

naked] By taking away their blanket, or upper garment, he left them naked; according to the mode of speaking in the east': that is, he left them only their tunic and shirt. A person also who was ill-clad, or in rags, was said to be *naked*; as Seneca tells us ².

Ver. 7. *Thou hast not given*, &c.] Entertainment of travellers and charity to the poor were looked upon by the Arabs, and by the ancient Greeks, as duties of the most sacred obligation. The Odyssee has some noble sentiments on this subject: and the poems of the Arabs abound with them. Wherefore the vilest of all characters among them was the inhospitable and avaricious man.

Ver. 8, 9. *But as for the mighty man*, &c.] Here he accuses him of shameful partiality in the administration of justice. The great were certain to carry their cause, when they set up a claim, however groundless, to the land of some defenceless widow or orphan.

the earth] *the land*, which he pretended to have a right to.

The honourable man] In the original, *He whose person is accepted*; that is, who is favoured on account of his wealth and power.

Ver. 10. *snares*] This was an established metaphor for destructive calamities; as also *darkness* and *floods of water* for overwhelming misery. Old Tiresias the soothsayer

---

¹ I Sam. xix. 24. II Sam. vi. 20. Isaiah xx. 2—4. Mic. i. 8. John xxi. 7.

² Qui male vestitium et pannosum, nudum se vidisse dicit. *De Benef*. lib. v. 13. quoted by Dr. Shaw, p. 226. of his *Travels*.

11. Hence black defpair, like night, around thee fpread,
And booming waters billowing o'er thy head.

12. Beholds not God, from his ethereal feat,
The ftars dim-twinkling far beneath his feet?
Yet mark the diftance, how immenfely far,
From this low dwelling to the neareft ftar!

13. Thy frenzy argu'd; can the ways of men
Lie in the compafs of his bounded ken?

14. Grofs foothfayer foretells the calamities that were coming on the royal family of Thebes in the following language:

" The deftroying minifters of vengeance *lie in wait for* thee, and *thou fhalt be caught* in the fame calamities with which thou haft overwhelmed others '."

abundance of waters, &c.] A drowning man, or a fhip foundering at fea, feems to be the image alluded to. The neighbourhood of thefe men's country to the Mediterranean and Arabian feas, and to the rivers Jordan and Nile, might furnifh them with thefe emblems of calamity: or they might be fupplied with fuch ideas by the torrents from their own mountains.

Ver. 12—20. *Is not God*, &c.] What Job had faid in the foregoing chapter, of the general impunity and profperity of the wicked, was matter of fact. But this calumniator mifreprefents his difcourfe, as a denial of a divine providence grounded on moft abfurd notions of the fupreme Being; as though he were limited in his prefence, and could not fee what paffeth in our world. Job therefore, in this man's account, held the fame atheiftical principles with the wicked who were deftroyed by the flood; whofe deftruction is here mentioned in vindication of the juftice of God, and as an admonition to him of his approaching fate if he did not fpeedily repent.

Ver. 12. *Is not God in the height*, &c.] The immenfe diftance of heaven, the habitation of God, is reprefented by its being far above the ftars.

Ver. 13. *And thou fayeft*, &c.] *Therefore thou faidft* ". Thy folly drew from its

---

' *Antigone*, ver. 1c86, &c.

" האמרת *therefore thou faidft*. ו *therefore*, as in chap. v. 17. *therefore defpife not thou the chaftening of the Almighty*.

CHAP. XXII.   THE BOOK OF JOB.   175

14. Grofs atmofphere, with interpofing fcreen,
    Conceals the profpect of this earthly fcene:
    He, veil'd in clouds, to his own cares confin'd,
    Walks round his azure realms unheeding human kind.
15. Haft thou, in boldeft profligacy bold,
    Follow'd the path trac'd out by atheifts old?
16. Whom vengeance feiz'd before the mortal day,
    Whofe column'd domes the deluge fwept away;

                                    17. Whofe

its own abfurd idea of God, as a finite being, a conclufion no lefs abfurd; that he is ignorant of the affairs of human kind.

Ver. 15. *Haft thou marked*, &c.] *Haft thou kept*[u] *the old way*, &c. Haft thou taken up the principles of thofe impious men, who lived at the time of the deluge? This interrogative form of expreffion is a vehement affirmation.

Ver. 16. *Which were cut down*] This verfion is authorifed by the Targum, " which were abolifhed from the earth." The Greek Bible renders the word, more agreeably to its true meaning[x], *which were taken*[y], or *apprehended*, as malefactors.

out of time[y]] The Chaldee turns it, " when their time was not yet;" that is, the time, or period, to which they might have lived according to the courfe of nature. They perifhed by an untimely death.

Ver. 16. *whofe foundation*] *whofe habitation*; denominated here from its effential part; the better to exprefs the durable materials of which their palaces were framed.

with a flood] The original makes ufe of the ufual word for *a river*: But that it was alfo ufed for the waters of the fea, appears from Jonah ii. 3. For
                                                                        thou

---

[u] הישמור *haft thou kept?* Chap. xxiii. 11. *his way have I kept.*

[x] קמישו *were apprehended.* See the note on chap. xvi. 8.

[x] Συλλαρβανεται.

[y] בלא עת See chap. xv. 32. Ecclefiaftes vii. 17. *why fhouldeft thou die before thy time.*

17. Whose madness said, " Away, thou deity,
" What blessings can our wants receive from thee?"
18. Ingrates! their fulness from his bounty flow'd;
Far be their counsels, far from my abode.
19. Then sang the righteous, glorying in the sight,
Atheists o'erthrown, and God's avenging might:
20. Thus fell those ancient rebels; but by fire
The wicked remnant shall at last expire.
21. Humble

thou hadst cast me into the deep, in the midst of the seas, and the floods [z] compassed me about.

Ver. 17. *Depart from us,* &c.] By describing the impiety of these men in the very terms of Job (chap. xxi. 14, 15.) he confronts their exemplary destruction to Job's assertion of the impunity and felicity of such characters.

Ver. 18. *But the counsel,* &c.] This is sneer. See the note on chap. xxi. 16.

Ver. 19. *The righteous see it,* &c.]

The righteous saw [a], and were glad:
And the innocent laughed them to scorn.

As we are to understand the foregoing verse of the deluge, by *the righteous and innocent* must be meant, Noah and his family. Aristotle remarks, that " no good man is troubled, when parricides, for instance, meet with their deserved punishment: for it is our duty to rejoice in such occasions."

Ver. 20. *Whereas our substance,* &c.] I apprehend the translation should be, *Was not [b] their rebellion [c] punished with destruction [d]?*

Schultens

---

[z] נהר It is used in the plural number as synonimous with ימים *the seas.* Psal. xxiv. 2.

[a] The LXX. translate the verbs in the past time.

[b] אם לא annon? אם is frequently interrogative. Vid. Noldium. See chap. iv. 17. vi. 30.

[c] קימנו *their rebellion.* (1) On the authority of the Septuagint, Syriac, and Vulgate versions I read קימו (?) קים is turned *obstinacy* by the Syriac interpreter. It may signify *insurrection,* or *rebellion;* as קמים signifies *insurgents,* or *rebels,* Ps. iii. 1. lxxiv. 23.

[d] נבחר It is englished *to be cut off,* chap. iv. 7.

CHAP. XXII. THE BOOK OF JOB.

21. Humble thyfelf to God, refign thy prey;
Rich harveft follows the repenting day:
22. Embrace

Schultens gives a very animated turn to this verfe, by fuppofing it to be the burden of a triumphal hymn, fung by Noah and his family on this awful occafion.

but the remnant of them, &c.] *but the remnant of them the fire fhall confume*[e]. Some interpreters apply thefe expreffions to the deftruction of Sodom and Gomorrah. But how could the inhabitants of thofe cities be ftyled the *remnant*, or all the remainder of the wicked? Whereas if we underftand it of the wicked that fhall be found remaining on the earth at the end of the world, we are prefented in this verfe with the two moft memorable and dreadful fcenes of divine vengeance, the deluge and the conflagration. Noah might learn the final deftruction of the wicked from the prophecy of Enoch, recorded by Jude ver. 14. and the manner of it from fome revelation to himfelf.

Ver. 21. *Acquaint thyfelf with him*] Crinfoz turns it *fubmit thyfelf to him*; Mr. Heath to the fame effect, *humble thyfelf before him*, grounding his verfion on the Arabic fenfe of the word.

and be at peace] *and make reftitution*[f]. It is a vulgar error, to imagine that Job was abfolutely impoverifhed. He ftill maintained a numerous family; and his three cenfors fuppofe him to have amaffed great treafures by bribery and extortion, which they exhort him to refund[g].

---

[e] אכלה *fhall confume.* It is the preter tenfe turned into the future by the influence of ן at the beginning of this claufe. Befides, according to the remark of Michaelis, the preterite and future were aorifts in the ancient ftate of the hebrew language. Michaelis in Prælect. p. 78. 8vo.

[f] שלמ Mr. Heath reads it *fhallem*, in the conjugation *pihel, make reftitution*. Or if we follow the Maforetic pointing *fhelom*, in the conjugation *kal*, yet as the fignification of this verb in *kal, to finifh*, is communicated to its conjugation *pihel*, I Kings ix. 25. On the contrary its fignification in *pihel, to make reftitution*, might be communicated to its conjugation *kal*.

[g] Chap. xi. 14. xv. 34.

22. Embrace his leſſons, his imperial word
   Deep in the table of thy heart record.
23. Vagrant from God, return; with ſparkling eyes
   Then ſee thy bow'r renew'd in beauty riſe:
   But hallow'd be thy tents, expell from thence
   All cover'd crime and manifeſt offence.
24. Leave Ophir's gold in her own ſtreams to ſhine,
25. God all-ſufficient be thy boundleſs mine.

26. To

Ver. 22. *the law—his words*] The divine revelations conveyed down by tradition from Noah, Abraham, &c. alſo perſonal favours of the ſame kind to Job [h], to Eliphaz [i], and to others [k].

Ver. 23. *Thou ſhalt be built up* [l].] He aſſures him of a re-eſtabliſhment of his ruined affairs, and particularly of a new race of children in ſupply of thoſe he had loſt.

thou ſhalt put away iniquity] By *iniquity* he means that which he ſuppoſed to have been Job's favourite ſin, *rapacity*. The tranſlation, I think, ſhould be, *put thou away iniquity*, &c. the future being often uſed for the imperative. He exhorts him to keep both himſelf and his family, for the time to come, from the vice of covetouſneſs; as well as from all other wickedneſs.

Ver. 24. *Thou ſhalt lay up*, &c.] He recommends to him a contempt of riches. But our public verſion makes him promiſe, that his avarice ſhall be gratified to the full. how abſurd is this! Mr. Heath's verſion is more juſt to the original,

---

[h] Chap. vi. 10. xxix. 4.

[i] Chap. iv. 12, &c.

[k] Chap. xxxiii. 14, 15.

[l] See the uſe of this metaphorical expreſſion in Jer. xxxi. 4. xxxiii. 7. Gen. xvi. 2. *it may be that I may obtain children* (marg. *be builded*) *by her*.

26. To him, in bleſt fruition of his grace,
Noble affiance ſhall erect thy face.
27. He'll crown thy pray'r, mature thy vows in praiſe,
28. Thy edicts ſtabliſh, and illume thy ways.

29. The

ginal, *Count*[m] *the fine gold as*[n] *duſt, and the gold of Ophir as the ſtones* (or pebbles) *of the brooks.*

Ophir] The *Ophir* here ſpoken of muſt be that which was in Arabia, on the coaſt of the red ſea[o]. Arabia had formerly its golden mines. We are aſſured by Sanchoniathon[p], ſays Mr. Crinſoz, that the Phœnicians carried on a conſiderable traffic to this Ophir even before the days of Job.

Ver. 25. *Yea the Almighty*, &c.] " Yea the Almighty ſhall be thy fine gold[q], and choice ſilver[r] unto thee." The verſe thus tranſlated contains a ſublime ſentiment. The favour of God ſhall be thy treaſure, an inexhauſtible mine of felicity.

Ver. 28. *Thou ſhalt alſo decree a thing*, &c.] Here he promiſeth the reſtoration of his princely authority. The word tranſlated *a thing* ſignifies a decree[s], an authoritative edict.

and

---

[m] שית על עפר *Set fine gold with duſt*, that is, count it of no more value than duſt. This verb is uſed in the ſame ſenſe chap. xxx. 1. *whoſe fathers I would have diſdained to have ſet* (לשית) *with the dogs of my flock.*

[n] על this prepoſition is uſed for עם *with* in Exod. xxxiv. 25. *Thou ſhalt not offer the blood of my ſacrifice with* (על) *leaven.* See Levit. ii. 2, 16. iv. 11. It is alſo uſed in a comparative ſenſe in Levit. xxv. 31. *But the houſes of the villages . . . ſhall be counted as* (על) *the fields of the country.*

[o] Bochart. *Phaleg.*   [p] and by Herodotus, quoted by Euſebius.

[q] בצריך (but all the ancient verſions read בצרך) it is the ſame word that is engliſhed *gold* in the preceding verſe.

[r] כסף תועפות *choice ſilver.* The LXX. turn it αργυριον πεπυρωμενον, *ſilver that hath been tried in the fire.* It ſignifies, as Schultens hath ſhewn, ſilver that is dug with great labour out of the deepeſt mines.

[s] אמר *a decree.* See chap. xx. 29. *his decree*, in the margin; that is, decreed to him by God. The verb גזר, *to decree*, is alſo uſed of a *royal edict*, or proclamation. Eſther ii. 1.

A a 2

29. The proud shall sink, on thy complaint depreft;
Affliction sing, redeem'd at thy requeft:
30. The righteous man shall stay th' Almighty's hand,
And turn the thunder from a sinning land.

CHAP.

and the light, &c.] Wisdom, succefs, joy, are all included in this beautiful metaphor. The administration of thy public and private affairs shall be ever prosperous and illustrious.

Ver. 29. *When men are cast down,* &c.] He assures him of the prevalence of his prayers with God, both for the overthrow of insolent oppreffors and deliverance of the oppreffed. This is an exalted idea of the high importance of a good man to fociety. The following verse exalts it still higher. The present verse will admit of the following tranflation,

Verily men *are cast down* ", *when thou shalt say* there is *pride* ".
And the dejected *person* ˣ, *he will save.*

Ver. 30. *He shall deliver,* &c.] The obscurity of this verse will vanish, if we turn it

The innocent shall deliver a country ʸ :
And it shall be delivered by the purenefs of his hands ᶻ.

Men of exemplary piety and virtue are sometimes the saviours of a whole
people,

ᵗ כִּי *verily, surely;* as in chap. viii. 6. *surely now,* &c. Chap. xxviii. 1. *surely there is a vein for the silver.*

ᵘ הִשְׁפִּילוּ *they are cast down;* as יַלְבִּינוּ If. i. 18.. *they shall be white.* Drusius.

ᵛ גֵּוָה *pride.* Isaiah xxv. 11. *he shall bring down* (וְהִשְׁפִּיל) *their pride* (גַּאֲוָתוֹ)

ˣ שַׁח עֵינַיִם *a perfon of downcaft looks.* The verb is used of a perfon who is bowed down with grief. Psal. xxxv. 14. xxxviii. 7.

ʸ אִי *a country;* Isaiah xx. 6. *the inhabitants of this country;* as it is englished in the margin.

ᶻ כַּפָּיו *thy hands.* The Syriac and Arabic versions read כַּפָּיו *his hands.* If we follow our prefent Hebrew text *thy hands,* there will be a very abrupt change of the perfon; and Eliphaz muft be imagined to addrefs thefe words to Job on suppofition of his becoming a pious and virtuous man.

THE BOOK OF JOB.

CHAP.
XXIII.
1, 2. The mourner anſwer'd, in lamenting ſtrain;
Still is it ſtiff rebellion to complain?
Alas! the mountain-weight of woes I feel,
Nor groans can equal, nor complaint reveal.

3. Guide people, by means of their favour with God. This grand idea of the efficacy of true religion, and the vaſt utility of virtuous men, is derived from the Patriarchal hiſtory. See Gen. xviii. 23, &c.

CHAP. XXIII.

This firſt part of Job's reply is the effuſion of a mind agitated by various ſtrong emotions:

By indignation, at the cruel ſlanders in the foregoing ſpeech, ver. 2.

By vehement deſire to argue his cauſe to God, ver. 3. to the end of ver. 7.

By diſtreſs, in that he could not obtain his deſire, ver. 8, 9.

By conſolation, in the teſtimony of his conſcience, ver. 10, 11, 12.

By conſternation and deſpair, on recollecting God's abſolute dominion and the Immutability of his deſigns, ver. 13, 14, 15.

And by apprehenſion that his life was preſerved for additional ſufferings, ver. 16, 17.

Ver. 2. *Even to-day*, &c.] *Still*[a] *is my complaint rebellion*[b]? Am I ſtill to be taxed with inſolence and impiety[c], for complaining of the ways of God?
Alas!

---

[a] היום *ſtill*. Pſal. cxix. 91. *They continue ſtill* (היום) *according to thine ordinances.*

[b] מרי Crinſoz and Mr. Heath juſtly render it *rebellion*, for the root is מרה *to rebel*. It cannot be derived from מרר *to be bitter*; there being no nouns in *this form* that are derived from verbs which double their ſecond radical. Vid. Guarin. *Gram. Heb.* vol. i. p. 393, 393.

[c] Chap. xxii. 2, 3, 4.

3. Guide me, O guide me to his dark recefs,
   Ev'n to his throne of judgement I would prefs;
4. A thoufand reas'nings, regular and ftrong,
   The flow of innocence, fhall fill my tongue.
5. His anfwer, welcome to my longing ear,
   Would the ftrange caufe of thefe ftrange fuff'rings clear.
6. Will he confound me with his dreadful might?
   No, but my courage at his bar excite:
7. There bold integrity may urge its plea,
   And there fhall triumph be ordain'd for me.

8, 9. Ah! Alas! *my ftroke*[d] *is heavier than my groaning*. His inflictions on me would juftify heavier complaint.

Ver. 3. *O that I knew*, &c.] He wifheth he could go to the tribunal of God, as one may go and demand trial at a human bar. *Crinfoz.* See chap. ix. 32—35. x. 2.

Ver. 6. *Will he plead againft me*, &c.] He will not bear me down with his authority, inftead of reafons: neither will he intimidate me with his great power. He will on the contrary exert his power to ftrengthen my mind, that I may have courage and compofure to argue my caufe with him. This is a worthy and fublime idea of the equity and condefcenfion of God.

he would put ftrength *in me*.] The original is elliptical. Our Tranflators fupply the word *ftrength* to perfect the fenfe. Other interpreters give a fomewhat different turn to the fentence, " *he will lay down* reafons *againft me*[e]; that is, he will fhew me his reafons for thus afflicting me. But I think he had expreffed this fentiment in ver. 5. *I fhould know the words which he would anfwer me*, &c.

---

[d] ידי *my hand.* The Septuagint, Syriac, and Arabic verfions read *his hand*, ידו

[e] בי *againft me.* Numb. xxi. 7. *We have fpoken againft the Lord* (ביהוה) *and againft thee* (ובך)

CHAP. XXIII.   THE BOOK OF JOB.   183

8, 9. Ah! fhould I journey this terreftrial round,
He no where in its eaftern coaft is found:
In vain I feek him on the weftern fhore,
In vain his footfteps in the north explore,
Or in the fouth: He, working in his might,
Wrapt in impervious fhades eludes my fight.

10. But, not unknowing in my ways, he knows
My truth his utmoft proving undergoes

As

Ver. 7. *So fhould I be delivered*, &c.] *So fhall I be delivered*[f] *for ever*[g] *by*[h] *my judge.*

He expreffeth the fulleft confidence that God would put an utter end to the difpute, by an honourable acquittal of him; provided God would favour him with an opportunity of making his defence to him.

Ver. 8, 9. *Behold I go forward*, &c.] Thefe verfes are not a meer defcription of the invifibility of God. They are intended to exprefs the vehement defire of confcious integrity to obtain fome vifible manifeftation of the Deity, and to expoftulate with him face to face on its unmerited fufferings.

The language will be more poetical, if, with the Chaldee Paraphrafe, we turn the words *forward, backward, on the left hand, on the right hand; to the eaft, to the weft, to the north, in the fouth.*

Ver. 10—12. *But he knoweth*, &c.] This is the glorious language of confcious piety. It derives powerful confolation from the omnifcience of God. The ftyle, however,

---

[f] אפלטה *apalletah*, in the conjugation *pihel*. But in that conjugation it is a tranfitive verb active *to deliver*; and requires after it an accufative of the perfon or thing delivered. I imagine our Tranflators read *eppaletah* in *Niphal*, or *appulletah*, in *pyhal*, *I fhall be delivered*.

[g] לנצח LXX. εις τελος *to an end*. But elfewhere, εις νικος *unto victory*.

[h] משפטי *by my judge*; or, as the Targum turns it, *by him who judgeth me*. The prepofition ב is englifhed *by* in Gen. xlix. 24. *by the hands of the mighty God of Jacob.*

As gold the furnace; and like gold shall rise,
Emerging, with new lustre, to his eyes.

11, 12. My foot hath been the follower of his own,
Unstraying from the path himself hath shown:
Unswerving from his high commands, I stor'd
Deep in my bosom his imperial word.

13. But who shall him, sole potentate, controll?
Resolv'd, he acts the purpose of his soul;

14. And will compleat my measur'd woes, assign'd
By the deep counsels of his awful mind:

In however, may be thought somewhat too lofty for an imperfect mortal. By the expression *I shall come forth as gold*, he cannot be understood to mean that he should be delivered out of his afflictions; otherwise than by death. he utterly despairs, to the very last, of recovering his health and prosperity. The sense of the comparison is, I apprehend, that his piety and virtue were like gold, and would endure the severest test.

Ver. 12. *the words of his mouth*] See the remark on Chap. xxii. 22.

Ver. 13. *He is in one* mind] In the original, *He* is *one* [1]. He inferreth from the unity of God, that his dominion is absolute, and his decrees immutable, as well as the reasons of them impenetrable. The Providence of such a Being oft times proceeds in measures, that confound all our ideas of wisdom, justice, and goodness.

Ver. 14. *For he performeth,* &c.] *Therefore he will bring to perfection, that which he hath decreed concerning* me. So Mr. Heath translates. Homer expresseth

---

[1] באחד Targ. יחידאי *unicus*, the only one. Vulg. *solus* est. It is the ablative put for the nominative, as in Exod. xviii. 4. בעזרי *my help*, and Exod. xxxii. 22. ברע *mischievous*. This enallage is very common in the Arabic language. The Arabians use *in potente* for *potens, in credente* for *credens, in negligente* for *negligens.* Vid. Erpenii *Prov. Arab. sent.* i. 67. Koran. *sur.* ii. ver. 69.

CHAP. XXIII.   THE BOOK OF JOB.

In acts like thefe, oft wont he to difplay
His boundlefs, abfolute, myfterious fway.
15, 16. Hence doubting, dreading, in confufion toft,
My courage melts and in amaze I'm loft:
17. For ftill in horrid ills I draw my breath,
Deny'd a refuge in the gloom of death.

feth the fame fentiment in almoft the fame language : " But Jupiter will accomplifh the evils, which he meditates both againft the Greeks and the Trojans [k]."

many fuch things, &c.] many defigns and proceedings of his Providence, as myfterious and unaccountable as his ways towards me.

Ver. 15. *Therefore am I*, &c.] *Therefore am I troubled by* [l] *him*; that is, reflection on fuch perplexing meafures of Providence dafhes all the hopes which innocence fhould give; and overfets me with prefaging fears, which guilt only ought to feel.

Ver. 17. *Becaufe I was not cut off*, &c.] *Becaufe I have not been cut off by* [m] *the darknefs*. By *darknefs*, in this member of the period, he means his affliction. *Darknefs* is an eftablifhed metaphor for calamity, not only among the facred poets but alfo among all others.

Neither hath he covered, &c.] *But he covereth the darknefs from my face*. The term, in the original, for *darknefs* here, is different from the foregoing. It is that by which Job expreffeth the darknefs of the fepulchral grot chap. x. 22. By *covering the darknefs from his face*, he means his not being permitted to fee death. God, he complains, denies him the only refuge from his forrows, a grave.

He was to the laft degree amazed, fays Mr. Heath, how he was able to fupport

---

[k] Αλλα κατα φρενων τεκμαιρεται αμφοτεροισιν. Il. vii. 70. Vid. Schol.

[l] בִּפְנֵי *by*, as in Judges vi. 6. *Ifrael was greatly impoverifhed by* (מִפְּנֵי) *the Midianites*.

[m] כפני See the foregoing note.

CHAP.
XXIV.
Ver. 1. Why does the sultan of the world refrain,
By vengeful seasons to assert his reign?
Why see not now observers of his ways
His drowning flood, or show'ring sulphur's blaze?
2. Landmarks:

port such a load of calamity; and that it did not put an end to his life: he dreaded further misery, for which he doubted he was reserved.

CHAP. XXIV.

Having somewhat eased his mind by the foregoing effusions, he makes one effort more to convince his adversaries by *reasoning* with them. The last verse demonstrates that he opposeth their sentiments, *And if it be not so now, who will make me a liar?* The first verse shews that the point he disputes with them is the constancy, and even the frequency, of the public judgements of God on wicked men. He produceth a catalogue of outrageous immoralities, which are fatal to the peace of society and threaten its dissolution. He instanceth invasion of property, cruel oppression of the poor, adultery, murder, and tyranny. Yet the Governor of the world seems to connive at these enormities, by forbearing to punish the authors of them. Toleration of such evils is by no means reconcileable to our notions of wisdom and justice, and is utterly repugnant to the system of providence maintained by his three antagonists.

A spirit of vehemence and indignation runs through the whole discourse. He could not speak of the lenity of God to the worst of men, and at the same time think of his own sufferings, without a considerable deal of warmth.

Ver. 1. *Why, seeing times*, &c.] *Why are not stated times*ⁿ *reserved*⁰ *by the Almighty? And why do they that know him not see his days*ⁿ *?* By *stated times* and
his

ⁿ Isaiah xiii. 22. Ezek. xxx. 3. Schultens.

⁰ נצפנו *are reserved*; *are laid up*; as in chap. xxi. 19. The primary idea, says Mr. Heath, is *sepsuit, to set apart:* the secondary idea is *occultavit, to hide; recondidit, to lay up*. See Psal. xxxi. 19, 20.

CHAP. XXIV.   THE BOOK OF JOB.   187

2.   Landmarks remov'd, and ravish'd fields behold!
The shepherd captiv'd with his bleating fold.
3.   Orphans lament, th' insolvent widow weeps,
Their only beast some ruthless harpy sweeps.
4.   Wrong'd

his days are meant signal seasons of divine vengeance. Such were those of the deluge and the destruction of Sodom. He asks, what is the reason why like displays of divine justice do not recur; as often as a like general corruption of morals prevaileth in the world?

Ver. 2. Some *remove the land-marks*, &c.] As their pastures and corn-fields were not inclosed [p], they had no other way of distinguishing the limits of each man's grounds but by boundary stones. He here describeth that sort of injustice which the prophet complains of, *They covet fields, and take them by violence; and houses, and take them away: So they oppress a man and his house, even a man and his heritage.* Mic. ii. 2.

and feed [q] thereof] *and him that feedeth* it. Mr. Heath. Juvenal complains of the rapines committed by the governors of the Roman provinces in language like this of our sacred poet;

> Nunc sociis juga pauca boum, grex parvus equarum,
> Et pater armenti capto eripiatur agello.
>
> Sat. viii. L. iii. ver. 108.

Ver. 3. *The ass—the ox*] This is another species of wrong. They deprive the fatherless and the widow of their only means of supporting themselves; who could not prepare their little farm for sowing, without an ox, or beeve, to till
it;

---

[p] See a late ingenious Publication, intituled *Observations on divers Passages of Scripture*, &c. p. 216.

[q] וירעו The Masoretic punctuation makes it the third person plural in the future of Kal. But Mr. Heath reads it in the third person singular. He takes ו for an affix, put instead of הו, and supposeth an ellipsis of the relative אשר *who, he who.* The LXX. probably read in the same manner: for they translate it, συν ποιμνι *together with the shepherd.*

B b 2

4. Wrong'd at tribunals, vex'd on every fide,
The fighing poor in friendly deferts hide:
5. There, like wild affes, in the dawn they ftray,
Hard toiling for the pittance of the day:
They browze the mountain roots, the fylvan food
Stills the loud clamours of their craving brood.
6. Others

it; or bring in their corn, if they had any, without an afs to carry the burden.

Ver. 4, 5. *They turn the needy,* &c.] Thefe two verfes reprefent moft iniquitous and oppreffive proceedings in the courts of juftice: infomuch that inoffenfive' and defenceleſs' perfons, having no protection from the laws, are forced to flee into the defert; for the fecurity of their lives, or to fave themfelves from flavery.

Ver. 4. *out of the way*] that is, the way or courfe of juftice. The very magiftrates refufe to redrefs their grievances, and to protect their property and perfons. Compare Ifaiah x. 1, 2. Amos ii. 7.

hide themfelves] In the caves of the defert. Compare Hebrews xi. 38.

Ver. 5. *Behold,* as *wild affes,* &c.] He defcribes the hardfhips which they fuffer in the wildernefs. The fimile, as *wild affes,* fhews that he is not fpeaking of the thievifh Arabs of the defert: for the wild afs is not a beaft of prey, but is itfelf the prey of the lion. It is a folitary timorous animal, whofe only defence is in the fwiftneſs of its heels. This is no fit emblem of the pillaging Arabs, but a very proper one for fuch harmleſs perfons as are mentioned in the foregoing verfe.

go forth to their work] Their daily toil in fearching for roots, and fuch vegetables as the woods and mountains afforded for their miferable fuftenance.

for

' עֲנִי *the inoffenfive*; LXX. ωπαυ; *the meek.*

' אָבִים *the defenceless*; LXX. αδυνατοι; *the weak,* perfons without power to defend their rights.

' Ecclefiafticus xiii. 19.

CHAP. XXIV. THE BOOK OF JOB. 189

 6. Others collect the grapes, or bind the sheaves,
  Of some hard churl, who not a gleaning leaves:
 7. Deny'd a shelt'ring hut in midnight cold,
  Deny'd a rug about their limbs to fold;
               8. On

for a prey] *for meat*^t, or eatables. Prov. xxxi. 15. *and giveth meat* ' *to her houshold.*

Ver. 6—8. *They reap*, &c.] The complaint in these three verses turns upon the barbarous usage of the *labouring poor*, who work in the fields and vineyards.

Ver. 6. *They reap every one his corn*^u, &c.] *They reap every one in a field which is not his own*^u. The persons described in this verse are such as are compelled by their poverty to work for wages in the fields and vineyards of the rich. The barley-harvest in those countries was in March; and their wheat-harvest was over by the latter end of May or the beginning of June ^w. Their vintage began in September and ended in October ^w.

they gather] without wages and without food, as the Septuagint explains it ^x. They are defrauded of both by their oppressive masters.

of the wicked] *of the oppressor*. The word frequently occurs in this acceptation in our author^y. It is also used in this sense Ezek. xxxiii. 15. *If the wicked restore the pledge*. It properly signifieth a doer of wrong Exod. ii. 13. *He said to him that did the wrong* ^z, *why smitest thou thy fellow?*

Ver. 7. *They cause the naked*, &c.] See the note on chap. xxii. 6.

they have no covering] no raiment for their bedding, nor tent nor miserable hovel

---

^t טרף

^u בלילו *his corn*. But the Chaldee Paraphrast and the LXX. read בלי לו *non sui*: For the former turns it בדלא דלהון *which is not their own*; and the LXX. ἐν αλλοτρίοις. The vulgar Latin, *agrum non suum*.

^v *Observations on divers Passages of Scripture*, &c. p. 27, 45, 54.

^x Αμισθοι και ασιτοι.

^y See particularly chap. xv. 20.

^z לרשע

8. On the damp clay, in dripping caves, they lie,
And hug that refuge left to poverty.
9. See orphans from the pap to bondage drawn,
The peasants vest detain'd in cruel pawn:
10. With naked limbs they toil, and starving bear
The golden burden of the foodful year:

11. To

hovel to shelter them. they are forced therefore to sleep on the damp ground, in the caverns of the mountains adjacent to the fields and vineyards where they slaved in the day.

in the cold] In those climates a very hot day was often succeeded by a very cold night [a].

Ver. 8. *with the showers*, &c.] The heavy rains which fall in spring and autumn produce torrents and inundations in that mountainous country. These oppressed wretches were obliged to secure themselves from those floods in holes of the rocks.

Ver. 9, 10, 11. *They pluck*, &c.] The injustice represented here is that of *unmerciful creditors*; who seize the persons of their poor insolvent debtors, and make them their slaves.

Ver. 9. *and take a pledge*, &c.] *and take that which is upon* [b] *the poor for a pledge*; that is, his upper garment or hyke, for security for a debt. See the note on chap. xxii. 6.

Ver. 10. *They cause him*] Namely, the poor man whose garment they keep in pawn, and the orphans whom they enslaved. They compel the former to drudge in their fields and vineyards in the most violent heats, to redeem their pawn: and they use the latter, as soon as they become capable of servile works, in the same cruel manner.

and

---

[a] Genesis xxxi. 40. Shaw's *Travels*, p. 439. 4to. Dr. Shaw tells us, that in Arabia Petræa, Job's country, the day is intensely hot and the night intensely cold. *Travels*, p. 438.

[b] עליו על id quod est supra pauperem, vestimentum ejus. R. Levi apud Schultens.

11. To noon-day labours in the vineyard curſt,
And while they ſtamp the wine-vat die with thirſt.

12. The city groans through all her ſtreets, the cries
Of wrongs and wounds and death aſſail the ſkies:
In vain; unheeded by the Pow'r above,
His wrath they wake not, nor his thunder move.

13. There

and they take away, &c.] *and thoſe who are ſtarving with hunger carry the ſheaves.* Mr. Heath. They are not ſuffered to eat ſo much as an ear of the corn they carry in.

Ver. 11. which *make oil*, &c.] *who labour in their vineyards*[c] *at noon-day*[d]. This was a grievous aggravation of the oppreſſion. The vintage began in September. From the beginning of May to the end of September, the air in thoſe countries is in general ſo hot, that it ſeems as if it came out of an oven. What then muſt it be at noon-day.? See Dr. Ruſſel's *Natural hiſtory of Aleppo*, p. 14.

and tread, &c.] Mr. Addiſon, in his letter from Italy, deſcribeth the miſery of the oppreſſed peaſants with the ſame beautiful energy: The poor inhabitant of that rich country

  Starves, in the midſt of nature's bounty curſt,
  And in the loaden vineyard dies for thirſt.

Ver. 12—20. *Men groan*, &c.] The principal ſcene of the foregoing violences was the country. In this paragraph he dwells upon the enormities which are committed in great cities, and their environs; under the very eye of the magiſtrate.

---

[c] שורתם Our public verſion turns it *their walls*; that is, the ſtone-walls with which they incloſed their vineyards. Prov. xxiv. 30, 31. In Arabic it ſignifies, according to Schultens, *the rows of pales* on which the vines were ſupported.

[d] יצהירו *they labour at noon-day.* צהרים in Hebrew ſignifies *noon-tide*; thence was formed the verb הצהיר *to work during the noon-tide,* as Mr. Heath renders it. This ſenſe is eſtabliſhed by the Arabic uſe of the ſame verb; as Schultens has proved.

192 THE BOOK OF JOB. CHAP. XXIV.

13. There are, like night's wild foragers, who shun
    Light's public walks, and bus'ness of the sun:
14. The ruffian, when the pilgrim quits his rest,
    Skulks in the dawn, and stabs the harmless breast:
    In the dead hour of sleep, no bolts withstand
    The practis'd cunning of his pilf'ring hand.
                                            15, 16. Th'

Ver. 12. *Yet God layeth not folly*ᵉ, &c.] The neglect of human rulers, to punish the authors of such crimes, seemed to render the interposition of divine justice necessary; for the very preservation of society. But God takes no notice, he says, of these flagrant violations of right and order: *God layeth not folly* to them.

Ver. 13. *They are of those who rebel*, &c.] There are those who rebel ᶠ against the light, &c. This verse is a description of those criminals, who seek the protection of privacy and darkness for the commission of their evil deeds. By light I understand here *the sun*, as it is translated in chap. xxxi. 26.

Ver. 14. *with the light*] very early, by break of day; as *the light* signifies in Mic. ii. 1. *wo to them that devise iniquity, and work evil upon their beds: in the light of the morning they practise it.*

as a thief ᵍ] *a very thief*; or *a perfect thief.*

ᵉ תפלה *folly*. (1) If, with Mr. Heath, we derive it from פלה *to separate*, his translation will be right; *God maketh no distinction*. (2) If, with Schultens, we take תפל *vain, futile*, for the root, the version must be; *God regardeth not their vain complaints*. or (3) If we follow Kimchi's etymology, and deduce the word from פלא *to do a wonderful thing*, we may translate; *God sets no extraordinary mark upon them*. The sense comes out the same in all these interpretations; namely, that God does not seem to pay any regard to these outrages.

ᶠ במרדי אור *lucifugæ*, persons who shun the light; as Grotius turns it. I take the ablative במרדי to be put for the nominative, as in chap. xxiii. 13. באחד for אחד. See the note.

ᵍ כגנב the *caph* כ is here what the Grammarians call *caph veritatis*: It denotes not *similitude*, but *emphasis* only.

CHAP. XXIV. THE BOOK OF JOB.

15, 16. Th' adulterer, conceal'd all day, prepares,
Watching for evening dusk, his fatal snares:
Fearful of jealous eyes, in twilight gloom
Muffled he steals into the guilty room:

17. Stranger

Ver. 15. *disguiseth his face*] The hebrew is, *he putteth a covering upon his face*. *This covering* was probably the hood of the *burnoose*: so the Arabs call the cloak which they sometimes throw over their other garments; and which has a hood or cowl to it [h]. The Arab dress was in all likelihood the same in the days of Job as now: For these people are remarkable for not having changed their customs for these three thousand years [i]. The Roman satyrist describes the adulterer just as our sacred poet has done here.

   Si nocturnus adulter
 Tempora santonico velas adoperta cucullo.
          Juv. *Sat*. viii. 144.

If you stroll about the streets a rank adulterer, with your head muffled in a Gallic hood.

Ver. 16. *In the dark they dig through houses*,] If I remember right, the sensible author of the *Observations on divers Passages of Scripture*, &c. remarks on this passage; that their houses being built of clay dried in the sun, it was easy to force a way into them in this manner. But I rather imagine, that the expression is figurative; and is intended to express stealing into the house of the adulteress like a thief in the night.

which they had marked, &c.] *They conceal themselves in the day-time* [k]. They dare not appear in such houses in the day: For *they know not the light*, when they practise their lewd amours.

---

[h] Shaw's *Travels*, p. 226. 4to.

[i] Ockley's *Preface* to *an Account of South-west Barbary*.

[k] יומם חתמו למו which Symmachus translates ὡς ἐν σφραγῖδι κρυψωσιν ἑαυτες, *they hide themselves as with a seal*, i. e. they keep as close as if they were shut up, and a seal put upon the door of the room.

17. Stranger to light, he dreads the morning beams;
  The morn to him as death's black shadow seems:
  And, haply by some conscious glance betray'd,
  Death's horrors his distracted soul invade.

18. Light as a bubble on the rolling sea,
  His pow'r should vanish, and his glory flee:
  Curse should his gardens and his fields pursue,
  Ne'er should his eye the flowing vintage view.

19. On

Ver. 18—20. *He is swift,* &c.] I do not apprehend that he here passeth to another vicious character. He declareth in these verses, if I mistake not, the punishments which ought to overtake all the foregoing delinquents, and especially *the adulterer.* He had a particular abhorrence of *the adulterer,* as appears from chap. xxxi. 9, 10, 11, 12. The verse before us should, I think, be turned;

> *Let him be* as *a light thing upon the water*[1]:
> *Let their portion in the earth be accursed:*
> *Let him not behold the way of the vineyards.*

Let him be as *a light thing,* &c.] The image which the sacred poet had in his thoughts seems to be the same that the author of *the Wisdom of Solomon* has expressed:

---

[1] קל הוא על פני מים *He is light upon the water*; ιλαφρος εστι, says the LXX. Symmachus renders על פני מים επιπλεον υδατι *a thing floating on the water.* I have ventured to translate, *Let him be* as *a light thing upon the water.* The Arabians express their benedictions and imprecations in the preter tense instead of the imperative mood: Thus they say, *he hath reigned,* for *let him reign; Thou hast had an easy labour,* for *mayest thou have an easy labour;* and, *thou hast not had an easy labour,* for *let not thy labour be easy to thee.* Pocock. *Spec. Hist. Arab.* p. 56, 57, 337. The Syrians also sometimes used the preter tense for the imperative mood; thus in the Syriac Testament, I Cor. iv. 1. הוין חשיבין *we have been accounted of;* for *let us be accounted of.* We likewise meet with some examples in the Hebrew Bible of the imperative put for the preterite, as in Psal. viii. 2. תנה for נתנת; and of the preterite put for the imperative, as in Psal xxii. 22. עניתני *Thou hast heard me,* for *hear thou me.* See Bp. Hare's note on Psal. viii. 2. and xxii. 22.

CHAP. XXIV.   THE BOOK OF JOB.   195

19. On such, all such, the yawning ground should close,
As hot sands swallow the dissolving snows:
20. Such, unremember'd by the parent womb,
Should feast the worm, hale victims of the tomb:
Their hated names should die; like trees o'erthrown,
A shiver'd ruin on the mountain strown.
                                                21. Unhappy

expressed: *For the hope of the ungodly is* . . . *like a thin froth that is driven away with the storm.*

Let their portion, &c.] I have followed the Septuagint, in translating this and the subsequent member of the period in the imprecatory form ᵐ.

Let him not behold, &c.] Or *let him not behold the treading* ⁿ *of the vineyards*; that is, such transgressors ought not to enjoy the produce of the vineyards, or any other felicity. The thought and turn of the expression resemble what Zophar had said chap. xx. 17. " *Let him not see the rivers, the floods, the brooks of honey and butter.*

Ver. 19. *The drought*, &c.] *Drought and heat snatch away the snow-waters:* so should *the grave* those who *have sinned*. According to our notions of justice, a swift and general destruction, he says, should sweep away from the earth such enemies to the peace of society. The image, by which he illustrates a swift and utter destruction, is very expressive: The snow which melts on the Arabian mountains at the approach of summer, rushes down in torrents which are quickly sucked up by the burning sands of the valleys. See the description in chap. vi. 15—18.

The grave] *Sheol*. It may here denote in general *the region of death*. See the APPENDIX *Numb.* II.

Ver. 20. *The womb*, &c.] This verse strongly paints an utter extermination. The

---

ᵐ Καταραται, αραφαιη.

ⁿ דרך The verb was used in the 11th verse for *treading the wine-press.* The noun substantive in Syriac is applied to *the treading of corn*, which was the eastern way of threshing it, in Levit. xxvi. 5.

C c 2

21.   Unhappy she, whose steril womb denies
   A filial patron in her cause to rise:

Unhappy

The verbs had better be translated in the imprecatory form, as the Latin Vulgate has rendered them:

> *Let the womb forget him,*
> *Let the worm feed sweetly on him,*
> *Let him be no more remembered,*
> *Let wickedness be broken as a tree.*

Or we may turn the verbs in Mr. Heath's manner, *The womb should forget him, The worm should feed,* &c.

Let the womb, &c.] What a strong idea do these expressions give us, of the detestation due to the profligate characters aforementioned; and of the oblivion in which they should be sunk? The mothers of such criminals should for ever cast them out of their remembrance, ashamed to have given birth to those monstrous productions.

Let the worm°, & c.] Or, *let his sweetness become corruption.* In either way of turning the sentence the meaning is, let him become the food of worms while his body is perfectly sound; that is, let him die in his full strength. But I think our version by far the most poetical.

Let wickedness, &c.] His adversaries had asserted, that atheistical and profligate men are suddenly and totally destroyed; like a tree that is torn up by a whirlwind or consumed by lightning ᵖ. Job here replies, It ought to be so, but is not generally so.

Ver. 21—24. *He evil intreateth,* &c.] This remaining part of the speech is exceedingly obscure. The twenty-second verse, however, seems plainly to describe a tyrannical prince who is a plague and terror to his people. The twenty-first

---

° מתקו   Our Translators understood it to be the verb in the preter tense (put for the future in the imperative sense, as קל in ver. 18.) with the affix of the third person singular, *methak-o.* It may however be a noun, if we read *mothk-o,* and be rendered *his sweetness.* רמה is turned *the worm* in our version: but it rather signifies *corruption* breeding worms.

ᵖ Chap. xv. 30. xviii. 16.

CHAP. XXIV.   THE BOOK OF JOB.   197

Unhappy she, whose solitary tear
Bewails a guardian on a husband's bier:
22. Each is the tyrant's prey. His savage might
Makes ev'n the strongest tremble in his sight:
Doubtful of life, they hang upon his breath,
His brow is terror, and his voice is death.

23, 24. Yet first verse, therefore, so closely connected to it in sense and construction, is, I think, the beginning of the description. A tyrant falls upon the weak and defenceless, before he ventures to attack the great and powerful among his subjects.

It was very judicious to close a catalogue of enormities, which threaten destruction to society, with *tyranny*. When kings and supreme magistrates abuse their power, by ruining those whom it is their duty to protect, there seems an absolute necessity for the governor of the universe to interpose. Strange then! that even *tyrants* are allowed by providence to reign prosperously and die in peace.

Ver. 21. *He evil intreateth*[q], &c.] The want of some word of transition is one cause of the obscurity of this whole paragraph. We may translate, Another *evil intreateth*, &c. just as our Translators supply the word *some* in ver. ii. *some remove the land-marks*, &c.

Ver. 22. *He draweth*, &c.] *He pulleth down*[r] *also the mighty with his power:* When *he riseth up*[s] (to judge) *there is no being sure of life.* Ezekiel styles a tyrant *the terror of the mighty*[t]. From a spirit of jealousy or avarice He invents accusations against them, and then condemns them to death.

---

[q] רעה *he evil intreateth;* rather, *he devoureth,* i. e. impoverishes by his oppressions. Mich. v. 5, 6. *They shall waste* (רעו *they shall devour, depascent) the land of Assyria with the sword.*

[r] משך *detraxit, he draggeth down;* so the Vulgate turns it: but the LXX. κατηρείψατο *he overthroweth.* Ezek. xxxii. 20. *Draw her (pull her down) and all her multitudes.* Compare Psal. xxviii. 3.

[s] יקום *he riseth up,* to pass sentence of judgement; as in chap. xxxi. 14. Psal. lxxxii. 8.

[t] Ezek. xxxii. 27.

23, 24. Yet safe in heav'n's indulgence, bold in crime,
   These miscreants to height of glory climb,
   God looking on; In height of glory, fall
   Soft to a peaceful grave, the home of all:
   Sudden and soft, as when some gentle hand
   Lops the tall ears that ripe for harvest stand.

                                                25. Rife

Ver. 23. *Though it be given him*, &c.] *It is given* [a] (permitted) *to him* (the tyrant) *to be in safety; whereon he resteth: and his eyes* (the eyes of God) *are upon their ways*. It is usual with this writer to mention the Supreme Being in this abrupt manner [w]. God, he says, suffers these wretches to continue in their prosperity, and seems an unconcerned spectator of their cruelties and oppressions.

Ver. 24. *They are exalted*, &c.] We may translate and point this period as follows;

   They are exalted; a little while and they are gone;
   [x] *After they are laid low* [y] *as all others, they are buried* [z] *:*
   And they are cut off as the tops of the ears of corn.

Here the complaint is, that the wicked are advanced to great preheminence; *They are exalted:* Secondly, that they are favoured with a death quick and easy; which is preceded by no reverse of their prosperity, is brought on by no
                                                disease,

---

[a] יֻתַּן *it is given*. The imperfonal form seems most proper here, as well as לֹא יֵֽאָמֵן (in ver. 22.) *there is no being sure*.

[w] Chap. xxiii. 3. xxv. 2. xxvi. 6.

[x] ו *after*. So in Joshua vii. 25. *and burned them with fire, after they had stoned them with stones*. Vid. Noldium.

[y] הֻמְּכוּ *they are laid low*, sc. by death. This verb signifies in the Syriac Testament (Luk. iii. 5.) *to level* a hill. Our poet useth it in a metaphorical sense, in opposition to *the exaltation* in the first sentence, *they are levelled*.

[z] יִקָּפְצוּן, literally, *they are shut up*, i. e. in a sepulchre. Psal. lxxvii. 10. *Hath he in anger shut up* (קפץ) *his tender mercies?* Or we may suppose it synonimous with the Syriac קפס *to gather up*, or *inclose* a dead body *in bandages*, in order to inter it; Acts v. 10.

25. Rise now, antagonist; who dares maintain
My facts are falshoods, and my reas'nings vain?

Chap. XXV.

1, 2. Bildad once more replies: To dictate law
High on a throne supreme, to hold in awe
Superior worlds, and order to maintain
Through boundless regions of ethereal reign,

3. Belongs

disease, nor imbittered with sharp and lingering pains; *a little while and they are gone.* This indulgent circumstance is happily illustrated, by the beautiful simile which closeth the period, *they are cut off as the tops of the ears of corn:*

And when they are brought to a level with all others by death, their bodies, instead of being exposed a prey to dogs and vultures, are honoured with the rites of sepulture; *After they are brought low as all others, they are buried.*

CHAP. XXV.

This short reply of Bildad represents, in a very lofty strain, the terrible majesty, supreme dominion, and infinite perfection of the Deity. Thence he infers the insufferable arrogance of a creature so frail and impure as man, to justify himself to God and impeach the rectitude of his government. He insinuates, that Job had thus done; and probably intended to impress the standers-by with a persuasion, that the sole point in dispute between Job and his opponents was; " Who was in the wrong, He, or God ?"

This speech is no sort of answer to the facts adduced in the foregoing chapter. They were indeed undeniable, and on the principles of these antagonists insolvable. I therefore incline to think, that the poet put Bildad on making this last feeble effort; merely to give occasion to the triumph of Job in the subsequent chapter.

Ver. 2. *He maketh peace*] His celestial kingdom is preserved in order, peace, and felicity, by an absolute and universal obedience to his laws.

in his high places] *in the high heavens,* as the Chaldee Paraphrast turns it. So

it

3. Belongs to God. What numbers can define
His winged armies, which around him shine?
Does not his glory fill those realms of day,
And each bright seraph glitter with his ray?

4. To this grand Being shall a mortal's tongue
Audacious say, " thy providence is wrong,
" My ways are equal?" Shall a thing of dust
Assume the lofty attribute of just?

5. Before his blaze the moon, abash'd, retires;
Before his blaze fade all the starry fires:

6. Yet shall pollution's worm his beam endure?
The child of woman in his sight be pure?

CHAP.

it signifies in chap. xvi. 19. *my witness is in heaven, and my record is in the high places.*

Ver. 3. *his armies*] his angels; who are called *the army of heaven*, Dan. iv. 35. *He doeth according to his will in the army of heaven, and among the inhabitants of the earth.*

upon whom doth not his light arise?] God is said *to cover* himself *with light as* with *a garment* [a]; and *to dwell in the light which no man can approach unto* [b]. His angels also are styled *flames of fire* [c] : But their lustre is only a faint reflection of his light. It is he who maketh them flames of fire.

Ver. 5. *Behold,* &c.] The fading of the sun (included here among the stars) and the moon when God appears in his visible glory, is a circumstance by which the prophet Isaiah heightens his grand description of the divine majesty: *Then the moon shall be confounded, and the sun ashamed, when the Lord of hosts shall reign in mount Zion . . . and before his ancients gloriously.*

---

[a] Psal. civ. 2. [b] I Tim. vi. 16.
[c] Psal. civ. 4. Hebrews i. 7.

Chap.
XXVI.
1, 2. Job anfwer'd keen: Incomparable tongue!
The babe in knowlege, with fuch aid, how ftrong!
3. Light of the blind! what fluency! what force!
What erudition beams in thy difcourfe!

4. Of

CHAP. XXVI.

Job infults his retreating adverfary; then takes up the fubject fo imperfectly touched by him. For whereas Bildad had fpoken only of God's kingdom in *heaven*; Job adds the counterpart, his kingdom in *Hades*, the world of death. Thence he afcends to the creation, the origin and foundation of divine dominion; and finifheth with a difplay of fome illuftrious operations of providence for the benefit and prefervation of our fyftem.

His defign in all this was not to make oftentation of his own fuperior eloquence: Schultens judicioufly remarks, that he had nobler views: He aimed to remove the ill impreffions made on the audience by the fpeeches of his opponents. He fhews them, that he firmly believed in the all-wife and almighty maker and governor of the world; and had too great and venerating ideas of his adorable perfections to be capable of being an atheift, as Eliphaz had cruelly painted him[d], or of entering into a conteft with fuch a formidable Being, as Bildad had injurioufly reprefented him[e].

Ver. 2, 3. *How haft thou helped*, &c.] The irony here is ftrong and exceffively ftinging. The expreffions are moft of them proverbial; and are intended to expofe the impertinent officioufnefs of perfons, who without talents are vain enough to fet up for inftructors of others; and to offer their affiftance where it is not wanted.

and haft plentifully declared, &c.] *and how haft thou fhewn fubftantial fenfe*[f] *in abundance!*

---

[d] Chap. xxii. 12—20.   [e] Chap. xxv.

[f] תושיה It is englifhed *found wifdom* in Prov. ii. 7. *He layeth up found wifdom for the righteous.* and again in Prov. iii. 21. *keep found wifdom*; LXX. ϭυλην counfel.

THE BOOK OF JOB. CHAP. XXVI.

4. Of whom hast thou harangu'd? whose breath has cast
Such wond'rous wisdom from thy mouth at last?

5, 6. God reigns above, beneath; yea far below
The deep abyss, in dark abodes of woe:

Hades

abundance! He ridicules the futility of Bildad's pompous harangue, as being nothing at all to the point in dispute.

Ver. 4. *To whom,* &c.] Or, *Of whom hast thou uttered words?* Thou hast presumed to teach me how to conceive and speak worthily of God. The subject is too lofty for thy abilities, neither do I need thy instruction in the matter.

and whose spirit [f], &c.] He laughs at him for giving himself the airs of a person who spoke by inspiration.

Ver. 5. *Dead things,* &c.] Seized with a glorious enthusiasm, he breaks out all at once in a magnificent description of God's almighty power and universal dominion. In this and the following verse, he displays God's terrible kingdom in *Sheol,* The region of the dead; that is, the grave and the mansions of departed souls. The translation I think should be,

Ver. 5. *The Giants are in anguish under the waters,*
together with their families.

Ver. 6. *Sheol is naked before him,*
and destruction hath no covering.

The Giants [h]] The mighty men of renown in the old world, who filled the earth

---

[f] אֵת *of,* or *concerning.* I Sam xii. 7. *that I may reason with you of all the righteous acts of the Lord.* Mr. Heath.

[g] נִשְׁמָה *spirit.* We turn it in chap. xxxii. 8. *inspiration;* the *inspiration of the Almighty giveth them understanding.*

[h] הָרְפָאִים *the Rephaim,* rendered by the Chaldee גִּבָּרַיָּא *the giants,* or *the mighty men;* by Symmachus ἀσεβεῖς *those who warred against God;* by the Vulgate *Gigantes.*

It is synonimous with *Nephilim* and *Emim* who were a race of men of great stature and a terror to all others. Gen. vi. 4, 13. Numb. xiii. 33. Deut. ii. 10, 20.

Hence

Hades and regions of perdition lie
Unveil'd, and naked to his flaming eye:

There earth with violence, and perished by the deluge. The punishment of those wicked men in *Sheol* is here mentioned, I imagine, as a sample and proof of the sufferings of all other bad men in that invisible world.

are in anguish [i]] or *are trembling.*

under the waters] I suppose he means the *abyss,* or subterraneous waters; which our poet calls *the springs of the sea,* and places thereabouts *the gates of the shadow of death* [k], that is, the entrance into *Sheol.* The expression *under,* or *from beneath, the waters* is equivalent, but more explicit, to *the depths of Sheol* Prov. ix. 8. and to *Sheol from beneath* in Isaiah xiv. 9. and to *the lowest part of Sheol,* in Deut. xxxii. 22. where our english bible turns it *the lowest hell.* For *a fire is kindled in mine anger, and shall burn unto the lowest hell.* In conformity to this popular creed of the ancients about the situation of *Sheol,* and in particular

---

Hence *tyrannical princes* came to be styled *Rephaim*; not indeed on account of their huge bulk, but for their causing terror by the power of their arms in the land of the living. Isaiah speaking of the king of Babylon sublimely says, *Hell, (Sheol) from beneath is moved for thee to meet thee at thy coming: it stirreth up the dead (Rephaim) for thee, even all the chief ones of the earth; it hath raised up from their thrones all the kings of the nations.* Compare Ezek. xxxii. 21, 23. It should seem also from Prov. ix. 18. that the *manes,* or ghosts, of all wicked men were called *Rephaim: But he knoweth not that the dead (Rephaim) are there, and that her* (the harlot's) *guests are in the depths of hell (Sheol):* Likewise, Prov. xxi. 16. *in the congregation of the dead* (Rephaim LXX. γιγαντων.)

[i] יהוללו it is turned by the Chaldee ומתממהין *who are trembling*; by the Vulgate *gemunt, they groan.* If the root be חול it is the Word by which the prophet expresseth the sufferings of the Messiah, Isaiah liii. 5. where our bible translates it *he was wounded.* But in Deut. ii. 25. where it is in the conjugation *Kal,* we render it *to be in anguish:* and in Habak. iii. 10. where it is in *hiphil,* it is englished *to tremble: The mountains saw thee, and they trembled.*

The word will likewise mean to be in a state of suffering, if we derive it from הלל *to pierce* or *wound,* Psal. cix. 22. *my heart is wounded within me.*

[k] Chap. xxxviii. 16, 17.

[l] שאול תחתית

There the old giants feel his wrath, and there
All wicked ghosts are trembling with despair.
7. He o'er the void heaven's lofty arch extends,
His arm the earth's unwieldy mass suspends,

8. Self-

cular of that portion of it which is allotted to wicked souls ᵐ, St. Luke calls the proper habitation of the devils *the abyss* ⁿ; and St. John *the pit of the abyss* °.

together with their families ᵖ] Or, *and their fellows*; those who dwelled on the earth at the same time with them.

Ver. 6. *Sheol is naked,* &c.] The meaning is not merely that the region of death lies in prospect to him; but that it is under his eye as part of his dominion. Death is the effect of his moral kingdom: and the consequences of death, the destruction of the body in the grave and the disposal of unbodied souls in *Sheol,* are operations of his power.

Ver. 7. *He stretcheth out,* &c.] The Poet now brings us out of the realms of darkness and scenes of putrefaction, to contemplate the glories of the creation; the origin and subject of divine dominion.

He stretcheth out the north, &c.] The *south* in chap. ix. 9. means the southern hemisphere of the heavens. By *the north* therefore he here intends the northern half of the heavens. The expression *he stretcheth out* is that which the hebrew poets generally use, when they celebrate the formation of the heavens. It is a metaphor from a superb pavilion. Isaiah xl. 22. *It is he . . . that stretcheth out the heavens as a curtain, and extendeth them as a tent to dwell in.*

upon

ᵐ Some of the Jewish Rabbis place Gehenna under the waters, which waters they suppose to be lower than the earth, and the earth to float in them like a ship. Vid. Windet *de vita functorum statu,* p. 243.

ⁿ Luke viii. 31. *the deep,* ης την αβυσσον.

° Revel. ix. 1. *the bottomless pit,* το φρεατος της αβυσσου *the pit of the abyss.* Compare Revel. xx. 2, 3.

ᵖ ושכניהם‎ *their families.* So the word signifies in Arabic, *their domestics.* Vid. Pocock. *in Carm. Tograi,* p. 18.

But Symmachus turns it, ϰ̓ οἱ γείτονες αυτων; *and their neighbours.*

CHAP. XXVI.   THE BOOK OF JOB.

8. Self-pois'd, on nothing. High in liquid air,
   His floating aqueducts their burden bear;
   So firm sustain'd, with such strong pressure bound,
   Their pendent waters burst not on the ground.
9. When empty fountains, and the with'ring plains,
   Ask the full bev'rage of nutritious rains;
   The splendors of his sapphire throne he shrouds,
   With wat'ry vapours, and a veil of clouds.

10. Old

upon nothing] without any thing to support it, as the Chaldee explains the hebrew word. Ovid, quoted here by Grotius, hit upon this great idea:
   Terra pilæ similis nullo fulcimine nixa.
   The earth hanging like a ball without any supporter.

   And earth self-balanc'd on her center hung.   Milton.

Ver. 8. *He bindeth up*, &c.] He here refers to the work of the second day of creation; the formation of the atmosphere, and the clouds to float in it. This verse, in short, comprehends the whole process of almighty power in making the air, raising the watry vapours, condensing them into clouds, and sustaining them in that form by a due balance of their pressure with that of the fluid in which they swim, so as their contents may not burst all at once upon the earth.

the cloud is not rent, &c.] as it was at the deluge, when the clouds burst in torrents upon the earth for the space of forty days.

Ver. 9. *He holdeth back the face of his throne*] *He shutteth* [q] *up the face of his throne.* The heaven, or sky, is styled in Scripture *the throne of God* [r]; which *he shutteth up* by spreading his clouds upon it. We are here presented with
the

---

[q] מאחז *he shutteth up.* So in Nehem. vii. 3. *let them shut the doors.* Schultens. The Syriac אחד is used in the same sense Rev. xx. 3. *And cast him into the bottomless pit, and shut him up*, ואחז. See also Rev xxi. 25.

[r] Isaiah lxvi. 1.

10. Old ocean, bounded by his circling line,
Reveres the limits which his laws define:
And shall revere them, till the rolling light
Fulfil its periods and is loft in night.

11. Yet,

the fame scene of nature which is defcribed in chap. xxxvi. 32. *with clouds he covereth the light, and commandeth it not to fhine, by the cloud that comes* betwixt. This is the magnificent preparation and fignal of Providence for the defcent of fruitful fhowers on the thirfty ground. Pfal. cxlvii. 8. *who covereth the heaven with clouds, who prepareth rain for the earth, who maketh grafs to grow upon the mountains.* Cloud-affembling Jove [1] is one of the lofty titles which Homer gives to the fupreme Being.

Ver. 10. *He hath compaffed the waters*, &c.] From the atmofphere, which furrounds this terraqueous globe, he paffeth naturally to the ocean; which more immediately encompaffeth the earth. Mr. Heath's verfion preferveth more exactly the image chofen by the infpired writer, *He hath defcribed a circle* [t] *on the face of the waters.* The powerful decree, or law, which God gave to the fea, that the waters fhould not pafs his commandment, determined the limits of that immenfe body of water with as much precifion, and keeps it within thofe precincts as exactly, as if a circle had been drawn round it.

until the day and night, &c.] Or according to the Chaldee, *until the end* [u] *of the light and darknefs.* By expreffing the confummation of all things in this manner, the poet turns our thoughts to another wonderful operation of Providence; the conftant viciffitudes of day and night: and this leads us up to the immediate natural caufe of that viciffitude, the diurnal revolution of the earth.

---

[1] Νεφεληγερέτα Ζευς.

[t] חק הג *he hath defcribed a circle.* חג, or חוג, which our bible tranflation renders *bounds*, fignifies *a circle*, or rather its circumference; chap. xxii. 14. where it is englifhed *the circuit*; Ifaiah xl. 22. where it is turned *the circle*. חק *he hath compaffed*, (according to our public verfion) fignifies *to draw letters, to write*, chap. xix. 23. *O that they were printed (infcribed) in a book!* See alfo Ifaiah xxx. 8. *note (infcribe) it in a book.* When therefore this verb is joined with הג, it moft naturally means *to draw*, or defcribe, *a circle.*

[u] תכלית, Targ. סוף *the end.*

11. Yet, when his anger bids the thunder roar,
   And his fierce lightnings flash from shore to shore;
   Heav'n's column'd frame with vast amazement quakes,
12. Wild horror the tumultuous ocean shakes:
   Through his great pow'r, with huge commotion rise
   The mountain billows foaming to the skies.

                                        13. His

Ver. 11—13. *The pillars*, &c.] His mention of the atmosphere and ocean suggests to his thoughts those terrible commotions in both, which seem to threaten the diffolution of the whole frame of nature and the reduction of all things to their original confusion. This gives him occasion to celebrate the wisdom and power of God in stilling these tumults, and restoring the order he at the first established.

The pillars of heaven tremble, &c.] I incline to think with Calvin, that the figurative expression, *the pillars of heaven*, represents the heavens under the idea of an immense fabric supported on stately columns. Their *trembling* and *astonishment* is the animated style of sublime poetry, to denote violent concussions of the air and agitation of the clouds. The cause is God's *reproof*, that is, thunder, lightning, and tempestuous winds; which are represented, by the heathen as well as sacred poets, effects and tokens of God's displeasure at the sins of men.

Ver. 12. *he divideth the sea*, &c.] A storm at sea, produced by those violent commotions in the atmosphere, and the laying of the storm, are painted here. Both are effects of divine agency. The first sentence of the period, I think, expresseth the calm; and the other the storm. For according to the most judicious interpreters the translation should be,

   He quieteth * *the sea by his power*,

                                        When

---

* רגע LXX. κατεπαυσε *he quieteth*. Our bible translation renders it *to rest* in Jer. xlvii. 6. *O thou sword of the Lord . . . rest and be still*. And likewise in Isaiah xxxiv. 14. The learned Dr. Hunt hath established this import of the word, and confirmed it by the Arabic. Vid Lowthi *Prælect*. p. 104..n.

13. His drying gale refines heav'n's troubled scene,
Renew'd in beauty smiles the blue serene;

The

*When by his understanding he hath dashed
together ' the proud ' waves.*

We meet with a parallel passage in Isaiah li. 15. *I am the Lord thy God who quieteth the sea, when the waves thereof roar.*

Ver. 13. *By his spirit,* &c.] If I mistake not, the first member of this period describeth a bright and serene sky, in opposition to its troubled state in ver. 11. and the second the floating of large and dead fishes on the surface of the sea, the effect of the storm and calm in ver. 12.

By his spirit he hath garnished, &c.] According to this version we are sent back again to the creation of the heavens mentioned ver. 7. But surely if this had been the poet's sentiment, he would have inserted it immediately after that seventh verse. The original will admit of a translation, which describeth the state of the heavens after laying the tempest in ver. 11, 12.

By his wind ˣ *the heavens become serene* ᵃ.

The

ˣ מחץ Symachus turns it Συγκλα *he dasheth together,* and the LXX. in II Sam. xxii. 39. ἐλαω *to dash in pieces.* In Arabic it signifies, as Schultens has shewn, *to agitate a fluid violently,* the water in a well, for instance, by plunging a bucket into it; or milk, by shaking violently the vessel that contains it. See his *Commentary* and his *Origines* Hebr.

ʸ רהב *the formidable pride,* or *the proud and formidable* waves, *l'orgueil de ses flots* as Crinsoz turns it. It is englished *the proud* in chap. ix. 13. where it imports both haughtiness and power. In Arabic it generally denotes *terror.* Egypt is stiled *Rahab* in scripture, because it was a haughty and formidable power. But there is no evidence that Egypt had this appellation in the days of Job.

ᶻ ברוחו *by his wind,* as in chap. xxxvii. 21. *the wind passeth and cleanseth them;* and in many other places.

ᵃ שפרה It may be a noun substantive, and so be rendered *serenity,* as Mr. Heath observes. Or it may be a verb in *pihel,* and then it signifies *to be serene,* or *to make serene.* In Arabic this word, as Schultens remarks, is particularly applied to *the whiteness* and *clearness of the sky.* It is used by the elegant Harir of a beautiful woman unveiling and shining out to her admirers. Harir Confess. v. p. 95. n. In Chaldee, שופרא is *beauty,* and שפיר *beautiful.* Targ. in ch. xlii. 14, 15.

CHAP. XXVI.   THE BOOK OF JOB.

The billows meekly, at his voice, subside,
And wrecks of monsters float along the tide

14. These

The sky is cleared of clouds by a drying wind, and the sun shineth out again in his glory. Chap. xxxvii. 21. *And now men cannot look on the lustre which is in the sky, when the wind hath passed and cleansed it.* By means of the north wind (cleansing the heaven of clouds) *the golden sun cometh forth.*

Sic ait, et dicto citius tumida æquora placat,
Collectasque fugit nubes, solemque reducit.
Æneid. I. 146.

The first line may serve for a translation of the first sentence of ver. 12. in our author, *He in a moment quieteth the sea by his power:* Virgil says, *he quieteth the swelling sea sooner than he could utter the command.*

The *collectasque—nubes* expresseth the collection of clouds which the Almighty spreadeth over his throne ver. 9; and the chasing them away (*fugit*) and causing the sun to break out again (*solemque reducit*) is the very image in this 13th ver. *by his wind the heavens become serene,* or *shine out with clearness.*

His hand hath formed, &c.] The appearance of the *sky,* after laying the forementioned storm, is the subject of the former clause. It is reasonable to expect that the appearance which the *sea* presents, is contained in this clause. The passage is extremely obscure. But our expectation is gratified, and the connection well preserved, by the interpretation which Schultens offers. According to that penetrating Critic, the words express the destruction made among the sea-monsters by the storm, and necessarily imply the floating of their carcasses on the surface of the water in the ensuing calm. Let us see how the original will bear this meaning. The translation may be,

His hand slayeth [b] *the bar-serpent* [c].

The

---

[b] חללה The bible translation is, *his hand hath formed;* the Chaldee, *created;* but the LXX. followed by the Syriac, ιθανατωσι *he slew.* This signification seems best adapted to the context. Our Translators were obliged to render the adjective, derived from this verb, *the slain,* in Ezek. xxxii. 21, 22, 23, &c.

[c] נחש ברח strangely rendred here in our bible *the crooked serpent,* and in the Vulgate *coluber*

14. *These are his ways, in these exterior lines
What wonders open! and what glory shines!
Yet,*

The word *serpent*, says the learned Gataker [d], is in the hebrew a general term common to all living creatures, in water or on land, that glide along in the one, and on the other, with a wriggling kind of motion, without use of feet or fins. The *bar-serpent* is some large fish. It is one of the descriptive characters of *Leviathan* in the passage cited from Isaiah in the marginal note: who also there calls it *the dragon*, that is, the great serpent *of the sea*. If by *the sea* the prophet means the Nile, which is sometimes so called, *Leviathan*, the *bar-serpent*, is the crocodile. But if *the sea* signifies the Mediterranean, the *bar-serpent* is that other *Leviathan* which is mentioned in Psalm civ. 25, 26, and which probably is the *tunnie*: for the tunnie is the largest fish in that sea, is of the whale kind [e], and the biggest fish, we may suppose, that Job and our poet were acquainted with. By God's *slaying the bar-serpent* seems, from the connection, to be meant his dashing them against the rocks, and destroying them in the storm mentioned ver. 12.

The Psalmist thought such a grand *sea-piece* to be a magnificent display of divine power: for he made choice of it as a proper emblem of the destruction of Pharaoh and his army in the Red Sea.

Psalm lxxiv. 13, 14. *Thou didst divide the sea by thy strength: Thou brakest the heads of the dragons in the waters. Thou brakest the heads of Leviathan in pieces, and gavest him to be meat to the people inhabiting the wilderness.*

The reader it is hoped, will pardon the length of this note, when he considers the difficulty of the passage which it aims to explain.

Ver. 14. *Lo, these are parts*, &c.] *Lo, these are the extreme parts* [f] *of his ways,
and*

---

coluber tortuosus. ברח (or בריח, for the plural is בריחים) signifies *a bar*. perhaps straitness of shape, as well as penetrating force, is intended by this epithet. Our Translators however have turned it much better *the piercing serpent* in Isaiah xxvii. 1. *Leviathan, that piercing serpent*. The Septuagint gives it here δρακοντα αποςταταν, that is, *the fugitive serpent*, εφιν φευγοντα, in Is. xxvii. 1.

[d] See his *Annotations* on Isaiah xxvii. 1.
[e] See Mr. Merrick's Annotations on Psal. lxxiv. 13, 14.
[f] קצות *the outlines*. Mr. Heath.

Yet, beyond these, what endless wonders grow!
For who the thunder of his might can know?

CHAP. XXVII.
Ver. 1. He paus'd; and then pursu'd his conqu'ring strains:
2. By him, Eternal Potentate, who reigns

Above;

and what a series of noble things [z] *have we heard of him! but the thunder of his power*, &c.

This is a sublime conclusion of a sublime discourse. We are acquainted only with the surface and outlines of the works of God. These indeed are grand: but the *thunder of his power*, the higher exertions of his power, in the internal structure of natural bodies, and the whole sum of their properties, and manner of their operation, are matters far beyond our reach.

Among the Greeks, when a great orator exerted the powers of his eloquence in their full strength, he was said to *thunder*. The Arabians were no strangers to this lofty metaphor [b].

CHAP. XXVII.

The foregoing chapter treated chiefly of God's dominion over the *material* world. Here the discourse turns to his *moral* kingdom, or providence; I mean that branch of his providence which had been the subject of altercation between Job and the three friends, *the ways of God toward wicked men in the present state.* He had all along maintained, in opposition to the others, that this world is not the scene of a regular distribution of good and evil, that virtue is often oppressed and vice triumphant; and that the major part of wicked men go unpunished here, and even grow hoary in affluence and ease, and at length die

in

---

[z] שמץ דבר. for שמץ, see the note on chap. iv. 12. דבר signifies not only *a word*, but also *a thing*, or *matter*.

[b] Schultens.

THE BOOK OF JOB. Chap. XXVII.

Above; who judgement in my caufe delays,
And who my foul imbitters with his ways,

3. I fwear; that while this bofom fhall inhale
The nurture of his animating gale;

4. Falfhood

in peace[i]. But now, having reduced his opponents to filence, he frankly owns, there are fome examples of fuch fort of divine vengeance on bad men in the prefent life as they had afferted. Left, however, this acknowledgement fhould be conftrued a giving up the caufe to his antagonifts, and fubfcribing to their condemnation of him; he prefaceth his *conceffion* with a folemn declaration of his innocence, of his refolution to defend it with his lateft breath, and of his abhorrence of a wicked character which they had endeavoured to fix upon him.

Ver. 1. *His parable*] His poetical ftrain; or his commanding eloquence, as the ingenious Mr. Peters[k] explains the original term.

Ver. 2. *As God liveth*, &c.] The folemnity and vehemence of this oath characterife the warmth and emotion of the fpeaker. It alfo fhews the aftonifhing force of innocence oppreffed by affliction and calumny; and gives a fublime idea of the fenfe a good man has of the ineftimable value of virtue, and of his own felicity in the poffeffion of it.

who hath taken away[l] *my judgement*] that is, refufeth to do me juftice. Thefe are harfh expreffions indeed, but not more harfh than thofe in chap. ix. 17. x. 3. I have however followed the fofter turn given to them by Codurcus, *Who hath fufpended my trial.* But the words even thus qualified are a complaint, and carry in them a reflection on the juftice of God which merited Elihu's caftigation chap. xxxiv. 5—7.

my judgement] *Judgement* here fignifies *the trial* in general, or *the paffing fentence*, which finifheth the trial.

---

[i] Chap. ix. 22—24. Chap. xii. xxi. xxiv.
[k] *Critical Differtation*, p. 45.
[l] הָסִיר It fignifies *to put away*, or *remove*, ver. 5. *I will not remove my integrity from me*,

CHAP. XXVII.   THE BOOK OF JOB.   213

4. Falſhood and guile ſhall ne'er employ my tongue
To flatter you, and my own conſcience wrong:
5. To juſtify your part, my own betray,
6. Forbid it, Heav'n! Firm to the mortal day
I'll hold my virtue, nor abate my zeal
In ſtrong apology and bold appeal:
My heart, which never yet a cenſure knew
From its own voice, diſdains reproach from you.

7. *Wicked*,

Ver. 4. *wickedneſs—deceit*] Thoſe are general terms for all kinds of iniquity and falſhood. But they are limited by the tenor of the diſcourſe to the particular crimes of calumny and falſe accuſation; that is, a man's calumniating and falſely accuſing himſelf. He means, that he does not intend, by the conceſſion he was about to make, to confeſs guilt whereof he was not conſcious.

Ver. 5. *God forbid*, &c.] *God forbid that I ſhould juſtify you*, in your notion of the courſe of providence; much leſs in your condemnation of me grounded upon that falſe principle. No; I will not to my dying day part with my claim to the character of an honeſt man; *till I die I will not remove my integrity from me*.

Ver. 6. *My righteouſneſs I hold faſt* ᵐ, &c.] I will be as tenacious of my innocence as a good ſoldier is of his ſhield.

My heart ſhall not reproach ⁿ *me*, &c.] My own conſcience has never yet upbraided me with any wickedneſs: and I am ſure, it never ſhall upbraid me with the wickedneſs of ſubſcribing to your verdict againſt me.

as long as I live ᵒ] *throughout my life*. It denotes the whole time of a man's life,

---

ᵐ החזקתי Pſal. xxxv. 2. *Take hold of* (החזק) *ſhield and buckler*. Schultens.

ⁿ יחרף לא *hath not reproached me ſince my life began*, or *in all my life* (מימי). The future is here uſed for the preter tenſe. Accordingly the Vulgate turns it, *Neque enim reprehendit me cor meum in omni vita mea*.

ᵒ בימי.

7. *Wicked, profane*—those hateful names bestow,
  Worst execration, on my deadly foe:
8. The wicked Great——although his eyes behold
  His boundless treasures of unrighteous gold;
  What can he hope, when stern decrees expell
  His trembling spirit from its earthy shell?
9. In that hard instant, will his piteous cry
  Pierce the deaf ear of angry Deity?

10. Will

'life, in chap. xxxviii. 12. *Hast thou commanded the morning since thy days?* ? that is, in any part of thy life-time.

Ver. 7. *Let mine enemy* ⁿ, &c.] Here he expresseth, in very strong terms, his abhorrence of a wicked character; which the three antagonists had endeavoured to fix upon him. He gives his reason in the three following verses, for detecting such a character.

Ver. 8. *For what is the hope of the hypocrite* ⁱ, &c.] *For what is the hope of a profligate*, &c. *hypocrite* here is evidently of the same import with *wicked* and *unrighteous* in the foregoing verse.

though he hath gained '] though he has been ever so successful in accumulating wealth, and enjoyed it throughout a long life '.

When God taketh away his soul] Is there not in this verse a clear intimation of
                                                                                  a future

---

ᵖ רחמימו

ⁿ LXX. *Let my enemies be as the overthrow of the ungodly; and those that rise up against me, as the destruction of transgressors.*

ⁱ LXX. ο = ἀσεβης *ungodly*; the Chaldee renders חנף throughout this book דילמור *a false ......* Mr Heath translates it here *a hypocrite*, but every where else *a profligate*.

ימיו The LXX. turn it ... *in habendo exsuperat he hath an overabundance*; the other Greek versions (says Olympiodorus) ... *he hath more than enough*; the Vulgate, *si avare rapiat if he greedily keep up riches by rapine*.

' Chap. xxi.

CHAP. XXVII.   THE BOOK OF JOB.   215

10. Will he then triumph in almighty pow'r,
    Unfought, unheeded in the prosp'ring hour?

11. Attend, while I my inmost thought reveal;
    Just to the ways of God I'll none conceal:

12. Persist to credit what your eyes attest;
    Why trifle you in proving things confest?

13. There
a future state of punishment and reward? The question *what is the hope*, &c. obviously imports, that the happiness of the most prosperous wicked man endeth with his life. The question seemeth also to imply, not merely that he hath no felicity to hope for in another world, but further that he will there be miserable. It certainly implies that a righteous man hath hope in his death.

Will God hear his cry, &c] His cries to God for mercy will then be unavailing. See Prov. i. 24—21.

Ver. 10. *Will he delight himself*, &c.] This verse seems to assign the reason of God's being inexorable to him: For the translation may be,

   Did he delight himself [u] *in the Almighty?*
   Did he always call [w] *upon God?*

To delight one's self in the Almighty signifies to seek his favour as our supreme felicity [x]. He who does so will be a sincere worshipper of him; not only in a time of distress, but throughout his whole life. See Psalm xxxvii. 4.

Ver. 11, 12. *I will teach you*, &c.] What is he going to teach them? somewhat relating to the administrations of providence, which he calls *the hand of God*; *I will teach you concerning the hand of God* [y]. But what does he mean to teach

---

[u] יתענג *did he delight himself?*

[w] יקרא *did he call?* The future and the preterite of the hebrew verbs were probably æorists in the primitive state of the language; and are to be rendered in the present, past, or future tense, as the context requires. See Michaelis on Bp. Lowth's *Prelections*, p. 78. 8vo.

[x] See chap. xxii. 26.

[y] ביד The preposition ב signifies *of* or *concerning* in chap. xxvi. 14. *how little a portion is heard of him?* See Noldius. By *the hand of God* is meant the operation of his power in his works of creation and providence.

13. There are, I yield, some dire examples giv'n,
    Some chosen victims of the wrath of heav'n;
14. Some lofty tyrants, from whose fatal bed
    A race increasing for the sword is bred:
    Vagrant and starving see the downward line;
15. See the last thin remains their breath resign,
                                        Without

teach them concerning those administrations? not surely what they had been teaching him; namely that great wicked men are *generally* overtaken by divine vengeance in the present world. He had proved this position to be false. By *teaching*, therefore, he means *not concealing that which is with* ᵃ *the Almighty*; that is, not suppressing the measures which the Almighty pursues towards *some* tyrannical princes and families in the present state. Thus, consistently with his former assertion of a promiscuous distribution of good and evil ᵃ, and of the worldly felicity of multitudes of bad characters ᵇ; he acknowledgeth that there are examples enow of God's vindictive justice here, to deter him and every one else from following such evil courses.

Ver. 14. *If his children*ᶜ, &c.] Statius introduceth the unhappy Oedipus thus apostrophising one of the Furies,

   ———natosque tibi, scis ipsa, paravi.   Theb. i. 97.

Thou thy self knowest, that I have brought up children for thy vengeance. History furnisheth several examples of this kind. They supplied subjects to the tragic poets.

Ver. 15. *shall be buried in death*] Or *by death*, that is, they shall have no burial. The mode of expression is singular and forcible. It probably comprehends

---

 ᵃ See chap. xxiii. 14.
 ᵃ Chap. ix. 22. xii. 17, &c.
 ᵇ Chap. xxi. 7, &c.
 ᶜ Compare Hos. ix. 13. *Ephraim shall bring forth his children to the murderer.*

Without a solemn dirge, without a bier,
Without a grave, without a widow's tear.
16. Where lie the silver heaps, and purple dies,
The proud progenitor's extorted prize;
17. Amass'd as dust? A worthier lineage wears
The robes of purple, and the silver heirs.
18. Wretch! as a moth, that ravages the looms,
Weaves her frail bow'r, and, as she weaves, consumes;
Or as the hireling warder of the vines
His green booth, lodging of a summer, twines;
With like vain toil, for a like fleeting date,
He builds his grandeur, and enjoys his state:

19. Wealthy

hends all those tragical circumstances which are accumulated in Jerem. xvi. 4. *They shall die of grievous deaths, they shall not be lamented, neither shall they be buried:* but *they shall be as dung upon the face of the earth, and they shall be consumed by the sword, and by famine, and their carcases shall be meat for the fowls of heaven, and for the beasts of the earth.*

Ver. 18. *as a moth*] He who buildeth his fortunes and greatness by methods of injustice, is such a builder as the moth; which, by eating into the garment wherein it makes its habitation, destroys its own dwelling. The simile represents the oppressor as working ruin to his own unrighteous acquisitions.

as a booth] The simile of the booth illustrates the short duration of such men's prosperity. A booth was an extempore hut made of boughs and reeds: It served for a shelter from the violent heat to the servant who guarded the summer fruits, when nearly ripe, from the birds, and other creatures of prey. As soon as the harvest or vintage was over, it was taken down or suffered to perish of itself[d].

---

[d] This custom is still kept up in Barbary. Shaw's *Travels,* p. 138. 4to.

19. Wealthy he lays him down; no more to rife;
   He wakes, he fees the glitt'ring fteel, he dies.
20. But O the terrors, which, that night, invade
   His foul, and drive him to infernal fhade!
   Sudden and furious like a midnight flood;
   Fierce as the ftorm which tears the mountain wood:
21—23. Upon him all at once the ftorm is caft,
   Boift'rous and burning as an eaftern blaft:
                                                    Fain

Ver. 19. *The rich man fhall lie down*] He *fhall lie down* (on his bed) *a rich man, but fhall no more*ᵉ. *It is for the laft time,* as Mr. Heath turns the original. He continueth indeed in his profperity fo long as he liveth: But then his death is fudden and terrible, in the night, and probably by affaffination. He is awakened by the noife of the confpirators rufhing in upon him, but he openeth his eyes only for a moment to fee his own deftruction; and then clofeth them for ever. So Mr. Heath well explains *he openeth his eyes and he is not.*

Ver. 20—23. *Terrors,* &c.] I think thefe verfes are an amplification of his fudden and terrible death; and not a reprefentation of his punifhment in another world. For *firft,* Job had told his opponents ver. 12. that he was going to fpeak of what themfelves *had feen. fecondly,* the image, ver. 20. of the *tempeft ftealing him away in the night* is proper to exprefs a fudden and violent death in the night; but has no affinity with the punifhments of a future ftate. And *thirdly,* all that the tempeft and the torrent effect is, *hurling him out of his place,* ver. 21. which muft be underftood of fending him out of this world, not of what he fuffers in another.

Ver. 20. *Terrors,* &c.] He refumes the topic of his fudden and violent death mentioned in the foregoing verfe. A fudden land-flood in the night, no uncommon thing in Arabia, and a furious ftorm of wind, are the ftrong images by which he reprefents fuch a death.

Ver. 21. *The eaft wind,* &c.] He fpecifies *the eaft wind,* only to heighten our
                                                                            idea

---

ᵉ יאסף LXX. ᴜ πρoσθησιι *he fhall not add*; viz. to lie down; *he fhall lie down no more.* They read יסף *jofip.* So chap. xxxiv. 32. *If I have done iniquity, I will do fo no more,* לא אסף

Fain would he flee, the winged wrath purfues,
Augments its vengeance, and its ftrokes renews:
The ftorm purfues him with remorfelefs rage,
And with loud infults whirls him off the ftage.

idea of the tempeft ver. 20. An eaft wind is the moft boifterous and the moft deftructive wind that blows in thofe countries ᶠ. (See the note on chap. xv. 2.) It is moft violent in the night ᵍ.

Ver. 22. *For God shall cast upon him*] Our Tranflators have inferted the word *God* which is not in the original. The agent fpoken of in this and the following verfe is *the eaft wind*, as Mr. Heath remarks. *It* (the eaft wind) *shall cast* itfelf *upon him, and not spare*. His violent death is the fubject ftill, but carried on in a ftyle of increafing force and exaggeration.

He would fain flee, &c.] *he would fain flee out of its hand*. He forefees the ftorm: His guilt prefages this fatal cataftrophe. He takes every meafure of human prudence to prevent it; but to no purpofe. The ftorm is irrefiftable, and his deftruction inevitable.

Ver. 23. Men *shall clap their hands*, &c.] *Men* is not in the hebrew. The verbs too are in the fingular number. Their nominative is ftill *the eaft wind*.

*It shall clap its hands at him
And it shall hiss*, &c.

The contempt with which this enemy to God and man is hurried out of the world, is here expreft in the boldeft ftyle of oriental poetry. The *eaft-wind* is made a perfon, is clothed with a human body, and has geftures and a voice afcribed to it fignificant of exultation and fcorn ʰ. A Greek or Roman poet, inftead of hazarding fo daring a profopopeia, would have feigned the wind to be a divinity; and attributed paffions and actions to it proper to the occafion: *lætus Eois Eurus equis, the east-wind exulting in his oriental steeds*.

ᶠ See Michaelis on Bp. Lowth's *Prælections*, p. 39. 8vo.

ᵍ *Hamasa*, p. 548. n.

ʰ Compare Pfal. xcviii. 8. Ifaiah lv. 12.

CHAP.
XXVIII.
1. The vein of silver, and the golden mine,
And how the metal from its ore to fine,

2. T' educe

ſhall hiſs him out of his place] This concluſion of the deſcription clearly ſhews, that the whole turneth upon the vengeance which ſometimes overtakes ſuch high delinquents in *the preſent world*.

CHAP. XXVIII.

The noble ſubject of this chapter is *wiſdom*; that is (if I do not miſtake) knowledge of the entire plan of providence, ſo as to be able to account for all its diſpenſations. The tranſition to this ſubject is abrupt, after the manner of the Arabian writers [i]. But a ſmall degree of attention will diſcover the connection. He had allowed in the former chapter, that God makes examples of ſome great wicked men in the preſent life: He had maintained in chap. xxi. that multitudes of others, equally culpable, eſcape with impunity and flouriſh to the laſt. He had alſo aſſerted chap. ix. 22. that general calamities involve the beſt and the worſt characters in one common deſtruction. Theſe are perplexing appearances. Hence his thoughts are naturally led up to thoſe impenetrable counſels which direct all this ſeeming confuſion. The powers of the human mind and perſevering application of them have made ſurpriſing diſcoveries, and performed wonders in *natural things*; for inſtance, in penetrating the bowels of the earth, and ſurmounting prodigious obſtacles to come at the wealth concealed in thoſe regions of darkneſs [k]. But neither can all theſe riches purchaſe, nor the utmoſt force of human genius and induſtry attain the knowledge of the whole plan of the divine adminiſtration of our world [l]. A future ſtate will afford ſome imperfect revelation of it [m]. But only he can comprehend the whole, to whom are known all his works from the beginning [n].

The inference is, that, inſtead of prying into myſteries which we cannot underſtand, the duty of man is to adore his Maker and practiſe univerſal virtue

in

---

[i] See Pocock. in *Carm. Tograi*. p. 50.
[k] Ver. 1—11. [l] Ver. 12—21. [m] Ver. 22. [n] Ver. 23—27.

2. T'educe hard iron from the rocky mafs,
And turn the ftone by fufion into brafs,

3. To

in obedience to his commandments. This is the Wifdom proper to man: for this is the only means of his happinefs °.

Ver. 1—11. *Surely there is a vein for the filver*, &c.] This firft verfe fpeaks of *mines*: The eleventh verfe, which concludes the paragraph, mentioneth man's bringing the riches of them into day-light: The intermediate verfes, therefore, muft in all reafon be fuppofed to relate to the fame fubject. The Poet is here difplaying the wonderful force of human genius and induftry. With great judgement has he chofen this fpecimen of both, as it furnifhed him with a profufion of glittering ideas wherewith to illuftrate the value of *wifdom*.

Ver. 1. *a place for gold*] fo the Arabians called the mine. Gold, fays one of their poets, *is thrown away like earth in its places* ᵖ.

It has no value in the mine.

where *they fine* ᵠ it] rather, which (both the filver and the gold) *they fine*. Neither filver nor gold are fined in the mine itfelf. The fining of thefe metals is mentioned as another inftance of man's ability, diftinct from his fearching them out in the mine. Arabia Felix had anciently its mines of gold. Pfal. lxxii. 15. *to him fhall be given of the gold of Sheba*; in the Septuagint and Arabic verfions, *the gold of Arabia*. Sheba was the ancient name of Arabia Felix. Job, who dwelt in Arabia Petræa, could be no ftranger to the riches of that neighbouring country.

Ver. 2. *brafs*] He means, I imagine, the natural or red brafs, which is copper. It was obtained, by fufion, out of two kinds of ftone called *cadmia* and

---

° Ver. 28.

ᵖ Pocock. in *Carm. Tograi.* p. 160.

ᵠ יָצֹק LXX. ἠθυται *percolatur*. The Greek word fignifies *to ftrain through a wicker fieve*. But Olympiodorus has χωνευει *conflatur*, *is fufed*. The hebrew word denotes feparation, of the ftony earth which adheres to the metal, by the action of fire; in Pfal. xii. 6. *as filver tried in a furnace of earth, purified* (מְזֻקָּק *refined*) *feven times*.

3. To man are known. Man, with gigantic pains,
Explores the depths where ancient darkness reigns,
Limits her kingdom, and with light invades
The marble caverns of the central shades.

4. They scoop the rock, and pendulous descend;
Lost from the sun their mazy way they bend,

4. Through

and *chalcites*¹. The modern brass, which the French name yellow copper, is factitious; being made of copper fused with the calamine stone¹. But where are we to look for these iron and copper mines within the compass of Job's geographical knowledge? Pliny says, that mines of iron ore are to be found almost every where¹: and as to brass or copper, he says, it was first discovered in the island of Cyprus. The traffic both of the Egyptians and Phœnicians to that island might be the means of Job's acquaintance with its productions.

Ver. 3. *He setteth an end to darkness*, &c.] *The stones of darkness* and *the shadow of death* must surely mean the metallic ore in the deep and dark parts of the earth. The agent, then, who searcheth them out must be man. He also it is, whose power and presumption *setteth an end to darkness*, that is, contracts its bounds by carrying light into the subterraneous caverns when he works the mines.

He searcheth out all perfection, &c.] Or as Cocceius more clearly translates it, *He searcheth to every extremity*ᵘ *the stones of darkness*, &c. He follows the vein of metallic ore as far as it goes.

Ver. 4. *The flood*, &c.] This is excessively obscure. By the assistance of

Cocceius

---

¹ Plin. *Hist. Nat.* xxxiv. 10. *Namque ipse lapis, ex quo fit æs, cadmia vocatur*: And in cap. 2. of that book, *Fit et ex alio lapide, quem chalciten vocant in cypro, ubi prima fuit æris inventio.*

¹ See Chambers' *Dictionary*.

¹ Plin. xxxiv. 14.

ᵘ תכלית *the end*, or *extremity*. Both the Chaldee and Syriac render it סופא *the extremity*. It is used in the same sense Nehem. iii. 21. *even to the end* (תכלית) *of the house of* Eliashib.

5. Through burning naphtha in the bowell'd earth,
Whose bosom gives the nodding harvest birth:
                                                6. Where

Cocceius and Schultens, we gain a more intelligible translation, agreeing happily with the context:

> He breaketh up ⃰ the valley ˣ near the bottom of the mountain ʸ:
> They are forgotten of the foot:
> They sink down ᶻ; they wander from men.

The first word, *he breaketh up*, denotes opening the ground for a passage into the mine.

The *place* is marked in the next words, *the valley near the bottom of the mountain*.

The manner of going down into the mine is intimated by that poetical expression, *they are forgotten of the foot*. They do not descend by their feet, but are let down by ropes or baskets.

The depth of the descent and their gradual disappearance are described in the third sentence, *they sink down*.

And by the last sentence, *they wander from men*, may be meant their winding progress in the subterraneous passages according to the course of the metallic vein.

Ver. 5. *As for the earth*, &c.] Here, I imagine, he represents the dangers to which miners are exposed, and which avarice is bold enough to venture
                                                                through.

⃰ פרץ *to make a breach, to break up*, or *through*. It signifies *to make a breach* in the wall of a vineyard, Psal. lxxx. 13.

ˣ נחל *the valley*. This is one known acceptation of the word.

ʸ מעם נגר *near the bottom of the mountain, de cum pede montis*. Schultens. I find in Golius and Castell, that רג in Arabic signifies *the foot of a mountain*.

ᶻ דלל *they sink down, subsidunt*. Cocceius. According to Castell, דלל in Arabic signifies *to humble* or *depress another*; and in the fifth conjugation *to let one's self down, to be submissive*. In the hebrew bible this verb occurs but seven times, and signifies, among other senses, *to be reduced to a low condition*, Psal. cxvi. 6. cxlii. 7. The noun דל denotes persons of a low rank, *the vulgar*, Judges vi. 15. I Sam. ii. 8. Hence we may conjecture with probability that the primary idea was *local descent*.

6. Where spangled sapphires in her flints are bred,
And golden glebes extend their shining bed:
7. A path, which fowl of rapine never try'd,
Not by the vulture's piercing eye descry'd;

8. Which

through. The surface of the earth produceth corn and other fruits for the sustenance of man and beast: But *underneath it is turned* [a] to be *as it were fire*. Its caverns abound with inflammable minerals, for instance sulphur. The sulphureous air in mines has been known sometimes to take fire from the candles of the workmen, and to destroy the miners. Or perhaps he referreth to *the slime-pits in the vale of Siddim* [b], near the place which was afterwards turned into a lake and called the *dead sea*. Those slime-pits were holes out of which issued a liquid bitumen or naphtha, an oily substance. Hanway, in his *Travels into Persia*, describes some fountains of Naphtha which were actually burning near Baku on the western coast of the Caspian sea. Chaldea abounded with them. The walls of Babylon were cemented with this bitumen or slime.

Ver. 6. *The stones of it are the place*, &c.] Here is the temptation to risk the aforementioned dangers: The rocky earth in those subterraneous caverns is the country and birth-place of *sapphires*, and other precious stones. There also men find *glebes of gold*, or golden ore.

Ver. 7, 8. *There is a path*, &c.] These two verses are a poetical illustration of man's intrepidity in penetrating these dangerous regions of darkness. The fiercest and most daring creatures of prey would not venture into them: *A path which* [c] *the fowls of prey know not*, &c. He means the path which leads to *the place of sapphires and golden ore*; the way into the mines.

no

---

[a] נֶהְפָּךְ *it is turned* or *changed.* Chap. xx. 14. *his meat in his bowels is turned*, it is the *gall of asps within him.* The translation may be, *But the lower parts thereof* (תַּחְתִּיָּה) *are turned* to be (נֶהְפָּךְ) *as it were fire.* The anomaly of a verb singular constructed with a nominative plural is common in Arabic.

[b] Genesis xiv. 10. See also the *Notes* of Michaelis *on the Prelections,* p. 108. 8vo.

[c] נָתִיב לֹא יְדָעוֹ here is an ellipsis. The compleat construction is אֲשֶׁר לֹא יְדָעוֹ נָתִיב

CHAP. XXVIII.   THE BOOK OF JOB.   225

8. Which beasts of fiercest countenance would fear,
   Nor dares to stalk the bold black lion here.
9. Man this explores: his hardy hand o'erthrows
   The marble roots whereon the mountain grows:

10. He

no fowl] *no fowl of prey* [e]. The expression comprehends all the kinds of ravenous birds. In the next sentence *the vulture* is specified as being one of the most rapacious and most daring.

Ver. 8. *The lion's whelps*] *The wild beasts* [d], as Mr. Heath rightly turns it. In the following clause *the black lion* is particularly mentioned, as one of the fiercest and most intrepid: *nor the black lion* [e] *walked upon it*.

Ver. 9—11. *He putteth forth*, &c.] These verses, I apprehend, describe the prodigious labour of working a mine: for the effects of the operations here specified is, man's *bringing forth to light the thing that is hid*; that is, the hidden treasure of the earth.

Ver. 9. *He overturneth the mountains*, &c.] The operation, described here, seems to be the breaking in pieces and dislodging, in order to come at the ore, the hardest flint or marble; which are the roots, that is, the foundation of the mountain. Or perhaps the poet means a still greater work; such as Pliny, quoted by Schultens, strongly paints: " Yet the labour of hewing the rock is comparatively easy. For there is an earth compounded of a kind of clay and grit, that is almost impenetrable. This the miners assail with iron wedges and mallets. Nothing is imagined to be harder, except the insatiable hunger after gold, which of all things is the hardest to subdue. Having finished this labour they cut the

props

---

[e] עיט *avis rapax a fowl of prey*; or ravenous bird, as it signifies Gen. xv. 11. and as our bible translates it Isaiah xlvi. 11. Indeed it comprehends all rapacious animals, quadrupede and volatile, being derived from a root in Arabic which signifies to *fly upon the prey*. See *Hierozoic.* p. i. 838. and p. ii. 165.

[d] בני שחץ *the children of pride*, as our Translators turn it, chap. xli. 34. where it plainly signifies, wild and fierce creatures. שחץ in Arabic denotes in general *elevation*, and, when applied to the mind, *pride, fierceness*. *Hieroz.* p. i. 719.

[e] שחל See the note on chap. iv. 10.

G g

10. He cleaves deep channels in the rocky ground,
    Collects the streams of all the springs around,
    And bids the torrent with impetuous roar
    Rend off the crust, and bare the precious ore:
11. Then with new law th' unruly flood restrains,
    To the last drop its raging waters drains;
    Breaks the strong seal of nature, and to light
    Triumphant brings the fulgent spoils of night.

12. But props of their arch-work, the prelude and signal of the fall of the mountain. The sentinel on the top of the mountain perceiving the ground under his feet to sink, immediately gives notice of it to the workmen below by his voice and repeated thumps. Away he flies. The mountain splits, and falls with a continued thundering sound and an incredible blast of wind. The victorious miners gaze upon the overthrow of nature."

Ver. 10. *He cutteth out rivers*, &c.] The next operation is to clear away the stones and rubbish, that *his eye may see every precious thing*; that is, lay bare the precious gems and the gold. The means by which this is accomplished, is turning a large body of water upon the ruins. But so wonderful is man's invention and so indefatigable his avarice, that he cuts a passage even through rocks to collect and convey a strong stream down to the mine for that purpose. " To wash the ruins, says Pliny [h], they bring rivers from the tops of mountains a hundred miles off. They carry aqueducts over the valleys, and sometimes hew a way for those pipes through the rocks: They gather the waters into large reservoirs, make sluice gates to those reservoirs; then let out such a torrent as bears down the largest stones with the violence of its course."

Ver. 11. *He bindeth the floods*, &c.] There remaineth still a third operation to exercise the art of man. The subterraneous waters sometimes burst into the mine in great abundance. These he must thoroughly drain off by machines, before *he can bring forth into light the hidden treasures*.

---

[g] *Hist. Nat.* xxxiii. 4.   [h] *Hist. Nat.* xxxiii. 4.

12. But where is Wisdom found? what happy coast
    The glory of this lovely birth can boast?
13. No mortal her unbounded value knows,
    Her value in no mortal climate grows:
14. The great abyss through her dark regions cries,
    " Not in my rich domains the purchase lies;"
15. Ocean, " nor yet in mine." Not golden sand,
    Nor silver ingots the exchange command:
                                                    16. Not

Ver. 12—14. *But where shall wisdom be found*, &c.] Having largely set forth the invention and powers of man in *natural things*, he now displays, with rhetorical amplification, man's utter inability to dive into the counsels of providence. That is what he meaneth here by *wisdom* and *understanding:* for he says, it is not attainable by man[l], and that it is to be found in God alone[k]. In this sense also Eliphaz had used the word *wisdom: Hast thou heard the secret of God? and dost thou restrain wisdom to thyself?*

Ver. 13. *Man knoweth not the price thereof*] that is, He hath no ability or means to obtain *this wisdom.*

neither is it found in the land of the living] This assertion clearly proves, that by *this wisdom* Job did not mean *religion*; as some interpreters have understood him.

Ver. 14. *The depth saith—the sea saith*, &c.] *The depth* being here distinguished from the *sea*, by the former surely is meant *the great abyss*, the subterraneous waters: by the latter, *the ocean*. The intention of this grand prosopopeia seems to be, that were man master of the most abstruse secrets of nature, and possest of its most hidden wealth, he would be never the nearer to understanding the reasons of the divine dispensations.

Ver. 15—19. *It cannot be gotten for gold*, &c.] It appears probable to me,
                                                                        that

---

[l] Ver. 13.   [k] Ver. 23—26. Compare Prov. viii. 22, &c.

16. Not Ophir's wealth, nor the clear sapphire's sky,
   Nor diamond's lightning with her beam may vie:
17. Or chryſtal vaſe, with golden circles bound,
   Or gold that heaves with ſculptur'd life around.

18. Beryls

that by a noble figure *the abyſs* and *the ocean* are repreſented ſtill ſpeaking; and declaring that all the riches in the depths of the earth and in the bottom of the ſea are inſufficient to purchaſe this *wiſdom*.

Ver. 15. *It cannot be gotten for gold*, &c.] The profuſion of brilliant and coſtly things here ſpread before us highly entertains the imagination. At the ſame time it ſets off, with glorious eloquence, the ineſtimable worth of the ſublime knowledge here intended; and the utter unattainableneſs of it by man.

Ver. 16. *the gold of Ophir*] See the note on chap. xxii. 24.

the precious onyx] It was obſerved on ver. 1. that Arabia Felix, now called Yaman, had formerly its golden mines. It ſtill boaſteth its gems. We are aſſured by an eye-witneſs [l], that precious ſtones for rings and bracelets are brought thence in great quantities, to the annual fair held at Mecca during the laſt ten or twelve days of the ſtay of the pilgrims there.

It is doubtful what gem is meant by that which we tranſlate *the onyx* [m]: The epithet *precious*, as Schultens remarks, gives a diſtinction to it; which the *onyx*, a ſort of agate [n], does not merit. The Chaldee interpreter renders it *beryls*. The beryl of the ancients was a tranſparent gem of a ſea-green colour [o].

the ſapphire] The *ſapphire* is of a beautiful ſky-blue. Some will have the hebrew word to ſignify the *ruby*; others the *carbuncle*, which is a ſtone of the ruby kind, very rare, and of a rich glowing blood-colour [p].

Ver. 17. *The gold and the cryſtal*] that is, *a cryſtal vaſe* ornamented with gold.
Schultens.

---

[l] Pitts in his *Account of the Mahometans*, p. 142.

[m] שהם

[n] Chambers' *Dictionary*.   [o] Ibid.   [p] Ibid.

18. Beryls and orient pearls no more be nam'd,
19. The blush of rubies, or the topaz fam'd
Arabia's verdant pride: nor crowns be laid
In loaded scale, with wisdom to be weigh'd.
20. Where

Schultens. But Dr. Shaw [q] thinks the *diamond* best answers the meaning of our author's term [r]. It may however be questioned, whether that gem was the produce of any country that Job was acquainted with.

jewels of fine gold] These must surely be some ornaments or vessels of gold that were of high value for the workmanship as well as for the materials.

Ver. 18. *coral—pearls*] The bottom of the red sea is in some parts covered with groves of *coral* [s]. But this is no gem. It is a marine plant. *Pearls* indeed are valued in the east beyond all other jewels [t]. It must however be owned that the signification of the hebrew words, translated *coral* and *pearls*, is altogether uncertain.

rubies] Either these or some other precious stone of a red colour must be intended. For the prophet compares the florid complexion of the Jewish Nazarites to this gem [u].

Ver. 19. *The Topaz of Ethiopia*] The *topaz of Cush*. *Cush*, according to Bochart [w], was that part of Arabia which bordered on the Red Sea, and was inhabited by the Saracen Arabs. *Topaz* was an adjacent island in the same sea, and gave name to the precious stone which grew there. Pliny says, it is of a singular green colour, and, when first found, was preferred to all other gems [x]. Chambers [y] tells us, the *topaz* is the third in order after the diamond ; and that it is transparent, and its colour a beautiful yellow, or gold colour. But we
may

---

[q] *Travels,* p. 54. 4to.
[r] זכוכית *lustre, purity.*
[s] *Arabian Proverbs,* cent. i. 15. n.
[u] *Lament.* iv. 7.
[x] *Nat. Hist.* xxxvii. 8.
[y] *Dictionary.*

[t] Dr. Shaw's *Travels.*
[w] *Geograph. Sacra.*

20. Where, then, is wisdom found? what happy coast
The glory of this lovely birth can boast?
21. Hid from all living, far beyond the height
Of strongest pinion in its loftiest flight.
22. Death and Destruction call, " learn somewhat here,
" The voice of wisdom vibrates in our ear:"

23. Herself may reconcile this seeming contradiction between the ancient and modern writer by observing, that there were two kinds of topaz: In the one [z], the prevailing colour was green; in the other [a], gold.

Ver. 21. *It is hid from all living*] See ver. 13.

and kept close from the fowls of the air] The residence of *wisdom* is beyond the flight of the swiftest and strongest birds. This is saying in a poetical, and perhaps a proverbial, manner, that this sublime wisdom is not to be found within the limits of our world. If any thing more is intended, it may be, as Crinsoz understands it, that the most exalted geniuses, the Astronomers for instance, are not able to reach this wisdom.

Ver. 22. *Destruction and death say, we,* &c.] Let it be remembered that he had before said, this wisdom *is not found in the land of the living*; and again, *it is hid from the eyes of all living.* Let it also be observed, that the phrase, *we have heard the fame thereof with our ears*, imports *imperfect* knowledge; like the evidence of report compared with the evidence of sight [b]. Hence the natural meaning of this verse seems to be, that the dead know more of this wisdom than the living: yet even their knowledge of it is imperfect. A future state, by its exact retributions, will clear some of the present difficulties in the ways of Providence [c]. But comprehension of the whole plan is the prerogative

---

[z] Called *prasoides.*
[a] *Chrysopteros.* Pliny, ubi supra.
[b] See chap. xlii. 5.
[c] " Wait the great teacher death, and God adore. *Essay on Man.*

CHAP. XXVIII.   THE BOOK OF JOB.   231

23. Herself acceſſible to God alone,
    To him her birth-place and her ways are known:
24. Earth's utmoſt bounds lay ſpread before his view,
    He with a glance look'd all creation through:
25. The wild winds balanc'd, weigh'd the ſwelling ſeas,
26. And gave the vapour and the cloud decrees;
    When rains ſhould fall, when ruddy lightning fly,
    And the big thunder roar along the ſky:
27. He ſaw the whole, he number'd every part,
    The finiſh'd ſyſtem of Almighty art,

Approv'd, rogative of him alone who formed it, as the following verſes remark. If, with the judicious Schultens, we ſuppoſe *Death* and *Deſtruction* to utter them, it will greatly add to the ſolemnity of the inſtruction.

Ver. 23—24. *God underſtandeth*, &c.] God alone ſees at one view the whole extent of the univerſe. He created it one perfect whole, and formed and placed every part in exact fitneſs to the deſign of the whole. He alone therefore is capable of knowing the uſe of every portion and appearance of nature, and the reaſon of every meaſure in his *moral* adminiſtration.

Ver. 25, 26. *To make the weight for the winds*, &c.] Theſe are ſelected as ſpecimens of the admirable wiſdom with which all the members of the univerſe were framed. The winds, the maſs of waters, the rain, the lightning and thunder, are endowed with their ſeveral qualities, and directed by diſtinct laws in moſt accurate fitneſs to the deſigns of providence in our world, and in regard to the whole creation.

Ver. 27. *Then did he ſee it*, &c.] (1) *Then did he ſee it*, viz. wiſdom. When he created the world, the entire plan lay in clear view before him. (2) *he declared it;* or rather, *he calculated it.* He took an exact ſurvey of all the parts of the plan; or of the various ſyſtems which preſented themſelves to his mind. (3) He prepared it; or, *he eſtabliſhed it.* He fixed his plan, by chooſing that ſyſtem which was upon the whole the wiſeſt and beſt.

Approv'd, and ſtabliſh'd his imperial plan:
28. Then ſpoke this leſſon to his creature man;
" Thy mighty Maker fear, from evil flee,
" This, Adam, is the wiſdom left to thee."

CHAP.
XXIX.
1, 2,   O happy months, and happy days, long fled!
When God, the guardian of my honour'd head,
3. Shin'd

Of ſyſtems poſſible, if 'tis confeſt
That Wiſdom infinite muſt form the beſt.

(4) *Yea, and ſearched it out*; rather, *for he had thoroughly ſearched it out.* He determined upon the preſent ſyſtem from unerring knowledge that it was the beſt.

Ver. 28. *unto man he ſaid*, &c.] Either to Adam by a vocal revelation; or to him and all his poſterity by the clear dictate of right reaſon.

that is wiſdom] Wiſdom is the knowledge and choice of the beſt ends and moſt fitting means. The beſt end that man can chuſe is his own everlaſting happineſs: the only means of obtaining it is the practice of his duty. This therefore is the wiſdom proper for man.

C H A P. XXIX.

The connection with the foregoing chapter is eaſy. His own caſe was an inſtance of thoſe incomprehenſible ways of providence of which he had been diſcourſing. He now gives an intire view of it[d], as a kind of *Epinicium*, or ſong of victory, as Schultens ſpeaks. His aim is to ſhew, that all his pleadings and complaints were juſtly founded. In the preſent chapter he ſets forth his former felicity in the ſingular favour of God to his perſon, family, and fortunes; and in the veneration paid to him by his tribe for the wiſdom of his counſels and

---

[d] Chap. xxix. xxx. xxxi.

3. Shin'd on his favourite with diftinguifh'd rays,
Difpell'd all darknefs, and illum'd my ways:
4. In autumn of my glory, when the Pow'r
Trufted his counfels to my hallow'd bow'r:

5. While and the juftice of his adminiftration. To which he adds the pleafing hope he had entertained of the permanence of all that happinefs, in reward of his virtue.

Ver. 3. *When his candle*, &c.] The extraordinary favour of God, and its effects, namely, conftant cheerfulnefs, profperity of condition, and luftre of character, feem to be all comprehended in thefe beautiful metaphors. The former, *his candle*, or rather *his lamp*, is probably an allufion to the lamps which hung from the ceiling of the banqueting rooms of the wealthy Arabs [e]. The latter, *by his light I walked through darknefs*, refers, it is likely, to the fires, or other lights, which were carried before the caravans in their night travels through the deferts [f].

darknefs] times of general calamity; war, famine, peftilence. The divine protection and guidance were his conftant fecurity and delightful confidence in fuch feafons of danger.

Ver. 4. *in the days of my youth*] *In my autumnal days* [g]; that is, as Mr. Heath freely turns it, *in the days of my profperity*. Autumn is a pleafant feafon in thofe hot climates: the heats are then abated, the rains fall, and the grapes and other fruits are in perfection.

When the fecret of God [h], &c.] Among men, communication of one's fecrets is

---

[e] See the note on chap. xviii. 6.

[f] See Pitts' *Account of the Mahometans*, p. 150.

[g] בימי החרפי *in the days of my autumn*. In the Arabic verfion of the Pfalms (lxxiii. 18) חרף ftands oppofed to *fummer*, and denotes *the winter half year*. It alfo fignifies, in that language, *the autumnal feafon*. (See Schultens, and Caftell. *Lex*.) The author of an *Effay towards a new Tranflation of the Bible* remarks, that this word fhould be rendered *the autumn* in Gen. viii. 22. it being the time of plowing, Prov. xx. 4. p. 187.

[h] *Quum mea tabernaculo familiaris effet Deus. Caftalio.*

5. While yet each morn his visits he renew'd,
   While yet, around me, I my children view'd;
6. While plenty stream'd in rivers through my soil,
   With milk my vallies, and my rocks with oil.

7. O

is a mark of the highest confidence and most intimate friendship. Accordingly the Psalmist expresseth the friendship of God to all good men by saying, *The secret of the Lord is with them that fear him, and he will shew them his covenant* [i]. The meaning is, I suppose, he will lead them into a clear knowledge of his will and of his gracious designs in favour of piety and virtue. A prophet enjoyed this divine intercourse in a superior degree: *shall I hide from Abraham that thing which I do* [k]? I incline to think, that Job was thus distinguished, and had the honour of being a divinely commissioned minister of religion to his tribe. Compare chap. vi. 10.

upon my tabernacle] *in*, or *within* [l], *my tabernacle*.

Ver. 5. *When my children* [m], &c.] He fetched a deep sigh, I doubt not, on mentioning this happy circumstance of his once happy condition. The sentiment is exquisitely tender. He could not bear to dwell upon it.

were about me] he probably refers to their sitting at table with him in a circle, after the eastern mode taken notice of by Shaw and Le Bruyn [n].

Ver. 6. *When I washed my steps*, &c.] Olive groves and abundance of cattle made the principal wealth of the Arabs. The best olives grow upon the rocky mountains.

---

[i] Psal. xxv. 14.

[k] Gen. xviii. 17. Compare John xv. 15. James ii. 23.

[l] עלי *in*, or *within*. The preposition על is equivalent to ב *in*, Exod. xxix. 3. Exod. xxxiii. 21. *upon a rock*, rather *within the rock*. See ver. 22. Nold. p. 698.

[m] נערי *my young people*, i. e. my children: so it signifies in chap. i. 19. *It* (the house) *fell upon the young men*; rather *the young people*, his sons and his daughters, ver. 18. Castalio there renders it *juvenes*. It is strange that he renders it here *famuli mei*, my *domestics*.

[n] See *Observations on divers Passages of Scripture*, &c. p. 189.

CHAP. XXIX.   THE BOOK OF JOB.

7.   O high enjoyment! on the folemn day,
When, with a princely train, I took my way
To the full forum, through the hailing ftreet,
And in the fenate fill'd a fovereign feat.

8. The

mountains [o]. Hence thefe bold figures, whereby the Arabs expreffed a condition of uncommon felicity. A Roman Poet would have conveyed the fame thought in the language of Perfius;

———quicquid calcaverit hic, rofa fiat [p].

Let rofes fpring beneath his feet. It is a proverbial expreffion, fays the commentator, for the higheft felicity. I am indebted to Schultens for great part of this note.

Ver. 7—17. *When I went,* &c.] Having defcribed his domeftic happinefs, he proceeds to reprefent the honours paid him in public life. This reprefentation is judicioufly intermingled with an account of his impartial and intrepid adminiftration of juftice; which is a noble anfwer to the particular accufation laid againft him by Eliphaz, chap. xxii. 6—9.

Ver. 7. *to the gate*] the court of juftice. But the Septuagint turns it, *in the morning*[q], Among the ancients the public affemblies for adminiftring juftice and tranfacting other public bufinefs were held early in the morning. Thus in the Odyffey, Telemachus goes to council at that time of the day.

through the city'] Mr. Heath turns it, *nigh the place of public refort*, the forum, or market-place.

in the ftreet] It fhould feem that thefe public affemblies were held in the open air, and in the wideft and moft frequented part of the city. compare Prov. viii. 3. Ruth iv. 1, &c.

---

[o] Deut. xxxii. 13, 14.

[p] Sat. ii. 38.

[q] שער *the gate*; LXX. ο;θρ;ος *early in the morning.* It was שחר in their copy.

[r] קרת *the place of public refort:* for קרא is *to call together*; and קרה fignifies *occurrere* to meet.

8. The youths, abash'd, retir'd; and, bent with age,
In dumb respect up rose the hoary sage:
9, 10. The ranks of pow'r stood all attention round,
And every tongue in every mouth was bound,
Princes and peers; all waiting to receive
The sentence wisdom in my voice should give:
11. Rapture in every ear the sentence rais'd,
And every eye with look applauding gaz'd:
12. The fatherless and friendless and distrest
13. Call'd me their saviour, while my name they bless'd:
Their blessings crown'd me; for I heal'd their wrongs,
And tun'd the widow's heart to grateful songs.
14. My robe was justice, justice my tiar;
This was my majesty, renown'd afar:
15. The feeble found in me a pow'rful stay,
16. The poor a father, and the blind man day:
The stranger's friend, I weigh'd his slighted cause;
17. Broke rapine's teeth, and snatch'd him from its jaws.
18. Thence

Ver. 14. *my judgement was as a robe*, &c.] His decisions in the court of justice procured him all the honour given to a king, without the dress and title. This beautiful manner of speaking is still preserved among the Arabs: One of their proverbs is, *Knowledge is a diadem to a young person, and a chain of gold about his neck* [1].

Ver. 15. *I was eyes to the blind*, &c.] When the cause of an ignorant and friendless person came before him, he assisted him, by his counsel and protection, to make his defence.

[1] Erpenii *Prov. Arab. cent.* ii. 22.

18. Thence I too fondly argu'd; here shall rest
My dying head, in this my lofty nest:
But countless as the sands my days shall run,
Without a cloud to their last setting sun.

19. The noble palm, whose laden boughs on high
Suck the sweet moisture of the midnight sky,
Whose op'ning roots imbibe the cryſtal rill,
Fearless of droughts, shall be my emblem still:

20. Still

Ver. 18—25. *Then I ſaid,* &c." At the eighteenth verſe begins a third diviſion of this chapter, and reaches to the end. Here he expreſſeth his hope of the continuation of his proſperity throughout a long life. I think, the whole paragraph is to be underſtood in the future time, not in the paſt. It contains the ſubject matter of his hope¹.

Ver. 18. *I ſhall die in my neſt*] Schultens remarks that the image is taken from the eagle who buildeth her neſt on the ſummit of a rock. Security is the point of reſemblance intended ᵘ. Longevity is expreſſed in the following clauſe, *I ſhall multiply,* &c.

Ver. 19. *My root was ſpread,* &c.] *my root* ſhall be *ſpread,* &c. *the dew* ſhall *lay* ʷ, &c. A tree planted by the rivers of waters, and bringing forth its fruit in its ſeaſon, is a beautiful emblem of proſperity. See Pſalm i. 3. The dews, which fall in the night very plentifully, contribute greatly to the nouriſhment of vegetables in thoſe hot climates; where they have ſcarce any rain all ſummer long ˣ.

---

¹ As Schultens obſerveth.
ᵘ See Numb. xxiv. 21. Obad. ver. 4. Job xxxix. 27, 28. Horace uſeth this metaphor, Quicunque celſæ nidum Acherontiæ, ſc. tenent.   Od. iii. 4.
ʷ ילין *ſhall lay all night.*
ˣ Shaw's *Travels,* p. 439, &c. 4to.

20. Still fresh in lustre shall my glory grow,
   And new in vigour be my conq'ring bow.
21. My eloquence shall flow, by all desir'd,
   Be heard with sacred silence, and admir'd:
22. Be heard without reply, and joy infuse
   Like heav'n descending in nutritious dews:
23. Crowds shall be eager to devour the strain,
   As the chapt soil to drink autumnal rain.

24. My

Ver. 20. *My glory was fresh*, &c.] *My glory shall be fresh* ˣ, &c. *and my bow shall be renewed*, &c. He promised himself a perpetuity of power, sufficient to subdue all who resisted his authority or invaded his possessions. A flourishing ever-green was the image in the foregoing verse, and is carried on in the first member of this verse; *my glory shall be fresh in me*. The warlike image in the second sentence, *my bow*, &c. is equally happy: It denotes increasing power and conquest. The eastern writers are fond of this image, as Schultens has shewn.

Ver. 21. *gave ear—waited—kept silence*, &c.] *will give ear—will wait—will keep silence*, &cʸ.

He refers to the attention with which he was wont always to be heard, when he spoke in the public assembly ver. 9, 10. He flattered himself that this veneration of his wisdom and eloquence would continue; and therewith his public influence and utility.

Ver. 22. *After my words they spake not*, &c.] *They will not speak again* ᶻ—*my speech shall drop* ᵃ *upon them*.

Ver. 23. *as for the rain—the latter rain*] *They will wait*, &c. *and will open*, &c.

ˣ חדש *shall be fresh*. This verb is here in the preter tense: but as it lies between two futures, ילין *shall lay*, and תחליף *shall be renewed*, it is to be construed, according to a known rule of the hebrew grammar, in the future tense.

ʸ וידמו, ויחלו, שמעו

ᶻ ישנו   ᵃ תטף

CHAP. XXIX.   THE BOOK OF JOB.   239

24. My fmile fhall tranfport raife, but check with awe
Left the bright funfhine fhould in clouds withdraw.
25. Their guide in council, and in war their chief,
In wants their father, and their hope in grief,

I'll

&c. In the foregoing verfe, the foft infinuating force of his political and religious inftruction was compared to the dropping dew [b]. Here the copioufnefs of his eloquence is likened to the abundant rains which fall in autumn in thofe countries [c]; and the high acceptablenefs of it, to the avidity with which the earth, burnt up by the fummer's drought, devours thofe rains. The alteration which they produce in the withered fields is fo aftonifhingly great, that Dr. Ruffel fcruples not to call it *a refurrection of vegetable nature*.

The fame ingenious Author informs us, that the firft rains fall about the middle of September; the fecond, or latter, about twenty or thirty days after. The firft are inconfiderable, the latter fall in great abundance.

They opened their mouth wide] This is a picturefque defcription of eager attention.

Ver. 24. *If I laughed*, &c.] *If I fhall laugh*, &c [d]. His authority and character were fo much reverenced, and his favour, which he calls *the light of his countenance*, was fo highly valued, that even familiarity did not leffen their veneration. His very fmiles were received with awe.

The light of my countenance they did not, &c.] *The light of my countenance they will not caufe to fall* [e]. In the hebrew idiom, *to lift up the light of the countenance* fignifies to fhew favour [f]. The oppofite phrafe therefore, *the falling of the light*, &c. denotes difpleafure; and *to caufe it to fall* muft mean, to provoke difpleafure by unbecoming behaviour.

Ver. 25. *I chofe out their way*, &c.] *I fhall choofe—I fhall dwell*, &c. He had flattered

---

[b] See Deut. xxxii. 2.
[c] Dr. Ruffel's Natural Hiftory of Aleppo, p. 14, 148, 154, 158, 159, 161.
[d] אשחק
[e] יפלון
[f] Compare Prov. xvi. 15.

I'll rule my tribe; and iffue my commands,
Great as a king amidft his martial bands.

CHAP. XXX.
Ver. 1. Now I'm become the game of boys: too bafe
I held their fathers with my dogs to place,

In
flattered himfelf that he fhould continue to be, what he once was; the director of their public councils, the commander in chief of their military expeditions, and a fupport to them in all diftreffing emergencies.

The phrafe of *choofing out their way* denotes fupremacy both in the ftate and in the affairs of religion. Exod. xviii. 20.

The next fentence reprefents him encamped with his fubjects, on fome military expedition; with the authority of a royal general: *I fhall pitch* ^g *my tent as a king in the army.*

The laft claufe, *as one that comforteth the mourners*, may mean, animating his troops when they were difpirited: or, in a larger and more noble fenfe, his being the father of his people; ever touched with their diftreffes, and ready to exert his utmoft ability for their relief.

CHAP. XXX.

This chapter is the contraft of the foregoing. It is a moving reprefentation of the miferable difappointment of his *hope* ^h, the infults he received, the deplorable condition of his body, and the defpairing ftate of his mind. The whole is in a ftrain highly querulous; and the paffions expreffed in it are grief and indignation.

Ver. 1—14. *But now*, &c.] This fection is, I apprehend, a ftrong and fpirited defcription of thofe villanous Arabs, who, when Job was in his profperity, had

---

^g אשכין, literally *I fhall pitch my tent*; as Mr. Heath renders it.
^h Chap. xxix. 18—25.

CHAP. XXX.   THE BOOK OF JOB.

In midnight fentry o'er my fleeping fold,
2. A flothful crew, in profligacy old.
3. The howling defert was of late their haunt,
   Where, ftung with hunger, and with famine gaunt,
4. They brows'd the bitter weeds, and hard befted
   On broom and berries of the foreft fed:
                                                5. Outlaws

had felt the feverity of his juftice; and fled into the lurking places of the defert. Upon the lofs of his authority, thefe mifcreants came out of their dens, to revenge themfelves upon him by the moft fcurrilous abufe.

In drawing their character, he infifteth much on the mifery of their habitation and way of living, as circumftances very expreffive of the turpitude and barbarity of their manners.

Ver. 1. *Younger*, &c.] The vaft refpect paid to their elders by the eafterns, quickened their fenfibility of contempt from their juniors.

Ver. 2. *Yea whereto*, &c.] The context obliges us to underftand *a reproach* to be here intended: and the *fathers* of thefe wretches being the neareft antecedent, the reproach, is probably defigned for them. He reprefents them as an idle good for nothing crew, who were grown old in profligacy: *in whom old age*[i] *is profligate*[k]. So I think the tranflation ought to be.

Ver. 3. *For want*, &c.] The defcription returns to the hopeful offspring of fuch worthy parents. Here, and in the following verfe, it reprefents the wretched fuftenance which they had in the defert where they fkulked.

For

---

[i] כלח *old age*, rendered chap v. 26. *in a full age*. See the note there.

[k] אבד *is profligate*. It feems to anfwer to the latin *perditus abandoned*. The hebrew אבד has the fignification of *perdo to corrupt* in Ecclef. vii. 7. *a gift deftroyeth (corrupteth) the heart*.

THE BOOK OF JOB. CHAP. XXX.

5. Outlaws and thieves, with outcry chas'd from men
6. To flooded vales and the dark mountain den:
7. To

For want and extreme ˡ famine, they lately ᵐ gnawed ⁿ the wilderness ᵒ waste and desolate.

He mentions their beggarly condition, as a heightening of the indignities offered to a person of his rank and character by such rabble.

Ver. 4. *Who cut up mallows*, &c.] *who cut up the brackish herbs among the shrubs*, that grow in the wild heath. Those deserts abound with saline particles which give a saltish bitter taste to the few hardy plants that live there. The original word denotes either in general all such brackish vegetables; or some particular plant of the desert that camels are exceeding fond of. See Schultens, and Pocock's Specimen, p. 79.

and juniper roots] The hebrew word, translated *juniper*, is *retem*; and in Arabic *ratam*, which is thought to be the same with the Spanish *retama broom*; and the name is supposed to have been imported into Spain by the Saracens when they conquered that country. It is sometimes high and large enough to afford shade; and might therefore be the plant under which Elijah rested himself and slept

---

ˡ גלמוד It is used in Arabic of *a bare rock* on which nothing grows, as Schultens shews in his note on chap. iii. 7. It seems to be here an epithet of *famine*, and to express the severity thereof.

ᵐ אמש *heri yesterday, the other day*.

ⁿ הערקים *they gnawed*. This verb signifies in Arabic *to gnaw*, a bone for instance (Castell.) In Chaldee *to flee*. But the former sense seems most eligible in this place.

ᵒ ציה *the wilderness*. The hebrew word signifies *drought*, or *a dry place*; it is a denomination of the desert from the scarcity of fresh water there. The two other terms ומשאה ושואה, *waste and desolate*, denote, that hardly any thing grows there. But I apprehend that the danger from wild beasts is also implied in those epithets: for they signify *tumultuous uproar*, that is, the confused yellings of those savage natives of the desert. The noun תשואה is rendered *noise* (it should be *noises*) in chap. xxxvi. 29. it there means claps of thunder. The verb שאו in Isaiah xvii. 13. is translated *to rush*. It there means the tumultuous uproar of the sea in a storm, and of torrents rushing down the rocks. Compare ver. 12.

7. To shelt'ring thorns in groaning crowds they press,
And huddled in vile heaps the thicket bless:

8. A

slept in the wilderness, 1 Kings xix. 4, 5 ᵖ. As to *the juniper tree*, Gerard in his Herbal says, on the authority of Dioscorides, it comes up for the most part in rough places and near to the sea. But whether it is found in the Arabian deserts, I know not.

Ver. 5. *They were driven forth*, &c.] They were cast out of civil society ᵠ, as pests not to be endured: and whenever they were discovered lurking about towns, an outcry was raised against them as against the pilfering Arabs of the desert; with whom, it is likely, they herded.

Ver. 6, 7. *To dwell*, &c.] To paint their infamous manners still more strongly, he returns to the description of the dismal places to which they were banished, and the hardships they suffered there.

Ver. 6. *in the clefts of the vallies*] In the hollows gulled by the winter torrents.

in caves of the earth and the rocks] Their habitation was sometimes under ground; at other times in the caverns of the mountains: There is a large cavern in mount Sinai ʳ. The rocks of Arabia Petræa abound with caves ˢ. At this day, the Arabs who dwell in the mountains of that country are a bad people, the worst of all the Arabs; as Dr. Pococke informs us ᵗ.

Ver. 7. *They brayed*] like wild asses pinched with hunger. This metaphor expresseth forcibly their distress for want of food. See chap. vi. 5.

among

ᵖ See Schultens, and Mr. Merrick's *Annotations on Psalm* cxx. 4.

ᵠ בְּנֵי בְלִי *from among men*. In the Syriac Testament Acts ii. 44. גוֹא denotes *the community*.

ʳ Exod. xxxiii. 22.

ˢ Michaelis *in Prælect*. p. 28. 8vo.

ᵗ *Travels into Egypt*, &c. vol. i. p. 137.

8. A herd of varlets, vagrants, without name,
Flay'd by the lash, the spurious brood of shame.
9. Now their lewd doggrel jests my name profane,
10. They stare aloof as though my breath were bane:
11. They

among the nettles" *they were gathered together* "] It is not known what species of plant is meant by the word translated *nettles*. It was, probably, some wild shrub of the heath*, which they thronged to for a sorry sustenance. Thickets of shrubs are sometimes met with in these deserts. See *Della Valle's voyage to the East Indies*, p. 262. fol.

Ver. 8. *children of fools*, &c.] He sums up their character in a few words; *flagitious*, *base-born*, *they were scourged out of the land*.

Ver. 9—14. *And now*, &c.] Having concluded their character, he proceeds to represent their contumelious usage of him. His indignation kindles as he goes along; and as that increases, his expressions grow more vehement and rise to lofty metaphors. But when were these insults offered to him? From the time that he was smitten with his disease, he was surely confined to his house. This treatment therefore must have happened to him before that time, yet after his overthrow. Whence it seems probable, there was a considerable

---

" חרול The Vulgate renders it *sentis a brier*. In Syriac חורלא signifies a kind of *small vetch*. *Castell*.

* יספחו this word signifies *to associate with*, Isaiah xiv. 1. *They shall cleave to (associate with) the house of Jacob*.

* The LXX. turn it φρυγανα αγρια *wild shrubs*.

y בני נבל Castellio renders it *infani fools*. But נבל is used of an *incestuous* person. II Sam. xiii. 13. of a *blasphemer* Psal. lxxiv. 22. and of a *malefactor* worthy of death II Sam. iii. 33. It must therefore mean here *very profligate fellows*.

z בני בלי שם Persons of obscure parentage, owned by no family, inrolled in no tribe, a spurious brood. Castellio translates it *ingenii*.

a נכאו מן הארץ turned by Schultens *flagellati sunt e terra*; by Mr. Heath, *they were whipped out of the country*. The verb נכה signifies in Exod. v. 16. to *beat* slaves with an instrument of correction. Castellio's version is *mortalium infimi* the meanest of mankind.

11. They hoot, they spit, for God hath cast me down;
Hence their contempt of my once dreaded frown.

12, 13. The derable interval between his first calamities and that last affliction; during which interval he met with these affronts, whenever he appeared abroad; as Cocceius, if I remember right, has observed.

Ver. 9. *now am I their song,* &c.] This and what follows to the end of ver. 14. is an amplification of the *derision* mentioned in ver. 1. here he tells us, they made him their *musical instrument* [a] to play upon and divert themselves; and their *by-word* [b], the subject of their lewd jests.

Ver. 10. *They abhor me, they flee far from me*] These expressions, doubtless, are significant of the highest aversion and contempt. But I cannot think, with Michaelis, that they refer to his *leprosy:* because it is not likely he would or could appear in public with such a disease as his was [c].

Ver. 11. *because he hath loosed my cord* [d], &c.] that is, God hath destroyed my authority by the afflictions he hath laid upon me. Therefore these profligates bid me defiance, and shew the utmost contempt of me in my presence. The phrase *he hath loosed my cord* seems equivalent to that other in chap. xii. 18. *he looseth the bond of kings.*

they have let loose the bridle before me] Or as the Greek version turns it, *they have cast away the bridle of my countenance* [e]. My very look was wont to curb their licentiousness; but they have now cast off all respect, and insult me to my face.

---

[a] נגינתם LXX. κιθάρα αυτων *their harp.* It is allowed to mean *a stringed instrument,* in the titles of Psal. iv. and vi. Compare Lament. iii. 14, 63.

[b] מלה LXX. θρυλλημα *proverbium vulgi.*

[c] See the notes on chap ii. 7. vii. 5.

[d] יתרו, but in the marginal correction יתרי; as also the Chaldee interpreter read, for he translates it *my chain.* The synonimous words כותרה *a band* and עבת *a cord* denote political authority in Psal. ii. 3.

[e] Χαλινον τε προςωπου μου εξαπεςειλαν.

רסן מפני *the bridle of my face* is the same construction as חרב פיהם *the sword of their mouth,* chap. v. 15.

12, 13. The spawn of vice start up, her shouting throng
Pelt me with sawcy malice of the tongue;
Besiege

Ver. 12. *the youth* '] Such as he mentions ver. 1. *they that are younger than I have in derision.* The insult they offered to him was reviling him, and giving him a kick when he chanced to be in their way; *they push away my feet.* Mr. Heath translates it, *they trip up my heels.*

they raise against me, &c.] In this sentence and throughout the two following verses he compares his situation, surrounded by these miscreants and overwhelmed with abuse, to that of a town which is besieged and stormed. Their *destroying troops* ⸺ *cast up* ᵇ *an high-way against me*; alluding to the throwing up of intrenchments and mounts by the besiegers, in order to engage the enemy on their walls, and more effectually to annoy the town with arrows and engines of war.

Ver. 13. *They mar my path*] *They destroyed my path.* These expressions seem to denote, in their literal meaning, the destruction of the fine walks, gardens, and vineyards about a town, by the besiegers as they make their approaches. In the metaphor, the words may import the havock these villains made in his character and dignity, by their opprobrious scurrilities. Their hideous hootings are represented by the shouts and exultations of the besieging army, when they have made a wide breach in the walls; *they triumphed* ᶦ *in my calamity.* His being

---

ᶠ פרחח The learned Schultens hath shewn from the Arabian writers, that this word signifies a *bastard.* The phrase *on my right hand they rise up* denotes their reviling language. They abused his character with foul reproaches. Thus Psal. cix. 6. *Set thou a wicked man over him, and let a false accuser* (in the Hebrew, *Satan) stand at his right hand.*

ᵍ ארחות אידם *the troops of their destruction*, i. e. *their troops of destruction.* We meet with the like transposition of the pronoun affix in the Syriac Testament, Luke xvi. 2. רבת ביתותך *thy stewardship.* ארחות chap. vi. 19. *The troops of Tema.*

ʰ יסלו It signifies *to make a causeway:* the noun מסלה *a highway,* or *causeway,* is understood. Compare Isaiah lvii 14. with lxii. 10. When the word is used as a military term, it means the works which are cast up by a besieging army, Isaiah xxxvii. 33. Ezek. xvii. 17.

ᶦ ויעילו Mr. Heath's version of this word, *they triumph,* agrees with the Syriac; *They rejoiced* (הדו) *in that which hath befallen me.* That interpreter read להיתי, as it is in our printed

CHAP. XXX.   THE BOOK OF JOB.   247

Befiege me, and with fouleſt ſcorn invade
My walks of honour, now bereft of aid,
Like war; when, roaring through the burſten wall,
14. It rolls with fury o'er the city's fall.

15. O the diſtracting terrors of that hour!
When evil like a whirlwind broke my pow'r;

When

being deſtitute of protectors againſt this outrage, he compares to the diſtreſs of a city that is without aſſiſtance in its utmoſt extremity: There is *no helper againſt* [k] *them.* And in the next verſe, he reſembles their numbers, rage, and violence, to the fury with which the troops of the enemy pour through the breach, and ſpread devaſtation over the unhappy town: *They came on as to a wide breach* [l], *they rolled themſelves along as* [m] *deſolation.* See Mr. Heath.

Ver. 15—31. *Terrors are turned*, &c.] He now paſſeth to a general review of his other afflictions, which takes up the remainder of the chapter. The ſtyle here abates ſomewhat in its vehemence, and is more the language of deſpairing grief than of indignation. This fifteenth verſe may be tranſlated,

Terrors were turned [n] *upon me :*
They purſued my dignity [o] *as wind :*

And

---

printed hebrew text, *in eo quod accidit mihi*; which the marginal correction changes into להותי *in my calamity.* Mr. Heath remarks, that Schultens hath illuſtrated ויעילו in his commentary on Prov. x. 1. and ſhewn that it ſignifies *culmen ſcandere to be at the heighth of their wiſhes.*

[k] למו *againſt them.* The prepoſition ſignifies *againſt* in chap. viii. 4. *If thy children have ſinned againſt him* (לו). See alſo chap. xx. 27.

[l] פרץ It is uſed for *a breach in a wall* I Kings xi. 27. and Iſaiah xxx. 13.

[m] תהת It denotes ſimilitude in chap. xxxiv. 26. *He ſtriketh them as wicked men.*

[n] ההפך *were turned*, הרדף *they purſued.* The firſt of theſe verbs is ſingular and maſculine: the other is ſingular and feminine: yet the nominative to both verbs is בלהות plural and feminine. This is an Arabic idiom.

[o] נדבתי The Chaldee turns it רבנותי *my lordſhip.* נדיב is *a prince* chap. xxxiv. 18. Job has that title given him chap. xxi. 28. נדבה therefore means his *princely dignity.*

When my blifs vanifh'd—like a cloud of rain
Big with falfe promife to the thirfty plain.
16. And now my foul in forrow melts away,
Left unfuftain'd in ill's diftrefling day:

17. My

And my welfare p *paffed away as a cloud.*
The terrible change which had befallen him, is expreffed in general terms in the firft member of the period; *Terrors*, &c. the particular lofs of his authority in the fecond; and in the laft, the ruin of his whole felicity.

as wind] that is, *a ftormy wind* q as the chaldee turns it. That this is the image, is evident from ver. 22. *Thou lifteft me up to the wind: thou caufeft me to ride upon it*, &c.

as a cloud] tranfient duration is expreffed by the fame emblem chap. vii. 9. But here *difappointment* may be alfo included r: For Schultens obferves, that it is ufual with the Arabian writers to compare hopes and promifes which are not fulfilled, to a cloud which raifes expectation of a plentiful fhower but is prefently difperfed by the wind. If we lived in the parched country of Arabia, we fhould be more fenfible of the propriety and force of this comparifon.

Ver. 16. *upon me*] *in me* s; as in Pfalm xlii. 4. *When I remember thefe things, I pour out my foul in me* t. We fay in our language, at leaft in poetry, fuch a one *is diffolved* in grief. The foundation of the metaphor is, that in exceffive grief, as well as fear, the mind lofes all confiftency. The Arabians ftyle a fearful perfon, *one who hath a watry heart*; or whofe heart melts away like water u. Compare Exod. xv. 15.

---

p עֶרְיָ֫ *my welfare*. It denotes in Arabic, as Schultens fhews, all that amplitude of fortunes which conftitutes a compleat worldly felicity.

q רוּחַ Chald. עַלְעוּלָא *a furious ftorm*. See Pfal. xviii. 43. where again the Targum has נְפָצָא Compare Job iv 9. where a fudden and deftructive calamity is likened to the havock made by a ftorm of wind.

r Jude ver. 12. *Clouds without water.*

s עָלָי

t עָלַי *in me*. So our bible renders בְּעָלַי ver. 17. *my bones are pierced in me.*

u Pococke in *Carm. Tograi.* p. 101.

17. My pain ne'er slumbers, all night long I groan,
It racks each sinew, and corrodes each bone:
18. My mantle, by my strong disease possest,
Hath chang'd its form, and girds me like my vest;

19. I'm

Ver. 17. *My bones*, &c.] This and the next verse relate to his *disease*, which tortured him by night as well as by day without intermission. Some of the symptoms which he describes, resemble those of the rheumatism. They might however, I suppose, all be the effects of his ulcers. See the note on chap. ii. 7. vii. 5.

my sinews] The hebrew word translated *sinews* occurs no more. I rather think, it should be turned *my gnawing* pains ʷ.

Ver. 18. *By the great force*, &c.] He here giveth us a strong idea of the violence and nauseousness of his disease. Foul matter issued from his ulcers in such abundance, as to soak through his robe and change its form. It no longer appeared like a garment, much less like a loose upper garment; but stuck as close to him as his tunic.

> *By the great force* of my disease *my upper*
> *garment is changed* ˣ :
> *It bindeth me about as* ʸ *my tunic.*

The

ʷ ערקי *my gnawers.* It seems to be the active participle of the verb ערק which signifies to *gnaw* ver. 3. *gnawing the wilderness*, that is, the roots of wild plants. See the note there. Castellio seems to have understood ערקי to mean *my tormentors* : for his version is, *infestorque sine ulla intermissione.* The Chaldee renders it בעטן *they which gnash their teeth:* The Vulgate, *et qui* (dolores) *me comedunt, non dormiunt,* And *those* (pains) *which prey upon me, take no rest.*

ˣ יתחפש *is changed.* It signifies *to put off a garment,* also to alter one's form and appearance, *to disguise.* See I Sam. xxviii. 9. I Kings xx. 38. יתחפש is here used passively, as יתחמם *was warmed* chap. xxxi. 20. Grinsoz turns the first member of this verse, *Mes habits sont tous penetrez de la matiere qui sort en abondance de mes plaies.*

ʸ כפי *as.* The Chaldee interpreter considered פי as expletive, אנב כתוני *secundum tunicam meam after the manner of my tunic.* Our bible translation renders it *according to* in Exod. xvi. 21. *according as* in Malachi ii. 9.

19. I'm held impure, as one bemir'd all o'er;
The public fcorn, like fweepings of the floor.
20. To thee my fervent fupplications cry,
Deaf is thy ear, and pitilefs thine eye.
21. Thou

The coat, or tunic, was a clofe-bodied frock. The *garment,* being here diftinguifhed from that, muft mean the *byke,* or loofe gown, which was worn over the tunic[z].

Ver. 19. *He hath caft me,* &c.] Here he complains of God, whom he mentions abruptly as in other places. See chap. xvii. 4. xxiii. 3. The complaint is, that the groffeft turpitude was thrown on his character, by means of his afflictions. He was held in abomination: He appeared to men as morally foul, as one appears foul in a literal fenfe who hath been rolled in mud; and as contemptible as the dirt of the ftreets and the fweepings of the hearth. This infamy lay heavy on his mind. Even his hope in the future judgement could not make him eafy to leave the world with the horrid character of a wicked wretch accurfed of God. He had often, therefore, and importunately begged of God to bring him to a trial before he died, but without effect; as he complains in the next verfe.

into the mire] He had reprefented the odium which his calamities had brought upon him, by the fame image and in the fame complaining way chap. ix. 31. *Yet haft thou plunged me in a ditch, fo that mine own clothes abhor me.*

like duft and afhes] This feems to be a proverbial expreffion for *vilenefs* and *contemptiblenefs.* Gen. xviii. 27.

Ver. 20—31. *I cry unto thee,* &c.] He now turns directly to God, whom he addreffeth on the fubject of his afflictions in very moving terms, to the end of the thirty-firft verfe.

Ver. 20. *I ftand up,*] *ftanding* being the ufual pofture in prayer among the Hebrews, *to ftand,* or *ftand up,* is fometimes put for *to pray,* as Grotius remarks in his note on Matt. vi. 5. See Gen. xviii. 22. Jerem. xv. 1.

---

[z] See Shaw's *Travels,* p. 226. 4to.

21. Thou once waſt gracious, why ſo alter'd now,
 To me ſo alter'd, ſo ſevere thy brow?
 Cruel to me; me, ſo belov'd of late,
 Thy ſtrong hand cruſhes with its dreadful weight.
22. Rous'd by almighty force, a furious ſtorm,
 Commiſſion'd thy ſtern purpoſe to perform,
 Upcaught me, whirl'd me on its eddying guſt,
 Then daſh'd me down, and ſhatter'd me to duſt.

23. I

Ver. 21. *Thou art become cruel*[a], &c.] This language to God is crude and irreverent. His ſpirit is far from being humbled as yet. The embarraſſment of the poem is ſtill kept up, but is on the eve of a ſolution.

thou oppoſeſt thyſelf[b], &c.] The differing verſions of the hebrew word ſhew its ambiguity. Mr. Heath preferrs the ſenſe it bears in the Ethiopic, *thou haſt overwhelmed me*.

Ver. 22. *Thou lifteſt me up*, &c.] *Thou liftedſt me up, thou cauſedſt*, &c. *thou diſſolvedſt*, &c. He refers to his cruel overthrow; which he repreſents by the forcible image of being caught up high into the air, by a ſtorm of wind, then thrown down and daſhed in pieces on the ground.

my ſubſtance[c]] The hebrew word ſeems to import *all that he once was, and poſſeſſed*; his riches, his authority, his honours, his health, and his good name.

---

[a] אכזר *cruel*. LXX. ἀνηλεημόνως *unmercifully*. We turn it *fierce* in chap. xli. 10. (Heb. ver. 2) but *cruel* in Iſaiah xiii. 9. *Behold the day of the Lord cometh, cruel both with wrath and fierce anger*. See alſo Deut. xxxii. 33.

[b] תשטמי LXX. μὲ ἐμαστίγωσας *thou haſt ſcourged me*. Chaldee תגזמנני *thou threateneſt me*. Vulgate, *adverſaris mihi, thou oppoſeſt thyſelf againſt me*. Syriac, מטמתני *thou haſt bound me with fetters*.

[c] תושיה *quod fuit mihi*, from יש *fuit*. Cocceius.

23. I know, that, foon, thy unrelenting doom
 Will bring me to man's common home the tomb:
24. But, O aſſwage theſe pains, with gentle hand
 In peace difmifs me to that dreary land:

25. Was

Ver. 23. *For I know*, &c.] If I do not miſtake, he expreſſeth here a firm perfuaſion that his difeafe would prove mortal [d]: I think he begs in the next verſe for a mitigation of his tortures, and an eafy death: And in the 25th verſe he urges his petition for that mercy, by the compaſſion which he himſelf had always felt for the wretched.

Ver. 24. *Howbeit*, &c.] The firſt ſentence of this obſcure period lies very clear in the Chaldee, *Only let him not ſend his ſtroke*[e] *in hot anger*[f]; that is, let him not inflict upon me a hard death. The Pſalmiſt, praying to God not to afflict him in ſeverity, expreſſeth himſelf in ſimilar terms: Pſalm vi. 1. *O Lord rebuke me not in thine anger, neither chaſten me in thy hot diſpleaſure.*

The hebrew text in the ſecond ſentence appears to me depraved. But not one of the ancient verſions will aſſiſt us to reſtore it. Poſſibly the following tranſlation may give it a ſenſe which agrees with the context; *O that*[g] *there might*

---

[d] See chap. vi. 21. xvi. 22. (conſult the note) xvii. 1.

[e] The hebrew is ישלח לא ידו *let him not ſend the ſtroke*. In chap. xxiii. 2. ידו *a ſtroke*, denotes his ſufferings in general. Here the connection ſhews it to mean the *ſtroke of death*.

[f] ברתחא *in hot anger*. The hebrew is בעי for בבעי, the ellipſis of the prepoſition being very common in the poetical books. רתחא is a metaphor for *violent anger* from the *boiling of water* over the fire. See chap. xli. 31. Heb. ver. 23. בעי may alſo be a metaphor for *wrath*, taken from the fame thing: for it may be derived from בעה *to cauſe to boil*. Iſaiah lxiv. 2. Heb. ver. 1.

[g] אם *utinam!* The engliſh bible renders אם *O that* in 1 Chron. iv. 10. *O that thou wouldeſt bleſs me indeed*, &c.

25. Was I unfeeling of another's woe?
Did not my sorrow with the mourner's flow?
26. Bright were the visions, which my fancy fram'd,
Of heav'ns unclouded and of hopes unsham'd:
But foul adversity, with sudden night,
Blotted those lovely visions from my sight.
27. Since when, my tortures no remission find,
Fire in my veins, and tumult in my mind:
28. I mourn,

might be, in his destroying stroke[b], *an alleviation*[i] *of these*[k] pains! He prayeth earnestly for a gentle death.

Ver. 26. *When I looked*, &c.] He expected to be made happy all his life through the divine benediction on his charity and other virtues. But instead of that, he was made most miserable. This is his complaint here. The verses which follow, are an enlargement on his miserable condition.

Ver. 27. *My bowels boiled*, &c.] *My inward parts boil without intermission: evil times have befallen me*[l]. These expressions, in their literal meaning, describe the violent inward heat caused by his inflammatory disease. They may likewise include the ferment of his mind ever since his afflictions came upon him.

The

---

[b] פידו *his destruction*. It means a calamity that brings death. For the verb in Arabic signifies *to die*, and in its fourth conjugation *to slay*. Vid. Castell. Compare Job xxxi. 19. Prov. xxiv. 22. *his destruction* means the destruction inflicted by him, i. e. God.

[i] שוע *an alleviation*. Schultens illustrates this word by the Arabic, and has made appear, with probability, that it means (1) easement of the throat from a stoppage; (2) easement in any other case of distress. See his *Commentary*.

[k] להן *as to these things*. The want of an antecedent to this pronoun is one cause of the difficulty of the whole sentence. But it cannot be thought, that a man in the most violent agitations of grief should express himself with accuracy. The antecedent was in his own mind. He had been speaking of his tortures: These were the things from which he wanted to be relieved.

[l] Castellio.

28. I mourn, with swelter'd countenance I mourn,
   In hotter flames than hottest suns I burn;
   And among crowds, unable to contain,
   Shriek in the anguish of outrageous pain.
29. In lonesome wastes, where mournful creatures yell,
   Where wails the screaming ostrich, let me dwell;

30. A

The heart and *the reins*, in the oriental figurative style, denote the thoughts and passions.

Ver. 28. *I went mourning, &c.*] *I am grown black* [m], *but not with the sun* [n]. *I stand up, and shriek out in the assembly.* His distemper had made his complexion as swarthy as that of the poor labourers in the field, who are exposed to the scorching sun in those hot climates: and so sharp were his pains, that he was not able to forbear shrieking out before company.

Ver. 29. *I am a brother, &c.*] Affinity in disposition and circumstances, as well as in blood, is denoted by this term among the eastern nations.

dragons—owls] *dragons—ostriches*. The hebrew name which is translated *dragons* is *Tannim,* or *Tannin* [n], and *Tannot* [o]. What species of animals is intended by it, has not yet been determined with certainty. Its being coupled with the *ostrich* here, and in several other places [p], shews it to be an inhabitant of the desert. It is expresly called so, in Mal. i. 3. *the dragons of the wilderness;*

---

[m] Mr. Heath. קדר הלכתי, קדר signifies *black* chap. vi. 16. *Which are black by reason of the ice.* The verb הלך denotes *custom* and *habit.* So it is used in the conjugation *hithpael* Psal. xxxv. 14.

[n] Lament. iv. 3. *Tannin,* which is with the Chaldee termination of the plural number; The marginal correction, however, reads *Tannim.*

[o] Malachi i. 3.

[p] Isaiah xiii. 21, 22. xxxiv. 13. xliii. 20. The reader will be pleased to take notice, that this word *Tannim* is twice used as a noun singular, viz. Ezek. xxix. 3. xxxii. 2. In the former of these two places our bible turns it *a dragon*; but in the latter, *a whale.* But it signifies in both *the crocodile.*

30. A skeleton, of bones bak'd dry within,
Scarce shaded with a swart and shrivell'd skin:
31. My pipe is broken, and my harp is dumb,
Grief with her weeping train to me is come:

And

ness; where by the wilderness is meant the deserts of Arabia Petræa, the country of Esau and of Job. It also is a creature that has a mournful voice, Micah i. 8. *I will wail and howl . . . I will make a wailing like the dragons, and mourning like the ostriches.* Lastly, the female hath breasts, and suckles its young. *Lamentations* iv. 3. Our Translators, sensible that the description there cannot agree to the *dragon*, render it *sea-monsters*. *Even the sea-monsters* (Tannin) *draw out the breast, they give suck to their young ones: the daughter of my people is become cruel like the ostriches in the wilderness.* The ingenious Dr. Shaw is of opinion, that *Tannim, Tannin,* and *Tannot* are to be taken for Jackalls [q]; which make a hideous howling in the night [r].

Owls] in the margin, *ostriches*. The hebrew term is *benot jaanah* [s], *the daughters of vociferation.* The males are called *jaanim* (Lament. iv. 3.) which our Translators render *Ostriches*. Dr. Shaw was an ear-witness to the hideous noises which ostriches make in the night: "During the lonesome part of the night, says that entertaining traveller, they often made very doleful and hideous noises; which would sometimes be like the roaring of a lion, at other times it would bear a nearer resemblance to the hoarser voice of other quadrupeds, particularly of the bull and the ox. I have often heard them groan as if they were in the greatest agonies." *Travels*, p. 450—455. 4to.

Ver. 30. *My skin,* &c.] As his disease made so large a part of his deplorable condition, he mentions again the violence of it; in the change it had effected in his complexion, and the intolerable heat which had dried, as it were, the very marrow in his bones.

---

[q] *Travels*, p. 431. 4to.

[r] See the english translation of Busbequius, p. 58, 59. where there is an account of Jackalls.

[s] יַעֲנָה *vociferation*, from יָעַן *exclamare, clamare fortiter.* Exod. xxxii. 18. *It is not the voice of them that shout* (עֲנוֹת) *for mastery.*

And sighs, and plaintive sounds, and funeral dole
Are now the music of my sadden'd soul.

CHAP.
XXXI.
Ver. 1. In solemn league I bound my roving eye;
" Beware the lovely maid, from beauty fly:"

2, 3. For

Ver. 31. *My harp*, &c.] These seem proverbial expressions for a most melancholy change of condition from happy to wretched. We cannot form an adequate idea of the force of the latter expression, *the voice of them that weep*, without reading the accounts which travellers have given us of the excessive lamentations of the easterns in their funeral processions. See Dr. Russel's *Natural History of Aleppo*, and Pitt's *Account of the Mahometans*.

my organ] *my pipe*. See the note on chap. xxi. 12.

CHAP. XXXI.

The apology contained in this chapter, and which turns chiefly on his behaviour in private life, is not the effusion of vanity and self-applause. It is, in regard to his antagonists, necessary self-defence and solid refutation. Yet, I think, from its connection with the foregoing account of his sufferings, and from verses 35, 36, 37, his favourite design evidently is to shew, that God *had multiplied his wounds without cause*[1]. In this view he is chargeable with justifying himself more than God; that is, making his own cause to be more just than that of Providence. However, if we except this fault, the picture he has drawn is a masterly piece of moral painting. Nothing can be more finished and amiable than the character here represented. It is an exemplification of the most benevolent virtue, inspired and ennobled by the most rational and exalted piety. In short, this apology may be justly styled a fine epitome of morality and religion.

There is a manifest dislocation of the 35th, 36th, and 37th verses; which are a bold desire of an inditement from God, and an appeal to this account of his

---

[1] Chap. ix. 17.

CHAP. XXXI.   THE BOOK OF JOB.   257

2, 3. For O what ruin, from the Pow'r above,
Hangs o'er the lewd, and bursts on lawless love!

4. Could

his life as an answer to it. Those verses therefore ought to close the whole. The 38th, 39th, and 40th verses, which are an exculpation of himself from the charge of oppression, come in very improperly after them; and should rather be subjoined to some other articles of injustice. The order in which I have ventured to arrange the several heads of his defence, is what appeared to me most natural:

First, Lewdness, falsehood, and adultery; ver. 1, 2, 3, 4, 5, 6, 9, 10, 11, 12.

Secondly, Injustice, in its several kinds; ver. 7, 8, 13, 14, 15, 21, 22, 23, 38, 39, 40.

Thirdly, Resentment of injuries; ver. 29, 30.

Fourthly, Inhumanity; ver. 16—20, 31, 32.

Fifthly, Avarice; ver. 24, 25.

Sixthly, Idolatry; ver. 26, 27, 28.

Seventhly, Protestation of sincerity in this defence; ver. 33, 34.

Lastly, His offer to bring his cause with God to an issue on the footing of this apology; ver. 35, 36, 37.

It is hoped, that the above transpositions will be excused; since they do not prejudice the sense, nor alter even a word of the inspired writer.

Ver. 1. *Why then*, &c.] *that* ⁎ *I would not* ⁎ *gaze upon* ⁎ *a maid*. Compare Matt. v. 28.

Sir

⁎ ומה Castellio renders מה *nequaquam*; *pactionem feci cum meis oculis nequaquam aspicere virgines*. This particle frequently signifies *non* in the Koran. It is also used in the sense of *né* in Cant. viii. 4. *that ye stir not* (מה) *up*, *nor* (ומה) *awake my love*, &c. See likewise Pocock. in *Carm. Togr.* p. 107.

⁎ אתבונן It means *to look wistfully upon*, in Psal. xxxvii. 10. where it is englished *to consider diligently*. It ought to have been rendered in some such way in ver. 20. of the foregoing chapter; *I stand up and thou lookest wistfully upon me*, without affording me any assistance.

4. Could shades conceal me? or, whene'er I stray'd,
    One step his all-observing sight evade?

5. If e'er I walk'd with Falshood, e'er my feet
    Stole to the winding paths of base Deceit——

6. Let

Sir Richard Steel has justly remarked, that when a man is accused, it is allowable not only to say as much as will refute his adversaries; but, if he can, he may assert things of himself praise-worthy: which ought not to be called vanity in him, but justice against his opponent; by proving it is not only false what is said as to the fault laid to his charge, but also that he hath exerted the contrary virtue.

Ver. 2. *portion—inheritance*] These are terms for divine punishments, chap. xx. 29. xxvii. 13.

Ver. 3. *the wicked—workers of iniquity*] These general expressions are limited by the context to mean *debauchers of virgins*.

a strange punishment '] The hebrew word comprehends all the tragical things intended by *destruction* in the former sentence.

Ver. 5. *with vanity*] *falshood*'. *Falshood* and *deceit* being here placed immediately after the crime of corrupting virgins, import, I apprehend, the false promises and other deceiving arts practised by the seducers of women. Otherwise, they may be understood as opposed to that *probity* which he had maintained in *all* his social intercourse. It may be proper to observe, this and all the following articles of defence are delivered in the form of a solemn oath; *If I have done thus and thus, God do so and more to me.* The imprecatory clause of the oath is for the most part expressed throughout the apology: And where it is omitted, it is understood; as in this place and some few more.

if my foot hath hasted, &c.] To *haste* to deceit can signify nothing less than promptitude and eagerness to deceive; which is the effect of inveterate habit.

' בכן in many copies. It means in Arabic *grievous afflictions, misery*. Vid. Schultens' Commentary.

² שוא. It means *dissimulation* and *false professions* in Psalm xii. 2. *They speak vanity* (שוא) every one with his neighbour: with flattering lips, and with a double heart do they speak. See also Psal. xliv. 8. xxvi. 4.

6. Let God, who knows me upright from my youth,
   Weigh me in his impartial scale of truth.

9. If, fir'd by wedded charms, the fav'ring hour
   I watch'd, in ambush at my neighbour's bow'r;

10. May

habit. But a vindication of himself from a *habit* of deceiving would be faint indeed. The tranflation I apprehend ought to have been, *if my feet hath gone in filence*ᵃ *to deceit*. The expreffion *to go in filence* characterifes the ftill and private manner of executing fchemes of fraud and feduction.

Ver. 7. *If my ftep*, &c.] The firft fentence expreffeth the commiffion of fome unjuft action: for *the way* denotes *the way of juftice*ᵃ. The fecond fentence mentions the corrupt defire and purpofe excited by fome vifible object. The laft fpecifies the tempting object, namely *a bribe*; *and if any thing*ᵇ *hath cleaved to my hands*, that is, as the Greek verfion explains it, *If I have touched gifts with my hands*. His adverfaries gave broad hints that he had been guilty of this crime, chap. xi. 14. xv. 34. xxii. 8.

Ver. 8. *let my offspring*, &c.] He now had no offspring. If this tranflation therefore be right, the meaning of the imprecation muft be; that he fhould have deferved the extirpation of his family, in cafe he had taken gifts to pervert the ways of judgement. But this latter member of the period will better tally with the former, if we turn the hebrew word according to its primary fignification; *let my produce*ᶜ *be rooted up*; by floods or other caufes of defolation.

ᵃ תחש *filenter ivit*, from השה *filere*. Mercer well expreffeth the meaning, *et furtive ac filenti pede ad fraudem ivi*.

ᵃ Amos ii. 6, 7. Prov. xvii. 23. *A wicked man taketh a gift out of the bofom, to pervert the ways of judgement*.

ᵇ מאום *any thing*. It feems to be the fame with מאומה in Deut. xiii. 17. *And there fhall cleave nought* (לא מאומה) *not any thing*) *of the curfed thing to thine hand*.

ᶜ צאצאי *my produce*. The Chaldee renders it *the fhoots of my young plants*; Crinfoz, *qu'en arrache entierement tout ce que je planterai*. We englifh it *that which cometh out of the earth*, in Ifaiah xlii. 5.

260   THE BOOK OF JOB.   Chap. XXXI.

 10. May the poor captive's lot my wife difgrace,
   Mean tafks by day, by night a forc'd embrace:
 11. For 'tis a crime, ye judges, which fhould fhare
   The fharpeft vengeance of the fword you bear;

12. For

Ver. 9. *If mine heart*, &c.] *If mine heart was allured*[d] *by* (*towards*[e]) *another man's wife*[f]. *A woman* here means *a married woman*. It ftands oppofed to *a maid*, in ver. 1. and is englifhed *wife* in ver. 10. *my wife*; in the hebrew, *my woman*.

Ver. 10. *Let my wife grind*, &c.] I meet with no evidence that the term *grind* is ufed in fcripture in an obfcene fenfe. The ancients ground their corn with hand-mills. This was the work of female fervants[g]; and captives were employed in all fervile works[h]. Some underftand the whole verfe of *voluntary proftitution*. An idea fo fhocking could fcarce enter into his heart. I rather think, he refers to the *compulfive* meafures that were ufed towards women captives[h].

Ver. 11. *an iniquity* to be punifhed by *the judges*] This verfion appears truly to exprefs the fenfe of the original. The hebrew word for *judges*[i] clearly means an authoritative judge in Exod. xxi. 22.[k] and the phrafe *an iniquity of the judges*[k] muft furely fignify an iniquity fit to be punifhed by legal judges[l].

---

 [d] נפתה *inefcatur*. Schultens.

 [e] על It denotes the motion of the heart towards the alluring object, in Cant. vii. 11. *his defire is towards* (על) *me*.

 [f] אשה, LXX. ει εξηκολουθησεν η καρδια μου γυναικι ανδρος ετερου, *If my heart went after the wife of another man*.

 [g] Exod. xi. 5. See alfo the Odyffey xx. 105, &c.

 [h] See Iliad. i. 29—31.

 [i] פלילים Alfo the verb in I Sam. ii. 25. fignifies to execute the office of a judge by legal authority: *If one man fin againft another the judge* (אלהים) *fhall judge him* (ופללו)

 [k] עון פלילים *an iniquity of the judges*.

 [l] So chap. xix. 29. עונות חרב *iniquities of the fword*, that is, *worthy of the punifhment of the fword*.

12. For 'tis a flame, whose furious wrath would shoot
Through all my substance and devour the root.

7. If, when I saw some glitt'ring prize display'd,
My eyes desir'd it, and my heart obey'd;
And, turning from the path where Justice stands,
The tempting bribe defil'd my venal hands;

8. Perish my crops! or let my harvests feed
The wasteful riots of an alien breed.

13. If I despis'd my slave, controlling right
By will imperious and a master's might;

14. How shall I face the righteous Judge of all,
Or how defend me at his dreaded call?

15. Was not our Maker one? and one our frame?
Was not the womb his mould? and mine the same?

21. If

Ver. 12. *A fire*, &c.] The psalmist represents ruinating calamities by the same simile. Psal. lxxxiii. 14.

Ver. 14. *when God riseth up*] to judgement. The phraseology seems to be taken from human judicatures. A judge, I suppose, stood up when he passed sentence. The scripture frequently expresseth God's judicial interpositions in this manner. See Psal. iii. 8. vii. 6. ix. 20. xii. 7.

Ver. 15. *Did not he that made*, &c.] I have met with this humane sentiment somewhere in Seneta, but cannot now recollect the passage. The equality of all men by nature, is a strong argument against tyrannical abuse of those distinctions, which divine Providence has established in the world for the good of society.

one] one God and father of all, who is no respecter of persons.

Ver. 18. *For from my youth*, &c.] His natural temper was humane, and grew to a habit in early life. The translation of this difficult verse should be,
I apprehend.

21. If at an orphan's head I shook my hand,
Secure the hall of judgement to command;
22. That arm be shatter'd, let my shoulder's ball
Disjointed from its guilty mortife fall:
23. I fear'd destruction: could my pow'r contend
With pow'r almighty the wrong'd orphan's friend?

38. Its

I apprehend, *For compassion ⁿ grew up with me, I brought it ⁿ from my mother's womb.*

Ver. 21. *my help in the gate*] He means his authority and influence in the court of judicature, in which he prefided. See chap. xxix. ver. 7, &c.

Ver. 22. *Then let mine arm,* &c.] *Then let my shoulder fall from the shoulder-blade, and my arm be broken from the elbow* °. There is a striking grandeur in this imprecation on the arm that was lifted up to threaten ᵖ an orphan in a court of justice.

Ver. 26—28. *If when I beheld the sun,* &c.] *Sabiism*, or the worship of the heavenly bodies, was doubtless the most ancient species of idolatry. The Arabs went early into it. They adored the sun, the moon, the planets, and the fixed stars. The principles on which this false religion was founded, were, that man must not approach the supreme Being without a mediator—That the angels are our mediators, who present our worship to God and convey his blessings to us—And that those intelligences, the angels, inhabit the fixed stars

---

ⁿ כאב The Syriac renders it *dolores*; the Vulgate, *miseratio*; Castellio, *misericordia*. They all read כאב which in the Syriac testament (Rom. ix. 2.) denotes *sorrow* for another's misery. The verb also in Hebrews x. 34. signifies *to compassionate: Ye had compassion of me,* כאב לכון Greek συνεπαθησατε.

ⁿ אנחנה V. *egressa est:* Castellio, *eam* (misericordiam) *eduxi.* The pronoun affix נה is feminine; because the antecedent כאב, like several other noun substantives with a masculine termination, was probably of the feminine or else of the common gender. Vid. Guarin's *Grammat. Hebr.* vol. i. p. 51.

° קנה LXX. τῳ αγκωνος.

ᵖ See Isaiah x. 32.

38. Its rightful owner if my land bemoan,
Held in hard bondage if its furrows groan;

39. If

stars and planets, the sun, and the moon; which are to them what our bodies are to our spirits, and are the medium of their communication with us [q].

Ver. 26. *the moon walking*, &c.] He seems to mention the moon with a sort of distinction and preheminence; perhaps, because the Arabs computed their year by the periodical revolutions of that planet, and regulated their religious festivals by her motion.

Ver. 27. *hath been secretly enticed*, &c.] *hath been enticed in secret*. This circumstance deserves attention. It leads to a right explanation of the following verse. He speaks, you find, of an inclination of the heart, which no man knoweth; and of a subsequent action done in privacy, which no man was witness of. I am obliged to the judicious Mr. Peters' for the substance of this remark.

or my mouth, &c.] *and my mouth hath kissed my hand*. Kissing the idol was an act of religious homage [s]. At this day the Mahometans, in their worship at Mecca, kiss the black stone which is fastened in the corner of the *Beat-Allah*, as often as they pass by it in their rapid walks round that sacred building. If they cannot come near enough to kiss it, they touch it with their hand and kiss that [t]. This seems a remain of the ancient idolatry, though not practised as such by them.

The heavenly bodies being at too remote a distance for a salute of the mouth, their worshippers substituted kissing their own hand in the place of that ceremony.

Ver. 28. *This also*, &c.] *Even this* [u]; even this inclination of the heart and kissing the hand, on looking at the sun and moon, were an heinous crime.

an e

---

[q] Pocock. *Specim. Hist. Arab.* p. 5, 138 to 145.

[r] See his excellent *Dissertation on the book of Job*.

[s] I Kings xix. 18.

[t] Pitt's *Account of the Mahometans*. Sale's *Preliminary Discourse*. Reland *de Relig. vet. Meham*.

[u] הוא גם *even this*. See the like emphatical sense of גם in Gen. xx. 5, Prov. xxii.

39. If the defrauded peafant curs'd my field,
Or blood of innocence my title feal'd;

40. May

an iniquity to be punifhed by *the judge*] I apprehend the tranflation fhould be; *Even this were iniquity to be punifhed* by *my judge* ᵂ; or, which comes to the fame meaning, *even this were iniquity, O my judge*. By *his judge* he muft furely mean God: For who elfe can take cognizance of the motions of the heart, or of hidden actions? ver. 27. It appears therefore clearly to me, that he is not fpeaking of *idolatry* as a crime punifhable by *human magiftrates*; but as worthy of punifhment by God.

for I fhould have denied, &c.] Polytheifm is a direct denial of the unity of God: And idolatry is, in every fpecies of it, a renunciation of his fole title to the religious homage of his reafonable creatures.

Ver. 29, 30. If I *rejoiced*, &c.] Not to rejoice in the ruin of an implacable enemy, nor even to allow ourfelves to give him reproachful language, or fo much as to wifh him ill, is virtue in no inconfiderable degree. But to wifh well to him, and to do him good offices, is a pitch of virtue known only to the moft benevolent of all religions; and recommended only by the greateft of all teachers and the moft perfect of all examples.

Ver. 31. *If the men of my tabernacle*, &c.] He appeals to his own domeftics for his bounty towards them and liberality to all others. Ikenius, quoted by Schultens, hath given the cleareft tranflation of this verfe: *If the men of my tabernacle do not fay, who can produce* ˣ *a perfon not fatisfied from his flefh* ʸ *? that*

ᵂ פְלִילִי *my judge*. We had פְלִילִים *the judges* ver. 11. the fingular number of which is not פְלִילִי For the plural of that, according to grammatical analogy, would be פְלִילִיִם פָּלִיל is its fingular number. Wherefore פְלִילִי is that fingular noun with the pronoun affix of the firft perfon, *my judge*. Vid. Guarin's *Grammat. Hebr.* vol. i. p. 64.

ˣ מִי יִתֵּן *quis dabit*, i. e. *exhibebit*, as in chap. xiv. 4. Schultens.

ʸ מִבְּשָׂרוֹ *from*, or *cf*, *his flefh*, that is, the flefh of his camels and fheep which he flew for entertainment of ftrangers, as well as for the fuftenance of his own family. Schultens compares the expreffion with that fimilar one in I Sam. xxv. 11. *Shall I then take my bread, and my water, and my flefh* (טִבְחָתִי *my flaughter*) *that I have killed for my fhearers*, &c.

40. May brambles, for a harveſt, choke the ſoil,
   And weeds unwholſome mock the ploughman's toil!

29. If when misfortune ſmote my deadly foe,
   I ſmil'd in ſecret, and enjoy'd his woe;
30. I, who forbad my tongue the ſpiteful word,
   And ev'n a revengeful wiſh abhorr'd——

16. Did I repulſe the lowly-bending poor?
   Or went the widow weeping from my door?
17. Have I e'er feaſted with a churliſh pride
   Alone, without an orphan at my ſide?
18. Humane affection from the womb I drew,
   And with my growth the tender paſſion grew:
19. Whenc'er a naked wretch before me paſs'd,
   His ſtarv'd limbs ſhivering in the wintry blaſt;
20. Has the warm life, new bounding in his veins,
   Not bleſs'd the woolly riches of my plains?

31. If my own houſe atteſt not; "When he din'd,
   "Who, unrepleniſh'd from his table, pin'd?"——
32. My gate flew open at the pilgrim's voice,
   Beneath my roof I bade his heart rejoice.

24. If

---

that is from his proviſions. The Chaldee interpreter underſtood it in the ſame manner, " who cutteth of his fleſh unſatisfied ?"

Ver. 32. *The ſtranger*, &c.] His family, he ſays, were witneſſes of his hoſpitality. This virtue was, and ſtill is, the national character of the Arabs. They

M m   value

24. If I e'er whifper'd to the precious duft,
Be thou my idol, thou my fovereign truft;
25. Or glory'd in the pow'r vaft wealth beftows,
My pulfe high beating as my treafure rofe——

26. If on the rifing fun, or filver moon
Majeftic walking to her ftarry noon,
27. I look'd; and, in the folly of my foul,
My palm the kifs of filent homage ftole;
28. This, O my Judge, were treafon; this denies
Thy fole dominion in the earth and fkies.

33. If my defence, like Adam's, is but art,
While, unconfeft, guilt rankles in my heart;
34. With

value themfelves upon it as their higheft glory. One of their poets expreffeth himfelf very warmly on this fubject: " How often, when eccho gave me notice of a ftranger's approach, have I ftirred my fire that it might give a clear blaze. I flew to him as to a prey, through fear that my neighbours fhould get poffeffion of him before me."

The learned Schultens, who has favoured us with this quotation from the *Arabian Anthologia*, remarks, that the *eccho*, here mentioned, refers to the practice of a ftranger who travels in Arabia by night. He imitates the barking of a dog, and thus fets all the curs in the neighbourhood a barking. Whereupon the people rufh out from all parts, ftriving who fhall get the ftranger for his gueft.

Ver. 33. *like Adam*] The Chaldee Paraphraft very juftly underftands him here, to appeal to *God* for the honefty of the defence he had been making. " If I have covered my tranfgreffion *before him* like Adam." Adam, when called to by God to give account of what he had done, endeavoured to palliate his crime. But how did Job come to the knowledge of that tranfaction? Adam might

relate

34. With vengeance let th' assembled clans pursue
My name; and, exil'd from the public view,
In lonely silence may I veil my head,
O'erwhelm'd with terror and with shame o'erspread!

35. Who now an umpire in my cause will find?
Behold my plea, with my own signet sign'd:

Let

relate it to Methuselah, into whose times he lived. From Methuselah the tradition might pass to Noah, then to Shem; from Shem to Abraham, and so to the several branches of the Abrahamic family; from which the three friends of Job descended, and probably Job himself.

Ver. 34. *Did I fear*, &c.] This passage seems to intimate, that it was customary among the Arabs to assemble all the families in a tribe for trying a delinquent of high rank. Job imprecates on himself such a solemn condemnation, in case he had concealed, in this apology, any crime whereof he had been guilty. The original will admit of the imprecatory form adopted by Schultens and Mr. Heath: *Verily let me fear the great multitude, and let the contempt of families terrify me: let me keep silence*, and *not go out of the door*. The punishment which he imprecates, is, execration by his whole tribe, a life of obscurity, and perpetual imprisonment in his own dwelling.

Ver. 35—37. *Oh that one would hear me*, &c.] His discontent with the ways of Providence, and his justification of himself, rise here to the highest pitch that the poet designed; and that the character of piety would allow. To use the words of the great Michaelis [*], " He challenges God to come into judgement with him, and to give his reasons for treating him with such severity. If God would condescend to this, nothing could be more desirable or more honourable for Job. For it would be evident from God's very accusation, that he was guilty of no fault but what is common to human frailty. Bolder words

than

[*] In his *Notes on Dr. Lowth's Prelections*, p. 216. 8vo.

Let God vouchsafe his answer; or indite,
And the just roll of my offences write:

36. Th'

than these Job had not uttered in the whole dispute. These provoked Elihu to renew the debate: and these are the expressions, for which the Almighty chiefly reprimanded him [a]; taking little or no notice of the rest."

Ver. 35. *Oh that one would hear me* [b] *!*] He wishes for a third person authorised to try the cause between God and himself. Compare chap. ix. 32, 33. and see the note.

behold my desire is] *Behold my signature,* or *my seal* [c]. This is a figurative way of expressing his readiness and engagement to take his trial. The figure is evidently borrowed from the forms of law; and alludes to some instrument signed by the accused party, whereby he gave security for his appearance on the day of trial.

that *the Almighty would answer me*] *Let the Almighty accuse* [d] *me.* This is the same challenge as that in chap. xiii. 22. *Then call thou, and I will answer.* See the note.

and that mine adversary, &c.] *and let my adversary* [e] *write a bill of accusation* [f]*.* By his *adversary* he must mean his *accuser,* that is, the Almighty; mentioned as such in the foregoing sentence. An adversary in law is the plaintiff.

---

[a] Chap. xl. 2, 8.

[b] שמע, *a hearer.* It is plainly the same in sense here as מוכיח chap. ix. 33.

[c] תו Michaelis translates it *sigillum meum*; Castellus, *designatio mea,* sc. ad causam meam defendendam. In Ezek. ix. 4, it denotes *a signature* made by a seal: *and he called to the man . . . which had the writer's inkhorn by his side . . . set a mark* (תו) *upon the foreheads of the men that sigh,* &c. Compare Rev. vii. 3. Olearius informs us, in his Travels, that the king of Persia seals his rescripts with ink instead of wax; and is therefore always attended by his secretary with a seal and inkhorn.

[d] יענני It is used in the sense of *accusing,* or *testifying against,* in chap. xv. 6. and Deut. xix. 16.

[e] איש ריבי

[f] ספר *a book or roll*; rendered by LXX. συγγραφην; by Grotius, *scripta accusatio*; by Michaelis, *accusatio.*

36. Th' accusing bill, upon my shoulder born,
   Or as a crown about my temples worn,
37. I'll show; and, dauntless in the noble strife,
   To the great Plaintiff I'll display my life.

CHAP.

Ver. 36. *Surely I would take it*, &c.] The original is much stronger, *If I do not take it*, &c. This is an oath. God do so and more to me, if I do not take *the bill of accusation* upon my shoulder, as a badge of honour. He means that it would afford him matter of triumph: For he was sure it would contain no criminal charge.

and bind it, &c.] The sentiment riseth in dignity. He says now, the *roll of accusation* would be as magnificent an ornament to him as a crown.

Ver. 37. *I would declare*, &c.] The actions of his whole life, or this very defence, shall be, he says, his answer to the inditement.

as a prince ᶠ] This noble expression denotes the courage and magnanimity, with which he would meet his great antagonist.

However daring and culpable this whole passage may be justly thought; yet it must be owned to have an astonishing grandeur, when it is considered as the language of conscious integrity and supereminent virtue.

Ver. 38—40. *If my land*, &c.] A small degree of attention will, I imagine, convince any one, that the speech ended with the foregoing verse. These verses therefore are out of their original situation. They would enter properly among the articles of *injustice*. Mr. Heath has placed them next after ver. 25. They might better, perhaps, be introduced next after ver. 23.

Ver. 38. *If my land cry*, &c.] His land could not reproach him with having gotten it by unlawful means, nor with defrauding of their wages those who tilled it for him; much less with having taken away any man's life by false accusation, or otherwise, in order to confiscate his estate. Compare James v. 4. Habak. ii. 11. I Kings xxi.

ᶠ נגיד Its verb in Arabic signifies *superavit, vicit; animosus, strenuus, magnanimus fuit*. Golii *Lex. Arab.*

CHAP.
XXXII.
Ver. 1.   Job ended ended his defence—They ceas'd reply—
He stood absolv'd in his own partial eye.

2, 3. A

Ver. 40. thistles] *thorns* [h]. It doubtless means some plant that has strong and sharp prickles. Chap. xli. 2. *canst thou . . . bore his jaw through with a thorn* [h]. Heb. xl. 26.

cockle [i]] This is well known, being a common and hurtful weed in our corn. But what particular sort of weed, or shrub, is intended by the hebrew word, cannot easily be determined.

In general, however, he imprecates barrenness upon his land. We meet with an imprecation of the same kind in *Œdipus Tyrannus* ver. 278. " Let not the ground bring forth any harvest to them."

CHAP. XXXII.

We left Job, in the close of the foregoing chapter, in high spirits, triumphing in the goodness of his cause against providence itself. We are now entering on the second part of the poem; which prepares the way for changing his too high opinion of his own rectitude into self-abasement, and his complaint of the ways of God into penitence and submission. For the management of this part, the poet introduceth a new personage; of whose extraction, and
motives

---

[h] חוח LXX. render it κνιδη *nettles*; Symmachus, ακανθα a kind of *prickly shrub*; Chaldee, סלוי *thorns*; Vulgate and Castellio, *tribulus land-caltrops*; so called from its resemblance of a military instrument, which has three spikes contrived in such manner that whatever way it falls on the ground it has one spike uppermost. It is thrown in passes to annoy the feet of the enemy's horses. See Gerarde and Johnson's *Herbal*, and Dr. Scott's edition of Bailey's *Dictionary*.

[i] באשה It is some noxious and stinking weed. For באש in Hebrew signifies *a fœtid smell* Joel ii. 20. and ביש in Chaldee is *mischief*. The verb also signifies *to stink* Exod. vii. 21. and its fifth conjugation in Syriac *to do harm*. LXX. render באשה βατος *the blackberry bush*; Castellio, *ebulus dwarf-elder*; Symmachus, ατελεσφορητα *plants which bring no fruit unto perfection*; Chaldee, חוה *noxious herbs*. See Buxtorf's *Lex. Talm.* under חוח

CHAP. XXXII. THE BOOK OF JOB. 271

2, 3. A youth attentive fate, Elihu nam'd,
Againſt them all with holy zeal inflam'd:
'Gainſt him, who full of ſelf-exalting praiſe,
Above his Maker's juſtify'd his ways ;
Them, who, inglorious, left this high diſpute ;
Fierce to accuſe, but feeble to confute.

4. Silent

motives for renewing the debate, he gives a brief account in the firſt five verſes.

Ver. 1. *becauſe he was righteous* [k], &c.] This tranſlation aſſigns the reaſon of the ſilence of the three friends to Job's laſt diſcourſe. They looked upon him as too ſelf-conceited and obſtinate for conviction. But Mr. Heath gives a different turn to the ſentiment; *wherefore Job was juſtified in his own eyes.* This tranſlation repreſents him as confirmed, by their ſilence, in his conceit of the goodneſs of his cauſe againſt God.

Ver. 2. *Then was kindled the wrath*, &c.] Theſe expreſſions do not mean, that he was in a paſſion. They are the ſtrong oriental manner of denoting high diſapprobation. At moſt, they ſignify no more than a becoming warmth.

the Buzite [l]] The Buzites were a Syrian or elſe an Arab family. Their ſettlement was probably in the neighbourhood of Dedan, Jer. xxv. 23. And Dedan was a city of Idumæa, Jer. xlix. 8. [m] Idumæa was that part of Arabia Petræa where Job lived [n].

becauſe

---

[k] צדיק *innocens*, as Caſtellio tranſlates it. It ſignifies in Prov. xviii. 17. one who has the better cauſe, or right on his ſide ; *He that is firſt in his own cauſe is juſt* (צדיק) *but his neighbour cometh, and ſearcheth him*.

[l] The LXX. ſeem to have read in their copy בעין, inſtead of הבוזי: for their verſion is, τῆς Αυσιτιδος χωρας *of the land of Uz*.

[m] See Bp. Lowth's *Prælect.* p. 417. n.

[n] See *note* on chap. i. 1.

THE BOOK OF JOB.   CHAP. XXXII.

4. Silent he sate, while Job his caufe difplay'd;
This honour to refpected age he paid:
5. At

becaufe he juftified himfelf, &c.] *becaufe he made himfelf more juft than God*°; that is, he had defended his own innocence in fuch manner, as to reprefent God to have done him wrong. Eliphaz thought the very complaint, chap. iii, implied as much. See chap. iv. 17. With greater reafon did Elihu put the fame conftruction on the far more querulous language that Job uttered after that, and on many daring expreffions which he dropped, efpecially his prefumptuous challenge chap. xxxi. 35—37. Here then we have one of Elihu's motives for entering into this difpute, namely, zeal for the honour of divine providence. The other motive is fpecified in the fubfequent verfe: It was the wrong meafures which the triumvirate had taken; who, to juftify God, had condemned Job for a wicked man. They had fo done without evidence: neither were they now able to offer any thing, in reply to the defence which he had made.

Ver. 4. *had waited till Job had spoken*] This is obfcure. We may offer two other tranflations; either of which is clearer, and connects better with the following member: *And Elihu waited to give an anfwer to Job*ᵖ, &c. He paufed a while, before he would anfwer Job; to fee whether any of the three friends would anfwer him.

Or thus, *Now Elihu had waited for Job during the difpute*ᑫ; that is, he had refrained

---

° על צדקו נפשו מאלהים   For the fenfe of the verb צדק fee the fignification of the noun צדיך in the marginal note on the word *righteous* in the foregoing verfe. Caftellio's verfion is clear, *qui fuam caufam juftiorem effe contenderet quam Dei*.

ᵖ This is the Septuagint verfion ἐπεὶ δὲ ὑπομένει ἔτι ἀπόκρισιν Ἰώβ (Alex. τῷ Ἰώβ) In the Hebrew, חכה את איוב בדברים The Septuagint verfion goes contrary to all the other ancient verfions in making בדברים (rendered δυναι αποκρισιν) the object of the verb חכה; and governed of it by the intervention of the prepofition ב Whereas when this verb is tranfitive, it conftantly governs its object by ל, except Hofea vi. 9. where it has no prepofition after it; as *troops of robbers wait for a man*, כחכי איש In fhort, the Septuagint tranflate as if the Hebrew had been, חכה בדברים את איוב *he waited for difputations with Job*.

ᑫ בדברים *in fermonibus*. The verb רבר fignifies to *plead*, or *difpute*, chap. xiii. 3. *furely I would fpeak to* (*difpute with*) *the Almighty, and I defire to reafon with God*. דברים *the difputations*, as in chap. xxxi. ult. *the words* (*the pleadings* or *difputations*) *of Job are ended*. It is ufed again in the fame fenfe ver. 11. of this xxxii. chap.

5. At length, none anfw'ring fuch a vain defence,
Ardent he rofe, and gave his modeft fenfe.

6. Fathers, my youth, thus long, through bafhful fear,
Refrain'd to reafon in your aged ear:

7. Reply,

refrained from attacking him, fo long as the debate was kept up between him and his antagonifts.

becaufe they were elder than he] This refpect for his feniors, and fuperiors, which the author himfelf affigns as the reafon of Elihu's filence, is an honourable teftimony to his *modefty*.

Ver. 6. *And Elihu . . . anfwered and faid*] Profeffor Michaelis is very fevere upon Elihu and his fpeech, as Codurcus had been before him. He charges this young man with high conceit of himfelf, and cenfures his difcourfe as little or nothing to the purpofe of the queftion in debate. But the facred writer bears witnefs to his *modefty*, in the foregoing verfe: and Job's patient attention to his long fpeech, without offering a word of reply, is a ftrong prefumption of the *pertinence* of it. Its good fenfe will perhaps further appear in the courfe of thefe notes. I will, now, only add that Elihu's plan for humbling Job is purfued and compleated by the Almighty.

I am young, &c.] For a youth to fpeak in fuch an affembly, on fo delicate and difficult a fubject, and after that his fuperiors in age, and men renowned for their wifdom, had given up the difpute; was an aftonifhing phenomenon in Arabia [r]. Elihu was confcious of this vaft weight of prejudice againft him. Like a fkilful orator he endeavours to remove that obftacle, and to fecure the favour and attention of his hearers, before he enters on the queftion in debate. To this end, he reprefents to the three elders his bafhful timidity, his reverence of age, and expectation of inftruction from them. He next alleges, that found judgement is the gift of heaven; that this quality is not a neceffary effect of years; and that, with all the wifdom for which they were famed, they had failed
in

---

[r] See ver. 15. and compare chap. xxix. 8.

7. Reply, I thought, beseem'd the head of snow,
   And wisdom's voice from ancient lips should flow.
8. But wisdom is a gift, the breath divine
   Moves on the soul and calls the light to shine:
9. The fam'd for wisdom are not always wise,
   Nor in grey locks the pow'r of judgement lies.
10, 11. Hear, then, my sense: I waited; while you fought
   For answers, and exhausted all your thought:
                                                    12. Yea

in this dispute. He therefore begs their indulgence of him to deliver his sentiments—He had patiently attended to them—They had not convicted Job—Neither was their argument, that *his afflictions were sufficient evidence of his guilt*, a proper means of conviction. This appears to me the sum of his address to the three antagonists, from ver. 6. to the end of ver. 14.

Ver. 8. *But there is a spirit in man*[1], &c.] He had taken notice in the foregoing verse, of the wisdom to be expected in *a natural way* from age and experience. Here he seems to oppose to that a superior sagacity derived from divine assistance. The ancients ascribed all extraordinary endowments to such an influence. This sentiment occurs frequently in Homer.

Ver. 9. *Great men*, &c.] This is an indirect and modest intimation, that they had mistaken Job's case and treated it in an improper way. He therefore intreats them, in the next verse, to hear his sentiments of it.

Ver. 10. *I said, hearken*, &c.] He had not said so before. The translation should be in the present time, *I say*[1]: I now therefore beg to be heard.

                                                    hearken

---

[1] Castellio's translation is, *verum afflatu aguntur homines*; *but men are acted by a divine influence*, &c.

[1] אמרתי This indeed is the preterite. But the hebrew preterites were aorists in the original state of the language, as hath been observed, from Michaelis, more than once in the course of these notes. Our bible translation renders them frequently in the present time. See chap. xxviii. 4. *He setteth—breaketh*, &c.

12. Yea still I wait, attentive—but I find
    Nor Job confuted, nor reply design'd:
13. Say not; " 'Tis wisdom, that we leave to God
    " To humble this stiff sinner with his rod—"
14. His words, unaim'd at me, shall meet reply
    Unlike to yours; a diff'ring path I'll try.
                                            15. Amaz'd

hearken] *hearken ye*[u]. He still addresseth the three elders, as appears from the following verse.

Ver. 12. *or that answered his words*] Not one of you hath answered his last words; his bold apology, wherein he offers to defend his cause against God himself.

Ver. 13. *Lest ye should say*, &c.] *say not*[w], &c. Do not excuse your ceasing to reply; by alleging, that the wisest course to be taken with Job is to leave him to be sifted and humbled by God, as being too obstinate to be reclaimed by man. *we have found out wisdom*; *'tis God must confute him*[x], *not man*. So Mr. Heath translates the hebrew.

Ver. 14. *Now he hath not directed*, &c.] His aim in this observation is to shew, that he enters not into the dispute with any personal animosity against Job, or with any other prejudice whatsoever.

                                                            neither

---

[u] שמעה *hearken thou*. But all the ancient versions, except the Chaldee (says Mr. Heath) read שמעו *hearken ye*. The MS. Oxford Bodley Archiv. A. 97. reads in this manner.

[w] פן תאמרו *say not*. The particle פן here signifies *né*; it is dissuasive. The same sense it has Isaiah xxxvi. 18. Jer. li. 46. Mr. *Heath*.

[x] ידפנו *Let* (God) *push him down*. Castellio has hit the sense, *cum a Deo persequendum he must be pursued by God*. We english the participle, *driven to and fro*. chap. xiii. 25.

It signifies in Arabic *to card* cotton, by shaking it with a proper instrument. Hence I imagine Schultens took his *excutio*, *Deus excutiet eum God will shake him thoroughly*. Vid. Castell. *Lex. Hep.* Horace useth the same metaphor; *te ipsum excute*, &c. *examine yourself, whether you have not faults either natural or acquired*. Sat. i. 3. ver. 34.

15. Amaz'd, confus'd, they fit; bereav'd of tongue—
16. Patient of this delay, I've waited long—
                                                    Dumb

neither will I anfwer him with your fpeeches] Their fpeeches were levelled againſt his whole moral character; aiming to prove him a *wicked* man, from the ſimilarity of his ſufferings to thoſe of notoriouſly wicked men. Elihu takes another courſe. He limits his cenſure to Job's anſwers in this diſpute. He fixes upon ſome of the moſt obnoxious paſſages; ſuch as ſeemed to betray too high conceit of his own virtue, want of reſpect to God, and diſhonourable ſentiments of Providence. He takes occaſion from thoſe paſſages to vindicate the divine goodneſs, equity, and juſtice. Towards the cloſe, he gives a magnificent repreſentation of the power and wiſdom of the Deity in his works ʸ. The whole diſcourſe is admirably fitted to ſilence Job's murmurs, to humble his vanity, and to produce in him reverent ſubmiſſion under the rod of the Almighty.

Ver. 15, 16. *They were amazed,* &c.] To ſuppoſe, with ſome, that the author here ſpeaks in his own perſon, would be to make a very inelegant and unuſual hiſtorical parentheſis in the middle of a dramatic ſpeech. Yet on no better foundation ſtands the notion, that Elihu was the writer of this poem. It is much more natural to tranſlate theſe verſes in the preſent time, as Caſtellio and Schultens have done.

Ver. 15. *They are amazed* ᶻ; *ſtill they anfwer not:
          Words are removed* ᵃ *from them.*

Ver. 16. *And I wait; but they ſpeak not:
          But they are at a ſtand; ſtill they anſwer not.*

Here Elihu turns to the *audience*; deſiring them to obſerve the confuſion of the three ſeniors, who, though he had waited and was ſtill waiting for their
                                                                              reply

---

ʸ Chap. xxxvi. 24. to the end of chap. xxxvii.

ᶻ חתו *they are in conſternation.* This and the reſt of the verbs in theſe verſes are in the preter tenſe; which is here uſed for the preſent. See *the marginal note* on ver. 10.

ᵃ העתיקו *are removed.* The original is, *they have removed words from them.* The impersonal active is very frequently uſed for the paſſive. This is the word which we engliſh *to remove,* chap. ix. 5.

Dumb they remain—not one essays to speak—

17. My meaner voice must, must the silence break:
18. My soul, so deeply and so long attent,
    Is crowded full, and labours for a vent:
19. My thoughts ferment like wine; restraint is vain—
    Pierce, pierce the vessel, or 'twill burst in twain:

20—22. My reply to Job, had nothing to offer. That there were others present at the meeting of the three friends at Job's house, is certain: For Elihu was present. It seems not improbable, that this was an assembly, like those which the literati among the Arabs used to hold, for conferences on points of philosophy, poetry, &c. Harir, the Cicero of the Arabians, intituled his work, from that custom, *the assemblies*.

Ver. 17. I said, *I will answer*, &c.] The words *I said* are not in the hebrew. They are very improperly inserted. Elihu is going on in his address to the audience; whose benevolence he endeavours to obtain, by pleading the fulness of his thoughts and the irresistable impulse he was under to give them vent.

Ver. 18. *The spirit within me*, &c.] I do not see that these expressions import a claim to *inspiration*, any more than those of Zophar, chap. xx. 3. The *spirit within me causeth me to answer*. The words imply courage, strong emotion, and powerful impulse of the thoughts.

Ver. 19. *my belly*] The hebrew word is the same that is englished *within me* in the foregoing verse. It denotes the interior part of the man, *the mind*. Prov. xxii. 18: *For it is a pleasant thing, if thou keep them* (the words of the wise, ver. 17.) *within thee*; in the hebrew, *in thy belly*, i. e. thy mind. The Arabian writers use this expression for the mind: One of them, speaking of the great stress which some laid on the ablutions prescribed in the Koran, observes, that while they were so scrupulously nice about the exterior purity of the body, the inward part lies uncultivated and over-run with pride, ignorance, and hypocrisy [b].

as

---

[b] Pocock. *Specimen. Hist. Arab.* p. 303, בטן.

20—22. My lips shall ease me, shall effuse abroad
   This honest heart by no man's person aw'd:
   Unskill'd in courtly titles, plain and free
   My phrase, expect no soothing arts from me;
   Lest he, who gives my heaving lungs to breathe,
   That instant hurl me to the shades beneath.

CHAP.

as wine, &c.] he means *new wine* [c] that is fermenting. This is a most lively image of a benevolent mind full of important thoughts, and impatient to communicate them for the benefit of others.

like new bottles] Their bottles being made of skins, either dressed or undressed, were not liable to burst till they were grown *old*. Compare Jos. ix. 13. with Matt. ix. 17. Grotius, in his note on Matt. ix. 17. inclines to understand *new bottles* here of bottles that have new wine in them.

Ver. 21. *Let me not*, &c.] He here assures the audience that he will deliver his sentiments with that noble freedom and impartiality, which truth and the honour of providence demanded.

Ver. 22. *flattering titles* [d]] The Arabs make court to their superiors by carefully avoiding to address them by their proper names; instead of which, they salute them with some title, or epithet, expressive of respect [e].

my maker would soon, &c.] The crime which he apprehended would expose him to such danger, could be no other than that respect to the persons of men, which would make him timid and unfaithful in the cause of truth and God.

---

[c] Symmachus, ωσπερ οινος νεος; so likewise Chaldee and Vulgate. LXX. translate the whole sentence ωσπερ ασκος γλυκυς ζεων δεδεμενος *as a leathern bottle full of sweet wine upon the fret, and close tied.*

[d] בנה Vid. Pocock. *in Carm. Togr. not.* p. 3.

[e] *Id. ubi supra.*

CHAP. XXXIII.

Ver. 1. Attend, O Job; with no unheeding soul
Receive my reas'ning, patient of the whole:
2, 3. Unmix'd with passion, from a tongue sincere,
No mean monition shall invite thy ear.
4. That forming spirit which all flesh inspires,
Breathes in my lungs and feeds the vital fires:
5. Me answer, if thou can; thy plea dispose,
Stand firm, and with thy fellow mortal close.
6. I to thy wish arise, for God I speak;
Fashion'd like thee, of elements as weak:

7. My

CHAP. XXXIII.

Ver. 1—7. Elihu proceeds with caution in this delicate affair. He now addresseth himself to Job, and solicits his candid attention by several engaging motives. Is this the manner of a vain presumptuous speaker?

Ver. 3. *My words, &c.*] According to this version, he promiseth to deliver his sentiments with *honesty* and *perspicuity*. But the latter clause may be turned, *and my lips shall utter knowledge purely*. *Good intention* and *sound instruction* seem to be the qualities, which, he says, shall recommend his discourse.

Ver. 4. *The spirit of God, &c.*] He repeats this sentiment in ver. 6. *I also am formed out of the clay*. It intimates that Job might engage such an adversary on equal terms; having nothing to fear but the strength of his arguments.

The *Spirit of God* is of the same import with *the breath of the Almighty!* just as *hath made me* is synonimous with *hath given me life*. Tradition had conveyed to these men the knowledge of man's formation. Compare Gen. ii. 7. Ps. xxxiii. 6.

Ver. 6. *according to thy wish*] See chap. xvii. 3. and the note. He may also possibly refer to those words in chap. xxxi. 35. *Let the Almighty testify against me:*

I *let*

7. My arm no thunder wields, my face difplays
   No godhead terrors and o'erwhelming blaze.

8, 9. I've heard thee vaunt thy purenefs, heard thee claim
   Unfully'd virtue and a faultlefs name;
10, 11. Heard thee accufe thy God, of hate complain,
   And ftudy'd quarrel, and his cruel chain.

12. Are

let mine adverfary write a bill of accufation. Elihu fays, *I am in God's ftead, and rife to fpeak in behalf of God:* I will teftify *againft thee.*

Ver. 7. *Behold my terror,* &c.] You are in no danger of being confounded by the terror of my appearance, nor of being born down by the greatnefs of my authority. We cannot enter into the beauty of this delicate reprehenfion, unlefs we recollect thofe daring expreffions in chap. ix. 34, 35. xiii. 20—22.

Ver. 9—11. *I am clean,* &c.] Thefe verfes contain the object of Elihu's cenfure in the prefent chapter. The language of the ninth verfe favours too much of pride. The tenth and eleventh verfes are a complaint of harfh treatment, which reflects on the *goodnefs of God.*

Ver. 9. *I am clean,* &c.] Job had not ufed thefe very expreffions, but he had ufed others equivalent to them. Chap. ix. 30. *Verily I have wafhed myfelf with fnow water, and have made my hands clean in innocence.* and ver. 21. *I am perfect.* chap. x. 7. *Thou knoweft that I am not wicked.* chap. xvi. 17. *Not for any injuftice in mine hands: alfo my prayer is pure.* chap. xiii. 23. *How many are mine iniquities and fins? make me to know my tranfgreffion and my fin.*

Ver. 10. *he findeth occafions againft me*] *He inventeth harfh things* [f] *againft me.* Thefe words are plainly fynonimous with thofe in chap. xiii. 26. *For thou writeft bitter things againft me, and makeft me to poffefs the iniquities of my youth.*

and

---

[f] תנואות *harfh things.* LXX. μεμψιν *accufation*; Chaldee, *matters of complaint*; Vulg. *querelas.* In Arabic, the verb, according to Caftell. fignifies in one conjugation *crudam reliquit, nec exit* carnem; in another conjugation *mutuas inimicitias* cum illo *exercuit.* See alfo *the Commentary* of Schultens.

CHAP. XXXIII.   THE BOOK OF JOB.   281

12. Are thefe a juſt man's murmurs? Mortal, know,
    God reigns above, our blindnefs creeps below:
13. Why doſt thou wrangle with a Pow'r, whofe throne
    Will juſtify its myſtic ways to none?

14. Once, yea again, when thoughtlefs man offends,
    Th' Almighty Sire his warning meſſage fends:
                                                But,

---

and chap. xxx. 21. *Thou art become cruel to me,* &c. Elihu doubtlefs glances at thefe obnoxious paſſages.

Ver. 10. *He counteth me for his enemy*] Chap. xiii. 24.

Ver. 11. *He putteth my feet,* &c.] Chap. xiii, 27.

Ver. 12. *in this thou art not juſt*] not juſtified. this language is utterly indefenſible. it is no evidence of your piety. it is too querulous and irreverent to be ufed to fo great a Being as God.

God is greater than man] This is one of thofe modes of fpeaking which imply much more than is expreſſed. There is a kind of ironical caſtigation in it. as if he had faid, You talk to God as to an equal: but methinks he is fomewhat fuperior to us.

Ver. 13. *Why doſt thou ſtrive,* &c.] Job's extravagant juſtification of himfelf and murmurs againſt providence (ver. 9, 10, 11.) are what Elihu juſtly calls *ſtriving againſt God.* The Almighty paſſeth the fame cenfure upon them chap. xl. 2. To convince Job how wrong and culpable this behaviour is; Elihu argues, firſt, that it is irreverent, and fruitlefs: God, fays he, will never ſtoop to defend his meafures againſt murmurers, nor will communicate the reafons of them to thofe who cavil at his difpenfations. *For he giveth not account of⁵ any of his matters.*

Ver. 14—18. *For God ſpeaketh,* &c.] He alledges another argument againſt
                                                                    ſtriving

---

ⁱ לא יענה *he will not defend.* It is ufed for *anfwering to a charge.* Chap. xiii. 22.

But, if despis'd, his monitory lore
Sollicits the averted ear no more.
15. In midnight shade, when sleep on mortal eyes
Sinks heaviest down, he bids the vision rise:
16. The vision, with celestial imprefs sign'd,
Conveys high mandate to the waking mind;
17. To

striving with God. There is no just cause for it. God has sufficiently manifested his goodness and care of human kind, by the methods which he takes to shew them their duty, to recover them from their wanderings, and thereby to save them from destruction. One method is, to reveal his will to them in *a dream*. By mentioning this, and dwelling upon it, he seems tacitly to reprove Job, for not having paid regard to the dream of Eliphaz. Chap. iv. 12, &c. That old Gentleman could not fail of being pleased with this piece of respect shewn to him.

Ver. 14. *God speaketh once*, &c.] The *Latin Vulgate* has given, I apprehend, a more just translation. *God speaketh once, but he does not repeat* [b] *the same thing a second time.* If the revelation be disregarded, we are not to expect a favour of that kind any more.

Ver. 15. *in a dream*] See Gen. xv. 12. xx. 6. xxviii. 12. xxxi. 24. The heathens, somehow or other, came to the knowledge of God's revealing his will to men in this way. Agamemnon's dream, in the second book of the *Iliad*, is a proof of the high antiquity of the notion among them.

Ver. 16. *and sealeth*, &c.] He puts his signet to the instruction. These divine dreams were accompanied with sufficient evidence of their original, and of the authority of the instruction they conveyed.

---

[b] לא ישורנה *he will not repeat it.* The author of the *Vulgate* read *jeshor* instead of *jeshur*, whom Mr. Heath follows. The root of *jeshor* is שרר, which in the Syriac language signifies *confirmavit* (vid. *Castell.*) *stabilivit*. *God will not confirm it*, by a second revelation. שריר in Chaldee is *firmum, ratum*. *Castell*. Castellio's version also agrees with the Vulgate, *siquidem semel loquutus Deus, iterare nescit*.

17. To heal man's follies, to abase his pride,
18. And turn the level'd shaft of death aside.

19. Or else, his grace commissions fierce disease
The sinner in his lusty bloom to seize.
Cast on his bed he groans in griding pain,
While raging fever boils in every vein:

20. The

Ver. 17. *his purpose*] rather, his *doing*, or *work* as the margin of our bibles has it; viz. all actions and words which proceed from *pride* mentioned in the next clause, or from any other corrupt affection. Pride may comprehend insolence towards God, and towards man. But I apprehend Elihu had his eye on the former; and that he glances at Job's too high opinion of his own rectitude and merit, which gave rise to his complaints against God. Elihu thought, that some of his expressions favoured of this vanity; and that his affliction was sent to correct that fault, and to teach him humility. See chap. xxxii. 2. xxxiv. 37.

Ver. 18. *the sword*¹] The sword *of the destroyers* (ver. 22.) that is the destroying angels. See APPENDIX, *Numb.* IV.

the pit ᵏ] This is one of the names of the sepulchral grot, denoting it to be a place of putrefaction. See Bp. Lowth's Prelections, p. 87. n. 8vo.

Ver. 19—30. *He is chastened also*ˡ, &c.] He passeth now to another method used by the goodness of God for healing moral disorder in his human offspring; namely, the discipline of bodily affliction. This comes home to the circumstances Job was in. The painting is strong, and the whole description highly
graphical

---

¹ שלח *the missive weapon*, Vulg. *gladius the sword*. It signifies in Arabic *any weapon of war*. Pocock. Specim. Hist. Arab. p. 356.

ᵏ שחת *the pit*. The verb נשחת signifies *to be corrupted*, or *retted*, in Jer. xiii. 7. where it is englished *was marred*.

ˡ ו, this copulative denoteth here transition to a new topic. It is well rendered by LXX. πάλι *again*.

20. The languid stomach turns, with sick'ning hate,
   From the plain viand and the flav'rous cate.
21. His flesh consumes away, the bones within
   Transparent starting through his shrivel'd skin;
22. His soul now trembles on the verge of fate,
   And death's dread angels for the signal wait.
23. If then some delegate of heav'n, renown'd
   For sacred skill (rare gift on human ground)

24. The graphical and affecting. It does honour to the powers of Elihu, or rather of the Poet.

Ver. 19. *and the multitude of his bones*, &c.] The original is, *and*[m] *(when) the multitude of his bones is strong*[n]. The hebrew word for *pain*, in the first sentence, signifies *affliction*[o] in general. He is seized with some dangerous distemper, when he is in his full strength.

Ver. 20. *His life—his soul*] These terms denote the person himself. They are equivalent to the personal pronoun *He*. Both the Greeks and Romans used this manner of speaking [p].

Ver. 22. *His soul—his life*] See the note on ver. 20.
the destroyers] See the note on ver. 18, and the APPENDIX, *Numb.* IV.

Ver. 23. *a messenger* [q]] One sent by the providence of God, or by special commission

---

[m] ו here signifies the circumstance of time, *when*; as in chap. i. 13. *And there was a day when* (ו) *his sons*, &c.

[n] So the Chaldee.

[o] מכאוב LXX. turn it μαλακια. It signifies *a violent bodily affliction* in Psal. xxxviii. 18. Compare ver. 3, 4, 5.

[p] Ατραν Ειος for λητται *robbers*. *Omnem medicorum vitam* for *omnes medicos*; *Nostra vita* for *ego*. Vid. Merric's *Annot. on Psalms*, p. 182.

[q] מלאך *a messenger*. This is the proper and very frequent meaning of the word. It is also frequently used for *an angel*, because angels are the messengers of God. But there is nothing

CHAP. XXXIII.   THE BOOK OF JOB.   285

24. The fick his duty fhew; the fav'ring Pow'r
Salvation wills:
  " Fly, Health, to yonder bow'r,
" Contrition hath appeas'd my wrath; go, fave
" The penitent, and difappoint the grave."

25. His commiffion from him, to affift the fick man with his inftructions and prayers. I cannot fee any thing in the character and office of the perfon introduced here, but what will agree to any good man eminent for wifdom and piety; and much more to a prophet.

an Interpreter] *an eloquent perfon*[r].

his uprightnefs[s]] his duty; what right reafon and religion required from a man in his fituation; repentance, fubmiffion, and prayer to God for pardon. The inftruction is fuppofed to be effectual; as appears from the following verfes.

Ver. 24. *Then he is gracious*, &c.] God mercifully accepts his repentance, and faith *Deliver him*, &c. that is, he fhall be delivered *from going down to the pit*.

a ranfom] or, *atonement*; as it is in the margin. Whatever is a means of averting punifhment and conciliating the divine favour, is termed in fcripture an *atonement*. The interceffion of Mofes[t] and the act of Phineas[u] are fo called; and here the fick man's repentance[w].

---

nothing in this paffage, or in the context, which obliges us to fuppofe that Elihu meant *an angel*. It is alfo remarkable, what Mr. Heath informs us; that in the Manufcript Oxon. Laud. A. 262. the word בְּלִאָךְ here is not acknowledged by the pointer; being not pointed, but dotted over (בלאך) he fuppofing it to be interpolated.

[r] מליץ *an eloquent perfon*, fo it fignifies in Chaldee. Vid. Caftell. *Lex*.

[s] ישרו *his duty, fuum officium* as Caftellio turns it.

[t] Exod. xxxii. 30.   [u] Numb. xxv. 13.

[w] Ecclefiafticus xxxv. 3. *To depart from wickednefs, is a thing pleafing to the Lord; and to forfake unrighteoufnefs, is a propitiation*.

25. His flesh, replenish'd with young juices, grows,
    And with a second prime his aspect glows:
26. Now in th' assembly of the just he stands,
    Before God's altar, with uplifted hands:
    His pray'r ascends, the Pow'r looks smiling down
    On new-born virtue, and with bliss will crown.
27. Sweet swells the carol'd hymn;
                              " With loudest praise
    " I sing thy mercy, and adore thy ways:
                                            " On

Ver. 25. *His flesh*, &c.] A beautiful description of the sick man's recovery. The word translated *shall be fresher*[x], is an elegant metaphor from plants, which having being withered by a long drought, recover their vigour and verdure upon the falling of a shower of rain.

Ver. 26. *He shall pray*, &c.] He is here represented offering a sacrifice to God, in the assembly for divine worship, accompanied with a prayer and a hymn. *The face*, or presence, of God means the place where he is publicly worshipped[y]. *To see the face of God with joy* is to offer up a thanksgiving hymn in the worshipping assembly[z]: and God's acceptance of him, and blessing him for returning to his obedience, is expressed by *rendering unto man his righteousness*.

Ver. 27, 28. *He looketh upon men*, &c.] *He shall sing*[a] *before men*, and say, &c.
                                                                                This

---

[x] רטפש *is fresher, revirescens augescit*; so Coccejus happily renders it. For, according to Schultens, it is a compound of two Arabic verbs; *tarah* (by transposition *ratah*) *viguit recenti succo*; and *push, crevit*.

[y] Gen. iv. 14. Exod. xxiii. 15. in the hebrew. Psal. xlii. 3. in the hebrew.

[z] Psal. xlii. 4. *I had gone with the multitude, I went with them to the house of God, with the voice of joy and praise, with a multitude that kept holy-day.* See also Psal. xcv. 1, 2. C. 2. *Come before his presence with singing.*

[a] שיר *cantabit*. It bears this sense in the conjugation *kal*, Psal. vii. 1. lxxxvii. 7. 1 Sam. xviii. 6. Schultens.

CHAP. XXXIII. THE BOOK OF JOB. 287

"On me, a sinner thy rebuke was laid;
"Light was the chast'ning, with the trespass weigh'd:
28. "Snatch'd from the gaping pit, unworthy I
"Live, and again salute the cheering sky."
29. In all these works, the Great Paternal Mind
Oft manifests his care of human kind;
30. And calls his offspring, when their footsteps stray,
From shades of death to live beneath his ray.

31. This refers to the *joy* ver. 26. The words of his confessional and thanksgiving hymn, or rather the substance and burden of it, are; *I have sinned,* &c. *and it profited me not*] rather, *and have not received according to my desert*[b]: for *he hath delivered my* [c] *soul from going into the pit, and my* [c] *life beholdeth the light.*

Ver. 28. *my soul—my life*] that is, me—I; *he hath delivered me—I beheld the light.* See the note on ver. 20.

Ver. 29. *oftentimes*] in the margin, *twice, thrice*; a manner of speaking which seems to import variety rather than frequency. The Greek version turns it, *three ways*[d]; namely, *dreams,* ver. 15. *bodily affliction,* ver. 19. and a divine *messenger,* ver. 23.

Ver. 30. *To bring back his soul,* &c.] He repeats from ver. 18. The merciful design of divine admonitions and corrections; in order to fix the persuasion of it in the mind of Job. Eliphaz and Zophar had hinted this, chap. v. 17, 18. xi. 11, 12. But Elihu expatiates on the subject. His aim likewise differs from theirs. The reclaiming of a *wicked man*, such as they supposed Job to be, was

---

[b] לא שוה לי Vulg. turns it, *ut eram dignus, non recepi*; Castellio, *illum non sibi par retulisse.* שוה imports equality between two things that are compared together, as in Prov. xxvii. 15. Isaiah xlvi. 5. *To whom will ye liken me, and make me equal?* So here, the sinner confesseth that his chastisement was not equal to his offence. In the Syriac Testament, Luke xii. 48. Acts xxviii. 18. it denotes desert of punishment, *worthy of stripes, worthy of death.*

[c] נפשי, היתי. So it is in the text, and so LXX. and Syriac read. Our marginal translation also adopts that reading.

[d] פעמים שלש *two times, thrice*. Gr. Schol. διὰ τριῶν τουτων τροπων. *Vid.* Drusium.

31. This ponder'd well; hear me, O Job, again,
32. Or anfwer make, if anfwer fit remain:
   To juſt defence I pledge a candid ear,
   Full loth to cenfure, but o'erjoy'd to clear.
33. Elfe give me audience; and the friendſhip prize,
   Which ſhews thee where the path of wifdom lies.

CHAP.
XXXIV.
1. He paus'd; then ſpake again, with zeal fevere:
2. Sages and men for knowledge fam'd, give ear;
3. A was the point they had in view. Whereas Elihu ſpeaks of thefe divine rebukes, as applied to the cure of faults which are not inconfiſtent with general goodnefs.

Ver. 32. *I defire to juſtify thee*] *I defire that thou fhouldſt be juſtified* [e]. It will be a pleafure to me to find you innocent of arraigning the goodnefs of God.

Thefe expreffions of Elihu difcover a candour and ingenuity too feldom to be met with in religious difputes.

Ver. 33. *I ſhall teach thee wifdom*] This language may appear too affuming for a young man to ufe to his fuperior. But it ſhould be confidered, that he thought it inconfiſtent with his duty to refpect any man's perfon in fuch a caufe as this. In the next place, the filence of Job was a tacit acknowledgement of the pertinence of what Elihu had already advanced: and thirdly, the words amount to nothing more, than an engagement to offer further what Job would ſtill approve as found fenfe and falutary inſtruction.

C H A P. XXXIV.

In the foregoing chapter Elihu vindicates the *goodnefs* of God; in this chapter his *juſtice*.

---

[e] צדקך LXX. δικαιωθηναι σε; Vulg. *Velo te apparere juſtum*; Caſtellio, *nam equidem te infontem effe cupio*.

CHAP. XXXIV. THE BOOK OF JOB.

3. A skilful ear its test to words applies,
   As the sound palate diff'ring sapors tries:
4. Let calm debate our wary sentence guide,
   And truth's own voice this weighty cause decide.

5, 6. " My innocence, unheard (thus Job complains)
   " Heav'n dooms to suffer a delinquent's pains;
   " Unmeriting I mourn a mortal wound."

7. Where can this scoffer's parallel be found?
   So lavishing of tongue, so bold to think,
   His pride a dropsy, cavilling his drink:

8. He

Ver. 1—4. *Hear my words, O ye wise men*, &c.] Job remaining silent, Elihu renews his addrefs to the three seniors; and appeals to their judgement. By this respectful method of interesting them in the debate, he effectually engages their favourable attention.

Ver. 5. *I am righteous, and God hath taken away*, &c.] See chap. ix. 15, 20, 21. xvi. 17. xxvii. 2. and the notes. His expressions imported in their obvious meaning an impeachment of *the justice* of God.

Ver. 6. *Should I lie against my right?*] Contrary to my right, I am cast ᶠ in my cause. He had complained, that God treated him as a wicked man, knowing him at the same time not to be so. Chap. x. 2, 3, 7, 15.

my wound is *incurable*, &c.] See chap. vi. 4, 26. ix. 17.

Ver. 7, 8. What man, &c.] Elihu's expressions may seem too severe in this
place.

ᶠ אכזב *causâ cado, damnor*, as Schultens interprets it. Castellio takes it in the same sense, *Dicit Jebus . . . sibi in suo jure injuriam fieri.* It has the signification of *overthrowing* in chap. xxiv. 25. *who will make me a liar?* who can overthrow what I have alledged?

P p

290   THE BOOK OF JOB.   Chap. XXXIV.

 8. He walks with atheists, he adopts their strain;
 9. " Vain is all virtue, all religion vain."

 10. Ye sages, hear me: Let us far remove
   Injustice from the scepter'd Pow'r above:
             11. Whose

place. But they are only a strong way of saying, that Job's complaints were too much akin to those of atheistical men, who revile providence and ridicule religion.

   Marmoreo tumulo Licinus jacet, at Cato nullo,
   Pompeius parvo. Quis putet esse Deos.

Licinus lies in a tomb of marble, Cato has none, Pompey a little one. Who can suppose that there are Gods? Licinus was a famous Roman barber whom Augustus made a senator for his hatred to Pompey [g].

Ver. 9. *For he hath said, it profiteth*, &c.] Job, so far from using such infidel language, had entered his protest against it chap. xxi. 14, 15, 16. Notwithstanding which, his complaint of hard measure from God, and of the frustration of all the hopes he had formed of a reward to his virtue, would scarce admit of any other construction. See chap. xix. 10. xxix. 18. xxx. 21, 26.

that he should delight himself [h], &c.] Or, *that he should set his affection* [i] *upon God*. It is not the same word in the original with that in chap. xxii. 26. *thou shalt have delight* [k] *in the Almighty*. But the meaning seems to be alike. It signifies to esteem the favour of God our supreme felicity, and to take pleasure in doing what will be pleasing to him.

Ver. 10—30. *Therefore hearken*, &c.] He enters on his defence of the divine *justice*, and continues it to the end of ver. 30.

---

 [g] Dacier's notes on Horace's *Art of Poetry*, ver. 301.

 [h] רצה ברצתו עם אלהים, occurs but once more constructed with עם, namely in Psal. L. 18. *then thou consentedst with him*. The interlineary version there is, *delectabaris eo, thou wast delighted with him*.

 [i] So our bible renders רצה in I Chron. xxix. 3. *I have set my affection to* (ב) *the house of my God*.

 [k] תתענג

11. Whofe retributions, with exacteft plan,
    Anfwer to virtue and to vice in man.
12. God injures none: his independent might
    Difdains to bend th' eternal rule of right.
13. Or is he viceroy of this puny ball?
    Who, then, the founder of the world's vaft All?
14. Were God a tyrant, would he not refume
    His quick'ning fpirit? terrible the doom!
                                        15. Which

Ver. 10. *far be it from God,* &c.] In our conception of an infinitely perfect being, we are to remove injuftice and tyranny to an infinite diftance from him. This pofition is the fame with Bildad's chap. viii. 3. But Elihu fupports it by feveral new arguments.

Ver. 11. *For the work of a man fhall he,* &c.] This is a neceffary confequence from the foregoing propofition.

Ver. 12. *will not do wickedly*] will not do *wrongfully*¹. He will not injure any.

Argument I.

Ver. 13. *who hath given him a charge* ᵐ, &c.] Elihu's firft argument, to prove that God cannot be unjuft, is taken from his *independence*. Were God a fubordinate governor, he might be tempted to commit injuries to gratify the avarice or refentments of his fuperior.

or who hath difpofed, &c.] Or who hath made ⁿ *the whole world?* If the God whom we worfhip be a delegated governor, who is the God above him, the maker of the univerfe?

---

¹ ירשיע Exod. ii. 13. *He faid to him that did the wrong* לרשע

ᵐ פקד   Ifaiah x. 28. *to Michmafh he hath committed* (יפקיד) *his carriages.* Job xxxvi. 23. *Who hath enjoined him his way?* מי פקד עליו דרכו What fuperior hath prefcribed to him Rules for his adminiftration. See alfo II Chron. xii. 10.

ⁿ שם *condidit,* Caftellio. See Exod. iv. 11.

15. Which in a moment would unpeople earth,
And into duſt reſolve all fleſhly birth.
16. This reas'ning ponder, and its ſequel weigh:
17. Unjuſt and cruel is almighty ſway?
18. Cruel·

ARGUMENT II.

Ver. 14, 15. *If he ſet his heart upon man, &c.*] *If he ſet his heart againſt* º *man, &c.* He argues now from the divine *benevolence.* Tyrants are malignant, revengeful, and cruel. If God were ſo, this earth, inſtead of being full of the goodneſs of the Lord, would become a dreadful ſcene of deſolation: inſtead of preſerving, he would extinguiſh the ſinful race of man. The author of the *Wiſdom of Solomon* ᵖ reaſons in much the ſame manner on God's tender mercies over all his works: *For thou loveſt all the things that are, and abhorreſt nothing which thou haſt made: for never wouldſt thou have made any thing, if thou hadſt hated it. And how could any thing have endured, if it had not been thy will? or been preſerved, if not called by thee? But thou ſpareſt all ; for they are thine, O Lord, thou lover of ſouls.*

Ver. 16. *If now thou haſt underſtanding*] This methinks is a rough kind of addreſs. Mr. Heath's verſion ſoftens it, *ſeeing then it is ſo, reflect* ᵠ ;

ARGUMENT III.

Ver. 17, 18. *Shall even he that hateth right govern?*] Is the governor of the world a hater of juſtice? This is a third argument to prove that God cannot commit wrong. The reaſoning is ſimilar to that of Abraham, *ſhall not the judge of all the earth do right?*

and wilt thou condemn him, &c.] He infers from the foregoing argument the culpableneſs of impeaching the juſtice of a Being who is ſupereminently great and juſt. Compare chap. xl. 8.

º אל *againſt.* Exod xiv. 5. *The heart of Pharaoh . . . was turned againſt the people.* Job i. 8. *Haſt thou ſet thy heart againſt my ſervant Job.*

ᵖ Chap xi. 24, 25, 2´.

ᵠ הבינה (for בינה) The imperative in *hiphil* with a paragogic ה and an aphærifes of the characteriſtic letter. (Vid. Guarin's Hebrew Grammar, vol. i. p. 2,8.) Pſal. v. 2. *conſider* (בינה) *my meditation.*

18. Cruel, unjuſt—in ſuch audacious ſtyle,
   What rudeneſs would an earthly prince revile?
19. Yet him revile, who, higheſt of the high,
   Sees prince and peaſant with impartial eye,
20. Maker of both! His equal judgements ſweep
   An impious city, in the midnight ſleep:

Then

Ver. 18. Is it fit *to ſay to a king*, &c.] He illuſtrates the inſufferable inſolence of taxing God with injuſtice. Such an affront even to an earthly ſovereign is not to be endured;

ARGUMENT IV.

Ver. 19. How much leſs to him *that accepteth not*, &c.] He paſſeth to a fourth argument, *the impartiality of God in his puniſhments*. If this verſe needed a comment, there cannot be a better than the following one of the *Wiſdom of Solomon* [r]: *For he who is Lord over all ſhall fear no man's perſon, neither ſhall he ſtand in awe of any man's greatneſs: for he hath made the ſmall and great, and careth for all alike. But afore trial ſhall come upon the mighty.*

Ver. 20. *In a moment*, &c.] This verſe is exceedingly obſcure. For the clearing of it we may obſerve,

(1) The connexion ſhews, that it is a confirmation by *example*, of God's *impartiality* in his puniſhments.

(2) The puniſhment deſcribed is capital and inſtantaneous. *In a moment they die.*

(3) To increaſe the terror, it is inflicted in the night. *the people ſhall be troubled at midnight.*

(4) It cauſeth a general conſternation and uproar. *the people ſhall be troubled.*

(5) Perſons of the higheſt rank periſh by it, as well as the meaneſt. *the mighty are taken away.*

Laſtly,

---

[r] Chap. vi. 7.

THE BOOK OF JOB. Chap. XXXIV.

Then uproar reigns; the mighty and the mean
That inſtant periſh, by a hand unſeen.
21. For human ways lie open to his view,
Each winding path his critic eyes purſue:
22. Nor

Laſtly, The ſtroke is given by an inviſible and ſupernatural agent. *without hand*.

It muſt be owned, that all theſe circumſtances may poſſibly ſuit the deſtruction of Sennacherib's army by an angel of the Lord in the night[s]. But the times of Job and his friends, who lived long before that cataſtrophe, forbid the application. May not the overthrow of ſome capital city, in the night, by an earthquake, fully anſwer the deſcription? An earthquake is repreſented chap. ix. 5, 6. as an effect and token of the wrath of God; and therefore the Power which is the firſt agent in producing it, is inviſible and divine. The ſlaughter of all the firſt-born of the Egyptians may perhaps be thought by ſome to be the calamity alluded to. But if the age of Job was poſterior to that event, or coincident with it, one might expect a clearer alluſion to that and other ſubſequent miracles, in a poem of this caſt. But I can find no ſuch alluſions.

ſhall be troubled[t]] This does not expreſs the full force of the author's word; which is a metaphor borrowed from the commotions of an earthquake[u], or from the tumultuous agitation of the ſea in a ſtorm[w].

without hand] by an inviſible and ſupernatural power. Lament. iv. 6. Dan. ii. 34.

ARGUMENT V.

Ver. 21—23. *For his eyes*, &c.] His fifth argument is taken from the divine *omniſcience*. God perfectly knows the perſons of men, all their moſt ſecret actions, and all the motives of them. He cannot therefore, through *ignorance*, puniſh the innocent, nor the guilty beyond their true demerit.

---

[s] II Kings xix. 35.
[t] יִגָּעֲשׁוּ
[u] Pſal xviii. 8.
[w] Jerem. v. 22.

CHAP. XXXIV.   THE BOOK OF JOB.

22. Nor dark difguife, nor ev'n the central fhade,
    Can hide the guilty, or his reach evade:
23. Nor will he punifh fave the foul mifdeed,
    Nor will his arm in punifhing exceed.
24. He, without procefs, hurls a tyrant down,
    And to a foreign line tranflates his crown :
25. Awaken'd by their crimes his anger burns,
    A night of evil he againft them turns;

26. With

Ver. 23. *that he fhould enter into judgement*, &c.] that man fhould have any juft complaint to bring againft his maker.

Ver. 24—30. *He fhall break in pieces*, &c.] That God will not *accept the perfons of men in judgement*, Elihu further proves from the examples of divine vengeance on tyrannical princes and other powerful oppreffors. Not that he means to infinuate, that Job came under that character and was fuffering for offences of that kind : For then he would have violated his engagement ch: p. xxxii. 14. *neither will I anfwer him with your fpeeches*. His only view is to eftablifh the *impartial juftice* of God, and thereby to convince Job of his pre- fumption in arraigning it.

Ver. 24. *He fhall break in pieces*, &c.] He *breaketh in pieces* ˣ, &c. *and fetteth others* ˣ, &c. Elihu refers to fome noted inftances of fuch cataftrophes; which fhewed, in his opinion, that it is the way of God to punifh tyrants by dethron- ing and deftroying them.

Ver. 24. *without number*] The marginal verfion, *without fearching*, is better. He in whofe fight all things are naked and open, ftandeth not in need of a long and formal examination to convict the guilty ʸ. The judgements of God are as rapid as they are unerringly juft.

ˣ ירע, יעמד. Our Tranflators might as well have rendered thefe futures in the prefent time, as they have יכיר in the next verfe, *he knoweth*.

ʸ Grotius.

26. With infamy thofe proud delinquents fall,
Exampled vengeance, in the gaze of all:
27, 28. For blind and impious they mifrul'd; the groan
Of fuff'ring innocence affail'd his throne:
He heard it, ever to affliction's cry
His ear is open and his vengeance nigh.

29. When

Ver. 25. *Therefore*, &c.] *For* ᵃ *he knoweth their deeds, and therefore* ᵃ *he turneth the night* ᵇ *upon them; fo that they are deftroyed* ᶜ. He brings upon them a fatal reverfe of condition, a calamity which ends in their utter ruin. The *night* and *darknefs* are in this and other writers ufual metaphors for times of great affliction. See chap. xxxvi. 20. where it means *the night of death*.

Ver. 26. *He ftriketh them*, &c.] Their punifhment is open and exemplary. It is the triumph of providence over tyrants. The expreffions of the facred writer allude to the public execution of malefactors. What is englifhed *in the open fight of others*, is, in the original, *in the place of fpectators*. And what is rendered *he ftriketh them* is literally *he clappeth his hands at them* ᵈ as in chap. xxvii. 23. and in the laft verfe of the prefent chapter. It is a gefture of exultation and derifion. Compare Lament. ii. 15. Ezek. xxv. 6.

Ver. 27, 28. *Becaufe they turned back*, &c.] The crimes which drew deftruction upon them were impiety and oppreffion. They paid no regard to the laws of God ver. 27. nor to the rights of men ver. 28. The manner of expreffing their impiety ver. 27. feems to charge them with *idolatry*. Compare Pfalm xliv. 17, 18, 20.

ᵃ לכן, Vulg. *enim*. Noldius, *quiá*.

ᵃ ן, Vulg. *et idcirco*. Noldius, *ideò*.

ᵇ הפך לילה *he turneth the night*. Mr. Heath renders it, *he turneth the night full upon them*. The Vulgate has, *inducet noctem*.

ᶜ *For the Lord knoweth all them that fin againft him, and therefore delivereth he them unto death and deftruction*. II Efdras xv. 26.

ᵈ ספקם, the fame with שפק עלימו chap. xxvii. 23.

CHAP. XXXIV.   THE BOOK OF JOB.   297

29. When on a man or people he bestows
His peace, what pow'r can trouble their repose?
And when he dooms to ruin and the grave
A people or a man, what pow'r can save?

30. Thus

Ver. 29, 30. *When he giveth*, &c.] These two verses are the epiphonema; or a concluding of his discourse, thus far, on the *justice* of God with a weighty aphorism. The aphorism is, that the decisions of his justice, in absolving or condemning nations or individuals, will take effect in spite of all opposition: And that in his punishments as well as in his benedictions he hath ever in view the welfare of human kind.

Ver. 29. *giveth quietness—can make trouble*] *When he acquitteth* [e], *who shall condemn* [f]? Mr. Heath. But the connexion shews, that *to condemn* signifies here *to oppress*; and, therefore, *to acquit* must here mean *to deliver from oppression*, that is, *to give quietness*, or rest. Psalm xciv. 13. *That thou mayest give him rest from the days of adversity.*

when he hideth his face, who can behold him?] Our Translators seem to have missed the sense. They have inserted *his*, thereby determining *the face* to mean the face of God. I apprehend the rendering should be,

When he hideth the face [g], *who can behold it* [h].

To

---

[e] ישקט Syriac, *he forgiveth*; Arabic, *he letteth go*.

[f] ירשיע LXX, καταδικασεται *shall condemn*; in which meaning all the other ancient versions interpret the word.

[g] יסתר פנים *he covereth the face.*

[h] ישורנו *shall behold it.* פנים *the face*, is one of those nouns which are plural in their termination but singular in their sense. Such nouns sometimes regulate the agreement of the verb, adjective, or affix, to them by their plural termination; and sometimes by their sense. אלהים *God* is plural in its termination: but as it means one being, the verb, &c. joined to it is for the most part singular. Vid. Guarin's Heb. Grammar, vol. i. p 54. I may add that it is a common idiom in the Arabic language, for the pronoun affix to differ from its antecedent noun in number and gender.

Q q

30. Thus he exerts his juſtice and his care,
Dethrones vile kings, and burſts the people's ſnare.

31. 'Tis fitting, ſurely, unto God to ſay;
" O ſpare the humble, for, behold, I pray:

32. " My

To *hide*, or *cover, the face* of a perſon ſignifies to treat him as a condemned malefactor [1]. It correſponds to *ſhall condemn* in the foregoing member.

To behold it, that is, to uncover the face that is hidden, ſignifies to reverſe the ſentence of condemnation; to ſave the condemned party. This anſwers to *giving quietneſs*, or delivering from oppreſſion and deſtruction.

I take the meaning to be, that when God appoints a nation, or ſingle man, to calamity and death, no power in heaven or earth can ſave them.

Ver. 30. *That the hypocrite*, &c.] *That the profligate*[k] *reign not.* Hypocrite is a very abſurd denomination of an openly profane and tyrannical prince, which is the character Elihu is ſpeaking of ver. 24—28.

leſt the people be enſnared] The original is, *that there be no ſnares* [l] *of the people*; that is, that the people may be delivered from the calamities which they ſuffer under the government of a tyrant. By deſtroying ſuch wicked rulers, God manifeſts his abhorrence of injuſtice and his care of human ſociety.

The connexion of this verſe with the foregoing ſtands thus: God's dethroning tyrants is the effect of his *covering the face* of ſuch; that is, adjudging them to deſtruction: And his deliverance of an oppreſſed people is the effect of his *acquittal* of them. It is *giving quietneſs* to them.

Ver. 31—33. *Surely it is meet*, &c.] He infers, from his doctrine of God's *goodneſs* and *juſtice*, the duty of a perſon in Job's ſituation. The petition and confeſſion which he recommends to him are remarkable. That which *I ſee not, teach thou me*; if *I have done iniquity*, &c. This would be very improper language

for

---

[1] Chap. ix. 24. and the note. See alſo Eſther vii. 8.

[k] חנף See the note on chap. viii. 13.

[l] בירקשי *ſnares*, a metaphor for *deſtructive miſchiefs*, chap. xviii. 8, 9, 10.

CHAP. XXXIV. THE BOOK OF JOB.

32. " My blindness heal, my latent sin explore,
  " In ought offending I'll offend no more."

33. His

for a man who knows himself to be guilty of heinous crimes; but highly fit for a person, who, though in the main good, has reason to suspect somewhat amiss in his temper and conduct for which God is displeased with him. The pious Psalmist prays in similar language, *Cleanse thou me from secret faults.* Again, *Search me, O God, and know my heart : try me, and know my thoughts. And see if there be any wicked way in me : and lead me in the way everlasting.* Pf. xix. 12. cxxxix. 23, 24.

It appears plainly, that Elihu did not suppose Job to be *a wicked man*, and to be suffering for his oppressions, bribery, inhumanity and impiety; which the three friends had accused him of.

Ver. 31. *I have born* chastisement, *I will not offend* ᵐ, &c.] *I lift up* my hands, *let me not be destroyed* ⁿ. Mr. Heath.

I prefer

ᵐ נשאתי *I lift up.* This is the word which is used for lifting up the hands in prayer Lament. ii. 19. The words *my hands*, which Mr. Heath supplies, have at least as good a claim as the word *chastisement* which our Translators have inserted. The authority of Isaiah xxxvii. 4. will warrant also the insertion of *my prayer* instead of *my hands* ; *lift up thy prayer for the remnant.* And here, *I lift up* my prayer.

ⁿ אחבל The Masorites have pointed it in the conjugation *kal*, and thereby have made it a word of two syllables, and embarrassed both the measure and the sense. Mr. Heath reads it in the future of *niphal.* It then becomes a word of three syllables, *ehabel*, and signifies *to be destroyed*; Prov. xiii. 13. as it does also in *pyhal*, Isaiah x. 27. and in *pihel to destroy*, Isaiah xxxii. 7. By making it a word of three syllables, *ehabel* in fut. of *niphal*, or *ehubbal* fut. of *pyhal*, this ver. 31. in conjunction with ver. 32. forms a stanza of four lines; the first line answering in its cadence or metre to the third, and the second to the fourth; according to Bp. Hare's idea of the hebrew metre.

		Feet.	
Ver. 31. ci el | él he | ámar - - - -	3	trochaic.
nasá | ti ló | ehá | bel - - - -	3 ½	iambic.
Ver. 32. bíl ya | dé eh | zéh at | táh ho | réni - - -	5	trochaic.
im yú | vel pá | altí | lo ó | sip - - - -	4 ¼	iambic.

Bp. Hare remarks, (in the preface to his edition of the Psalms, p. 48.) That the Masorites in pointing the verbs are frequently mistaken, by making a verb to be in one conjugation when the metre requires it to be in another.

33. His rod chastises some offence of thine;
   Scorn or submission be thy choice, not mine;
   Reveal thy thought.

34.   Ye men of prudence, speak;
35. *Are not Job's answers libertine and weak?
                                       36. Again

I prefer Mr. Heath's version, because it avoids the tautology *I will not offend any more* ver. 31. *I will do no more* iniquity ver. 32. and because I cannot find that the word which our bible renders *to offend*, has any where that acceptation.

Ver. 33. Should it be *according to*, &c.] The hebrew leads us to the following translation,

> He hath requited that which is from thee, but thou hast despised it.
> But thou must chuse, and not I.
> Wherefore speak what thou knowest.

The meaning seems to be, " God has chastened thee for some fault of thine. I have recommended to thee submission; and mentioned a form of confession. But thou must chuse for thyself whether to submit or not, and not I for thee. Speak therefore what thy conscience dictates."

hath requited, &c.] Elihu supposed that affliction is always *correction*. So far he was under the same mistake with the three friends. But though he believed the sufferings of Job to be a divine chastisement of something wrong in him, he did not join with those censors in concluding from his sufferings that he was a *wicked* man.

that which is from thee] somewhat found in thee which has offended God.

thou hast despised it] It is the same word by which Eliphaz expresseth *contumacy* under divine corrections. chap. v. 17.

Ver. 34, 35. *Let men of understanding*, &c.] He appeals to the sensible and judicious hearers, whether he had not clearly proved Job's expressions to be
                                                                    rash

36. Again (I counsel) let us try their sense;
37. Try to the utmost: for his first offence
Is grown rebellion; petulant to God
This babbler triumphs, and insults his rod.

CHAP.
XXXV.
1, 2. And wilt thou join presumptuous issue here;
" The wrong is God's, my juster cause is clear?"
3. Yet

rash and foolish. He withal begs they would go along with him in a thorough examination of Job's speeches, *because of his answers for* °, or after the manner of, *wicked men.* His complaints were too much in the spirit and style of infidels, and gave too much countenance to the cavils of such against the ways of God.

Ver. 37. *For he addeth,* &c.] Job's discontent with the measures of Providence towards him broke out in his very first speech, grew more loud and vehement in the course of the dispute; and arrived to its height in his presumptuous challenge of God chap. xxxi. 35—37. This progress and increase are what Elihu marks by the expression, *he addeth rebellion to his sin.* The phraseology denotes continual augmentation; like that in Pfalm lxix. 27. *add iniquity to their iniquity.* Compare Pfalm lxxxiv. 7.

He clappeth his hands, &c.] He exults not only over his three opponents, but also over God himself, particularly in chap. xxxi. 35—37.

CHAP. XXXV.

In this chapter Elihu correcteth Job for talking so highly of his own virtue and importance *'*; and for complaining of God's neglect to punish the wrongs and

---

° באשׁוּ LXX. render ב *ωστε ας, like.*' They seem to have read כ instead of ב. But Mr. Heath remarks that כ denotes similitude in Isaiah xliv. 4. *as among the grass.* xlviii. 10. *not as silver.*

*' Ver. 2—8.

3. Yet fpeaks thy murmur lefs? " what boafted hire,
" Better than fin's, can virtue's toils acquire?"
4, 5. Thee and thy fect I anfwer: Infect, rife;
Look from thy duft, furvey yon lofty fkies:
6. Trembles

and violence which are committed in the world [1], He is ftill vindicating the *juftice* of God.

Ver. 2, 3. *thou faidft my righteoufnefs,* &c.] He had brought this charge againft Job before, chap. xxxiv. 9. But there he cenfured the complaint as an arraignment of *the juftice of God.* Here he takes it in another point of view, namely, as laying God under obligation. The charge is, that Job had in effect faid, " I have been more juft to God than he hath been to me. I have difcharged my duty to him, but have not met with a proper return from him: My innocence hath been of no advantage to me." Elihu replies, firft, that fo great a Being cannot poffibly be hurt by the fins, or benefited by the fervice of men: And fecondly, that our vice and virtue can harm or profit our fellow mortals only. ver. 5—8.

Ver. 2. *thinkeft thou this to be right*] *thinkeft thou this to be a caufe*[2], or matter of difpute; a queftion fit to be tried; " Whether thy righteoufnefs is more than God's?"

my righteoufnefs is more than God's] He had not faid thefe very words. But this was the amount of his vehement complaints againft God and juftification of himfelf. See particularly chap. xiii. 18, 22, 23, &c.

Ver. 3. *what advantage,* &c.] See the note chap. xxxiv. 9.

what profit, &c.] *what am I profited by not having finned*[3]? See chap. ix. 30, 31. x. 15.

Ver. 4. *thy companions*] Thofe who entertain the fame unworthy fentiments of God and his providence. Chap. xxxiv. 8.

---

[1] Ver. 9—13.

[2] משפט *a caufe,* or matter of litigation, chap. xiii. 18. xxiii. 4.

[3] מחטאתי *á peccato meo.* The fenfe feems to require us to read it as an infinitive with the prefix מ, *á non peccando,* or *quod non peccavi.* Caftellio turns the whole verfe with elegance and freedom, *Negans tibi prodeffe aut conducere innocentiam.*

CHAP. XXXV.   THE BOOK OF JOB.   303

6. Trembles his empire, if thy sins increase?
7. Or to thy virtue must he owe his peace?
8. Thy sins, vain worm, a fellow worm may wound;
   Thy virtue bless a brother of the ground.

9. " This earth (thou cavill'st) is fill'd full with wrong,
   " Cries of the weak, abandon'd to the strong."

10. But

Ver. 5. *Look unto the heavens*, &c.] This is a sublime sentiment in a plain dress. One view, says he, of the magnificent scenery of the lofty sky will extinguish all low conceptions of its Almighty author. It will strike the mind with a vast idea of his infinite superiority to all other beings, and of the impossibility of his gaining or suffering by the good or bad behaviour of his reasonable creatures.

behold the clouds, &c.] *behold the sky* [t], which *is*, &c.

Ver. 7. *If thou be righteous, what givest thou him?*] Eliphaz had touched this argument chap. xxii. 2, 3.

Ver. 9—13. *By reason of the multitude*, &c.] He passeth abruptly to another topic, Job's complaint of God's disregard of the numerous oppressions commited in the world [u]; the authors of which he suffers to escape with impunity. Elihu replies; that when God avengeth not the oppressed, it is owing to their want of piety. He neglecteth them, because they neglect him. They murmur, but they do not pray. They are clamorous but they are not humble [v]. This seems an oblique hint to Job, that the continuation of his sufferings was owing to his unsubmitting behaviour.

Ver. 9. *By reason of the multitude*, &c.] *By reason of violence* [x] *the oppressed* [y] *cry*, &c.

---

[t] שחקים *æther*, as Castellio turns it. It is another word for *the heavens*. Psal. lxxxix. 38. E. T. ver. 37.

[u] Chap. xxiv. 1—12.   [v] Ver. 10—13.

[x] רוב *violence*, Mr. Heath. It answers to *the arm of the mighty* in the next member of the period. רב is rendered ϐια, *violence*, by LXX. in Isaiah lxiii. 1.

[y] עשוקים *the oppressed*. It is the passive participle in *kal*, as Schultens remarks.

THE BOOK OF JOB. CHAP. XXXV.

10. But none their Maker and his ways desire,
    Whose gracious acts the midnight song inspire:
11. Him they neglect; who dignify'd our mind
    With reason far above the speechless kind:
12. Their cry is clamour of unhumbled grief,
13. God hears not clamour, nor will deign relief.

14. Thou say'st; "He gives no midnight song to me,
    His healing day I ne'er, alas! shall see."

Submit,

Ver. 10. *where is God my maker, &c.*] They neglect the most obvious dictate of reason; *O come, let us worship, and bow down: let us kneel before the Lord our maker.*

who giveth songs in the night] The *night* may signify, here, as in chap. xxxiv. 25. a time of calamity. The *songs* are thanksgivings to God for deliverance. Compare Psalm xxxii. 6, 7. xl. 2, 3.

But if *the night* is to be taken literally, there may be a reference to the nocturnal devotions of the pious. See Psalm xlii. 8. lxiii. 5, 6. lxxvii. 6. cxlix. 4, 5. Isaiah xxx. 29.

Ver. 11. *Who teacheth us, &c.*] By bestowing the noble gift of reason, God hath qualified us for religion; and laid us under the highest obligation to be religious.

Ver. 12. *There they cry, &c.*] *There they cry;* but *he answereth not, because of the pride of evil men.* The sufferers themselves are persons of no religion, and too proud to apply humbly unto God for deliverance. Therefore he pays no regard to their complaints, which are *vanity* [x] (as they are termed in the next verse) that is, void of real piety. *The wicked through the pride of his countenance will not seek after God: God is in none of his thoughts.* Psalm x. 4.

Ver. 14. *Thou sayest thou shalt not see him, &c.*] He endeavours to recover

Job

---

[x] שוא *nequitia*, as Castellio turns it. The Chaldee renders it by שקרא, *falshood*; by the same word that interpreter translates און *iniquity*.

Submit, and hope; thy caufe before him lies.

15. As yet unchaften'd for his ftout replies,
16. Or lightly chaften'd, Job exalts his tone,
Loquacious trifler with vain-glory blown.

CHAP.

Job from his defpair, and to infpire him with hope of reftoration on condition of humble truft in God for deliverance. *To fee God* muft here mean to enjoy his faving power. The Syriac tranflation however is clearer, and the hebrew will warrant it; *Thou fayeft thou fhalt not praife him*[a]. "He will give no *fong in the night* to me."

Elihu, it is plain, did not underftand the words in chap. xix. 25—27. to exprefs a hope of *temporal deliverance*. He fuppofeth Job to be ftill in defpair of fuch a reftoration.

judgement is *before him*] *The caufe is before him*. So our bible englifheth the fame hebrew word in Pfalm ix. 4. For *thou haft maintained my right and my caufe: thou fitteft in the throne judging right*. cxl. 12. *The Lord will maintain the caufe of the afflicted*.

Ver. 15. *But now*, &c.] This whole paffage is very dark. The ancient verfions differ widely. Not one makes any tolerable fenfe of it. Perhaps the following tranflation may meet with acceptance:

Ver. 15. *But now becaufe his anger hath not vifited, neither hath noticed*[b] *great exceffes*[c];

Ver. 16. *Therefore doth Job open his mouth*, &c.

Elihu

---

[a] לא תשורנו *thou fhalt not fing unto him.* It is the fame word which fhould have been rendered *he fingeth*, chap. xxxiii. 27. See the note.

[b] לא ידע *hath not noticed.* It is ufed for *taking into confideration*, chap. xxxiv. 4. *to take cognifance*, or judicial notice, of; Pfal. i. 6. but there in order to reward, here in order to punifh. Crinfoz renders it, *& qu'il ne prend point connoiffance de l'excés de vos plaintes*.

[c] בפש מאד *great exceffes*; that is, Job's intemperate fpeeches both of complaint and felf-juftification. Schultens remarks, that the verb fignifies literally in Hebrew *to be overgrown with fat*, Jer. l. 11. Cromarus obferves, that in Arabic the verb fignifies *to toaft*; one of its derivative nouns, *a beafter*; and another of them, *boafting*, or *vain-glory*. The verb in Chaldee (in the conjugation *aphel*) fignifies *to caufe to increafe*. See the Targum on Pfal. cv. 24.

R r

306   THE BOOK OF JOB.   CHAP. XXXVI.

CHAP.
XXXVI.
1—4. Indulge me ſtill; much argument remains
On God's behalf, and lofty are the ſtrains.
I'll

Elihu cenſures Job's behaviour as having been the very reverſe of patient waiting on God. It was murmur; it was vain-glorious exaltation of himſelf. God however had not manifeſted his diſpleaſure againſt him for it, or not in any ſevere degree. But this lenity (Elihu adds) has but encouraged Job to be more bold and clamorous.

Ver. 16. *in vain*^a] *raſhly*. Mr. Heath. It anſwers to *words without know- ledge* in the next ſentence. The Almighty paſſeth the ſame cenſure on Job's complaints^c. They did but diſcover his ignorance and preſumption.

CHAP. XXXVI.

At the third verſe Elihu reſumeth his defence of *the juſtice of God*, and cloſeth it with the twenty-third. He had given us his idea of the juſtice of God ver. 11. of the xxxivth chapter. *For the work of a man ſhall he render unto him, and cauſe every man to find according to his ways.* God's puniſhments and bleſſ- ings correſpond to the moral behaviour of men.

At the twenty fourth-verſe, he enters on a train of ſublime reflections on the *natural works* of God, that come within the reach of our obſervation. He pur- ſues this ſubject throughout the ſubſequent chapter.

Ver. 2. *Suffer me a little*] Literally, *wait for*^f *me a little*; wait a little longer for the ending of my diſcourſe to you.

Ver. 3. *I will fetch, &c.*] In a free tranſlation we might render it, *I will carry back my reflections to what I began with*^g (chap. xxxiv. 10.) namely, juſtifica- tion of my Maker; *and will aſcribe righteouſneſs to my Maker*.

But

---

^a הבל, LXX. ματαίως *fooliſhly*.

^c Chap. xxxviii. 2.

^f כתר לי׳ The Targum turns it, אמתן לי *wait for me*; in like manner LXX. μεῖνόν με; Vulgate, *ſuſtine me bear with me*; Mr. Heath, *have patience with me*. It ſignifies in Chaldee and Syriac *præſtolatus eſt*; Caſtellus. In the Syriac Teſt. Rev. xvii. 10. כתר; is the tranſ- lation of μένω *to tarry*.

^g אשא דעי למרחוק Vulgate, *Repetam ſcientiam meam à principio*.

I'll justify my Maker, without art,
Truth I explore, and faithful I impart.

5. Th' Almighty Mind, in all perfections great,
Above low envy and capricious hate,

6. An

But perhaps the original will warrant the following version, *I will utter* [h] (or *will go on to utter*) *my knowledge of that which is high* [i]; that is, of a sublime subject. He may well honour his subject, which is *the justice of God*, with the epithet *sublime*. He had discoursed on it in the two preceding chapters, he had dropped it during his address to Job and the audience chap. xxxiv. ver. 31—37. and interrupted it again chap. xxxv. 14—16. Now he says, he will resume it.

Ver. 4. *He that is perfect in knowledge*, &c.] One who will honestly speak the sentiments of truth in discoursing with thee; *He that is upright* [k] *in knowledge is with thee*. Elihu means himself. See chap. xxxiii. 3.

Ver. 5. *God is mighty, and despiseth not any*, &c.] He asserts that God cannot be warped by prejudice or caprice in his administrations of justice. The argument to prove the assertion is, that such weaknesses are incompatible with the transcendent wisdom and grandeur of the divine mind [l].

despiseth

---

[h] אשא *I will utter*. So it signifies Num. xxiii. 7. although it is there englished *to take up*.

[i] למרחוק *of that which is high*. ל is sometimes the particle of the genitive case; as a *psalm of David*, (לדוד) a *psalm of praise* מזמור לתודה. It also signifies *de*, *of*, or *concerning*, Esther iii. 2. Gen. xx. 13. מרחוק *longinquum*, denotes great distance in respect to *height* ver. 25. and in respect to *length*, I Kings viii. 41, 46. In metaphor it may denote a high and extensive subject. A sublime and boundless matter of enquiry is compared to the height of heaven, the depth of hell, the length of the earth, and the breadth of the sea, chap. xi. 7—9.

[k] תמים *upright*, (II Sam. xxii. 24.) *secum agitur sinceris sententiis*, Castellio.

[l] כביר כח לב *mighty in strength of heart*, or *understanding*. Mr. Crinsoz finely remarks, that the expressions in the original denote an elevation of mind, which is not capable of any thing unbecoming a noble, generous, and magnanimous character. But, says he, these are epithets too much beneath the Deity, to be used when we speak of him. Castellio's version, however, is beautiful; *Quum sit Deus excellens, quum sit inquam et excellent et magnanimus.*

6. An equal judge, no saviour of th' unjuſt,
Upraiſes weeping virtue from its duſt.
7. He marks the righteous whom the ſhade conceals,
Inthrones with kings, as blazing noon reveals
Their worth, and bids recording Time proclaim
Their titled offspring and imperial name.
                                            8, 9, 10.

deſpiſeth not any] he refers, no doubt, to Job's own expreſſions chap. x. 3. *Is it good unto thee that thou ſhouldſt oppreſs? that thou ſhouldſt deſpiſe the work of thine hands? and ſhine upon the counſel of the wicked? To deſpiſe* there means to take up an averſion to a perſon without cauſe, from caprice.

Ver. 6—15. *He preſerveth not the life*, &c.] He proceeds to eſtabliſh the juſtice of God by *facts* in the courſe of providence. It is proper to carry along with us Elihu's idea of divine juſtice chap. xxxiv. 11. *For the work of a man ſhall he render unto him, and cauſe every man to find according to his ways.*

The wicked are, in this book, perſons whoſe character is in general bad, but particularly *oppreſſors. The poor* mean not merely indigent perſons, but all who are injured, and withal innocent and friendleſs. *To preſerve the life of the wicked* is to protect and proſper the wicked and injurious: And *to give right to the poor* is to redreſs the wrongs of the innocent and humble.

Ver. 7. *He withdraweth not*, &c.] The ſufferings of religious and virtuous men are apt to raiſe in our minds hard thoughts of the Providence of God. Job had diſcovered ſentiments of that nature. When therefore we behold men of excellent piety and moral worth remarkably delivered from their afflictions, drawn out of their obſcure condition, and advanced to high and illuſtrious ſtations; ſuch inſtances ought, in all reaſon, to be conſidered as proofs of God's *rendering unto man according to his work*. Elihu, I ſuppoſe, refers to ſome known examples of ſuch a ſtrange revolution in Arabia, or in Egypt, or in ſome other neighbouring country.

but with kings, &c.] *but he ſetteth them with kings on the throne, and they are exalted for ever*. Mr. Heath, who thus tranſlates the paſſage, remarks, that the alluſion is *certainly* to David and his poſterity. Strange indeed! that this excellent

8, 9, 10. When erring mortals in his bonds he holds,
Their ear he touches, and their sins unfolds;
Humbles their pride, their self-deception breaks,
And slumb'ring conscience to its charge awakes.

11. If to his high commands their ear they bow,
And faithful keep the penitential vow;
Sweet days ensue, bright is their evening scene,
And death comes late and with a look serene.

12. Indocile else, and stubborn in their ways,
A fatal blow their heavy forfeit pays.

13. For stubborn sinners but augment their pain,
Sullen or fuming in th' Almighty's chain:

14. Inflam'd,

excellent poet should so far confound times and characters, as to make Job and his friends acquainted with the history of that monarch. Grotius supposes, with much greater probability, that Elihu alludes to the advancement of Joseph.

Ver. 8—14. *And if they be bound,* &c.] He seems to pass here to another character, the opposite of the foregoing, the doers of unrighteousness. God *causeth* such also *to find according to their ways.* He afflicts them; but with a merciful design to reclaim them. If they are penitent, their repentance makes a change in their character, and a corresponding change in God's treatment of them: he restores them to their former felicity. But if they prove too corrupt and stubborn to be reclaimed, he cuts them off by some calamitous death. Thus he manifests his justice, *by rendering to every man according to his work.* Compare chap. xxxiii. 26.

Ver. 12. by the sword] by the sword of the angel of death. See the note on chap. xxxiii. 18.

Ver. 13. *the hypocrites in heart*] *the profligates in heart;* men of very corrupt minds,

14. Inflam'd, the holy minifters of death
    By violent pangs prefs out their guilty breath.

15. How fwift his faving arm, when meekly ftill
    The man of forrow learns celeftial will!

16. Thee too he calls; for thee prepares releafe,
    Fulnefs, and feaft, and virtue's heav'n-born peace:

17. But
minds, incurably wicked, who will not humble themfelves under the mighty hand of God when *he bindeth them in the cords of affliction.* It is a variation of the expreffion in ver. 12. *if they obey not.*

Ver. 14. *They die in youth,* &c.] This is an amplification of *they fhall perifh by the fword* ver. 12. The tranflation of this verfe fhould be, I apprehend,

> *Their breath dieth by violence*
> *And their life is deftroyed by the holy* beings.

See the APPENDIX, *Numb.* IV.

Ver. 15—23. *He delivereth,* &c.] The obfervation in ver. 15. is an epitome of ver. 10, 11. He introduceth it as being the leaft offenfive tranfition to the exhortation, which he addreffeth to Job in this portion of his difcourfe. For it would have been too harfh to make the application immediately after thofe fevere expreffions in ver. 13, 14. *But the profligates in heart heap up wrath,* &c.

the poor[m]] This paffage clearly fhews, that by *the poor* are meant perfons in a fuffering condition *whofe ears are opened,* that is, who humbly receive the admonition which the difcipline of heaven conveyeth to them.

Ver. 16. *Even fo,* &c.] *the ftrait place* meaneth his prefent afflicted condition; *the broad place* his deliverance: The phrafe *where* there is *no ftraitnefs* expreffeth the completenefs of the deliverance: And *the table furnifhed with fatted things,* fignifies the affluence and enjoyment in which he fhould fpend the remainder of his life. The parallel paffages are Pfalm cxviii. 5. xxiii. 5.

---

[m] עני It is rendered by LXX. πραυς *meek,* Zach. ix. 9. Compare Pfal. xxxiv. 7. lxxxvi. 1.

17. But thou, litigious (not the wicked more)
Wilt wrangle for thy right, thy wrongs deplore:
Thy right is yielded thee, thy suff'rings laſt,
And juſtice in her fetters holds thee faſt.
18. Curb thy impatience, wrath already burns;
Beware its fury, which no ranſom turns:
19. Wrath, which defpiſes all the wealth of kings
And all the force that wide dominion brings.
20. Wiſh not that difmal night, which ſweeps away
The race of mortals from the walks of day.
21. Leave, leave thy murmurs; theſe thy peeviſh tongue
More than affliction's ſtyle has lov'd too long.

22. God

Ver. 17. *But thou haſt fulfilled,* &c.] *But thou art full of the ſtriving*[n] *of the wicked.* The ſenſe is the ſame as in chap. xxxiv. 36. *his anſwers like wicked men.* Thou haſt abounded in wranglings with Providence, after the manner of irreligious men. Elihu tells him, that the continuance of his ſufferings was owing to his murmurs; *Judgement and juſtice take hold* on thee.

Ver. 18, 19, *Becauſe* there is *wrath,* &c.] *Verily* there is *wrath,* &c. God is highly offended with your undutiful behaviour in this trial. Take heed, leſt your perſeverance in this froward temper provoke him to cut you off by ſome exemplary deſtruction. If things come to that extremity, not all the wealth and power of the world will be able to ſave you.

Ver. 20, 21. *Deſire not the night,* &c.] He farther warns him, both againſt his impatient wiſhes for death and murmurings at God. This was Job's *iniquity.* by *the night* is meant the *night of death.*

---

[n] ריב *ſtriving,* or *ſtrife.* Compare Eccleſ. vi. 10. This noun is engliſhed *ſtrife,* Prov. xxii. 10.

THE BOOK OF JOB. CHAP. XXXVI.

22. God reigns fupreme, above the ftarry fky,
Where is the fovereign who with him may vie?
23. Who gave his fcepter, and his fteps o'erfees?
Who dares pronounce, " unjuft are thy decrees?"

24. O Job, the grandeur of his work admire,
Hymn'd in loud anthems by the righteous choir:
25. Aloft

Ver. 22, 23. *Behold God exalteth*, &c.] Thefe verfes contain the argument by which he enforceth the foregoing admonition. God is the fupreme lawgiver. His dominion is abfolute. It tranfcends all comparifon, and is above all difpute and objection. The verfion of ver. 22. fhould be, *Behold God is exalted° in his power: who is a lawgiver ᵖ like unto him?*

Ver. 23. *Who hath enjoined*, &c.] God is not a deputy governor of the world. He is fupreme, independent, accountable to none. It is the higheft infolence to tax him with doing wrong. the expreffion *who hath enjoined him his way*, is of the fame import with *who hath given him a charge over the earth*, chap. xxxiv. 13. See the note there.

Ver. 24. *Remember*, &c.] This verfe ought to have begun a new chapter: for it begins a new head of difcourfe, which is continued to the end of the enfuing chapter. The fubject is the incomprehenfible wifdom and power of God, in forming the meteors of rain, thunder, &c. and ufing them to ferve the ends of his moral government. The fcope of the difcourfe is, to convince Job of his ignorance of *the ways of Providence* by his ignorance of *the works of creation*; and to humble him for his prefumption in finding fault with what he did not, could not, underftand.

his work] the vifible creation, the heavens in particular; in which he has
made

° ישגיב בכהו Vulg. *excelfus in fortitudine fua.* LXX. ο ισχυρος ο ισχυι αυτω *mighty in his power*.

ᵖ מורה LXX. render it δυναστης *a potentate*; Vulg. *nullus ei fimilis in legiflatoribus.* תורה *is the law*, מורה *he that maketh the law*.

CHAP. XXXVI.   THE BOOK OF JOB.

25. Aloft prefented to all mortal eyes,
    Above all mortal thought his wonders rife:
26. The work proclaims; the workman is divine,
    Whofe boundlefs years no numbers can define.

27. Refin'd by him the wat'ry atoms rife,
    Run into clouds, and flow along the fkies:

28. And
made manifeft his eternal power and godhead. Pfalm xix. 1. cii. 25. Rom. i. 20.

which men behold] *which men celebrate with fongs*ᵠ. It is the fame word that fhould have been rendered *to fing* chap. xxxiii. 27. xxxv. 14. See the notes.

Ver. 25. *Every man may fee*, &c.] *feeth—beholdeth*. The phrafe *beholdeth afar off* denoteth literally a vaft diftance, and figuratively incomprehenfibility. Our fight of an object which is afar off is very indiftinct; our knowledge of the works of God is very imperfect.

Ver. 26. *Behold God is great*, &c.] The creation demonftrates its author to be an eternal, almighty, incomprehenfible being.

Ver. 27. *For he maketh fmall*, &c.] The tranflation, I apprehend fhould be,

*He draweth up*ʳ *the exhalations*ˢ *of water*,

Which

ᵠ שררו Targum, *which righteous men do praife*. Vulgate, *de quo cecinerunt viri*. The root is שור *cecinit*. It is here in the conjugation *pihel*.

ʳ יגרע Vulgate *aufert carrieth*, or taketh, *away*. Schultens has fhewn that גרע fignifies in Arabic *forpfit, fublimavit*.

ˢ נטפ The root in Arabic fignifies *ftillavit, deftillavit, exftillavit*, præfertim per exfudationem & exhalationem. Schultens.

28. And thence diſtilling in benignant rain,
   Swell the brown harveſt of the ſhouting ſwain.
                              29, 30. What

Which *are fined*¹ for *the rain of*ᵘ *his cloud*ᵛ.

The exhalations of water are the watery vapours. Theſe are the materials of *clouds* and *rain*.

According to Profeſſor Hamilton*, evaporation is nothing more than the gradual *ſolution* of water in air, produced and promoted by attraction, heat, and motion, by which other ſolutions are effected. The attractive power of the air *draws up* the watery particles that are in contact with it. By attracting them, the air at the ſame time *fineth* them; ſeparating and leaving behind their ſaline and other heterogeneous parts. By this divine chymiſtry they become qualified for the purpoſes of a *rainy cloud*. When the air has drawn up the watery vapours, it diſſolves them, that is, unites them with itſelf. It keeps them ſuſpended, in this ſtate of ſolution, until by cold or ſome other cauſe it is forced to let ſome of them go. They then run together by their own mutual attraction and form a *cloud*. They continue in that form until the *cloud* is ſo much accumulated, by a freſh acceſſion of more watery vapours, as to become heavier than the air; or until the heat or denſity of the air itſelf is ſo diminiſhed as to become lighter than the cloud. The cloud then falls in *drops of rain*.

This beautiful theory is advanced by the very ingenious Dr. Hamilton, who has ſupported it by a train of curious and accurate experiments, obſervations, and reaſonings.

But ſtill *attraction*, which is ſuppoſed to be the firſt mechanical agent in this wonderful proceſs, is itſelf little underſtood. For who will preſume to define the

---

¹ יְזֹקּוּ The LXX. turn it in the paſſive voice but miſſed its meaning, ἐπιχυθήσονται. זָקַק is properly to fine metals by fuſion, chap. xxviii. 1.

ᵘ לְ *ef*, as in Pſal. cxlviii. 14. *the horn of his people*, לְעַמּוֹ

ᵛ לְאֵדוֹ, LXX. τις νεφέλης.

ˣ In the firſt of his *philoſophical Eſſays*.

CHAP. XXXVI. THE BOOK OF JOB.

29, 30. What lofty genius can the scene unfold,
When his dark tent of vapours is unroll'd?
About their king aërial clangors sound,
Thick-bursting flames spread terribly around,
Tempestuous winds th' affrighted ocean sweep,
And from its bed upheave the roaring deep.

31. These the precise bulk and shape of those minute particles of the air, which endow them with an attractive power: and as for *heat* and *cold*, so instrumental in producing rain, who knows what are the first natural causes of them? *Rain* therefore, which is the origin of fountains and rivers, and one principal means of carrying on vegetation and supporting animal life, must still be reckoned among the great and incomprehensible works of God.

Ver. 29, 30. *Also can any understand the spreadings*^y, &c.] that is, covering the sky with clouds, the prelude to a thunder-shower. These two verses are a lofty description of a storm of thunder and lightning: the great Author of nature is represented sitting in a pavillion of clouds. The clouds burst, the lightning flashes, the thunder roars, and tempestuous winds turn up the sea from its bottom.

> Ipse pater, media nimborum in nocte, corusca
> Fulmina molitur dextra——   Georg. I. 328, &c.
>
> The father of the gods his glory shrouds,
> Involv'd in tempests and a night of clouds;
> And from the middle darkness flashing out,
> By fits he deals his fiery bolts about.   Dryden.

the noise of his tabernacle] By *his tabernacle* are meant the clouds. Psal. xviii. 11. *He made darkness his secret place: his pavillion round about him* were dark

---

y מִפְרְשֵׂי *the spreadings*. It is a metaphor taken from extending the curtains of a tent. LXX. ϲυνϵτασιν.

31.   These are his servants; these for wisest ends,
   To feast the nations, or afflict, he sends:
   These meteors his judicial will perform,
   Bless in the show'r, and punish in the storm.

32.   God holds a flaming dart with both his hands,
   Forbids its flight where'er a suppliant stands;

33. But

dark waters, and *thick clouds of the skies*. See the following verses, *At the brightness*, &c. *the noise* [a] is well rendered by Crinsoz *the claps of thunder*.

Ver. 30. *Behold he spreadeth*, &c.] *Behold his lightning* [a] *bursteth* [b] *around him* [c]; *he turneth up* [d] *the bottom of the sea*. Mr. Heath. The latter sentence, *he turneth up*, &c. represents the effects of a thunder-storm upon the ocean.

Ver. 31. *By them judgeth he*, &c.] Fruitful showers, continual rains with consequent inundations, thunder, lightning, and tempestuous winds (ver. 27—30) are employed by God in his moral government, for the benefit or punishment of men according to their moral behaviour.

To judge a people is the phrase used by the Psalmist for punishing them, Psalm ix. 19. Compare ver. 15, 16.

Ver. 32, 33. *With clouds*, &c.] Thunder and lightning being looked upon, in those ancient times, as the most awful token of the divine displeasure against

the

---

[a] תשאות *the noises*. שאון, which is derived from the same root שאה, denotes the *roaring of the sea* in a storm Psal. lxv. 8. According to Castell. שאון signifies *strepitus, qui irruptionem et ruinam consequitur*.

[a] אורו It signifies *lightning*, and is so rendered chap. xxxvii. 3.

[b] פרש אורו *he scattereth his lightning*. פרש, *paras*, signifies to break a whole into parts and disperse them abroad. Ezek. xvii. 21.

[c] עליו LXX. ἐπ' αὐτῷ *over him*. Vulgate, *desuper*. Crinsoz, *autour de lui*. Prov. vi. 22. *it shall keep watch around thee* עליך. See Noldius.

[d] כסה *sodit*. By this word the Samaritan Pentateuch renders הפר in Gen. xxvi. 22. Mr. Heath.

CHAP. XXXVI.   THE BOOK OF JOB.   317

33. But hurls the forked vengeance at the proud,
And deep-mouth'd thunder speaks his wrath aloud.

CHAP.

the sins of men, Elihu takes up that subject again; and dwells upon it to the end of ver. 5. of the subsequent chapter. I can make no sense however of our bible translation of these verses 32, 33.

They will be more intelligible, and of a piece with the context, in the following version;

Ver. 32. *He holdeth* [e] *the lightning with both his hands* [f],
And giveth it commandment concerning him that prayeth [g].

Ver. 33. *His thunder* [h] *announceth, concerning him, jealousy and anger* [i] *against the impious* [k].

The

---

[e] כסה *he hideth,* or *covereth;* that is, he holdeth so as to cover, with his hands, the lightning.

[f] כפים

[g] מפגיע *maphgiy him that prayeth.* This version, which is supported by the Chaldee, presents a fine contrast between *the impious* at whom the thunderbolt is levelled, and *him that prayeth* whom it is commanded to spare. פגע in *Kal* signifies *to pray*, chap. xxi. 15. But, if I mistake not, the author of *the Wisdom of Solomon*, cited in the note, read *miphgay a mark,* as in chap. vii. 20. The translation then must be,

God holds with both his hands a flaming dart,
Gives it command to strike th' offending part;
Then hurls the forked vengeance at the proud,
And deep-mouth'd thunder speaks his wrath aloud.

[h] רעו *fragor ejus* (à רוע), or רוע *clanxit, personuit) his noise;* Mr. Heath turns it, with more dignity, *his thunder;* which certainly is the particular *noise* intended.

[i] מקנה אף *jealousy* and *anger;* so the Targum renders it. מקנה for מקנא, as מקוה *netum, filatum* for מקוא. See Guarin's *Hebrew Grammar,* vol. i. p. 400.

[k] על עולה *against,* or *upon, the impious.* The Syriac read yavlah and so did LXX. who render it ἀδικία *unrighteousness,* i. e. *the unrighteous,* as the Arabic turns it.

But it comes to the same thing, if we follow the Masoretic pointing yoleh *elatus, him that is high;* who in the pride of his countenance will not humble himself before God. Compare chap. xl. 11—13.

CHAP.
XXXVII.

Ver. 1. Ev'n while I paint this dreadful scene, I start;
My bosom scarce can hold its panting heart.

2. Hark !

The Divine Being is represented here in the attitude of vengeance, holding a thunderbolt with both his hands, and aiming it at the appointed mark, the obstinately wicked. I fancy the author of *the Wisdom of Solomon* chap. v. 17. 21. had this passage in view: *He shall take to him his jealousy for compleat armour, and make the creature his weapon for the revenge of his enemies. Then shall the right-aiming thunderbolts go abroad, and from the clouds, as from a well-drawn bow, shall they fly to the mark.*

Ver. 33. *Jealousy* and *anger*] Those appearances in nature which carry terror in them, and are calamitous to mankind, were ever thought, by pagans as well as worshippers of the true God, to be signs of divine wrath.

But Jove averse the signs of wrath display'd,
And shot red lightning thro' the gloomy shade:
Humbled they stood; pale horror seiz'd on all,
While the deep thunder shook th'aërial hall.
            Pope's *Homer's Iliad.* B. vii. 573, &c. Gr. ver. 478, 9.

The source of these apprehensions, with regard to thunder, was perhaps a tradition, that the first thunder heard by man was immediately after his disobedience. *They heard the voice of the Lord God going in the garden,* Gen. iii. 8. The knowledge of this fact was transmitted, it is probable, by the sons of Noah to their posterity. *The voice of the Lord* is thunder, Job xxxvii. 2, 4. Psalm xxix. 3, &c.

CHAP. XXXVII.

Ver. 2. *Hear attentively,* &c.] If these words are to be understood *literally,* an address to the *ear*; we must adopt Mr. Heath's ingenious conjecture, that it now began to thunder and lighten from the cloud in which the Almighty was about to make his appearance. Such an incident would greatly heighten the propriety and animation of this sublime description. The address, however,

CHAP. XXXVII.   THE BOOK OF JOB.

2. Hark! tremble; murmurs in the distant air,
   Whisper of God, his awful way prepare:
3. He fires the heav'ns, earth to her utmost shores
   Feels the broad flashes, now his thunder roars;
4. His voice, exalted with majestic sound,
   Augments its terror through the vaulted round:

We may be to the *imagination* only, after the poetic manner of representing things as though they were actually present.

The noise] The hebrew word is not that which is translated *noise* chap. xxxvi. 29. It signifies the first grumbling, or lower sound, of the thunder which gives warning of louder and more terrible explosions [l].

The learned Dr. Hunt, however, inclines to render this clause, *Hear attentively his voice with trembling* [m].

The sound[o]] If the foregoing word rendered *the noise* must give way to the authority of Dr. Hunt's criticism, we recover the idea of a *murmur*, or low grumbling noise, in the word which is here translated *the sound*.

Ver. 3. *He directeth it*, &c.] The translation should have been, *The flash thereof is under the whole heaven; even his lightning unto the ends of the earth.*

The *electric matter*, which, when discharged from a cloud, we call *lightning*, moves with such a velocity as we cannot measure: for it has been found to pass through a wire two miles and a half in length, as it were instantaneously [p].

---

[l] רין *the murmur*. Schultens in his commentary affixes this sense to it from the Arabic.

[m] Dr. Hunt is of opinion that the verb שׁמע does not here govern ברגז because in that construction, viz. when it is followed by ב, it signifies *to obey*. Bp. Lowth's *Prelections*, 457. n.

[n] הגה *the murmur*. See Clodii *Lex. Selectum*. Crinsoz renders it *le grondement*. The verb הגה signifies *to speak with a low voice*. Psal. cxv. 7.

[o] ישׁי, *rectus impetus ejus*. Chald. תריצותיה Vid. *Comment*. Schultens.

[p] Dr. Hamilton's *Philosophical Essays*, p. 125.

We hear, we shudder, but in vain enquire
How form'd his voice, and how inflam'd his fire.

5. Great is the thund'ring God, and great his deeds,
Nor less his work our loftiest thoughts exceeds,
6. When he commands ; " descend, my fleecy snow,
" On the sown fields thy rich manure bestow:
" Heav'n, ope thy sluices ; ye impetuous rains,
" Pour down my strength upon th' autumnal plains."
7. Seal'd

Ver. 4. *And he will not stay them*, &c.] *They cannot be searched out* [q], *when his voice is heard.*

The electric matter, which by its violent discharge produceth both the flash and the explosion, is but imperfectly known: it is far from being *searched out*. Some few properties and effects of it have been discovered. The discovery serves to enlarge and aggrandize our ideas of the Almighty Maker, and to convince us how little we understand of his boundless works.

Ver. 5. *great things*, &c.] He proceeds to mention other wonderful operations in the natural world, which we can but very imperfectly account for.

Ver. 6—8. *To the snow*, &c.] Here he paints a winter-scene. The son of Sirach gives a beautiful description of a shower of snow: *As birds flying he scattereth the snow ; and the falling down thereof is as the lighting of grasshoppers.*

Snow and heavy rains are joined together, as here, by the prophet Isaiah [r]; who

---

[q] עקבם The Vulgate turns it, *non investigabitur.* Symmachus led the way, ουκ ιξιχνιασθω̄σεται. The impersonal active, with an accusative of the noun after it, is used for the passive with the nominative of the same noun. עקב signifies to *track*. It is here a metaphor, from the chase, and means *to investigate.*

[r] Chap. xliii. 17.

7. Seal'd is each rural hand, reftrain'd from toil,
That men may own the fovereign of the foil:

8. Then

who reprefents them as inftruments of providence for promoting vegetation, of bread-corn in particular.

Homer, in the beginning of the tenth book of his Iliad, mentions a ftorm of thunder and lightning in fnowy weather. Barnes, in his note, tells us, that he himfelf had feen the fame phænomenon at London; and quotes Boffu as another witnefs of the like appearance at Senlis in France.

"Sometimes the clouds are frozen before their particles are gathered into drops, and then fmall pieces of them, being condenfed and made heavier by the cold, fall down in thin flakes of *fnow*, which appear to be fragments of a frozen cloud: but if the particles be formed into drops before they are frozen, they become *hail-ftones*[1]."

to the fmall rain, &c.] *to the great rain*[t], *even to the great rains of his ftrength.*

He defcribes the winter rain, called the *latter rain*. It was periodical, and fell in great abundance, foon after feed-time, in the month of October[u]. It caufed the feed which had been fown to take root; and by filling the ponds and cifterns furnifhed a fupply of water for the winter feafon. Its fhowers therefore are ftiled *fhowers of bleffing*, Ezek. xxxiv. 26[*].

Ver. 7. *He fealeth up*, &c.] The lands being laid under water by thefe heavy and continual rains, a prefent ftop is thereby put to the works of the field. This is the meaning of that beautiful metaphor *he fealeth up the land*, &c.

---

[1] Dr. Hamilton's *Philofophical Effays*, p. 30.

[t] גשם *a heavy fhower*, 1 Kings xviii. 45. The epithet *overflowing* is given to it, Ezek. xiii. 11.

[u] Or the latter end of September, Joel ii. 23. See the *note* on chap. xxix. 23. of this book.

[*] See Cant. ii. 11. Ifaiah lv. 10. Jer. v. 24. LXX. renders גשם מטר χειμαρρον the *ftormy rain*.

8. Then beasts of rapine to the mountains scud,
   Couch in their dens, and fast a while from blood.

9. Sharp wind, no longer in its cells controll'd,
   Scatters abroad his all-subduing cold:
10. Keen blows the breath of God, the floods congeal
    To solid pavement like refulgent steel:

11. The

Ver. 8. *Then the beasts*, &c.] This is picturesque. The low grounds are covered with water. The beasts of prey flee to the caverns of the mountains for safety. they couch there; and watch impatiently for the drying of the valleys.

Ver. 9, 10, 11. *Out of the south*, &c.] These verses are a description of stormy, cold, and frosty weather. Wind, cold, and freezing are still among *the great things which God doeth, and which we cannot comprehend.* The general cause of *wind*, which is only air put in motion, is said to be the atmosphere's being heated over one part of the earth more than over another. For in this case the warmer air, being rendered specifically lighter than the rest, rises up into the superior parts of the atmosphere, and there diffuses itself every way; while the neighbouring inferior air rushes in from all parts at the bottom, to restore the equilibrium[x]. But yet it holds true, that *the wind bloweth where it listeth, and we hear the sound thereof, but cannot tell whence it cometh, nor whither it goeth.*

As to *cold*, philosophers are not agreed in their definition of it[y] : And the various hypotheses to account for *freezing*[z], shew that it has not yet been accounted for.

Ver. 9. *Out of the south*, &c.] The marginal rendering is juster. The period will then be,

Out

---

[x] Rowning's *Natural Philosophy*, part ii. 116.
[y] See Chambers' Dictionary, art. COLD.
[z] Id. art. FREEZING.

CHAP. XXXVII. THE BOOK OF JOB.

11. The burnish'd ether sheds a smarter day,
And not a cloud endures the vivid ray.

12. The

Out of the chamber [a] *cometh the storm* [b],
And cold from the dispersing [c] *winds.*

The chamber, or rather *the secret chamber*, denotes those unknown regions whence the winds have their origin. Or the meaning may be, that winds are part of the treasures of God; which he hath always in readiness wherever he pleases to employ them. *He bringeth the wind out of his treasuries . . . stormy wind fulfilling his word.* Psalm cxxxv. 7. cxlviii. 8.

The *dispersing* winds are supposed to be those which blow from the northern points, and by scattering the clouds or dissolving them, make such a clear sky in sharp frosty weather, as is described ver. 11.

Ver. 10. *the breath of God*] The stormy, cold, freezing winds mentioned in the preceding verse. A tempestuous wind is, in the lofty style of the eastern poetry, called *the breath of God* chap. iv. 9.

is straitned] This version cannot be right. Water is not straitned by freezing, but dilated. It takes up more room, when frozen, than in its state of fluidity [d]; as hath been proved by many experiments. The translation, I apprehend, should be,

And the broad waters become *hard* [e].

Snow,

---

[a] מן החדר LXX. εκ ταμιειων *out of the store-houses.* חדר is properly the inner and most retired apartment of a dwelling-house Gen. xliii. 30. Thence it was applied to the remote and unknown regions of space. In chap. ix. 9. it is coupled with הימן *the south*, and there means *the southern hemisphere*.

[b] Chap. xxi. 18. xxvii. 20. סופה *the storm*.

[c] מזרים קרה Castell. in his Lexicon turns it *dispergentes frigus*, the winds *that scatter cold*. He seems to have understood מזרים to be the active participle in *pihel* of the verb זרה *dispergere*, and קרה to be governed by it.

[d] Chambers' Dictionary, art. FREEZING.

[e] במוצק *in* a state of *hardness*, or *cohesion.* Chap. xxxviii. 38. *when the dust groweth into hardness*, למוצק. It is a metaphor from fused metals, which, when cooled, cohere into a firmer mass.

12.   The Lord of nature at her helm prefides,
    Her feafons turns, the circling meteors guides;
                                                                    While

Snow, cold, froft, and ice were no ftrangers in Judæa[f]; which bordered on Arabia Petræa, Job's country: nor yet in Arabia Petræa. See chap. vi. 16.

the waters] the ponds, lakes, and winter rivers. It may be thought incredible, that there fhould ever be fuch fevere cold in thofe warm climates as to freeze lakes and rivers. But the Rev. Mr. Dawes informs us, that in 1756-7 at Aleppo (Lat. 32°. o' North) they had a very fharp winter, which deftroyed all the fruits of the earth. The cold was fo very intenfe, that the mercury in Fharenheit's thermometer, expofed a few minutes to the open air, funk entirely into the ball of the tube. Millions of olive trees, that had withftood the feverity of fifty winters, were blafted in this: and thoufands of fouls perifhed merely through cold.

Was not this a froft fufficient to freeze a lake, or river? And yet Aleppo is fo warm a climate, that the fame author tells us, " They were obliged to fleep on the terrace of their houfes in the fummer [g]."

Ver. 11. *Alfo by watering*, &c.] Here we have a picture of the fky in a clear, fharp-freezing day,

    Alfo the clear fky[h] *difpelleth*[i] *the thick cloud,*
    His fun[k] *fcattereth the extended clouds*[l].
                                                                    The

---

[f] I Chron. xi. 22. Pfal. cxlvii. 16, 17.

[g] *Letter to Dr. Littleton.*

[h] בְּרִי *the clear fky*. The interlineary verfion renders it *ferenitas*; Targum, *in puritate*. This is the acceptation of it in Arabic, according to Schultens in his *Commentary* and Pocoke *in Carm. Tegr.* p. 123. Its root *Barea* fignifies, fays Schultens, to give a high and elegant polifh to the furface of bodies.

[i] יַטְרִיחַ in Arabic *difpellit*. Schultens.

[k] אוּרוֹ *his fun*, as in chap. xxxi. 26. It comes however to the fame thing, whether we underftand it of the body of the fun or of his rays.

[l] עָנָן *tractus nubium*. Vid. Schultens on chap. iii. 5. A collection and arrangement of clouds, chap. xxxviii. 9. The Maforites have pointed עֲנַן *in regimine*. But LXX. read it in the *abfolute form*, διασκορπίζει πρὸς φῶς αὐτοῦ *his light difperfeth the cloud*. Thus אוֹר is the nominative to the verb יָפִיץ, and the parallelifm of the diftich becomes perfect: For אוֹר and בְּרִי, יָפִיץ and יַטְרִיחַ, עָנָן and עָב correfpond to each other.

While these and those his high behests obey,
And through earth's peopled climes assert his sway;
13. Whether as scourges of a rebel race,
Or sent as tokens of paternal grace.

14. O Job

The clearness of the sky in frosty weather is owing to the check of evaporation by cold. Hence the air becomes transparent, and the heavenly bodies are seen through it with undiminished splendour; there being no dense vapours to reflect back the rays of light, and thereby prevent their coming all down to us. (See Dr. Hamilton's *Philosophical Essays*, p. 18, 19.) In the language of poetry, therefore, *the clear sky* may be said *to dispell the thick clouds*, and *the sun to scatter them*.

Ver. 12. *And it is turned round*, &c.]

  And he turneth the revolutions by his counsels,
  That they may do all which he commandeth them on the habitable parts
   of the earth.

This noble sentiment represents the governor of the universe directing all its motions; and guiding the periodical returns of summer and winter, heat and cold, fair and foul weather, thunder and lightning, so as they shall prove punishments or blessings to mankind in proportion to their moral conduct.

the revolutions ᵐ] or *circuits*.
by his counsels ⁿ] literally, *by his steerings* ⁿ.
upon the face, &c.] *upon the habitable parts of the earth* °.
Ver. 13. *Whether for correction*, &c.] The *moral* use which God makes of
                   meteors,

ᵐ מסבות LXX. κυκλωματα.

ⁿ בתחבולתיו Symmachus turns it ἐν τῇ κυβερνήσει αὐτοῦ *by his piloting.* He understood the word as modern interpreters do, to be a metaphor from *navigating a ship.* רב החבל is *a ship-master*, or *steersman*, Jonah i. 6.

° תבל ארצה So Prov. viii. 31. בתבל ארצו *in the habitable part of his earth*, i. e. the part inhabited by men. תבל is used for mankind, or the world of mankind, Isaiah xiii. 11.

14. O Job, thefe wonders weigh; erect thy mind,
More wonders rife in boundlefs view behind:

15. Knows thy weak reafon, how he ftains his bow
When among clouds its fevenfold colours glow?

16. Or
meteors, wind, rain, &c. can be but twofold. They are either for *correction*,
or for *mercy*. The fituation of the words *or for his land* between thofe members
of the partition, feems very uncouth and perplexes the fenfe. A fmall tranf-
pofition will render the period clear and eafy.

Whether for correction or for mercy,
Verily [p] *for his earth he caufeth it* [q] *to come.*

it] that is, *correction or mercy*; the work *which he commandeth* the meteors *to
do upon the habitable parts of the earth.*

Ver. 15. *Doft thou know*, &c.] By God's *difpofing them* he means God's difpofing his *wondrous works*, or operations (ver. 14) in fuch manner as to produce
fuch and fuch effects.

and caufeth the light of his cloud, &c.] *and caufeth his luminous clouds* [r] *to fhine.*
He means perhaps, thofe bright clouds, fringed with gold and ftained with the
richeft tints, which often in a fummer evening attend the fetting fun. Some
eminent commentators explain this paffage of the *rainbow*. The expreffions indeed may appear too vague to allow that limitation. Neverthelefs, as it feems
very unlikely fuch a wonderful phænomenon as the rainbow fhould be taken
no notice of in this poem, and as this is the only place where it can be fuppofed
to be mentioned; I have adopted this fenfe in the verfe tranflation.

We know that thefe beautiful appearances are caufed by various reflexions
and refractions of the fun-beams. But why fome rays are more refrangible than
others,

---

[p] אם *certé*. Schultens. See alfo Noldius.

[q] יִמְצִאֻהוּ The relative affix הוּ *it* refers to שֵׁבֶט and חֶסֶד for its antecedents taken
feparately.

[r] אוֹר עֲנָנוֹ *lucem nubis ejus*, i. e. *nubem ejus lucidam*; or rather *nubes ejus lucidas*: for עָנָן
is *a range of clouds*, as Schultens fhews in his *Commentary* on chap. iii. 5.

16. Or knows, what balancings thofe clouds confine,
Amazing workmanfhip of art divine?
17. How fouthing day inflames the breathlefs air,
When fcarce thy limbs their glowing raiment bear?
18. Art

others, how their different refrangibility produceth different colours, and what peculiar texture in the fmall parts of bodies fitteth fome to reflect one kind of rays, others another kind, are problems which philofophy is not able to folve.

Ver. 16. *the balancings of the clouds*] The clouds remain fufpended, fo long as their preffure is exactly balanced by the counter-preffure of the air which is underneath them. When the equipoife is deftroyed, either by a diminution of the denfity and weight of the fupporting air, or by condenfation of the watery vapours; they often precipitate in rain. But the law of the equilibrium and the caufes which deftroy the balance, are fo myfterious in their operation, that our knowlege of thefe matters is extremely fuperficial. Elihu argues all along from our ignorance of the works of nature to our incapacity for judging of the counfels of providence. The fame kind of argumentation is beautifully purfued in the *Effay on Man*.

Prefumptuous man! the reafon wouldft thou find,
Why form'd fo weak, fo little, and fo blind?
Afk of thy mother earth, why oaks were made
Taller or ftronger than the weeds they fhade?
Or afk of yonder argent fields above,
Why *Jove*'s fatellites are lefs than *Jove*.

Ver. 17, 18. *How thy garments are warm*, &c.] He defcribes an Arabian noon-day in the heighth of fummer; when the fun is in his full ftrength and not a breath of wind ftirring to cool the fultry air.

When he bringeth a calm upon the earth from the fouth[1]. that is, from the fouth quarter of the heavens; when the fun is in the meridian.

The

---

[1] דרום *the fouth*. Ecclef. i. 6. *the wind geeth towards the fouth, and turneth about to the north*. I cannot find that the word ever fignifies the *fouth-wind*. Befides, a fouth-wind is tempeftuous

18. Art thou affifting, while he fpreads the mafs
Of ether fplendent as the polifh'd brafs,
Bright as the mirror, as the metal ftrong?

19. O man of courage, aid our fault'ring tongue;
Confus'd we cannot reafon in his ear,
Dark cloud defcends, the coming God we fear.

20. Should

The exceffive heat and bright tranfparency of the air in a fummer's noon, efpecially in the warmer climates, perplex philofophy with many difficult queftions. How do the fun's rays operate, to produce calmnefs in the air and a ferene fky? What quality in bodies raifes in us the fenfation of heat? And how does that quality act upon our nerves; and by what procefs is the fenfation excited in our minds?

Ver. 18. *Haft thou with him fpread out*, &c.] *Doft thou*, or *wilt thou, with him fpread out*, &c.] Wilt thou undertake to be his affiftant, in giving to the noon-day fummer fky its high polifh and infufferable effulgence? The elegant fimile of the mirror cannot be underftood, without recollecting that their looking-glaffes were made of metal highly polifhed.

The ftate of the fky in a long drought feems more particularly the fubject of the defcription. *The heaven that is over thy head fhall be brafs, and the earth that is under thee* fhall be *iron*. Deut. xxviii. 23.

Ver. 19—ult.] Thefe verfes are the peroration: wherein he reprefents to Job the rafhnefs and danger of difputing with God, fets forth the incomprehenfibility of the fchemes of providence, infifts that they are planned and executed with moft perfect equity and juftice; and exhorts him and all mankind to annihilate themfelves before their Maker, in profoundeft reverence of his adorable majefty.

---

tempeftuous in thofe climates, Ifaiah xxi. 1. It muft, however, be owned, that in the fummer feafon a fouth wind produced *heat* in thofe climates, Luke xii. 55. Dr. Ruffel remarks, that the coldeft winds at Aleppo in the winter, bring with them, when they blow from the very fame points from May to the end of September, a degree and kind of heat which one would imagine came out of an oven. *Natural Hift. of Aleppo*, p. 14.

CHAP. XXXVII. THE BOOK OF JOB.

20. Should some bold mouth presume to speak for mine,
Perdition will confound the rash design.

21, 22. When

Ver. 19, 20. *Teach us*, &c.] I do not clearly understand these verses.

Cur nescire, pudens pravè, quam discere malo?

We may however, partly by the assistance of Schultens, make out the following explanation:

Teach us what we shall say to him.

This is an ironical reprimand of Job, for wishing the Almighty would appear by some visible manifestation, that he might *reason*, that is, dispute, *with him*[w].

We cannot order [x] *our speech.*

He declares himself to be in too much terror and confusion to speak to God at all, much more to dispute the fitness of his proceedings.

He next assigns the cause of his perturbation:

by reason of the darkness.

meaning perhaps the dark cloud which now overshadowed them, and which was the sign of the Deity's near approach[y]. This is Mr. Heath's remark. If *the darkness* is to be taken literally, the remark appears probable, and is withal so ingenious and beautiful, that I have formed the verse-translation upon it.

Elihu adds, to shew the danger of disputing with God about his ways;

If any one speak, surely he shall be destroyed[z].

If

---

[w] Chap. xiii. 3.

[x] ערך It signifies (1) to *form*, as an army does when it prepares for battle, chap. vi. 4. *The terrors of God do set themselves in array against me.* (2) *to be in readiness* for engaging in a dispute, chap. xxxiii. 5. *If thou canst answer me, set* thy words *in order before me, stand:* Put thyself in readiness to dispute with me. (3) *to arrange* arguments in pleading, chap. xiii. 18.

[y] See the note on chap. xlii. 5.

[z] יבלע It is rendered *to destroy*, chap. ii. 3. In the Syriac Testament, Rev. viii. 12, is the translation of καταληγη, and signifies to be smitten so as to be destroyed.

U u

21, 22. When heav'n's expanse the sweeping north-wind clears,
And, flaming forth, the golden sun appears,
Whose optic on the dazzling scene can gaze?
How, then, abide a God's terrific blaze?

23. In

If any one should venture to be my proxy, and carry my complaints of God to his ear; he will certainly perish for his rashness. By *speaking* we must understand speaking of God as Job had done, cavilling at his providence. Otherwise it would not have merited such a punishment.

Ver. 21, 22. *And now*, &c.] He illustrates the terrible majesty of God in a visible manifestation of it, which Elihu seems to be now expecting.

Ver. 21. men *see not*, &c.] men cannot look [a] at the bright light *which* is *in the sky* [a], *when the wind hath passed and cleansed it* [b]. That is, when the sky is in such a clear and dazzling state as he had described ver. 18. He beautifully applies that resplendent image to the purpose of shewing the insufferable splendor of the Divine Majesty.

Ver. 22. *Fair weather* [c]] Our Translators meant, I suppose, by *fair weather* such a serene sky as is painted in the foregoing verse. But the original presents us with a new and more glorious object, the sun itself.

By means of the north-wind [d] (cleansing the sky ver. 21.) *the golden sun cometh forth: with God is terrible majesty.*

---

[a] לא ראו *they cannot look at*, as ver. 19. לא נערך *we cannot order* our speech. *Quum ne fulgentem quidem lucem aspicere possint homines, quæ est in æthere.* Castellio.

[a] שחקים *the sky*. It is translated so ver. 18.

[b] In ver. 22. he calls it the north-wind. The winds that blow from the northern parts bring with them a large quantity of dry air, which drives before it the saturated air and clouds; or imbibes the watery vapours which the saturated air, whose place these dry winds occupy, had let go. In this manner the wind *passeth and cleanseth the sky*.

[c] זהב *gold*. The connection shews that the *sun* is meant by this term. For it is the cause of the *dazzling brightness* in the sky, ver. 21. and is brought in between that and God's terrible majesty; with a view to heighten the infinitely superior lustre of the latter.

[d] צפון *the north*, that is the *north-wind* as in Cant. iv. 16. If we translate, as some, *the golden sun cometh out of the north*, that is, the northern parts of the heavens; the meaning

CHAP. XXXVII.   THE BOOK OF JOB.

23. In vain we pry, in vain our reason toils,
Immensity the force of reason foils:
Justice and boundless pow'r exalt his throne,
Beneficent to all, unjust to none.
24. Therefore let men adore him; in his eyes
To nothing shrinks the wisdom of the wise.

CHAP.

Ver. 23. Touching *the Almighty*, &c.] This great and worthy sentiment is the sum of his whole speech in justification of God. The incomprehensibility and infinite perfection of God silence all objections to his government. This is a sufficient answer even to those two perplexing difficulties in the measures of providence, which Job had started; the destruction of the righteous with the wicked in general calamities, and the prosperity of so many profligate men to the very end of their lives. *For as the heavens are higher than the earth, so are his ways higher than our ways, and his thoughts than our thoughts* [e] : And the ways and thoughts of an infinitely perfect Being cannot be otherwise than right.

WHATEVER IS, IS RIGHT.   *Essay on Man.*

he will not afflict] He *will not oppress* [f]. See chap. x. 3.

Ver. 24. *men do therefore fear him*] *Let men therefore fear him,* who beholdeth all the wise in heart as *a nothing* [g].

This

will be, that he *riseth* on the northern points of the compass, or to the north of the east, as he does throughout the summer. But the sun at his rising is not bright enough to shed *a dazzling light* on the sky: And the sun in his full strength, upon or near the meridian, is the only proper object to set forth the glory of the Divine Majesty.

[e] Isaiah lv. 9.

[f] לא יענה *he will not oppress.* It signifies to afflict unjustly and tyrannically, Exod. i. 11. Psal. lxxxix. 23.

[g] לא *a nothing,* so Schultens renders it here. And so it signifies and is englished, chap. vi. 21.

Chap.
XXXVIII.
Ver. 1. Now the black shadowing cloud, descending fast,
Shot fiercer flames and roar'd a stormy blast:

The

This great instruction is the point of aim throughout Elihu's speech. This is the sublime moral of the whole poem. To establish this primary duty of all religion by his own authority, the Deity himself at last appears; the design of whose speech to Job is to reduce him to this reverent submission; and by his example to enforce it upon all others.

I appeal now to the sensible reader, whether upon a review of this discourse of Elihu it does not appear pertinent and judicious. Job certainly thought it so. He never once interrupts him. He remains silent. It certainly therefore made some impression upon him. He was convinced by it, that he had exceeded both in his justification of himself and in his complaint of God. The conviction however was not full and strong enough, to produce the requisite humiliation. A higher authority was wanted to work that effect; and to bring the poem to its crisis. Hence appears the necessity of the Almighty's interposure.

CHAP. XXXVIII.

The poem is now hastening to its catastrophe. Elihu's discourse had prepared the mind of Job for the change that was to be wrought in him. The speech of the Almighty bears down all obstacles, that remained in the way of his repentance and submission.

The design of *this* appearance of the Almighty is not to vindicate the injured character of his servant Job. That is done by a *second* appearance, which was afterwards made to Eliphaz singly[h], and which comes not within the limits of the poem.

Neither is it the design of this *speech* to decide the controversy, in the dialogue, about the ways of providence: For the decision of that dispute was not

intended

---

[h] Chap. xlii. 7—9.

The voice almighty through the whirlwind broke,
And thus to Job with lofty accent spoke:

2. Who this, whose blindness, in so bold a strain,
Judges my ways, and teaches God to reign?

3. Advance,

intended by the *poem*; but was reserved for the subsequent *history*. The scope of the speech is to *humble Job*; and to teach others, by his example, to acquiesce implicitly in the disposals of God, from an unbounded confidence in his wisdom, equity, and goodness. This surely is an end worthy of the interposition of the Deity.

——dignus vindice nodus.

The method taken in the speech to accomplish its design, is a series of questions and descriptions, relative to *natural things*, admirably fitted to convince this complainant, and all others, of their incapacity to judge of God's *moral* administration, and of the danger of striving with their Maker.

The poet had given, in the course of the poem, glorious specimens of his talent for the sublime. But he seems to have reserved the full exertion of his powers to this concluding part. Here he has collected all his fire, as it were, in a focal point. I imagine it will be easily granted, that, for majesty of sentiment and strength of expression, this speech has nothing equal to it in the most admired productions of Greece or Rome.

Dr. Young has translated it with dignity and spirit. Nothing but the propriety of making an *uniform* version of the whole poem could have prevailed on me to attempt this part after so great a master.

Ver. 1. *out of the whirlwind*] *out of the stormy cloud*[1]. That the Almighty manifested himself on this occasion by some *visible* token of his presence, may be inferred, I should think, from what Job says, chap. xlii. 5. *But now mine eye seeth thee:* And *a cloud* was generally his mode of appearance. Compare Ezek. i. 4. Nahum i. 3.

Ver. 2. *that darkeneth counsel*, &c.] The reproof is, that he had taken upon him

---

[1] מסערה, LXX. διὰ λαιλαπος καὶ νεφων (*MS. Alex.* νεφων) *in a storm and a cloud*. It signifies *a storm at sea*, which is always attended with dark clouds, Jonah i. 4.

334 THE BOOK OF JOB. Chap. XXXVIII.

3. Advance, display the hero, gird thy loin;
  My part the learner's, to instruct me thine.

4. Where thou, when earth's foundations I began?
  Say, knowing creature, how design'd the plan:
5. Who laid its measures, and the line apply'd?
  Did thy vast genius o'er the work preside?
6. What ground sustains the massy pile? who plac'd
  The corner-stone, and its strong framing brac'd?
7. Myriads of starry forms the builder sang,
  My raptur'd sons, and heav'n with chorus rang.

8. Where

him to judge the ways of God, the reasons whereof he was utterly in the dark about: And that he had given vent to his rash judgement in complaints equally rash and inconsiderate. A free translation of this passage might, be,

Who is this that *judgeth in the dark*[k], *and* whose *words* are *without knowledge*.

Ver. 3. *I will demand of thee*, &c.] These expressions refer, no doubt, to that daring challenge, *Then call thou, and I will answer: or let me speak, and answer thou me.* chap. xiii. 22.

Ver. 4—7. *Where wast thou*, &c.] The sentiment conveyed in these pungent interrogations is, that only He who made the world, or at least was present and assisting in that great affair, is capable of judging how it ought to be governed. These verses, 4, 5, 6, 7, speak of the creation of the *earth*, and in terms of architecture, which denote exact proportion, nice arrangement and durable solidity.

Ver. 7. *The morning stars*] They are styled *the sons of God* in the next sentence.

The

---

[k] מחשיך עצה Symmachus turns it σκοτινος γνωμη *of a dark judgement*, or understanding. עצה seems to mean here *thought* in general, or *thoughts* in the form of *judgments* or propositions.

8. Where thou, when ocean from the womb I fent,
When burfting forth roar'd the huge element?

9. A

The fons of God are the angels[l]. I fuppofe, they are called *the morning ftars* on account of the luminous vehicles with which they are cloathed. The morning ftar is exceedingly bright. What a grand appearance does the poet here prefent to our view, ten thoufand times ten thoufand and thoufand of thoufands of glittering angels attending the birth of our world, and finging hallelujahs to the Almighty Father.

Ver. 8—11. *Or who fhut up the fea,* &c.] The waters were coæval with the earth, and covered it in the beginning. The gathering them together into a proper receptacle was the great work of the third day of creation. They then took the denomination of *feas,* or *the fea,* and likewife retained the name of *the deep.* This operation of Almighty power, together with the meafures taken to prevent the fea from overflowing the earth, is the fubject of thefe verfes, 8, 9, 10, 11.

Ver. 8. *with doors*] ver. 10. *and fet bars and doors.* The fhores [m], promontories in particular, and high rocky coaft, are a reftraint upon the ocean and a fecurity to the earth. Thefe are the *barred doors,* which in part keep the waters of the fea within the bounds affigned to them.

When it brake forth [n]] The original word denoteth an *impetuous eruption.* It is the fame that is ufed in Dan. vii. 2. *the four winds of the heaven ftrove (rufhed forth) upon the great fea.* The prophet's defcription is like that in Virgil,

Una Eurufque Notufque ruunt, creberque procellis
Africus: et vaftos volvunt ad littora fluctus.

out of the womb] Had *the creation* of the whole mafs of waters been the thing fpoken of, *by the womb* muft be meant *nihility, non-entity.* But the fubject here is

---

pofitions in the mind; more particularly Job's *thoughts* about the ways of God. עָטֶה בְּחֹשֶׁךְ is *one who judgeth darkly,* as מֵיטִיב צַעַד *one that goeth well,* or *moveth gracefully,* Prov. xxx. 29.

[l] Chap. i. 6. ii. 1.

[m] Prov. viii. 29. Jerem. v. 22.

[n] בְּגִיחוֹ, LXX. ιμαιμασσεν *impetu ferebatur.*

9. A night of swathing clouds I threw around,
And in those folds the wond'rous infant bound:
10. Its fury tam'd with laws, with rocky land
Embarr'd the raging flood, then gave command;
11. " Thus

is the collection of part of the mass into a channel, to form the *sea* and surround the earth. The *womb* therefore, out of which the waters of the *sea* issued, seems to have been the subterraneous abyss, *the sea under ground*, as the Arabs call it [o]. Thus Drusius explains it, *The Abyss was as it were the womb thereof.*

Dr. Woodward supposeth, that there is an immense cavern in the earth, and that this is the *one place* into which the whole mass of waters was gathered on the third day. He further supposeth the abyss to communicate with the bottom of the sea, by vast hiatuses or chasms in the earth [p]. Through these passages, we may conceive, the waters of the abyss *brake forth* and filled the channel of the sea.

Ver. 9. *When I made the cloud,* &c.] The poet had compared the eruption of the sea from the great abyss, to the breaking forth of an infant out of the womb. This astonishing image gave rise to *the garment* and *the swadling band*, to which he resembles those thick and dark clouds, which frequently arise over the sea and encompass it.

Ver. 10. *and brake up for it my decreed* place] If the boundary or channel of the sea had been intended by our author, he would have said, I imagine, *its decreed* place. I prefer therefore the marginal version,

And

---

[o] Shaw's *Travels,* 67. 4to. That curious traveller informs us, that even in the *Sahara* (the desert, south of the kingdom of Algiers) by digging wells to the depth of one hundred, and sometimes two hundred fathoms, they never want a plentiful stream. In order therefore to obtain it, they dig through different layers of sand and gravel, till they come to a flaky stone, like slate, which is known to lie immediately above the *sea below ground,* as they call *the abyss.* This is easily broken through; and the flux of water, which follows the stroke, rises generally so suddenly and in such abundance, that the person let down for this purpose hath sometimes, though raised up with the greatest dexterity, been overtaken and suffocated.

[p] See Chambers' *Dictionary,* art. ABYSS.

11. "Thus far, ye mountain waves, no further, roll,
"My bulwarks shall your haughty foam control."

12. Ancient of days, did Morn thy voice obey
From whence to journey with the dawning ray?

13, 14. Mantled

And established my decree upon it[q]. The decree which God imposed on the mighty ocean, is that wonderful law of gravitation in fluids, by which all the parts of them exerting an equal pressure upon one another, the equilibrium of the whole mass is maintained.

Ver. 11. *And said, Hitherto,* &c.] What a sublime conception does this command give us of the power and majesty of that Being who speaks it!

Ver. 12—15. *Hast thou commanded the morning,* &c.] The transition from the *sea* to *the morning* is not so abrupt as it appears. For the ancients thought, that the sun sets in the ocean, and at his rising cometh out of it again. These verses however are difficult. But I apprehend, *the morning* is described here by three remarkable characters; First, its constant return to its appointed station the east.

Secondly, its making visible the forms and colours of things, which are confounded and lost in the night.

Thirdly, its being the time of the day when justice was administered.

Ver. 12, 13. *the morning—the day-spring*]

Ver. 12.

---

[q] אשבר עליו חקי This surely is a phrase of the same import with that in Prov. viii. 29. בשומי לים חקו *When he gave to the sea his decree.* שבר *to break off,* which our author uses instead of שום *constituit,* is synonimous with חרץ *præcidit, statuit, decrevit,* Daniel ix. 26. *desolations are determined,* נהרצת. But as שבר also signifies figuratively to *enervate* or *break the force* of a thing; Crinsoz translates, *Lorsque je la domptai par mes loix, when I tamed it by my laws.*

THE BOOK OF JOB. Chap. XXXVIII.

13, 14. Mantled in gold she wings her beamy flight,
Holds in her hand the beauteous seal of light,
From east to west the clear impression gives,
And earth like clay the colour'd forms receives:

15. Then

Ver. 12. *Haſt thou commanded the morning in thy life-time*[1]*? Haſt thou cauſed the day-ſpring to know its place?*

Ver. 13. *To take hold of the ends of the earth, That the wicked might be ſhaken out of it?*

In ver. 12. *The morning* and *the day-ſpring* are but different terms for one single thing; break of day until ſun-riſing. Its regular appearance in the eaſt is here marked. In the firſt ſentence of ver. 13. the diffuſion of the morning light over the whole face of the earth, is expreſſed by the beautiful figure of *taking hold of the ends of the earth*. In the ſecond ſentence, the *moral* benefit of the morning to mankind is taken notice of; *That the wicked might be ſhaken out of it.* In thoſe times and countries the courts of Juſtice ſate in the morning[2]. This ſingular circumſtance gives a dignity and importance to the deſcription of the morning, worthy to come from the mouth of the righteous governor of the world.

Ver. 14. *It is turned as clay,* &c.][3]

It (the earth) *is changed*[4] *as clay* by *the ſeal,*
When they (the morning and the day-ſpring) *preſent themſelves as it were* in *magnificent attire.*

During the darkneſs of the night the earth is a perfect blank; in which ſtate it reſembles clay that has no impreſſion. By the morning light falling upon the earth,

---

[1] מימיך *atate tua.* Caſtellio.

[2] Judges vi. 31. Pſal. ci. 8. *I will early (in the morning) deſtroy all the wicked of the land.* Alſo, Jer. xxi. 12.

[3] תתהפך. Vertitur terra et mutatur ut lutum ſigilli; quod facilé cedit, et varias formas recipit pro libidine imprimentis aliquid in eo. *Druſius.*

[4] הפך denotes a change from one ſtate to another that is oppoſite; when *the ſea,* for inſtance, *was turned,* or changed, *into dry land,* Pſal. lxvi. 6.

CHAP. XXXVIII. THE BOOK OF JOB.

15. Then juſtice from the world ejects the vile,
And breaks the giant arm inur'd to ſpoil.

16. Haſt earth, innumerable objects make their appearance upon it: It is then changed, like clay which has received the ſtamp of the ſeal. Thus I underſtand this elegant ſimile. Sealing upon *clay* is ſtill practiſed in the eaſt. When the corn-granary at Grand-Cairo, belonging to the Sultan, is full; the inſpectors (ſays Mr. Norden) having ſhut the door, put on their ſeal, upon a handful of clay, which they make uſe of inſtead of wax[a].

They preſent themſelves as it were in magnificent attire[x]. In the original the verb is plural, merely in conformity to grammatical conſtruction; there being two nominatives to it, *the morning* and *the day-ſpring* ver. 12. But as thoſe two nominatives mean but one thing, namely, *the morning*; the tranſlation would be juſtified, and the ſenſe clearer, if the verb is turned in the ſingular number: *ſhe preſents herſelf*, &c.

We have here a grand poetical image. The *Morning*, in the figure of a beautiful perſonage, cloathed in a garment of light, preſents herſelf in the eaſt: She holds a ſeal in her hand, as the miniſter of providence; and is on the wing to enlighten the earth, and to renew with her ſeal the appearance of things in their proper forms and colours.

Ver. 15. *And from the wicked*, &c.] The poet blends together in his deſcription of the morning, the *moral* and *natural* benefits of it. He now returns to the moral benefits, which he began to mention ver. 13. By cutting off ſome wicked men, in the morning, and putting a ſtop to the oppreſſions committed by others, a happy change is made in the ſtate of ſociety; correſponding to the beautiful change in the face of nature, when the morning effaces the horrors of night and reſtores the pleaſing ſcenes of day.

---

[a] Norden's *Travels*, p. 72. 8vo.

[w] ויתיצבו *they preſent themſelves*, to perform their miniſtry, as in chap. i. 6. ii. 1.

[x] כמו לבוש for כמו בלבוש. The ellipſis of the prepoſition is very common in the poetical books of ſcripture. See an inſtance in chap. xxxviii. 30. *the waters are hid as with a ſtone*, כאבן. Schultens has obſerved, that לבוש ſignifies *magnificent apparel* in Eſther vi. 8, 10, 11.

16. Haſt thou gone down th' immeaſurable ſteep?
Travers'd the windings of the central deep?
17. Unbarr'd death's portal? and from thence ſurvey'd
The ghoſts that colonize the world of ſhade?

18. Or

Ver. 16, 17. *Haſt thou entered,* &c.] We now deſcend into the lower parts of the earth. For I apprehend (1) that by *the ſea,* or *deep,* we are to underſtand the *ſea below ground,* the waters of the great abyſs. (2) that by *the gates of death* and *the doors of the ſhadow of death* is meant the entrance into *Sheol* the world of ghoſts. (3) that in the creed, at leaſt the poetical creed, of theſe men, *Sheol* was placed under the waters of the abyſs. The interrogation therefore is, *Haſt thou gone down into Sheol?* The reproof contained in this interrogation is, that it is folly and preſumption to interpoſe our judgement upon the diſpenſations of good and evil in the preſent world; unleſs we perfectly knew the connection of theſe diſpenſations with a future world, the world of final reward and puniſhment.

Ver. 16. *the ſprings of the ſea* ʸ] This verſion is ſupported by the Septuagint, which turns it *the fountain of the ſea:* By *the fountain,* or *ſprings of the ſea,* is meant, I ſuppoſe, the abyſs, or maſs of waters in the bowels of the earth. See the note on ver. 8. But I rather think the tranſlation ſhould be, *the intricate paths of the ſea,* i. e. of the abyſs.

in the ſearch ᶻ *of the depth*] *in the depths of the abyſs.* Mr. Heath.

Ver. 17. *the gates of death—the doors,* &c.] Iſaiah calls them *the gates of Sheol* ᵃ; that is, the entrance into the region of the dead, the world of departed ſouls. The Hebrews named it *Sheol,* and the Greeks *Hades.* The Septuagint verſion of the ſecond ſentence, *Haſt thou ſeen the doors of the ſhadow of death,* is remarkable and ſtriking; *Were the door-keepers of Hades terrified when they ſaw thee* ᵇ?

What

ʸ נבכי *the intricate paths.* The Chaldee turns it *the intricate places.* That interpreter makes the root to be נבך *to be entangled* in difficult ways, Exod. xiv. 3.

ᶻ חקר, LXX. επι ιχνιων *in the paths;* Crinſoz, *les gouffres.*

ᵃ Iſaiah xxxviii. 10.

ᵇ Πυλωροι δε αδε ιδοντες σε επτηξαν.

18. Or is the furface of the globe, fo wide,
A landfkip in thy view from fide to fide?
Do thy paternal eyes, ftill watching o'er,
Vifit each clime, and coaft along each fhore?

19. The palace where imperial light renews
Her golden treffes, and her glitt'ring hues;.
The fhadowy realm whence darknefs from her bed
Afcends, new horrors on the world to fpread,

20. Reveal:

What Hebrew text this interpreter followed I cannot guefs. But he is certainly right in underftanding it of *Sheol*[c]. For as *the gates of death* are here connected with *the abyfs*; fo in chap. xxvi. 5, 6. the ghofts of the old giants, which are in *Sheol*, are faid to be *under the waters:* And that by *the waters* are meant the waters in the cavern of the earth, *the abyfs*, is evident; inafmuch as Ifaiah gives to *Sheol* the epithet *from beneath*[d], and Ezekiel calls it *the nether parts of the earth* and *the pit*[e]. Alfo in the *Apocalypfe*, *The keys of Hades and death* (chap. i. 18.) are ftiled (chap. ix. 1.) *The keys of the pit of the abyfs*.

Ver. 18. *Haft thou perceived*, &c.] We now afcend from below the center of the earth to its furface; from the region of death to the world of life. *Haft thou confidered*[f] *the breadth of the earth*, &c. The queftion relates not to a fpeculative knowledge of the earth's extent, but to a providential furvey of it; fuch as he alone can take who created it, and who alone is a competent judge how it ought to be provided for and governed.

Ver. 19—21. *Where* is *the way* where *light dwelleth?*] This queftion differs from that in ver. 12—15. That related to the *morning* and its benefit to mankind,

---

[c] See Windet *de vita functorum ftatu.* p. 73—75.
[d] Ifaiah xiv. 9. שאול מתחת *Hell* (Sheol) *from beneath.*
[e] Ezekiel xxxi. 14, 16, 18.
[f] התבננת *Haft thou confidered?* chap. xxxii. 12. *Yea, I attended* (אתבונן) *unto you.*

20. Reveal: their well-diftinguifh'd paths define,
   Guide us along th' inviolable line.
21. Skill in all this, O antemundane fage,
   Befeems thy venerable length of age.
22. Inform us if thy curious travels know
   My treafur'd hail, and magazines of fnow;

23. Spar'd

kind, this to fettling the precife boundary of light and darknefs, that is, day and night. One half of the earth is enlightened, the other half is in darknefs at the fame inftant. This is owing to the fphæroidical form given to the earth at its creation. Job is now afked, whether he was witnefs to this operation by which the limits of light and darknefs were fixed, and knew the extent both of the one and the other. But the queftion is dreffed in the glorious ornaments of fublime poetry: *Light* and *Darknefs* are reprefented as perfons: Each has its feparate dwelling and peculiar jurifdiction: The bounds of one never encroach on thofe of the other.

Ver. 19. *Which is the way to the habitation of light? and the place of darknefs, where* is *it?*

Ver. 20. *Surely thou canft guide* (take) *us to its border; yea, certainly thou canft fhew the roads* which lead *to its houfe.*

Ver. 21. *Thou muft know, for thou wert born at that time; as to the number of thy years,* they are *many.* Mr. Heath.

This is lofty irony.

Ver. 22—38. Haft thou entered, &c.] This whole paragraph relates to thofe changes in the ftate of the atmofphere, which we call the weather.

Ver. 22. *The treafures of the fnow,* &c.] Snow is the watery vapours frozen in the cloud; hail the fame vapours frozen after they have run into drops large enough for rain. The clouds therefore are the *treafures,* or rather *treafuries,* of fnow and hail. Job is ironically afked whether he has ever been among them, to affift in, or at leaft obferve, thofe wonderful operations.

CHAP. XXXVIII. THE BOOK OF JOB. 343

23. Spar'd for the day of evil, when with ftorms
Winter the foreft and the fields deforms:
Or when ftrange battel on my foes I pour,
And armies perifh in the wrathful fhow'r.

24. When the hot caft-wind wheels its boift'rous courfe,
Who drives the tempeft and directs its force?
Or by what arm is ruddy lightning hurl'd?
How burft the flafhes, and inwrap the world?

25—27. Who

Ver. 23. *Which I have referved*, &c.] The infpired poet ftill keeps in view the *moral* purpofes for which the Deity employs his *natural* works. *The time of trouble* may fignify not winter in general; but thofe fevere winters, in which there falls fuch abundance of fnow and hail as does infinite damage to the fruits of the earth, to cattle, and to human kind.

Leo Africanus affures us, that the caravans which travel through the African deferts, are fometimes fuddenly overtaken with fuch furious ftorms of fnow, that their beafts and carriages and themfelves are caft away in it.

the day of battle and war] Thefe expreffions may only import that in fuch a *time of trouble* as was mentioned in the former fentence, God himfelf makes war upon his enemies; that is, punifhes the fins of men by ufing fnow and hail to deftroy their fuftenance. Extraordinary and miraculous fnow or hail may alfo be intended, like that with which he punifhed the Egyptians and the Canaanites[r]. There might be inftances of the fame kind before thofe times, and which might fall within the compafs of Job's experience or information.

Ver. 24—27. *By what way*, &c.] The wind, rain, and thunder which accompany, or immediately follow *the light* here mentioned, might have led our Tranflators to render it *the lightning*, as in chap. xxxvii. 3.

That.

---

[r] Exod. ix. 23. Jof. x. 11.

25—27. Who fashion'd the canals, which spout the rain
In flame and thunder on the desert plain?
The howling wild, by human foot untrod,
Pours out green pasture from each teeming clod.

28. Tell

That ingenious traveller and naturalist Dr. Russell informs us, in his observations on the weather at Aleppo, that March 1743 set in with variable spring weather (though somewhat cooler than usual) which continued till the 23d; from which time till the end a great quantity of rain, hail and thunder.

On the 16th of October, at night, the second rains fell with a good deal of thunder.

In January 1753 more rain fell in the day time than usual in this month. Wind generally *north-east* or *east*, and moderate [g].

Ver. 24. *the light*] rather *the lightning*. How imperfect a solution of this phænomenon philosophy is able to give, see in the remark on chap. xxxvii. 4.

which *scattereth*, &c.] when *the east wind scattereth itself*, or *is scattered* [h]; &c.

Ver. 25. *Who hath divided a water-course*, &c.] *Who prepared* [i] *an aqueduct* (or *conduit* [k]) *for the overflowing of waters*. The sublime metaphor of *the aqueduct* signifies, I suppose, the ways through the atmosphere, in which the power of God conducts the heavy inundating clouds to their appointed vent.

for the lightning of thunder] *for the blaze* [l] *of thunder*. Mr. Heath.

---

[g] Dr. Russell's *Natural History of Aleppo*.

[h] יפץ LXX. διασκιδάνυται *is scattered*. Verbs active which have no nominative express or understood, must be turned in the passive voice.

[i] פלג *prepared*. So Mr. Heath renders it, and remarks that LXX. translate it ητοιμασεν. The root פלג, he says, signifies *separavit, divisit*; and has likewise the signification of *setting apart to a particular use*. I could wish however he had produced a voucher for the latter acceptation.

[k] תעלה Some Greek versions rendered it ὑδραγωγον *an aqueduct*, or *conduit*, as our bible turns it in II Kings xx. 20.

[l] חזיז *the blaze*. But Aquila renders it κτυπον *the crack*; Symmachus ψοφον *the sound*. But it signifies in Arabic *scuit crenatim to cut a thing like the jagged edge of a leaf*. The noun חזיז denotes

28. Tell, who the father of the rain; and who
    The plaſtic parent of the dropping dew.
29. What is the womb of ice? and whence is born
    Hoar-froſt, that whitens in the wint'ry morn?

                                            30. A

Ver. 26, 27. *To cauſe it to rain*, &c.] This circumſtance, where *no man is*, &c. is dwelt upon, to ſhew the proviſion which the creator makes for the ſuſtenance of *wild beaſts*. Compare Pſalm civ. 10, 11. Joel ii. 22. This inſtance of the power and providence of God might alſo be intended to ſuggeſt, that he who turns the barren wilderneſs into fruitful paſture, is equally able to change a miſerable condition into a happy one. Such an inſtruction is a ſtrong motive to confidence in God in the moſt deſperate ſituation, as Job thought his own to be. Compare chap. v. 9—11. and ſee the note there.

Ver. 28. *Hath the rain a father?*] The queſtion cannot be whether the rain hath a father, but *who is the father of the rain* º *?* as appears by the next ſentence, *or who hath begotten the drops of the dew?*

The firſt mechanical agents in the production of *rain* and *dew* are known only to him whoſe name is wonderful. With regard to *rain*, ſee the remark on chap. xxxvi. 27. As to *dew*, all the diſcoveries of philoſophy concerning it are couched in theſe few words; " If the vapours, after they are exhaled from off the waters, do not riſe very high in the atmoſphere, but hover near the ſurface of the earth, they then conſtitute what we call *a fog*. If they fall to the earth, being condenſed by the cold of the night, without uniting into drops large enough to be called rain, they are then ſaid to fall in *dew* ᵖ."

Ver. 29. *the ice—the hoary froſt*] *Hoar-froſt*, or white-froſt, is the dew frozen

or

---

denotes *a flaſh of lightning* as it appears in the hot climates, in a jagged or zigzag form Our engliſh bible tranſlates it *bright clouds*; but in the margin *lightnings*, in Zach. x. 1. *The Lord ſhall make bright clouds, and give them ſhowers of rain*. It certainly means there *flaſhes of lightning* burſting from the clouds, the prelude and concomitant of rain.

º היש *is there?* LXX. פי יש τις εςιν, *who is?* ſo likewiſe the Vulgate, *Quis eſt?*

ᵖ Rowning's *Natural Philoſophy*, p. ii. 142. Chambers' *Dictionary*, article Dew.

30. A marble covering on the ſtreams is caſt,
And the broad lake with cold is fetter'd faſt.

31. When milder ſtars the gentle feafon bring,
Canſt thou withold the beauties of the ſpring?

Or

or congealed early in cold mornings; chiefly in autumn ⁹. Our ignorance in the mechanical production of ice and froſt was taken notice of in the remark on chap. xxxvii. 9, 10, 11.

Ver. 30. *The waters are hid*, &c.] Mr. Heath turns it, *The waters cover themſelves ʳ as it were with a ſtone*. The ſon of Sirach has given a beautiful deſcription of this wonderful operation and appearance of nature: *When the cold north wind bloweth, and the water is congealed into ice; it abideth upon every gathering together of water, and clotheth the water as with a breaſt-plate.* Eccleſiaſt. xliii. 20.

the deep ˢ] *The deep* cannot here mean *the ſea*. A frozen ſea was never ſeen in Arabia or its neighbourhood. Neither could ſuch a phænomenon be ſo much as heard of in thoſe days; when navigation had not reached to the high northern latitudes. But our author's word ſignifies, in the Arabic language, any deep gathering together of water, whether fountain, river, or lake. *A frozen lake*, &c. might be known even in Arabia, or in ſome of the adjacent countries. See the remark on chap. xxxvii. 10.

Ver. 31, 32. *Canſt thou bind*, &c.] He is now aſked, whether he has power over the heavenly bodies, to direct their motions, control their action upon the earth, and prevent the feaſons and weather which they are wont to produce.

The

---

⁹ Chambers' *Dictionary*, article HOAR-FROST.

ʳ יתחבאו The Vulgate ſeems to have read יתקפאון *congelantur*; having rendered it *durantur*.

ˢ תהום It is uſed for any large body of water. The ſtreams which ran from the rock ſmitten by the rod of Moſes, are called תהומיא רברבן *great deeps*, or fluxes of water; in the Targum on Pſal. lxxviii. 15.

Or when Orion lifts his ſtormy ſphere,
Canſt thou with flow'rs adorn the froſt-bound year?
32. By monthly ſtages doſt thou learn the ſun,
Through the vaſt orbit of the ſigns to run?
Or lead Arcturus and his ſons, to roll
In ſhining ranks around the northern pole?
33. Thy laws do theſe fulfil? with pow'rs from thee,
Hold they dominion in the earth and ſea?

34, 35. Come,

The gueſſes of the learned concerning thoſe aſtronomical terms which we tranſlate *Pleiades, Orion,* and *Arcturus,* were mentioned in the note on chap. ix. 9. Chryſoſtom explains *Mazzaroth* [1] of *the twelve ſigns* of the zodiac. Our marginal verſion adopts that explanation. *Bringing forth* the twelve ſigns each *in its ſeaſon,* or month, is an expreſſion accommodated to the then received ſyſtem of the world. The earth was ſuppoſed to be at reſt in the center; and the heavens to revolve annually round it, carrying with them the ſun, planets, and fixed ſtars.

Ver. 31. *the ſweet influences,* &c.] *The ſweet influences* are the pleaſant ſeaſon of ſpring; *the bands* are the rigours of winter when the earth is bound with froſt. The chief attention of the Arabs was not ſo much to the planets, as to the fixed ſtars, their riſing and ſetting, and their ſuppoſed influence in producing rain, wind, heat, cold, and all other changes of weather. See Pococke's Specimen Hiſt. Arab. 164. where we are told, that one of the three branches of knowledge which the ancient Arabs chiefly applied themſelves to, was the influence of the ſtars in producing rainy weather.

Ver. 33. *the ordinances of heaven,* &c.] By *heaven* is meant the celeſtial ſphere, or the heavenly bodies contained in it. *The ordinances of heaven* are the laws

by

---

[1] מזרות Some will have the root to be אזר to *gird.* אזור is *a girdle.* Hence (ſays Caſtell.) אזיר המזלות *the girdle,* or belt, *of the* conſtellations, i. e. the zodiac. See other derivations in Clodius' *Lexicon Sel-ctum,* p. 335.

34, 35. Come, to its pitch thy thund'ring voice extend,
Summon the clouds from heav'ns far-diftant end:
Involv'd in darknefs, and begirt on high
With feas of vapours, bid the lightnings fly:
Hark! do they anfwer, "Here?" and diftant bear
Thy awful mandates through the trembling air?

36. Vague

by which thofe bodies perform their revolutions: And *the dominion thereof in the earth* denotes their real, or fuppofed, action and effects upon our atmofphere and terraqueous globe.

Ver. 34—38. *Canft thou lift up thy voice,* &c.] Thunder-fhowers were the fubject in ver. 25—27. The fame fubject feems to be refumed here. But there the operation was, the guiding of the rainy clouds, through the air, to the place appointed for the difcharge of their contents: Here a body of dark clouds is collected, to form, as it were a pavillion for the Lord of thunder. The rain is mentioned there as poured down on the defert, for the benefit of wild beafts: Here it is fent to mollify the hardened glebe, and prepare the field for plowing and fowing. The lightnings alfo are here fent forth with greater pomp of divine majefty. One is apt however to think, that thefe verfes fhould have been fubjoined immediately after ver. 27. and that this divifion of the fpeech would be clofed with more propriety and dignity by verfes 31, 32, 33. which mention the courfe of the fun, and thofe conftellations which were thought to produce rain and all the other variations of weather.

Ver. 34. *Canft thou lift up,* &c.] What can be more humiliating than fuch interrogations as this? What muft Job, what muft any man, think of himfelf, for daring to enter into a ftrife with God, and to find fault with his ways; when his own ignorance is thus contrafted with his wifdom, his own weaknefs with his power, and his own littlenefs with his tremendous majefty?

Ver. 35. *Here we are*] This furprizing figure of fpeech, which gives intelligence and a voice to the lightnings, expreffeth, with great fublimity, the punctuality with which inanimate creatures obferve the laws prefcribed to them, and perform the fervice enjoined them by their Creator. The author of *Baruch*

has

36. Vague meteors, wild phenomena, who taught
 Thefe not to err, as though endow'd with thought?

37. Who ranges the celeftial urns, and pours
 In wifdom's feafon their emollient fhow'rs;

38. The

has imitated this wonderful profopopeia, chap. iii. 34. *The ftars fhined in their watches, and rejoiced: when he calleth them they fay, Here we be.*

Ver. 36. *Who hath put wifdom*, &c.] This profe may be turned into the following diftich,

Who planted reafon in the human breaft?
Who on the mind ideal forms imprefs'd?

But the fentiment bears no fort of analogy to what goeth before and cometh after. The learned Schultens therefore has, by the help of the Arabic, offered another tranflation; which carries on the grand figure that clofed the preceding verfe.

Who put wifdom in wild motions[u]?
Or who hath given to a phænomenon[v] *underftanding?*

By *wild motions* and *a phænomenon* are meant thunder, lightning, rain, and other meteors. Their motions are faid to be wild and vague, becaufe they feem fo to us. Philofophy has not been able to reduce their operations to any certain theory. Neverthelefs they are governed by laws, as fteady as thofe which regulate the motions of the heavenly bodies. This the poet has fuggefted by the noble expreffions, *putting wifdom and underftanding* into thefe wild phænomena.

Ver. 37, 38. *Who can number*, &c.] The work of providence defcribed in thefe

---

[u] בטחות *wild motions*. The root טחא in Arabic fignifies *vagari, eberrare fine certa lege.*

[v] שכוי *a phænomenon*, or *appearance, adfpectabile, apparens.* The root שכה is in Chaldee, *fpectavit, imaginatus eft.* The noun שכיות in Ifaiah ii. 16. fignifies *fpectacula*, or *fpectabiles figuræ, pictures.* Vid. Schultens, & Clodii *Lex. Select.*

38. The glebe to loosen, when the glowing ray
Hath harden'd into rock the binding clay?

39. Does thy all-pow'rful impulse drive along
The mother *lioness*, so swift and strong?
                                                    Furious

these verses is, the collecting and arranging the clouds in the most fitting season, and then disposing them in the most proper manner for emptying themselves in beneficent showers upon the arable lands. The beautiful images with which the description is adorned, are as follow: (1) *The collecting* and *arrangement* of the clouds is exprest by a metaphor taken from a civil or military enrolment, *who can number*, &c. See II Sam. xxiv. 10. (2) *The clouds* themselves are compared to those earthen jars in which the eastern people keep their water and their wine, *the bottles* (or *pitchers*) *of heaven*. See I Sam. x. 3. Isaiah xxx. 14. Lament. iv. 2. (3) *The disposing* the clouds in a proper manner for emptying themselves, is denoted by the position into which which a pitcher, or jar, is put for pouring out its contents: who can *lay along* the pitchers of heaven? This image is similar to the inclined urn which the heathen poets place in the hand of a river-god. The urn represents the fountain from which the river flows; and what fountains are to rivers, the clouds are to rain. I am indebted to Schultens for the substance of this note.

Ver. 38. *When the dust*, &c.] These showers are sent to mollify the glebe, and prepare it for plowing; when it has been baked and hardened by the long drought of summer. Compare Psalm lxv. 9—13.

Ver. 39, 40. *Wilt thou hunt*, &c.] Verse 39 should have begun a new chapter. For we there pass to quite a new topic, the brute animals which inhabit the air, the land, and the water. This subject is continued, with a few short interruptions, unto the end of the Almighty's speech. The judicious Poet has selected those species of animals, in which the wisdom, power, and providential care of the Creator are most eminently displayed. The tendency of the descriptions is, to raise in our minds such admiring sentiments of the Deity as will effectually extinguish discontent, and silence murmurings against his dispensations.

Furious at eve she hunts the yelling wood,
And swells her empty pap with milky food.
Is it thy hand the *lion colts* sustains,
And pours the carnage through their greedy veins;
40. When couchant in the shaggy mountain lair,
In watch of quarry, o'er the vale they glare?

41. Lo,

Ver. 39. *Wilt thou hunt,* &c.] *Wilt thou hunt the prey for the lioness*[x]*?* The question turns upon making provision for the lioness and her family of sucking whelps. The wonderful providence of God effects this, by the tender feelings of parental affection which he has infused into this savage animal, and the peculiar fierceness and swiftness which he has given to it, to hunt the prey that she may have a supply of milk for her young.

Or fill the appetite, &c.] This is a different question. It relates to qualifying the young *weaned* lions [y] to provide for themselves.

Ver. 40. *When they couch,* &c.] Statius finely describes a lion in this attitude:

    Qualis ubi primam leo mane cubilibus altis
    Erexit rabiem, & sævo speculatur ab antro
    Aut cervum aut nondum bellantem fronte juvencam [z].

    So the fierce lion, at the rising day,
    His hunger wakes, and meditates the prey:
    Close ambush'd in the mountain den he lies,
    And darts along the vale his glaring eyes;
    If chance some stately stag his claw invite,
    Or heifer yet unbudded for the fight.

---

[x] ללביא Vulg. *leænæ.* See Ezek. xix. 2. and Hieroz. part i. 719.

[y] כפירים, Ezek. xix. 3. Hieroz. ubi supra.

[z] Theb. vii. 760.

41. Lo, the young *ravens*, from the nest exil'd,
On hunger's wing attempt th' aerial wild:
Who leads their wand'rings, and their feast supplies?
To God ascend their importuning cries.

CHAP. XXXIX.
Ver. 1.   When did the *mountain goat*, or bounding *roe*,
In their hard travail thy assistance know?

2. Thou

Ver. 41. *Who provideth for the raven*, &c.] The raven, one is apt to think, has slipped in here by mistake. Should he not rather have been joined with some of his feathered relations, in the subsequent chapter? But perhaps he is mentioned here, because he lives on carrion, and may be supposed to feed on the carcasses which the lion leaves. The difficulty of meeting with such kind of food renders the divine power more illustrious in preserving this species of creatures. Compare Psalm cxlvii. 9.

CHAP. XXXIX.

Ver. 1. *Knowest thou—canst thou mark*] Not meer knowledge, but providential care and protection is intended here[a]. *To know* is used in this sense in Ps. xxxi. 7. The other expression *canst thou mark*, &c. should have been *canst thou watch over*, or *preserve*[b], the calving of the hinds? i. e. the hinds when they calve.

the wild goats[c] *of the rocks*] The kind of *wild goats* here mentioned is the *Ibex*, the *Eveck*. Its habitation is on the tops of the highest rocks, where its perpetual

---

[a] See verses 26, 27.
[b] Chap. x. 12. *Thy visitation hath preserved* (שמרה) *my spirit*. Grotius expounds חלל אילות תשמר, *An obstetricari potes cervis fœminis?*
[c] יעלי, V. *ibices*.

CHAP. XXXIX.   THE BOOK OF JOB.   353

2. Thou to their fwelling womb its moons ordain?
Thou watch the burden to the hour of pain?
3. Bending they ftrain t' emit the ftruggling birth,
And caft their forrows on the rugged earth:

4. Faft-

tual leaping from precipice to precipice, together with the kids, expofes them to fo many perils, that without a fingular care of providence the breed muft perifh. It is remarkable for its fwiftnefs and agility, for the largenefs of its horns, which bend backward and extend to the buttocks, and for its affection to its parents and young[d].

the hinds] The *hind*, or roe, is the female of the hart. It is a lovely creature, of an elegant fhape, and its hair is of great price. It is noted for its fwiftnefs and the furenefs of its ftep. The rutting time is at the coming in of autumn. They go eight months in their pregnancy, and bring forth in the fpring. This creature is timorous, perpetually fleeing from wild beafts or men, and jumping among the rocks[e].

Ver. 2. *Canft thou number—knoweft thou,* &c.] *Canft thou number* is here equivalent to *Canft thou appoint the number,* &c. See chap. xiv. 5. And *knowing* means operative providential care, as in ver. 1.

Ver. 3. *They bow themfelves,* &c.] The difficulty with which thefe creatures bring forth their young, is taken notice of by Pliny[f], as Grotius remarks. That difficulty is here painted by our poet in very expreffive terms:

They bow themfelves, they burft[g] with their pangs, they caft out[g] their young ones.

---

[d] I Sam. xxiv. 3. Pfal. civ. 18. Hieroz. p. i. 917—920.

[e] II Sam. xxii. 34. Pfal. xviii. 34. Cant. ii. 8, 9. viii. 14. Habak. iii. 19. Hieroz. p. i. lib. iii. cap. 17.

[f] *Nat. Hift.* lib. viii. 32.

[g] תשלחנה and תפלחנה. Mr. Heath obferves, that thefe words are marked in fome MSS. with a circle (o) to fhew, as he imagines, that they have changed places.

354 THE BOOK OF JOB. CHAP. XXXIX.

4. Fast the hale infants thrive; then leave their home,
Hang o'er the cliffs, and through the vallies roam.

5. Who from the *forest-ass* his collar broke,
And manumis'd his shoulder from the yoke?

6. Wild

Ver. 4. *are in good liking*[h]] This verfion gives the force of the original word, which denotes *healthfulnefs* and *plumpnefs*.

They grow up with corn] *They grew up in the defert*[i]. Bochart remarks[j], that in Arabia the corn is cut (or plucked up) in March and April, at which time thefe kids and fawns are not yet brought forth, or but juft littered. They grow up therefore not with corn, but with the few fhrubs and hardy plants which the deferts afford: a circumftance which renders their prefervation and *good-liking* the more wonderful.

They go forth] into the wide world to cater for themfelves.

return not unto them] unto their parents.

Ver. 5. *the wild afs*] The beautiful variety in the works of God is apparent in this animal, which though ranked under the fame genus with the domeftic afs, differs widely from it; in the liberty it enjoys, the place of its habitation, and its manners.

free] The word does not imply here an antecedent ftate of bondage. It fignifies freedom in oppofition to flavery; an exemption from the fervitude to which the domeftic afs is made fubject; which exemption is expreffed in the next fentence by *loofing the bands of the wild afs*.

---

[h] יהלמו In the Syriac Teftament III John 2. הוה חלים is the tranflation of ὑγιαίνειν. Clodius alfo in his *Lexicon Selectum* obferves, that this verb fignifies both in Syriac and Arabic *to be fat*.

[i] בר It fignifies *the defert* in the Arabic Pfalter, Pfalm xlix. 11. as likewife ברוך Pfalm xxviii. 7. Caftell. likewife informs us in his *Lex.* that עשל אלבר is *wild honey*. And חיות ברא are *the wild beafts, the beafts of the defert*, in the Targum on Pfalm lxviii. 23, 14.

6. Wild tenant of the waste, I sent him there,
   Among the shrubs, to breathe in freedom's air.
7. Swift as an arrow in his speed he flies,
   Sees from afar the smoking city rise;
   Scorns the throng'd street, where slav'ry drags her load,
   The loud-voic'd driver and his urging goad:
8. Where'er the mountain waves its lofty wood,
   A boundless range, he seeks his verdant food.

9. The savage *reem*, in thy own deserts bred,
   Shakes the tall terrors of his horned head:

The

Ver. 6. *the wilderness*] The deserts of Arabia, as well as Africa and India, are the habitation of this creature. He is a gregarious animal: For they go in herds to pasture and to watering. Yet in Hof. viii. 9. he is said to be *solitary* because he frequents lonely places. In some countries the wild ass is very tall and beautifully striped, in others they are grey or of an ash colour and low of stature [k].

The barren land] In the hebrew, *salt places*. The soil of deserts, those of Arabia in particular, abounds with salt; as appears from the brackish taste of the springs and plants that are found there. Salt was a metaphor to express barrenness, because the plains bordering on the lake of Sodom are the most barren spots in all Palestine. When Jordan overflows its banks this lake also overflows the neighbouring shores, and leaves a coat of salt upon the land [l].

Ver. 7. *He scorneth*, &c.] This is a very animated amplification of the *freedom* mentioned ver. 5. which freedom is here contrasted with the bondage and drudgery of the tame ass.

---

[k] Hieroz. p. i. lib. iii. cap. 16.
[l] See Judges ix. 45. Jer. xvii. 6. Michaelis in Prælect. p. 40. n. 42. and Maundrel's *Journey*, &c.

The mighty monarch of the mountain groves,
And brawny-limb'd, with furious gait he moves.
Will he forget his fierceness, at thy call?
Accept thy hire, and slumber in thy stall?

10. Foam

Ver. 9. *the unicorn*] *the wild bull.* The hebrew name is *Reem*, which appears from the allusions to it in scripture to be a creature of great strength, with high and terrible horns, and of the beeve kind ᵐ. It cannot therefore be the *unicorn*, which is a fish in the north seas. the land unicorn is a meer fiction. Neither can it be the *Rhinoceros*, which hath but one horn, and that a very short one placed just over the nose ⁿ. Neither is it the *Arabian Reem*, which is a species of *roe* and a weak timid animal. It is most probably the *wild bull*, bred in the Syrian and Arabian deserts; which answers perfectly well to the characters of the *scripture Reem*. The Arab poets are very copious in their descriptions of the hunting of this animal, and borrow many images from its beauty, swiftness, strength, and the loftiness of its horns. They represent it a very fierce and untameable beast, white on the back, with large shining eyes. The reader however ought to be informed, that one of the Arabian poets joins it with the *roes*; perhaps because they are both wild creatures. Damir, their great naturalist, in the chapter which he entitles *Of the wild bull*, describes no other than *a wild stag*. But so Cæsar speaking of the *Urus*, of the black forest in Germany, calls it *bos cervi figura*, 'a beeve shaped like a stag ᵒ. The *Reems* are in effect called *wild bulls* by the Psalmist Psalm xxii. For those whom he stiles

bulls

ᵐ Numb. xxiii. 22. xxiv. 8. Deut. xxxiii. 17. Psal. xxii. 13, 22. xxix. 6. xcii. 11. Isaiah xxxiv. 6, 7.

ⁿ We learn from Dr. Parsons, in the *Philosophical Transactions* for the year 1743, that there is in Africa a species of Rhinoceros that hath always a double horn upon the nose. The doctor produced to the members of the Royal Society a double horn, of this creature, brought from the Cape of Good Hope. But neither Job nor the writer of the poem can be supposed to have heard of such an animal; nor will this circumstance of a double horn intitle it to the description of the *Reem*.

ᵒ Schultens *in loc. Hieroz.* p. i. 965, 966. Clodius in his *Lex. Select.* says, that the *Reem* occurs nine times in the hebrew bible; and that its name is derived from רום *altus*, on account of the tallness of its stature or the loftiness of its horns.

10. Foam in thy harness, tremble at thy rod,
Harrow the vale and break the stubborn clod?
11. Wilt thou, relying on his force, demand
His hoof to thresh the harvest of thy land?
12. Or to his shoulder trust the loaded wain,
Which fills thy garners with the precious grain?

13. The *camel-bird*, with her broad quiv'ring vans,
In stately pride, her heated body fans:

But

bulls of Bashan, i. e. of the mountains of Bashan, ver. 13. he calls *Reems* ver. 21. as though they were synonimous terms. In short the *Reem* must be supposed to be of *the beeve kind;* since it is represented in our author's description as qualified by its make and strength for the business of agriculture like the tame ox.

Ver. 9. *or abide by thy crib?*] The original may be rendered, *or will he lie all night on thy threshing floor?* i. e. to guard it. Mr. Merric has made it appear probable, that bulls were in the earliest ages employed, as dogs, to guard fields. Oxen are actually put to this use by the Hottentots [p].

Ver. 11. *thy labour*] the labour of threshing the corn. The eastern nations do not bring their corn in the straw to the barn. They separate the grain on a round level plat of ground, in or near the field where it grew, and in the open air. Neither do they use a flail, but the hoofs of beeves to tread it out [q]. This is still the practice in Syria, Egypt, and Barbary; excepting that in the latter country they employ horses and mules, instead of beeves, in this service [r].

Ver. 12. *gather it into thy barn*] The original is, *and gather thy threshing-floor;* that is, the increase, or produce, of thy threshing-floor, as in Numb. xviii. 30. Will he cart thy corn, after it has been threshed, to thy barn?

---

[p] See Merric's *Annotations on the Psalms*, p. 28.
[q] Deut. xxv. 4. Hof. x. 11.
[r] Shaw's *Travels*, p. 139. 4to. Pococke's *Description of the East*, vol. i. p. 208.

358   THE BOOK OF JOB.   CHAP. XXXIX.

But does her wing the ſtork's wife inſtinct ſhare ?
14. For to the ſand ſhe truſts her oval care ;

                                                    15. Warms

Ver. 13—18. Gaveſt thou *the goodly wings*] The great deſcriptive powers of our ſacred poet ſhine out with increaſing luſtre. This ſhort deſcription of the *Oſtrich* is rich in poetical ornaments, and is a finiſhed piece of miniature painting.

Ver. 13. Gaveſt thou *the goodly wings*, &c.] The words *gaveſt thou* are inſerted by our tranſlators. Mr. Heath renders the ſentence more juſtly,

The wing of the oſtrich ' *is triumphantly expanded* '.

The word which our engliſh bible renders the *peacock* is one of the hebrew names ' of the *Oſtrich* '. The peacock was not known in Syria, Paleſtine, or Arabia before the reign of Solomon, who firſt imported it. It was originally from India. Beſides, the *oſtrich*, not the *peacock*, is allowed on all hands to be the ſubject of the following parts of the deſcription. Neither is the peacock remarkable for its wing, but for the beauties of its tail : Whereas *the triumphantly expanded*, or as Dr. Shaw turns it, *the quivering expanded wing* is one of the characteriſtics of the *Oſtrich*. "When I was abroad (ſays this entertaining writer) I had ſeveral opportunities of amuſing myſelf with the actions and behaviour of the *Oſtrich*. It was very diverting to obſerve, with what dexterity and equipoiſe of body it would play and friſk about on all occaſions. In the heat of the day particularly, it would ſtrut along the ſunny ſide of the houſe with great majeſty. It would be perpetually fanning and priding itſelf with its *quivering expanded wings*, and ſeem at every turn to admire and be in love with its own ſhadow. Even at other times, when walking about or reſting itſelf on the ground, the wings would continue theſe fanning and vibrating motions, as if they were

deſigned

' רננים. The other name is יענה. Theſe two names diſtinguiſh this creature by its vociferation, the noiſes it makes being loud and ſonorous. The verbs רנן and ענה ſignify *exclamare, clamare fortiter*. In Arabic רנן ſignifies *ſonum tremulum et tinnulum edidit, clamavit*, quod Struthiones fœminæ maximé faciunt. Hieroz. p. ii. lib. ii. cap. 16. Shaw's *Travels*, p. 450—455. 4to. Clodii *Lex. Select*. p. 480. See the note on chap. xxx. 29.

' נעלסה. It is engliſhed *to rejoice* in chap. xx. 18. and *to ſolace one's ſelf* in Prov. vii. 1°. According to Buxtorf, in his *Concordance*, it anſwers to the Latin *exſultare* ; which denotes joy expreſſing itſelf in leaping and dancing.

CHAP. XXXIX.   THE BOOK OF JOB.   359

15. Warms it a while, improvidently leaves,
Nor peril from the crushing paw conceives:

16. Unus'd

designed to mitigate and aswage that extraordinary heat wherewith their bodies seem to be naturally affected."

The *Oſtrich* is called by the Perſians the *Camel-Bird* : becauſe it reſembles a camel in its neck, height, and walk; and a bird in its bill and feathers. See Shaw's *Travels* p. 450, &c. 4to. and Hieroz. p. ii. lib. ii. c.16.

Or *wings and feathers*, &c.] The tranſlation, I apprehend, ſhould be,
    Is it *the pinion and feathers of the ſtork*°?
The Oſtrich prideth herſelf in her quivering expanded wing, but without reaſon, ſince it does not, like the wing of the *ſtork*, provide for the ſecurity and education of her young. Natural affection is as remarkable in the *ſtork* as the want of it is repreſented to be (ver. 16.) in the *Oſtrich*.

Ver. 14, 15. *Which leaveth*, &c.] As for *the ſtork*, the lofty *fir-trees* are *her houſe*. But the improvident Oſtrich *depoſiteth* ʷ her eggs in the earth.

The Oſtrich buildeth her neſt on ſome ſandy hillock, in the moſt barren and ſolitary receſſes of the deſert; expoſed to the view of every traveller and the foot of every wild beaſt. She ſits upon her eggs, as other birds do; but then ſhe ſo often wanders, and ſo far, in ſearch of food, that frequently the eggs are addle by means of her long abſence from them ˣ. Leo Africanus ſays, they lay about ten or a dozen eggs at a time. But Dr. Shaw ſays, that by the repeated accounts

° אם אברה הסידה ונצה *Is it the pinion of the ſtork, and the feathers?* Caſtellio turns the whole verſe, *Utrum generoſiores ſunt alæ ſtruthio-cameli, an pennæ plumæque ciconiæ?* אם is interrogative in chap. xxxviii. 33. *Canſt thou ſet* אם תשים, and in many other places. See Noldius. אברה or אבר ſignifies *a wing*, or *pinion*, and נצה *feathers*, in Ezek. xvii. 3. אברה is here uſed in the abſolute form inſtead of the conſtruct. Guarin produces ſeveral inſtances of this anomaly; in his hebrew grammar, vol. i. p. 121. הסידה *the ſtork*, is ſo rendered in the margin, and elſewhere by our tranſlators. See Pſal. civ. 17. Jer. viii. 7.

ʷ תעזב *ſhe leaveth*. Dr. Shaw juſtly renders it *ſhe depoſiteth:* for the word ſignifies *to truſt*, or *commit*, *to*, in ver. 11. *wilt thou leave thy labour to him?*

ˣ Hieroz. part ii. 253, 257.   3.

16. Unus'd a mother's tender fears to feel,
Afar she wanders for her morning meal;
Adopts, in her return, some casual brood,
Mother in vain, and cruel to her blood.

17. God counts which he received from his conductors, as well as from Arabs of different places, he had been informed they lay from thirty to fifty. He adds " We are not to confider this large collection of eggs, as if they were all intended for a brood. They are the greateſt part of them reſerved for food, which the dam breaks and diſpoſeth of according to the number and cravings of her young ones."

Ver. 16. *She is hardened*[y], &c.] " On the leaſt noiſe (ſays Dr. Shaw) or trivial occaſion, ſhe forſakes her eggs, or her young ones: to which perhaps ſhe never returns; or if ſhe does, it may be too late either to reſtore life to the one or to preſerve the lives of the others. Agreeable to this account, the Arabs meet ſometimes with whole neſts of theſe eggs undiſturbed: ſome of them are ſweet and good, others are addle and corrupted; others again have their young ones of different growth, according to the time, it may be preſumed, they have been forſaken of the dam. They (the Arabs) oftner meet with a few of the little ones, no bigger than well grown pullets, half ſtarved, ſtraggling and moaning about like ſo many diſtreſſed orphans for their mother. In this manner, *the Oſtrich* may be ſaid *to be hardened againſt her young ones, as though they were not hers*; *her labour* (in hatching and attending them ſo far) *being in vain, without fear*, or the leaſt concern of what becomes of them afterwards. This want of affection is alſo recorded Lament. iv. 3. *The daughter of my people is become cruel, like the Oſtriches in the wilderneſs*[z]."

To this account we may add, When ſhe has left her neſt, whether through fear or to ſeek food, if ſhe lights upon the eggs of ſome other Oſtrich, ſhe ſits upon them, and is unmindful of her own[a].

---

[y] הקשיה Vid. Iſ. lxiii. 17. *præduruſ fuit*, phyſicé & moraliter. Arab. قسح and קשה idem notant. conf. Schult. ad h. l. Clodii *Lex. Select*.

[z] Dr. Shaw, in the pages of his *Travels* above referred to.

[a] *Hieroz.* p. ii. 254, 255.

17. God in his wisdom form'd this stupid kind,
   Creation's fool, all body without mind.
18. Yet when her sudden enemy she sees,
   Uprising like a tow'r away she flees;

In

Ver. 17. *Because God hath deprived her,* &c.] Natural affection and sagacious instinct are the grand instruments, by which providence continueth the race of other animals: But no limits can be set to the wisdom and power of God. He preserveth the breed of the Ostrich without those means, and even in a penury of all the necessaries of life.

"Those parts of the *Sahara* (the desert) which these birds chiefly frequent, are destitute of all manner of food and herbage; except it be some few turfs of coarse grass, or else a few other solitary plants of the *laureola, apocynum* and some other kind, each of which is destitute of nourishment, and, in the Psalmist's phrase, even *withereth afore it is plucked* [b]. So that considering the great voracity of this Camel-Bird, 'tis wonderful not only how the little ones, after they are weaned from the provision I have mentioned [c], should be brought up and nourished; but even how those of fuller growth, and much better qualified to look out for themselves, are able to subsist [d]."

Ver. 18. *When she lifteth up herself,* &c.] "Notwithstanding the stupidity of this animal, its Creator hath amply provided for its safety; by endowing it with extraordinary swiftness, and a surprizing apparatus for escaping from its enemy. They, *when they raise themselves up* [e] for flight, *laugh at the horse and his rider.* They afford him an opportunity only of admiring at a distance the extraordinary agility, and the stateliness likewise, of their motions, the richness of their plumage,

---

[b] Psal. cxxix. 6.

[c] The eggs. See the note on ver. 14.

[d] Shaw's *Travels,* p. 450—455. 4to.

[e] במרום תמריא LXX. ὁ ὑψῶν ὑψώσει Vulg. in *altum alas erigit.* Mr. Heath, *when she extendeth herself in height.*

In clouds of whirling sand, to fav'ring gales
She spreads the volumes of her plumy sails:
With native spurs she stimulates her speed,
And mocks, aloof, the hunter and his steed.

19.   Hast thou with prowess fill'd the *martial horse?*
Thou ton'd his throat with roaring thunder's force?

20. Light

age, and the great propriety there was in ascribing to them an *expanded quivering wing*. Nothing certainly can be more entertaining than such a sight; the wings, by their rapid but unwearied vibrations, equally serving them for sails and oars; while their feet, no less assisting in conveying them out of sight, are no less insensible of fatigue."

Ver. 19—25. *Hast thou given the horse,* &c.] The fire and sublimity of this passage are perhaps no where equalled, except by the great author himself in his description of *Leviathan*. The present situation however of verses 22, 23. throws the whole into confusion. For those parts of the description which precede and follow ver. 22, 23. represent the horse in his *rank*, smelling the battle *afar off*; and paint him in every attitude of ardour and impatience for the fight. But in ver. 22, 23. he is in the very midst of the engagement, intrepidly keeping his ground against all its terrors. In propriety of order therefore those verses, 22, 23. should conclude the description.

Ver. 19. *hast thou clothed his neck,* &c.] I understand this of the *neighing* of the war-horse, which though shrill is compared to thunder for its loudness and terror. An ingenious gentleman assured me, that he has heard his own horse perfectly *roar* when he was provoked by blows.

The *neck* is here put for the throat through which the voice passeth, as in Virgil (quoted by Bochart) when he is describing the swans:

Dum sese a pastu referunt, et longa canoros
Dant per colla modos ——

Thunder

20. Light as the locust, in the field he bounds;
   His snorting with majestic terror sounds:

21. Ardent

Thunder means the terrible modification of the voice of the war-horse when he *neighs*.

His throat is said *to be clothed with thunder*; which may seem a harsh expression. But the hebrews denoted any permanent quality or circumstance by this metaphor. Thus it is said in Ezek. xxvi. 16. *they shall clothe themselves with trembling*; that is, they shall tremble every moment.

Ver. 20. *Canst thou make him afraid*, &c.] *Canst thou make him leap as the locust*? This agility expresseth his joy to find himself in the rank of battle. Ælian says of the war-horse, " when he hears the sounding of the reins and the clattering of the bits, and sees the breast-plates and forehead-pieces, he neighs, and *leaping* makes the ground to ring with his hoofs." The simile of *the locust* is illustrated by Dr. Shaw. This insect, he says, hath the two hindermost of its legs, or feet, much stronger, larger, and longer than any of the foremost: In them the knee, or articulation with the leg and thigh, is distinguished by a remarkable bending, or curvature, whereby it is enabled, whenever prepared to jump, to spring and raise itself with great force and activity.

the

רעמה Theodotion renders it χρεμετισμον *neighing*; and the Vulgate *hinnitum*. It may be רעם, *thunder*, with a feminine termination; as אברה אבר a wing, and אורה אור light, according to Bochart's remark in *Hieroz.* P. i. p. 126. I find in Castell. *Lex.* that the verb רעם signifies in Syriac, *iratus est, infremuit, tonare fecit;* and רעם, in *Arabic, ira percitus est, vociferatus est* camelus. Castellio's version is, *aut ejus clamosam cervicem induisti?*

התריש The verb is used for *the dancing motion* of the ground in an earthquake, Ps. lxviii. 9. The noun for *the brandishing* of a spear, Job xli. 21.

ארבה, always in other places rendered *the locust*. It seems to denote the genus. There are three species of them, as Dr. Shaw remarks; סלעם, הרגל, and הגב.

i Hieroz. p. i. 122.
k Shaw's *Travels*, p. 420. 4to.

21. Ardent for fame, and glorying in his might,
He paws, he stamps, impatient for the fight:

24, 25. The ground he swallows in his furious heat,
His eager hoofs the diftant champain beat:
He fcarce believes that the fhrill trumpet blows;
He neighs exulting as the blaft ftill grows;
Trembling with rapture, when the fhouts from far
And thunder of the chiefs aroufe the war:

22. Deriding

the glory of his noftrils, &c.] *the ftrength*[l] *of his fnorting* [m] *is terrible.* Mr. Heath. This action of the horfe denotes joy heightened to a pitch of fury.

  Et fremitum patulis fub naribus edit ad arma.   *Lucret.*

  ——*When by fierce alarms*
  He fnorts, and bears his rider on to arms.   Creech.

Ver. 21. *He paweth in the valley*] The valley, or plain [n], is mentioned, becaufe cavalry cannot act in a hilly country. His *pawing* expreffeth his impatience for the fignal of battle.

He rejoiceth in his ftrength] confcious of his powers, and fill'd with the profpect of victory and glory.

He goeth on to meet, &c.] *He would go out* [o] *to meet the armed men.* He can hardly keep his rank, fo eager is he to charge the enemy.

---

[l] הוד de *vigore* quoque ac *vehementia vocis* dicitur *Job* xxxix. 20. ubi de equo, *magnificentia ronchi ejus eft terribilitas.* Clodii *Lex. Select.*

[m] נחרו *his fnorting.* The feminine is fo rendered Jer. ix. 16. The word for *noftrils* is נחירים Job xli. 12.

[n] עמק, LXX, ἐν πεδίῳ.

[o] יצא *he would go out,* fo in chap. xx. 24. ברח *fhould be rendered, he would flee.* The Hebrews having no optative, or fubjunctive, or potential mood, often employ their fimple future indicative to exprefs the powers of them all.

CHAP. XXXIX.   THE BOOK OF JOB.   365

22. Deriding death, he rushes undismay'd
Where flames with horrid wheel the slaught'ring blade,
23. Where quivers clang, and whizzing arrows fly,
And spears and jav'lins lighten in his eye.
                                            26. Does

Ver. 22, 23. *neither turneth he back*, &c.] *The sword from which he turneth not back*, must surely be the sword lifted up to strike him, the sword therefore of the enemy: and *the quiver which rattleth against him*, must mean the quiver and arrows which rattle against him, or are shot at him, when the battle is begun. His courage and daring spirit, which urge him on amidst these horrors, is plainly the finishing stroke in the description. Accordingly Dr. Young has in his translation closed the description with these two verses, and I have followed his example.

Ver. 23. *the shield*] *the javelin*, which is a short spear. It undoubtedly means some such offensive weapon, in Josh. viii. 18, 26. where it is translated *a spear*.

Ver. 24. *He swalloweth the ground*, &c.] This verse should have been joined to ver. 21. There the horse was represented in the utmost eagerness *to go out to meet the armed* men. Here his impatience grows stronger, his imagination devours the space between him and the hostile army, and he fancies himself in the midst of the engagement.

    Stare adeo miserum est, pereunt vestigia mille
    Ante fugam, absentemque ferit gravis ungula campum.
                 Thebaid. VI.
    Delay such misery is; that ere he starts
    A thousand steps are vanish'd, and his hoof
    Smites the far distant plain.

neither believeth he, &c.] This sentence and the subsequent verse mark the passions of this noble animal, when the trumpets sound a charge. He doubts, he hopes, he is transported; and at last is fixed in his conviction and joy, by hearing the thunder of the captains and the shouts of the soldiers coming on to battle. Then *mocking at fear*, he bears his rider with impetuosity on the foe: neither *turneth he back from the* lifted *sword*, &c. ver. 22, 23.

neither

26. Does thy contrivance on the *falcon*'s wing
Bestow its swiftness, and unweary'd spring?
Or guide his voyage, when he shoots away
With outspread pinions to the southern ray?

27. Mounts the imperial *eagle* with thy might,
When among clouds he bounds his trackless flight?

28. On

neither believeth he, &c.] When some great good fortune befalls us, in our transport we scarce believe it. It is too good, we say, to be true. Thus Job xxix. 24. *If I smiled on them, they believed not.* This animated figure applied to the horse, represents with energy and beauty his excess of joy.

Ver. 25. *Among the trumpets*] *When the trumpet soundeth amain*ᵖ. Mr. Heath.

He smelleth, &c.] The sense of smelling, when perfect, is exceeding quick and subtile. Hence in other languages, as well as the hebrew, it is used to denote sagacity of mind, acuteness of discernment, and sound judgement. The war-horse immediately concludes from the thunder of the captains, &c. that the engagement is on the point of being begun.

Ver. 26. *Doth the hawk*, &c.] Most of the species of hawks, we are told, are birds of passageᵠ. The hawk therefore is produced here as a specimen of that astonishing instinct, which teacheth birds of passage to know their times and seasons, when to migrate out of one country into another for the benefit of food, or [a warmer climate, or both. The stork is of this kind, Jerem. viii. 7.

by thy wisdom—at thy command] These expressions clearly prove, that the questions in this speech do mostly relate, not to speculative knowledge but providential power and government.

ber

ᵖ בדי שפר *in sufficientia tubæ, when the trumpet soundeth loud and long.* Drusius.
ᵠ *Hieroz.* p. ii. 270.

28. On the sharp rock's sharp edge he builds his dome,
    The craggy summit forms his pleasing home:
29. From that strong citadel, he darts abroad
    His eyes on earth and o'er th' aerial road:
30. His glance is instant death; his callow brood
    Gape at the prey, and lap the reeking blood.
    Where chance the carcase flings, his banquet see;
    And where the field of slaughter, there is he.

CHAP.
XL.
Ver. 1. Th' Almighty paus'd; then question'd Job again:
2. Dumb is the man who dar'd my ways arraign?

The

her nest] *his nest, he* dwelleth, *he* seeketh, &c. as the word our Author useth for *the eagle* denotes *the kind*, it seems most proper to follow him in employing the masculine, rather than the feminine, gender, as the most noble.

Ver. 28. *abideth*] *delighteth himself* '.

Ver. 29. *her eyes behold afar off*] From the highest promontories, and his loftiest flights, he discerns his prey on the ground '.

Ver. 30. *Her young ones also suck up blood*] He sees and pounces his prey and bears it alive to his nest almost in the same instant. The eagle is fond of flesh and sucks the blood, with both which he nourishes his young '.

C H A P. XL.

Ver. 1. *Moreover the Lord*, &c.] The insertion of these words seems to imply, that the Almighty paused a while; and upon Job's remaining silent resumed his discourse.

' יתלנן *elle se plait*, Crinsoz. לון in Arabic signifies *mollis fuit*. Schultens ad c xxxix. 12. In the Arabic Psalter (Psal. xxiv. 14. Heb. xxv. 13.) יעני, in the second conjugation *delectari faciat*, is the rendering of תלין *shall dwell at ease*.

' *Hieroz.* p. ii. 174, 175.

The disputant with God, no answer find?

3, 4. *Ah! what am I? what answer* (Job rejoin'd)
Shall I presume? my guilty lips I close,
And humble silence on my tongue impose:

5. Too

Ver. 2. *Shall he that contendeth,* &c.] It is clear from Job's reply, that he understood these expressions to be a demand of an answer from him; *What,* says he, *shall I answer?* The terms in which the demand is made, are a severe sarcasm on his courage in daring to enter into a contest with God; and on his presumption in having desired to reason ᵗ with the Almighty about his ways. The translation, I think, should be;

Does he that contendeth with the Almighty draw back ᵘ *?*
Let the disputer ʷ *with God, answer him* ˣ*.*

The answer required was, a solution of the foregoing questions relative to the *natural works* of God. He who cannot account for these, much less perform or amend them, is utterly incapable to solve the difficulties in God's moral providence; and is therefore guilty of the highest presumption in complaining against it. Job now felt the force of this inference.

Ver. 3—5. *Then Job,* &c.] The nature of the preceding interrogations, the pungency of their rapid succession, the majesty of the speaker, and the circumstances

---

ᵗ Chap. xiii. 3.

ᵘ יסור, *jissor, shall instruct,* from the root סר. But the LXX. read יסור *jasur,* from the root סור *recessit:* for they turn it εκκλινει *declinat.* The Vulgate also gives a sense expressive of the same reading, *tam facilè conquiescit?* is he that contendeth with God, *so easily satisfied,* or stilled? Mr. Heath in his note has, *should he draw back?* though he does not approve that translation.

ʷ מוכיח *Celui qui vouloit disputer,* Crinsoz. It is a participial noun derived from the verb הוכיח, which signifies *to reason, to argue a point,* chap. xiii. 13. *Surely I would speak to the Almighty, and I desire to reason* (הוכח) *with God.*

ˣ יעננה The Chaldee, the Complutensian LXX, and Vulgate read יעננו *respondebit ei.* The meaning however will be the same, if we translate the present hebrew text, as Schultens, *respondeat ad hocce, let him reply to this,* to the foregoing questions relating to the natural works of God.

5. Too oft I spoke, too rashly spoke before;
I will not answer, I'll offend no more.

6. Again the whirlwind roar'd, in lofty tone
Again th' Almighty from his cloudy throne:

7. Advance, display the hero, gird thy loin;
My part the learner's, to instruct me thine.

8. Wilt thou my judgement disannul? and must,
To prove thee righteous, I be prov'd unjust?

9. Hast

stances of terror that accompanied his speaking, could not fail of having a powerful effect. Job now begins to be sensible of his own blindness, weakness, and littleness; of the rashness of his complaints, and the excesses of his self-justification. These convictions produced the confession here related.

Ver. 4. *I am vile*] This translation appears to me too strong for our author's word; which does not import, I think, *a moral pravity,* but *lightness of estimation*. He retracts by this expression the too high value he had set on his own rectitude. *I am of small account*[y] in the immensity of thy works, and am so now in my own eyes.

Ver. 5. *Once have I spoken—yea twice*] This is an acknowledgement of all his rash speeches, his complaints, his demands of a trial, and his offers to defend the justice of his cause against God himself.

but I will not answer] *To answer* means here *to put in a defence,* as in chap. xiii. 22. *Then call thou,* do thou bring the accusation, *and I will answer.* He retracts that daring expression, and declares he will not be guilty of offering to justify himself any more; *I will proceed no further.*

Ver. 6. *Then answered the Lord*] It seems, the foregoing confession was not thought

---

[y] בלתי *Levis, & nullius sum pretii.* Aq. ἐλαφρύνθην *levis factus sum.*

THE BOOK OF JOB. CHAP. XL.

9. Haſt thou an arm omnipotent, like mine?
And like my voice, does thunder burſt in thine?

10—12. Go,

thought adequate to the offence. A deeper humiliation and more compleat ſubmiſſion were required. To effect this, the Almighty aſſumes a ſeverer tone,
and ſets before this man *the danger* he had incurred by contending with his
Maker.

Ver. 8. *Wilt thou alſo diſannul my judgement*, &c.] By *diſannulling God's judgement* is meant *condemning* ᵃ God, as the latter ſentence explains it. Job's complaints and manner of juſtifying himſelf amounted to charging God with injuſtice.

Ver. 6—14. *Haſt thou an arm*, &c.] Here the weakneſs and littleneſs of mortal man are brought into compariſon with the almighty power and majeſty of
God. By this means the infinite diſparity becomes more glaring; and the prodigious madneſs of entering into a competition with ſuch a Being is diſplayed
with overwhelming conviction ᵇ.

Ver. 10. *Deck thyſelf*, &c.] The magnificent ſcenery preſented to us in this
and the four following verſes, is the Almighty, arrayed in the ſplendors of
divine majeſty, exerting his ſupreme dominion, and manifeſting his righteous
vengeance; by thundering and lightning on the heads of haughty tyrants,
and hurling them down to the bottom of Hades. In the ſame grand manner,
the ſublime prophet deſcribeth the vengeance of God upon the Aſſyrian monarch.
See Iſaiah xxx. 30.

with majeſty and excellency—with glory, &c.] Job is ironically required to inveſt
himſelf with the attributes of Deity, and to aſſume the glorious inſignia of divine majeſty; that *he* may execute judgement on proud oppreſſors, and other
profligate men, of whoſe impunity and proſperity he had ſo loudly complained ᶜ. The terms *majeſty* and *excellency* ᵈ mean, I think, thoſe high perfections,

natural

ᵃ תרשיעני, Symm. αδικον με ποιησεις; *wilt thou make me unjuſt?*
ᵇ See Bp. Lowth's *Prelections*, p. 200. 8vo.
ᶜ Chap. xxi. 7, &c. and chap. xxiv. throughout.
ᵈ גאון וגובה.

CHAP. XL. THE BOOK OF JOB. 371

10—12. Go, deck thyself with pomp, aſſume the rod,
And fulgent form, and majeſty of God;
Thron'd amidſt ſplendors heav'n and earth control,
Thy wrath in flaming inundation roll;
Abaſe the lofty, wither by a frown
The tow'ring creſt, and daſh fierce tyrants down:
13. Down in the duſt rebelling nations throw,
And whelm them all in endleſs ſhades below:

14. Then
natural and moral, which exalt the poſſeſſor to the ſummit of all being, power,
and dominion : The other terms, *glory* and *beauty* ᵈ, when uſed of mortal po-
tentates, ſignify the external pomp of royalty; the crown, the ſcepter, the
purple robe, the guards, &c. But when applied to God, they denote, I ſuppoſe, the *Shechinah*, the numberleſs retinue of angels, thundering clouds, lightning, &c.

Ver. 11. *the rage of thy wrath*] In the original, *torrents* ᵉ *of wrath*; that is,
lightning. Compare Exod. xv. 7.

Ver. 12. *Look on every one that is proud*] This is that γοργον ομμα (as Æſchylus ᶠ calls it) " that formidable look, at which the mountains, the earth, the
depths of the ſea, and the height of heaven tremble." Compare Pſalm civ.
32.

tread down] *break in pieces* ᵍ.

in

ᵈ הוד והדר

ᵉ עברות *torrents; exundationes*, from עבר *tranſivit to paſs over*, ſc. its banks, when a
river is alluded to, as here: for הפץ *caſt abroad* has for its theme פוץ *excrevit, exundavitque,
aqua*. Vid. Schultens *ad h. l.*

ᶠ Quoted from Clemens Alexandrinus by Mr. Merrick, in his *Annotations* on Pſal. civ. 32.

ᵍ הרוך Clodius, in his *Lexicon Selectum*, compares it with the Arabic *hadaka contrivit*,
inde etiam *diruit*, ſc. ædificium, a conterendo & comminuendo.

Bbb 2

THE BOOK OF JOB. CHAP. XL.

14. Then own'd by me thy deity shall stand,
    Safe in the prowess of thy own right hand.

15. Behold my *Behemoth* his bulk uprear,
    Made by thy Maker, grazing like a steer.

16. What

in their place] In the very place of their exaltation, as Crinsoz explains it.

Ver. 13. *Hide them in the dust*, &c.] Cast them down from their splendid elevation into the obscure abodes of death, as condemned malefactors.

To bind the face is a phrase for treating a person as a convict condemned to die[h]. *The dust* is the grave[i]; and *the secret place* (bind their faces in the secret place) is another expression for the sepulchre; or else it means the secret abodes of *Sheol*, the receptacle of departed souls.

Ver. 14. *that thy own right hand can save thee*[k]] That thou art self-sufficient, the author and preserver of thy own happiness; therefore a God, and a match for me. This humiliating sarcasm makes way for another mortification: For the Almighty next sends him to two of his creatures *Behemoth* and *Leviathan*, and bids him prove his high courage in an *open encounter* with either of them.

Ver. 15. *Behemoth*[l]] This name signifies *the beast* by way of eminence, or the *greatest among beasts*. The *Elephant* and the *River-horse* lay claim to it, and to the honour of being the original of the following grand description. But with regard to the name, the *River-horse* seems to have no title to it: For Leo Africanus

---

[h] See the note on chap. ix. 24.

[i] Chap. xvii. 16.

[k] תושיע *can make thee happy*. Schultens informs us, that the nouns וישע and שעה in Arabic signify *possession of all the ingredients of happiness*. Comment. ad cap. v. 4.

[l] בהמות. This is the plural of בהמה, which in Arabic (says Clodius in *Lex. Select.*) signifies a *dumb animal*, from בהם *bahama*, in conjug. iv. *clausit*, in conjug. x. *obmutuit*. The plural number was sometimes used by the Hebrews to denote *greatness* and *preheminence*. So that בהמות is *bestiarum maxima*. Vid. Guarin's *Heb. Grammar*, vol. i. p. 476, 477.

16. What strength is seated in each brawny loin!
What muscles brace his amplitude of groin!
17. Huge

Africanus assures us, that both in the Nile and the Niger they are no bigger than an ass. Thevenot indeed, quoted by Mr. Heath, says, he saw one of these animals at Cairo, that was as tall as a camel with a body twice as large as that of an ox. But this was an extraordinary phænomenon. Nor did even this equal the bulk of a full-grown *Elephant*. Moreover, several characters in the description of the *Behemoth* by no means agree to the *River-horse*, whereas all of them, if I mistake not, are applicable to the *Elephant*. The principal objection to the *Elephant* seems to be, that this animal was never seen in these parts of Asia before the reign of Seleucus Nicanor, about A. D. 312, to whom an Indian prince made a present of five hundred of them [m]. To this we may reply that Elephants breed in those parts of Africa which border upon Egypt [n]. They were therefore well known to the Egyptians; and by the intercourse of Palestine and Arabia with Egypt were doubtless known also to Job and his friends, and to the writer of this poem.

whom I made with thee] whom I made thy fellow-creature. This is a humbling stroke.

He eateth grass, &c.] The expression seems to imply, that grass is his constant food; and the wonder is, how a creature of such enormous bulk can be supported by a meer vegetable diet. The simile, *as an ox*, naturally leads one to suppose some analogy in the form of the *Behemoth* to that of an ox. Accordingly the Romans called it *Bos Luca*, the Lucanian beeve; Lucania being that part of Italy into which Pyrrhus, in his war with the Romans, brought them, and where the Romans first saw this creature. The *Elephant* is known to be of the grazing kind. But the usual food of the *River-horse* is fish; though he will sometimes steal out of the river in the night into the neighbouring fields of corn, and devour a vast quantity. The *River-horse* is carnivorous and a beast of prey, the *Elephant* is not [o].

Ver. 16, 17. *Lo now, his strength*, &c] I apprehend, these verses are descriptive

---

[m] Hieroz. p. i. 256.
[n] Plin. *Nat. Hist.* lib. viii. cap. 11.
[o] Schultens' *Comment*.

17. Huge like a cedar fee his tail arife,
   Large nerves their meshes wreathe about his thighs:
                                                        18. His

criptive of the great powers and mighty apparatus with which the *Behemoth* is furnished for propagating his kind. In the *Elephant* the organs of generation doubtless bear proportion, in their magnitude and strength of texture, to the huge bulk of that animal; and therefore far exceed those of the *River-horse*, and consequently better correspond to the description.

*his strength—his force*ᵖ] that is, as Mr. Heath explains these terms, his generative vigour. He might have produced, in support of his interpretation, Gen. xlix. 3. *Reuben, thou* art *my first-born, my might* ᵠ, *and the beginning of my strength* ʳ.

Ver. 16. *in the navel* ˢ *of his belly*] *in the ligaments of his belly.* Mr. Heath. The strong muscular fibres of his belly are not mentioned as rendering the creature impenetrable in those parts, but as qualifying him with extraordinary vigour for propagation.

Ver. 17. *He moveth his tail like a cedar*] Mr. Heath translates, *He erecteth* ᵗ *his tail like a cedar.* In the literal sense, *the tail* both of the *Elephant* and the *River-horse* is too contemptible to be compared to a cedar, or even at all taken notice of in this description. It is therefore to be understood figuratively for the principal organ of generation; like the latin *cauda;* according to the remark of Mr. Mudge quoted by Mr. Heath. I wonder that neither of those learned gentlemen alleged the following passage in Horace,

———quin

ᵖ און, כח   ᵠ כח   ʳ און, כח

ˢ שרירי This is not the hebrew word for *the navel*. The root in Syriac signifies *to be firm and strong*. One of the derivatives in Arabic is אשראדה *opus plexum ex junco, wickerwork*. wherefore שרירי most probably denotes *the muscular fibres variously twined together*.

ᵗ יחפץ *he erecteth*. Three MSS. mentioned by Mr. Heath read יחפן. Now חפן, he observes, signifies, in the eighth conjugation in Arabic, *cum impetu erupit, se proripuit*. The Vulgate seems to have had some such idea of חפץ or חפן. For that author translates it, *stringit he unsheaths* his tail. LXX. ιστησιν ουραν ως κυπαρισσον, *He erecteth* his tail *like a cypress*.

18. His ribs are channels of unyielding brass,
   His chine a bar of iron's harden'd mass:
19. My sovereign work; prime of the bestial kind
   In pow'r of body, and in gifts of mind.
   I with a tusky falchion arm'd his jaw,
   His foe to humble, and the desert awe:

20. In

—quin etiam illud
Accidit, ut cuidam testes caudamque salacem
Demeteret ferro.   Sat. I. 2. ver. 45.

the sinews, &c.] *the sinews* ᵗ *of his thighs* ᵘ *are twisted together.* Mr. Heath.

Ver. 18. *His bones,* &c.] The description seems too strong for the *River-horse*. whose teeth indeed are remarkably hard, as likewise are those of the *Elephant*; But the former cannot enter into competition with the latter, for the largeness and iron-like strength of its ribs, spine, and thigh-bones. Mr. Heath's translation is,

His bones are like brazen pipes ˣ,
His back-bone ʸ *is like a bar of iron.*

Ver. 19. *He is the chief,* &c.] that is, the chief of all the beasts which God hath made. The grandeur of the Elephant and his mental endowments give him surely the sole title to this character of preheminence.

He that made him, &c.] *He that made him, hath furnished* ᶻ *him with his scythe.*

ᵗ גידי LXX. νεῦρα *the nerves.*

ᵘ בחדו *his thighs.* So it signifies in Arabic, as Bochart has proved. There is not sufficient warrant for our english version of this word.

ˣ אפיקי *tali,* Cocceius. אפק signifies, among other things, *the channel of a river.* .

ʸ גרמיו LXX. ἡ δὲ ῥάχις αὐτε *his back-bone.*

ᶻ יגש, Vulg. *applicabit gladium ejus.* It signifies *to be brought into close contact,* chap. xli. 16. (Heb. ver. 7.) *one is so near to another;* rather, *they* (his scales) *are in close contact* (יגשו) *are with one other.* It signifies *to put into, to insert, to make fast by insertion,* II Sam. iii. 34. *Thy hands were not bound, nor thy feet put into fetters.* .6

20. In peaceful majesty of might he goes,
And on the mountain tops his forage mows:
Where beasts of every savage name resort,
And in wild gambols round his greatness sport.

21, 22. In

scythe. Mr. Heath. The *River-horse* has two tusks with which he cuts the corn, when he chuses that diet. But the *Elephant* has also two teeth, much larger, which project from his jaws, are shaped like a sickle, and which Nonnus, in his description of this animal, calls *a sharp sword*. With this instrument the *Elephant* defends himself when attacked[a] by any other beast.

Ver. 20. *Surely the mountains,* &c.] Three characters of the *Behemoth* are marked here (1) He frequents the mountains. This is so true of the *Elephant*, that one sort are called mountaineers. (2) The mountains supply him with food. The *Elephant* lives there upon grass, plants, and the tender branches of trees which he breaks off with his trunk. (3) He is a gentle and sociable animal. The *Elephant* will graze freely with other animals whether wild or tame. Among the latter, if they are near enough to be hurt by his sudden movement he puts them gently by with his proboscis. None of these characters suit the *River-horse*, who is a solitary creature, never goes far from the river, and leaves it only in the night; who has no mountains on the banks of the Nile, frequented by wild beasts[b] to resort to, were he inclined to visit such eminences, and who is of a savage nature and carnivorous.

---

[a] Their long teeth Nature hath given them for their defence. Their trunks are to them as a hand by which they feed themselves: With these they tear off boughs from trees, and eat the tenderest part of them. With these also they pull up green corn and grass by the roots, and then against their legs beat off the earth and dust that hangs about them before they eat thereof. See *A Voyage to East India* by Sir T. Roe's Chaplain.

[b] Beasts of prey are very rare in Egypt. Bp. Pococke mentions only a few tygers and Ahenas, which haunt the deserts near Alexandria. Description of the East, vol. i. p. 207. Moreover the mountains on each side the Nile are barren rocks. See Sandys' *Travels*, p. 92.

21, 22. In moory vales, befide the reedy pools,
Deep plung'd in ooze his glowing flanks he cools:
Or in umbrageous groves enjoys repofe,
Or bow'r'd in willows where the torrent flows.
23. Not fwelling rivers can his heart difmay,
He ftalks fecure along the wat'ry way:

Should

Ver. 21, 22. *The fhady trees*[c], &c.] Thefe verfes defcribe the *Behemoth*'s places of fhelter and repofe. If the vegetables here mentioned did neceffarily mean fuch as grow on the banks of the Nile, the *River-horfe* might juftly lay claim to this part of the defcription. But they fignify in general marfh-plants, as reeds, tamarifks, and others, that grow in fens and by the fides of lakes and torrents in thofe countries. The *Elephant* is called by Ælian the Fen-animal, becaufe he is fond of retiring to marfhy places, in the heat of the day, to cool his body in the ooze. He loves the banks of rivers, and ftanding waters in the fandy deferts.

Ver. 21. *He lieth*, &c.] It is objected to the *Elephant* that he never *lies down*. But our author's word[d] denotes *a fleeping or refting pofture*. The Elephant's is kneeling. Bochart allows this. After all, it is certain that Elephants lie down and rife again at their pleafure as other beafts do[e].

Ver. 23. *Behold*, &c.] What is faid here, feems intended to convey a fublime idea of the lofty ftature, great force, and intrepidity of the *Behemoth*.

Behold

---

[c] צֶאֱלִים *fhady trees*. Schultens fays, this is an Arabic word, and the name of the *Lotus* tree. He adds, the *Lotus* tree grows plentifully in the Cyrenaica (now the kingdom of Barca) the country of Elephants. It is a tall, prickly tree.

[d] וישכב It is ufed of *fleeping*, without any reference to the pofture, in Prov. xxiv. 33. *a little folding of the hands to fleep*, לשכב

[e] We are affured of this fact by Sir T. Roe's Chaplain in the Eaft Indies. See his *Voyage to Eaft India*, publifhed along with Della Valle's *Travels*, p. 381. Yfbrants Ides attefts the fame, in his *Travels*, p. 80. As alfo does Mr. Bell in his, *vol.* ii. p. 26.

Should Jordan heap its overflowing waves
Against his mouth, the foaming flood he braves.

24. Go-

Behold a river overfloweth ᶠ, yet he maketh not haste ᵍ.
Although Jordan breaketh forth ʰ against his mouth, he is in security.

We may remark on this passage (1) that the common height of the Elephant is ten feet and a half. There were some in the stables of Cosroes king of Persia, twelve cubits high ⁱ. A credible traveller assures us that in Indostan he had seen some which he conceived to be at the least twelve feet high, and was informed there were others fourteen or fifteen feet in height. *Voyage to East India* by Sir T. Roe's Chaplain, p. 380. The Elephant therefore can ford most rivers.

(2) He will walk with great composure through deep and rapid rivers, provided he can but carry his trunk, through which he draws in fresh air, above water ᵏ.

(3) The *Jordan* is here mentioned, not as frequented by Elephants, but only as put for any deep and violent river: for such the *Jordan* is in the time of its overflowing. This river is instanced rather than any other, as being in the neighbourhood of Job's country, and therefore well known to him.

Lastly, This part of the description will appear trifling, if applied to the *River-horse*. For where is the wonder, that a native of the *Nile* (compared

to

ᶠ עשק *to oppress, to do wrong by violence.* By a grand metaphor this is applied to a river, which breaks over its banks and destroys the neighbouring fields. The Arabians associated these ideas *injustice* and *an inundation* For the word which in their language signifies *to oppress*, is also used of *the overflowing of a river.* Schultens. LXX. ιαν γινηται πλημμυρα *if there be an inundation.*

ᵍ יחפז *maketh haste*, or *is afraid*. The word, in the Hebrew use of it, denotes, says Schultens, *to make haste*, or *to be in a hurry, through fear.*

ʰ יגיח *breaketh forth* It denotes a violent eruption, chap. xxxviii. 8. *when it* (the sea) *brake forth*, as if *it had issued out of the womb.*

ⁱ Hieroz. p. i. 271.

ᵏ The Elephants delight much to bathe themselves in water; in which, when they find depth enough, they swim as well as any other creature. *Voyage to East India* by Sir T. Roe's Chaplain, p. 381.

8

24. Go now, thy courage on this creature try,
Dare the bold duel, meet his open eye:
Sublime on thy gigantic captive ride,
And with a slender string his vastness guide.

CHAP.

to which the *Jordan* is a brook) which stems that river in its most furious rapidity, should not shrink at swimming or walking through any other much smaller body of water?

Ver. 24. *He taketh*, &c.] Job is here called upon, in most humiliating irony, to try his courage on this huge and powerful creature, to take him by open force, and guide him when taken, with a cord, as he used to manage his camels.

> *Let* a man *take him openly*¹,
> *Let him draw* ᵐ *a cord* ⁿ *through his nose.*

The second sentence alludes, I imagine, to the *hair-noose*, or ringle, which the Arabs put through the nose of their camels; and by which, a line being fastened to it, they bring them to their beck °.

In justice to the learned Schultens, I must apprize the reader that most of the foregoing remarks, relative to the *Behemoth*, are extracted from his Commentary; where proper authorities for the several particulars are to be met with.

---

¹ בעיניו in oculis ejus, i. e. *aperté*, non *ex insidiis*. Schultens.

ᵐ ינקב *let him perforate*, or *pierce through*.

ⁿ במוקשים *with snares*. By an easy figure it might come to be used for *cords*, the materials of which snares are made. Both LXX. and Symmachus read the word in the singular number. The former translates, ισκολιευομενος τρησει ρινα, *Let a twisted* line *bore* his *nose*. But Symmachus understood מוקש to mean the boring instrument, ιν πιρον τρυπηθησεται την ρινα *Let his nose be bored with a bodkin.*

° Hamasa, p. 325. n.

Chap.
XLI.
1, 2.   Doubtlefs, with hook and cordage, thou art bold
To drag *Leviathan* from his wat'ry hold;

To

C H A P. XLI.

The irony is continued. Job is now addreſſed as a man of prowefs fuffi- cient to combat and fubdue another creature, much more formidable than the *Behemoth*; in regard of the armour with which it is furniſhed, both for defend- ing itſelf and attacking its enemy. This creature is named *Leviathan*. The *Crocodile* has found fo powerful an advocate in Bochart, that all other claim- ants are put to filence. The characters in the defcription perfectly correfpond to that animal, allowance being made for poetical ornaments and heightenings. The defcription is not intended for a difplay of the author's fublime talents, and meerly to embelliſh his poem. It has a nobler defign. That defign is clearly explained ver. 10. *None is ſo fierce that dare ſtir him up: who then is able to ſtand before me?* Hence Job is taught to tremble at his danger, in having provoked, by his murmurs and litigation, the difpleafure of the Maker of this dreadful ani- mal. His high fpirit is now brought down, his conviction is completed, and his repentance and fubmiſſion fatisfy the Almighty.

Ver. 1, 2. *Canſt thou draw out*, &c.] It is no eafy matter to fix the precife meaning of the feveral terms here uſed. They feem however in general to de- note the inftruments to be made uſe of partly for taking him alive in the water, and partly for governing him when brought on the land.

*with a hook*ᵖ] The irony will be ftronger, if we turn this and the following verſe in the affirmative form, *Thou canſt draw out*ᵠ *Leviathan*, &c. *or thou canſt faſten a rope in his tongue.*

Or

ᵖ הכה *a hook.* LXX. ιν αγκιϛϱν. It occurs but twice more, viz. Iſaiah xix. 8. and Habb. i. 14, 15. Our bible there renders it *an angle*. But it rather fignifies, I apprehend, *a fiſh-hook*.

ᵠ תמשך *Thou canſt draw up.* Jer. xxxviii. 13. *ſo they drew up* (וימשכו) *Jeremiah with cords, and took him up out of the dungeon.*

To strain the noose about his dreadful jaw,
And tame his fierceness with domestic law.
3. Will he, in humble parle, before thy feet,
With mollifying words thy grace intreat?
4. And, if thy clemency his life but spare,
Eternal service to his victor swear?

5. What

Or his tongue, &c.] *Or thou canst fasten*' *a rope in his tongue*. These expressions import, I should think, a way of taking this creature in the water different from the foregoing, and more dangerous; namely, fastening a rope within his mouth. *The tongue* is put for the whole inside of the mouth, as Mr. Heath remarks.

Ver. 2. *Canst thou put a hook*, &c.] *Assuredly thou canst put a muzzle on his nose, and bore his jaw through with a thorn*'. The muzzle was to secure his mischievous jaws, when he was landed: and the thorn, Mr. Heath says, was to make the muzzle fast; by pinning it, I suppose, to his cheeks.

Ver. 3, 4. *Will he make*, &c.] Here the irony is very apparent. The sacred poet shews a wonderful address in managing this deriding figure of speech in such manner, as not to lessen the majesty of the great Being into whose mouth he puts it.

Ver. 4. *a servant for ever*] There is no necessity of understanding this to be a reference to the Mosaic law of perpetual bondage. The allusion in these verses, 3, 4, is evidently to a person or people, who offer to submit to an enemy on certain terms, and to yield perpetual allegiance to him.

' חשקיע It signifies in Chaldee *firmiter infixit*. Castell. *Lex*.

' אגמן *a pool, reeds and rushes* growing near pools, and *ropes* made of rushes. Schultens. We english it *a rush*, Isaiah ix. 14. *a bulrush*, Isaiah lviii. 5. Pliny informs us (lib. xix. cap. 2.) that the Greeks at first made their ropes of rushes. Probably the Egyptians did the same. They certainly made boats of the *paper-reed*, which Isaiah (xviii. 2.) calls *vessels of bulrushes*.

' חוח This word signifies properly *a thorn upon a plant*; probably made use of for bodkins: Or their bodkins were called by this name from similitude of form.

5. What duty wilt thou to this slave assign?
 Ty'd like a houshold bird, with silken twine,
 His gamesome mood thy weighty cares may ease,
 Or his soft touch thy gentle damsels please.

6. Or wilt thou send him into foreign lands,
 Barter'd to Zidon's ships or Tema's bands?

7. Is open war thy choice? what fame is won,
 If thou invade him basking in the sun!

Ver. 5, 6. *Wilt thou play with him*, &c.] Here he is asked, how he will dispose of his captive: Whether he will retain him in his family, for his own amusement and the diversion of his maidens; Or whether he will sell him, as a rare curiosity, either to the Phænician merchants or to the caravans.

Ver. 6. *Shall the companions*, &c.] *Will the companies of merchants*" *drive a bargain*" *for him? shall he be portioned out* × *among the Canaanites?* By *the companies of merchants* Mr. Heath understands the caravans who traded to Egypt by land; By the *Canaanites* ʸ, I suppose, are meant the Phænicians of Zidon who trafficked thither by sea. *The dividing*, or *portioning him out*, among the latter, means, I apprehend, selling this creature in separate pieces or members.

Ver. 7—11. *Canst thou fill*, &c.] These verses relate, I think, to attacking this formidable creature two ways; (1) At a distance, as he lieth sunning himself

---

" חברים *the companies of merchants.* So Mr. Heath translates it. It signifies *associates,* persons who join in any undertaking and are united in their counsels and designs. See Judges xx. 11. Cant. viii. 13. Isaiah i. 23.

ʷ יכרו Mr. Heath remarks that it is the future in *kal* of the root כרה which signifies *to buy,* Deut. ii. 6. Hosea iii. 2. It has, however, a different construction in those passages.

ˣ יהצוהו, αγορασουσιν αυτοι, *they will purchase him.* Theodotion.

ʸ כנענים LXX. φοινικων ὁτι, *the Phœnician people.* Aquila, μεταξυ χαναιαιων, *among the Canaanites.*

CHAP. XLI.   THE BOOK OF JOB.   383

Surely thy javelins will tranfpierce his hide,
And fhow'rs of fang'd harpoons his fkull divide.
8. Affail him, but remember well the foe,
Fell him at once, or aim no fecond blow.
9. Deceiving hope! his look thy heart appalls,
The foe appears, the fwooning champion falls.
10. Not ev'n the fierceft chief, with war's whole pow'r,
Dares roufe this creature in his flumb'ring hour.
11. Who then fhall face my terrors? where is he,
Whofe rafh prefumption will contend with me?
Where is the giver to whofe gifts I owe,
Owner of all above and all below?

12. Come

felf on the mud iflands in the Nile. Pococke and Norden faw many of them in thofe places in their voyage up that river. (2) Engaging him in clofe fight, when he lieth on the bank of the river, ver. 8.

Ver. 7. *barbed irons—fifh-fpears*] The impenetrability of *Leviathan*'s fkin is here intimated, and is afterwards defcribed at large. The attempt to wound him with miffile weapons is ridiculed. This is a circumftance which will agree to no animal fo well as to the *crocodile*. The weapons mentioned are undoubtedly fuch as fifhermen ufed, for ftriking large fifh at a diftance. The *fifh-fpears* are fuppofed by Schultens to be *harpoons*.

Ver. 8. *Lay thine hand upon him*, &c.] An engagement hand to hand is plainly marked in this verfe.

Ver. 9. *The hope of him*] The hope of maftering him is abfurd.

Ver. 11. *Who hath prevented me*, &c.] The fentiment in this verfe demonftrates the folly and impiety of contending with God, as Job had done. He is all-fufficient and independent, and therefore cannot be indebted to any for their fervice.

THE BOOK OF JOB. CHAP. XLI.

12. Come forth, *Leviathan*, harness'd for the fight,
In all thy dread habiliments of might:
Behold his limbs, their symmetry survey,
For war how well adjusted his array:
13. The temper'd morion, o'er his visage brac'd,
What hardy valour ever yet unlac'd?

Who

service. He is the proprietor of all beings: He therefore cannot injure any one by taking away his possessions and enjoyments: For he takes only what he gave. Submissive resignation, therefore, to his disposals, is the duty of every reasonable creature.

Ver. 12. *I will not conceal*, &c.] We now enter upon *the description* of *Leviathan*; which takes up the remainder of the speech, and is immediately followed by Job's submission that closeth the poem.

It is not beneath the dignity of the great Creator to display his own wonderful work; and to call upon man to observe the several admirable particulars in its formation, that man may be imprest with a deeper sense of the power of his Maker.

Ver. 13. *Who can discover*, &c.] This verse is obscure. The first sentence however seems to describe that terrible helmet which covers the head and face of the *Crocodile*. The translation might be, *Who can uncover his mailed face*[a]? If in Job's days they covered their war-horses in complete armour, the question

will

---

[a] פני לבושו *faciem loricæ ejus*, i. e. *faciem ejus loricatam*. The latter of two substantives in this construction is frequently to be construed as an adjective. Thus ver. 19. *burning lamps*, in the original *lamps of fire*. Schultens also refers us to Deut. i. 41. Isaiah ii. 20. Ezek. xxvi. 16. for other instances of the same hebraism. לבוש signifies in general *a garment*. but the garment, or cloathing, of a warrior and a war-horse is *a coat of mail*. Such probably was that which Joab had on, II Sam. xx. 8. and such a garment seems alluded to, Isaiah lix. 17. lxiii. 1. as that learned commentator remarks.

CHAP. XLI. THE BOOK OF JOB.

Who near his mouth, with double rein, will draw,
14. And lift the huge portcullis of his jaw?
Behold he yawns, the hideous valves difclofe
Death's iron teeth imbattled rows on rows.
15, 16. Proud o'er his mailed back his fcales are clafs'd
Like ferried fhields, lock'd each in each fo faft,

And

will refer to the taking off the armour, and *Leviathan*'s fkin be reprefented by fuch an image. Then the fecond fentence may denote bridling him, after his armour is ftripped off, for fome other fervice. The moft eafy verfion of this latter fentence is that which our englifh Bible and Schultens give,

Who will bring ᵇ *his double bridle?*
Or, *Who will come with his double bridle?*

Ver. 14. *His teeth,* &c.] The apparatus of teeth in the crocodile, to the number of threefcore ᶜ, perfectly fatisfies this formidable defcription.

Ver. 15—17. *His fcales,* &c.] The indiffoluble texture, and perhaps the largenefs alfo, of the fcales, which compofe the Crocodile's hide, are reprefented by the powerful images and figures in thefe verfes.

Ver. 15. *His fcales* are *his pride*] rather, *His body* ᵈ is like *ftrong fhields* ᵉ, that is, his back and fides are covered with fcales that refemble the ftrong plates of fhields.

ᵇ בוא׳ *veniet in,* &c. *Venire* in vel *cum aliqua re* is a common eaftern phrafe for *eam adducere.* Schultens.

ᶜ Hieroz. p. ii. 778.

ᵈ גאוה Aquila, whom the Vulgate follows, renders it σωμα αυτω *his body.* They perhaps read גאותו (taking א for a vowel) from גוה *gevah the body,* as in chap. xx. 25. Bochart and Mr. Heath turn it, *his back,* from גב *dorfum.*

ᵉ אפיקי מגנים, LXX. ασπιδες χαλκιναι *brazen* (i. e. ftrong) *fhields.*

D d d

And feal'd together, that no breath of wind
17. Infinuates: So clofe the plates are join'd,
So folder'd, that the ftouteft force were vain
To pierce the tight-wedg'd joints and burft the chain.
18. His fneeze is lightning, from his eye the ray
Streams like the pupil of emerging day.
19, 20. He belches flame, and fire at every blaft
Leaps fparkling out: A fmoke his noftrils caft,
Like clouds which from a boiling caldron rife,
Or marifh mift beneath the morning fkies.
21. His

Ver. 17. *They are joined*] *They* (the fhields, or fcales) *are foldered* [f] *one to another*.

Ver. 18. *By his neefings a light doth fhine*] Such is the violence and heat of the air, that is repelled from his nofe when he fneezes, that it fparkles in the fun-beams. This circumftance marks the force and fury of the *Crocodile*.

his eyes, &c.] This may happen, fays Schultens, when the *Crocodile* lifts his head above water in the night. His ftaring eyes, which are the firft object that ftrike the beholder, may then be compared to the dawning light. The eyes of the *Crocodile* are faid to be fmall. But, as Bochart obferves, they are fo remarkable; that when the Egyptians would reprefent the morning by an hieroglyphic, they painted a Crocodile's eye [g].

Ver. 19—22. *Out of his mouth*, &c.] Here the creature is defcribed in purfuit of its prey on the land; as appears, I think, from ver. 22. *Deftruction danceth before him*. His mouth is then open, his blood inflamed, his breath is thrown out with prodigious vehemence, it appears like volumes of fmoke, and is
heated

---

[f] ירבקו *ferruminantur* they are foldered, Ifaiah xli. 7. *it is ready for the foldering*, דבק. Schultens.

[g] Hieroz. p. ii. 781.

21. His breath enkindles coals; so hot it steams,
That his wide mouth a furious furnace seems.
22. Strength on his neck is thron'd; where'er he turns,
Woe springs before him and the carnage churns.
23. His flesh coheres in flakes, with sinews barr'd
Compact as steel, indissolubly hard:

24. His heated to that degree as to seem a flaming fire. The images which the sacred poet here useth, are indeed excessive strong and hyperbolical; especially that in ver. 21. *his breath kindleth coals*. But Ovid [h] did not scruple to paint the enraged boar in figures equally bold:

Fulmen ab ore venit, frondesque adflatibus ardent.

Lightning issueth from his mouth, and the boughs are set on fire by his breath.

Ver. 22. *In his neck*, &c.] *Strength* and *Destruction* are here represented as animated beings. The former is seated on the neck of the *Crocodile*, to signify the extraordinary inflexibility of that part. The other leaps and dances before him, when he pursues his prey, to express the terrible slaughter which he makes.

Strength abideth upon his neck,
And Destruction [i] *danceth* [k] *before him.*

Ver. 23, 24. *The flakes*, &c.] The muscular flesh and viscera of this animal, are here represented to have a firmness of cohesion like that of stone and metal [l]. The sentiment stript of its poetical dress amounts to no more, than that the flesh and inward parts are remarkably compact and tough. Theocritus, quoted by Schultens, says of a robust gigantic man " he hath flesh of iron."

---

[h] Quoted by Schultens.

[i] דאבה, LXX. απωλια *destruction*.

[k] תדוץ *leapeth for joy.* דוץ is the word by which the Syriac Testament translates the Greek σκιρταω, Luke i. 41, 44. vi. 23.

24. His heart is from the quarry hewn, comprefs'd
Hard as the nether milftone in his cheft.
25. The valiant tremble, when he lifts his head,
Down fink the mighty, impotent with dread.

26. The

Ver. 24. *his heart is as firm*¹, &c.] Thefe ftrong fimiles may denote not only a material but alfo a moral hardnefs, his favage and unrelenting nature. Ælian, quoted by Schultens, calls the *Crocodile* a *voracious devourer of flefh and the moft pitilefs of animals*.

Ver. 25—30. *When he raifeth up himfelf*, &c.] The terror of this creature debilitates the ftouteft heroes. For no arms or weapons can fecure them, or make any impreffion on him. They know him to be invulnerable in every part but his belly, which is not eafy to be come at. This impenetrability is amplified in a rich vein of fublime poetry.

Ver. 25. *When he raifeth up himfelf*ᵐ] When he lifts his head above water, as though he meant to come out on the fhore.

*by reafon of breakings*ⁿ, &c.] *for very terror they fall to the ground*°. Mr. Heath.

---

¹ The word englifhed *are firm* ver. 23. *is firm* ver. 24. is צוק, which is a metaphor borrowed from fufed metals. See I Kings vii. 46. Job xxviii. 2. In the firft of thefe paffages יצקם is rendered *did caft them*, viz. the veffels of brafs, in the latter יצוק *is molten*.

ᵐ משרו The root is נשא *fuftulit, to lift up*. It does not neceffarily import great elevation; for it is ufed to exprefs *lifting up the feet* in walking, Gen. xxix. 1. *Jacob went on his journey*; the hebrew is, *lifted up his feet*.

ⁿ משברים, Crinfoz paraphrafes it, *through fear of being torn in pieces*. The Vulgate turn it *territi*, as though it were the participle in pyhal *mefhubbarim*. The root is שבר *frangere*. But Bochart obferves, words which fignify *frangere* fignify alfo *timere*, as חתת in hebrew, and *fractus* in latin. Caftellio's verfion is, *fracti*; which is fynonimous with *territi* in the Vulgate. Schultens tranflates it, *præ confractionibus*, i. e. *ftragibus*; *by reafon of the deftruction*, which he makes. שבר *fheber* fignifies *deftruction*, in Ifaiah xv. 5. Jer. iv. 20. Lament. iii. 47.

° יתחטאו *labefactantur*, Caftellio. Their fear is fo great, that they have not power to flee, but inftantly drop down. This agrees with ver. 5. *Shall not one be caft down even at the fight of him*. It is alfo countenanced by the fenfe of חטא in Arabic, *lapfus eft*. Vid. Hamafa. p. 446.

7

CHAP. XLI.   THE BOOK OF JOB.   389

26. The sword at hand, the missile arms from far,
Will thunder on his skin an idle war:
The sword breaks short, the blunted spears rebound,
And harmless clank the javelins on the ground.
27. Iron as straw, and brass as mould'ring wood,
28, 29. He scorns; nor flees, nor flinches to elude
The whurring shaft: as stubble is the stone,
From the strain'd sling with forceful eddies thrown;
As stubble is the pounding mace, his hide
Death's every brandish'd weapon will deride.

30.   Sharp ragged pebbles are his downy bed,
On pointed rocks his flimy couch is spread. .

31. What

Ver. 26. *the habergeon*] rather, *the javelin* [p].

Ver. 29. *Darts*] *The club*, or *mace* [q]. .

Ver. 30. *Sharp stones*, &c.] The belly of the Crocodile is penetrable by a bullet, and perhaps also by a sword. Nevertheless it is hard enough to be insensible of pain when he lieth on sharp stones and ragged rocks which are in the bed of the Nile. In that part of the Nile where the cataracts are, and which the Crocodiles mostly frequent, its bed is of granite marble; as is evident from the ridge of granite rocks, which there runs across its channel and is the cause of those falls of the water. See Norden's *Travels into Egypt*, p. 115. 8vo. and Pococke's *Description of the East*, vol. i. p. 114, 115, 122.

---

[p] שריה *spiculum*. Bochart observes that it is so explained by the Arabian Lexicographers.

[q] תותח LXX. σφυρα *mallets*. Bochart renders it *fustis*, from the Arabic ותח *fuste percussit*.

31. What time he flounces in the wave and mire,
    He boils the water like the rage of fire:
    The boiling water to a thick perfume
    Works, as he dashes the discolour'd spume.
32. The flood turns hoary while his way he cleaves,
    And in his rear a shining path he leaves.

33. Dire

Ver. 31, 32. *He maketh the deep to boil*, &c.] To give us a further idea of the force of this creature, the poet describes the effects of its motion in the water. By *the sea* is meant the Nile, which is called *the sea* by the hebrew prophets and by the Arabs [r]. *The deep* is the deep places in that river. When a Crocodile fifty feet in length [s] dives to the bottom, the violent agitation of the water is justly compared to liquor boiling in a cauldron. The mud raised by that agitation thickens the water and gives it a consistency like that of ointment: *He maketh the sea* (the Nile) *to boil like a pot of ointment*. The simile will be still more exact, if, as it is said, the Crocodile emits a strong scent when he plungeth into the river [t]. When a Crocodile of the size above-mentioned is swimming upon or near the surface, he cuts the water like a ship; and makes it white with foam. At the same time his tail, like a rudder, causeth the waves behind him to froth and sparkle like a trail of light: *He maketh a path to shine after him*, &c. These images are common among the poets.

————tumultuous boil the waves :
They toss, they foam, a wild confusion raise,
Like waters bubbling o'er the fiery blaze [u].

---

[r] Hieroz. p. ii. 787, &c. See also the note on Job vii. 12.

[s] Captain Norden saw, in the upper Egypt, twenty Crocodiles extended on banks of sand in the Nile. They were, he says, of different sizes, namely, from fifteen to fifty feet. *Travels*, p. 61. 8vo.

[t] Hieroz. p. ii. 787.

[u] Pope's Odyss. b. xii. ver. 282, &c. in the original, ver. 235—237.

33. Dire reptile, on the duſt without a peer,
    Fill'd with a ſoul incapable of fear;
    All beaſts of lofty ſtature he diſdains,
    And fierceſt o'er the fierce ſupreme he reigns.

Ver. 33, 34. *Upon earth*, &c.] The deſcription cloſeth with three characters, which complete our idea of this creature as the moſt terrible of animals.

1. He hath not his match among any of the creatures upon earth. *Upon earth there is not his like*, either for defence or attack.

2. He is a ſtranger to fear, *Who is made without fear*. This may ſeem an objection to the *Crocodile*'s claim. Pococke and Norden tell us, that thoſe which they ſaw on the mud-iſlands in the Nile went ſlowly into the water at the approach of their ſhips, and when ſhot at plunged in [w]. But had any one of thoſe animals been in a ſituation for ſeizing his prey, he would have ſet the crew of both veſſels and all their fire-arms at defiance.

3. He deſpiſeth and as it were holds in ſubjection the talleſt and fierceſt animals.

> *He beholdeth all that is high:*
> *He is king over all the creatures of fierceſt*[x] *look.*

The firſt of theſe ſentences deſcribes a look of contempt, as in chap. xl. 11. *behold every one that is proud, and abaſe him*. The other ſentence declares the ſuperiority of his power. No animal, not even the talleſt or the moſt ſavage, can cope in fight with the *Crocodile*. Bochart produceth ſeveral vouchers to prove, that this creature will attack and bring down with his tail not only men, but camels, and even elephants and tigers, when they approach his river[y]. This confirms the aſſertion, *that he is made without fear*.

---

[w] *Deſcription of the Eaſt*, vol. i. p. 111, 114, 202. Norden ſays, that ſome, before he could get within gun-ſhot of them, *darted themſelves* into the water. *Travels*, p. 84. 8vo.

[x] בני שחץ. The word שחץ in Arabic implies in it both *height of ſtature* and *fierceneſs of aſpect*. Vid. Schultens' *Comment*. Hieroz. p. i. 718.

[y] Hieroz. p. ii. 750.

CHAP. XLII.

1, 2. Jehovah ceas'd. Then Job, submiss, reply'd:
I know 'tis thine to humble human pride;
Thine is the pow'r Almighty, thine the throne
Whose counsels are controllable by none.

3. " *Who he, that with impenetrable skill*
" *Plans the high purpose of his sov'reign will?*"

'Tis

CHAP. XLII.

Ver. 1—6. *Then Job answered, &c.*] A new chapter should not have begun here, but at ver. 7.

This *complete* submission contains the following particulars:

I. A full acknowledgment of God's almighty power and supreme dominion.

Ver. 2. *I know that thou canst do every thing, and that no purpose of thine* [z] *can be hindered.*

By thus glorifying the sovereign authority of God, he tacitly condemns himself for not having meekly submitted to it.

II. A like acknowledgment of the unsearchable wisdom of divine providence, with an explicit condemnation of himself for his objections and murmurings against it.

Ver. 3. *Who is he that hideth counsel which cannot be known?*
Therefore have I uttered that I understood not, things too wonderful for me which I could not know.

The

---

[z] מִמְּךָ מְזִמָּה Our marginal translation, *no thought of thine can be hindered*, is justified by Gen. xi. 6. Nothing of theirs (לֹא מֵהֶם כֹּל) which they have purposed (אֲשֶׁר יָזְמוּ) *will be hindered*, יִבָּצֵר. מְזִמָּה signifies *wise thought* or *purpose, prudential schemes*, in Prov. v. 2. viii. 12. where it is englished *discretion*, and *witty invention*. זִמָּה bears the same sense in Job xvii. 11. my *purposes*.

'Tis so—I censur'd what the wise adore,
Wonders which far above my reason soar.

4. *Indulge my pray'r, a gracious ear incline,*
   " *My part the learner's, to instruct me thine:*"

5. *Before,*

The Almighty began his speech to Job with a sharp reprimand of his presumptuous complaints against providence: *Who is this* that *darkneth counsel by words without knowledge* [a]? that is, who is this ignorant man, that discovers his ignorance by finding fault with what he knows nothing of? Job, in this reply, turns that reproof into a noble acknowledgment of God's inscrutable counsels, and in such manner as necessarily implies humble acceptance of the reproof.

1. By changing the expression *who is this that darkneth counsel*, into *who is this* that *hideth counsel?* The former is a phrase for an ignorant man, one whose thought, or mind, is in the dark; the latter denotes one who is *secret in counsel*, or whose *counsel is secret* [b], which is a character of wisdom.

2. By omitting the terms *by words*, which could not be introduced here with any propriety. These two remarks belong to Schultens.

3. By altering the sense of the expression *without knowledge*, into *beyond* [c] *knowledge*, or which cannot be known.

Here then he condemns the rashness of his interrogating God concerning the reasons of his inflictions. *Who is he* that *is secret in counsel, beyond* my *knowledge? Therefore,* &c.

III. He humbly begs of God to vouchsafe a gracious audience to his confession, and to instruct him further in his duty.

Ver.

---

[a] Chap. xxxviii. 2. See the note there.

[b] מעלים עצה *whose counsel is hidden*, or *who is secret in counsel*, as in Isaiah xxviii. 29. עצה והפלא *He is wonderful in counsel*, or *his counsel is wonderful*.

[c] בלי This particle, says Mr. Heath, signifies here *supra, ultra*; so Isaiah v. 14. חק בלי *supra medum*.

5. *Before, I knew thee by the ear alone;*
By vision now, and in thy glory known.
6. *Lo, self-detesting in the dust I lie,*
And mourning breathe the penitential sigh.

Ver. 4. *Hear I beseech thee, that I may speak:*
I will ask of thee, and do thou instruct me.

He refers to the sarcasm in chap. xxxviii. 3.

IV. He declares, that this *visible* manifestation of the Almighty to him had imprest him with a deeper and more reverent sense of the divine perfection and majesty, than what he had before conceived by means of *instruction* only.

Ver. 5. *I have heard of thee by the hearing of the ear*, &c.

In which words there is an implied comparison of the evidence of report with the evidence of sight, greatly to the advantage of the latter,

> Segnius irritant animos demissa per aurem,
> Quam quæ sunt oculis subjecta fidelibus——
>
> *But what we hear moves less than what we see.*   Roscommon.

Lastly, He expresseth his repentance in the strongest terms of self-condemnation and humble sorrow:

Ver. 6. *Wherefore I abhor myself*[d], &c.

This complete submission may not improperly be called the *catastrophe* of the poem. It is not indeed a change of Job's outward condition. It is an alteration infinitely more important and beneficial; an alteration, I mean, in the temper and state of his mind. He is brought back to his duty, and his soul returns to its rest. The restoration of his health and prosperity quickly followed, and is the subject of the ensuing narrative.

---

[d] אמאס, LXX. εφαυλισα εμαυτον *I despise myself.* It is added ν̓ ετακην and *I am dissolving*, which is another sense of מאס and seems to be a marginal gloss that crept into the text.

7. THE cloud now difappear'd. But when the Sun
Had a few more diurnal ftages run,
God call'd to Eliphaz: Difpleas'd I heard
What thou and thy affociates have averr'd,
Erroneous, of my ways; not thus offend
The reas'nings of your rafhly-cenfur'd friend,

8. My

Ver. 7, 8. *And it was* fo, &c.] The poem being finifhed, the ftyle changes here to hiftorical profe; and the tranfition is made by a form of fpeech familiar to the hebrew hiftorians, when they begin a narration, *And it was* fo, or *And it came to pafs.*

When the Almighty had ended his fpeech to Job, and Job his confeffion; the cloud, I fuppofe, afcended out of fight, and the affembly broke up. After which, it pleafed God to reveal his mind perfonally to Eliphaz, who had taken the lead in the uncharitable difpute with Job. The contents of the revelation are related in thefe verfes, 7, 8. and are as follow;

Firft, A condemnation of their unrighteous cenfures, and a decifion of the controverfy about the courfe of providence.

Ye have not fpoken of me the thing that is right, as my fervant Job hath.
They had reprefented Job's afflictions as laid upon him by God for his wickednefs. This was not *right*.

They likewife grounded their cenfure on a notion, that wicked men never profper long in the prefent world; and thence inferred, that great calamities are proofs of great antecedent guilt. This was not *right*.

Job on the contrary had maintained, that all things happen alike to all; and that therefore no man's moral character can be afcertained by his external condition. This was *right*, and is here pronounced to be the truth.

Bp.

8. My servant Job. Go, let sev'n heifers bleed,
Sev'n rams in social sacrifice succeed:
My servant Job, while yet your victims burn,
Shall with atoning pray'r my vengeance turn:
Him I accept; your folly, else, shall rue
Those falshoods which my servant Job o'erthrew.

9. They all obey'd, and sought the Pow'r Divine;
The Pow'r, appeas'd, display'd the fav'ring sign.

10. Then God began the mourner to restore,
And gave, and doubled what he gave before.

11. His

Bp. Hare remarks [c], that Elihu's speech is neither praised nor censured by the Almighty: and thence concludes, that Elihu was the writer of the poem. But Elihu is not commended, because he was in the main of the same opinion, concerning the course of providence, with the three friends. Neither is he blamed, because he had not condemned Job for a wicked man, but censured only his behaviour towards God in his affliction.

Secondly, The Almighty now vindicates the *innocence* of Job, by styling him three times *my servant*; that is, my sincere worshipper.

Thirdly, The three false accusers are commanded to offer a sacrifice in acknowledgment of their offence: To which is added the mortifying declaration, that their injured friend should make intercession for them, and on that condition their sacrifice should be accepted and their sin forgiven.

Ver. 9. *The Lord also accepted Job*] that is, accepted his intercession for his three adversaries; and began his restoration from the time of his performing that charitable office, as appears by the next verse.

Ver. 10—17. *And the Lord turned*, &c.] Here we have an account of Job's restoration

---

[c] Not. ad Psal. cvii. 40.

11. His brethren, sisters, friends, a cheerful band,
　　With golden gifts in each saluting hand,
　　Crowded his house; on the rich feast regal'd,
　　Condol'd his sorrows, his deliv'rance hail'd:
12. Job now, beyond his former blessings blest,
　　Number'd twice o'er the wealth he first possess'd:
13. Seven sons his patriarchal sway rever'd
　　His houshold cares three lovely daughters cheer'd;
14. Distinguish'd each, by some expressive name,
15. All grac'd with beauty of unrival'd fame:

And restoration to a state of prosperity far superior to that from which he had fallen, of his enjoyment of it to a very great old age, and of his peaceful conclusion of the scene in an easy death.

Ver. 10. *turned the captivity*, &c.] This seems to have been a proverbial phrase for a happy reverse of condition. For certainly it here includes all that God did for this excellent man; and among other blessings, giving him a new family of children equal in number to those he had lost.

Ver. 11. *every man also gave*, &c.] It was an ancient custom, which is still observed in the east, never to visit a person of distinction without paying him the compliment of a present. It is uncertain whether one kind of present made to Job on this occasion, was *a sheep*, or *a piece of money* [e] that had the figure of a sheep stamped upon it.

Ver. 12. *fourteen thousand sheep*, &c.] Michaelis [f] remarks, that this exact doubling of his former possessions, and also giving him exactly the same number of children that he had before, looks more like fiction than history. Such precision is seldom known in the ordinary course of things.

---

[e] קשיטה, LXX. αμναδα *an ewe lamb*. But by comparing Gen. xxxiii. 19. with Acts vii. 16. one would rather imagine it to have been some species of current coin.

[f] In *Prælect.* p. 17'.

      And each beyond a daughter's dowry fhar'd,
      For each the portion of a brother heir'd.
16. Twice feventy years, from this bright æra, fhed
      Health and pure joys upon his favour'd head:
      His chidren's children flourifh'd at his fide,
17. Then, full of days, in hoary peace he dy'd.

APPENDIX.

APPENDIX.

NUMBER I.

Queries *and* Observations *concerning the Author of the Book of* JOB; *in order to determine whether he was an* Arabian, *or a* Hebrew *Prophet.*

IN the narrative part of this book, that is to say, the first and second chapters, and the eleven last verses of the concluding chapter (all which are written in prose) the name *Jehovah*, the LORD, is used no less than twenty-six times. But in the *poem*, which begins with the third chapter and endeth with the sixth verse of the forty-second chapter, *this name* occurreth only in chap. xxxviii. 1. and xl. 1, 3, 6. and xlii. 1. where the writer speaks in his own person; and once in the *dialogue* of the poem, chap. xii. 9. where this name is put into the mouth of Job: *The hand of Jehovah (the* LORD*) hath done this.* Thus stands the fact, on which we may ground the following queries and remarks:

I. Why is the name *Jehovah* so cautiously avoided in the *dialogue* of the poem?

The reason, I think, must be, that the persons of the dialogue, being *Arabians*, were not acquainted with *this* appellation of the Supreme Being, which was peculiar to the *Hebrew* nation. If then the author of the poem was an *Arab*, no wonder that he did not use this name of God in framing his dialogue. If the author was a *Jew*, he has shewn great judgment in such exact attention to propriety of character in his speakers.

II. How

APPENDIX.

II. How happened it, that this name, *Jehovah*, is found *once* in the *dialogue*, and there in the mouth of Job?

This muſt have happened, ſurely, either through a miſtake of the ſcribe or a ſlip of the author. If the former was the caſe [g], the author of the *poem* might be an *Arabian*, and a different perſon from the writer of the *hiſtory*. But if the name *Jehovah* ſlipped into the dialogue through caſual inattention of the author, it will follow, I preſume, that the poet and hiſtorian were one perſon, and he a *Jew*. For how ſhall we account for ſuch a lapſe; otherwiſe than by ſuppoſing the uſe of the name *Jehovah* to have been ſo habitual to this writer, that in ſpite of all his caution it did for once, improperly, fall from his pen?

III. If the author of the *whole* book was not an *Hebrew* and a *reputed prophet*, how ſhall we account for its admiſſion into the canon of the Hebrew Scriptures? The Hebrew nation was exceedingly jealous of its religious prerogatives. *Unto them were committed the oracles of God.* Would they have inrolled in their ſacred volume a *poem* written concerning a foreigner by a foreigner?

IV. But how came this wary and judicious writer to put the name *Jehovah* three times into the mouth of Job the *Arabian*, in the *narrative* part of his work, chap. i. 21?

Perhaps he judged, that the laws of hiſtory are not ſo ſevere in this particular as the laws of a dramatic poem.

V. Doth not the *ſtyle* of the *poem* indicate its origin from an *hebrew* pen?

This poem, after the manner of all the hebrew poems [h], is broken into ſhort periods, conſiſting, in general, of two ſhort ſentences; the latter of which correſponds to the former, either as ſynonimous with it, or antitheſis to it, or agreeing in the number and diſpoſition of the words. Till therefore the learned
produce

---

[g] Perhaps the learned Dr. Kennicott's various lections, when the world ſhall be favoured with that invaluable labour, will determine this queſtion.

[h] See that learned and elegant work, Bp. Lowth's *Prelections on the ſacred poetry of the Hebrews*, p. 39. 8vo.

produce a very old *Arabian* poem, in the same caſt of ſtyle with this; may we not juſtly ſuppoſe, that a *hebrew poet* was the author of the *poem* in the book of Job?

VI. Doth the *language* of the *poem* prove the writer to have been an *Arabian?*

There are, I confeſs, many words, phraſes, and idioms in this compoſition, which appear no where elſe in the hebrew bible : Neither can they be explained without the aſſiſtance of the Chaldee, Syriac, and Arabic dialects. The Arabic, more eſpecially, has preſerved thoſe and many other remains of the primitive tongue. But, I apprehend, the argument only proves the great ability and addreſs of this author. He was perhaps maſter of the *old language*; and the perſons of his dialogue being known to have lived in very early times, he has given a venerable antique air to his poem, by making them ſpeak the language which was ſpoken in their days.

APPENDIX.

NUMBER II.

An inquiry into the notion of Sheol *in the book of* JOB.

*F*IRST, *Sheol* is reprefented to be a portion of fpace, vaft and deep.

Chap. xi. 8. It (the counfel of God) is *as high as heaven what canft thou do? deeper than hell* (Sheol) *what canft thou know?*

Secondly, Sheol is fpoken of as the common receptacle of human fouls after death.

Chap. vii. 9. As *the cloud is confumed, and vanifheth away; fo he that goeth down to the grave* (Sheol) *fhall come up no more.*

Job defired earneftly to be there:

Chap. xiv. 13. *O that thou wouldft hide me in the grave,* (Sheol) &c.

The *wicked* alfo go down thither:

Chap. xxi. 13. *In a moment they go down to the grave* (Sheol).

xxiv. 19. *Drought and heat confume the fnow-waters: fo fhould the grave* (Sheol) *thofe which have finned.*

Thirdly, This region of difembodied fouls feems to be placed in the bowels of the earth, under the great abyfs:

Chap. xxvi. 5, 6. *The Rephaim are in anguifh under the waters, together with their families. Hell* (Sheol) *is naked before him,* &c. See the note on this paffage.

I apprehend, that this paffage not only determines the fituation of *Sheol*; but alfo implies, that wicked fouls are in a ftate of fuffering there, and confequently are feparated from the good: whofe refidence therefore is fuppofed to be in a different part of this fubterraneous region. Thus Virgil, in the fixth book of

his

APPENDIX.

his *Æneid*, placeth the *Elysian fields* and *Tartarus* in the bowels of the earth, but allotteth to each a separate situation. Thus likewise the Chaldee Paraphrase (Job xxviii. 6.) divides *Sheol* into *Gehenna* and *Paradise*, and representeth both to be under ground.

It seems to have been a very ancient opinion among the Hebrews, that the dwelling of unbodied souls is within the earth: For in I Sam. xxviii. 13. the witch of Endor says to Saul, *I saw the judge* (Samuel, ver. 14.) *ascending out of the earth*.

I beg the favour of the reader to turn back to the note on chap. xxxviii. 16, 17.

Fourthly, It appears to me doubtful, whether Job and his friends believed good souls in *Sheol* to be in a state of *consciousness* and enjoyment. The contrary opinion seems implied in chap. xiv. 13.

O that thou wouldst hide me in Sheol, that thou wouldst keep me secret, until thy wrath be past, that thou wouldst appoint me a set time, and remember me! See the note.

The famous passage however chap. xix. 25—26. leads one to imagine, that they expected some future period; when the souls of good men will be removed out of *Sheol* into a more happy situation.

It is not my business to impugn or defend these notions, but only to trace out the ideas affixed to the word *Sheol* in my author. If the reader desires a more enlarged view of the Hebrew notions of the state of the dead, he will meet with full satisfaction in the ingenious Mr. Peters' *Critical Dissertation on the book of Job*. And if he would be entertained with an account of the conformity between the *Sheol* of the Hebrews and the *Hades* of the Greeks, let him peruse Windet's learned treatise *de Vita Functorum Statu*.

Lastly, The *sepulchral grot*, being a part of the world of death, is sometimes called *Sheol*. I think, *Sheol* is rightly rendered the *grave* chap xvii. 13—16. (see the note) and that this is the *land of darkness* described with such solemn horror chap. x. 21, 22.

The foregoing account of the situation of the mansion of souls departed, may perhaps be thought inconsistent with what Solomon says in Ecclesiast. iii. 21. *Who knoweth the spirit of man that goeth upward, and the spirit of the beast that goeth downward to the earth?* But these words, I apprehend, relate not at all to the *habitation* of departed souls; but either (1) to their *existence after death* " Who considers the great difference between a human spirit and that of a beast? the former is immortal, the latter perisheth with its body." Or (2) the expressions relate to *the accountableness* of human souls to God; " Who considers that the spirit of man returneth to God who gave it, to render account of the deeds done in the body? whereas beasts are not free agents, not therefore under moral government, nor subjects of reward or punishment."

APPENDIX.

NUMBER III.

Explication of Chap. xix. 25, 26, 27.

Ver. 25. *F*OR *I know, my redeemer* is *the living* one: *and* he *the Last will over the dust rise up.*

Ver. 26. *And my skin,* which *is thus torn,* shall become *another : and in my flesh I shall see God.*

Ver. 27. *Whom I shall see, even mine eyes shall behold, on my side and not estranged. my reins are consumed within me.*

Some interpreters understand this famous passage, of a *temporal* salvation. But Job had all along despaired of *such* a deliverance. Even after uttering these words, he continued in the same despair. See the note on chap. xxx. 23, 24. Moreover, Elihu addresseth to him as a person still without hope of a recovery. See the note on chap. xxxv. 14. xxxvi. 20. This therefore cannot be the true interpretation of the words.

Neither can they be justly applied to the manifestation of God in his favour, which is related chap. xlii. 7, 8. For that manifestation is not said to have been a *visible* one : and if it were, Job saw it not. It was made to Eliphaz alone.

Neither can this passage be referred to God's appearance to Job himself in the *poem.* For the whole design of that appearance was to reprimand and humble him. There is not the most distant hint in the Almighty's speech of an intention to vindicate and restore him.

In short, these words are no anticipation of the *history* which is subjoined to the poem ; much less of the *catastrophe of the poem* itself : for the catastrophe of the poem is Job's repentance. See the note on chap. xlii. 1—6.

It remains therefore, that in this passage the good man is supporting himself, under a heavy load of calumny and other afflictions, by the faith of a *resurrection* from the grave and a *future judgement*; when his innocence should be fully cleared and his integrity amply rewarded.

Let

Let us now examine the foregoing version of these words.

Ver. 25. *my redeemer*, &c.] The term *redeemer* denotes in general a *deliverer* [1]. The sense in which Job styles God his redeemer or deliverer must be determined by the nature of the deliverance described in the words that follow.

The epithet *the living* one [k] is a title of the supreme Being, expressing his eternity; as likewise the other epithet *the Last* [l]. These titles have a peculiar propriety and emphasis here; on supposition that Job is speaking of the resurrection and final judgment.

The *dust* signifies the *grave*, in chap. xvii. 16. By a common figure of speech it is put for *them who dwell in the dust*, the dead. Psalm xxx. 9. *Shall the dust praise thee? Shall it declare thy truth?*

The expression *shall rise up* presents to us an idea of God acting in the capacity of judge of the world. It is used again, and, if I mistake not, in reference to the general judgment, chap. xxxi. 14. *What then shall I do when God riseth up?* The phraseology seems to be derived, as Mr. Peters observes, from the custom among human judges to *stand up* when they pronounced sentence. Here then Job declares his belief, that the everlasting God will raise the dead and judge them.

Ver. 26. *And my skin* which *is thus torn* [m], &c.] According to this translation, which is taken from the learned Michaelis, Job here compares his body

in

---

[1] גאלי It is rendered by LXX. ο εκλυειν με μελλων, *He that shall deliver me*; by the Chaldee, פריקי *my deliverer*.

[k] חי, LXX. αιωνιος *eternal*. See Deut. xxxii. 40. Joshua iii. 10.

[l] אחרון *the Last*, Isaiah xliv. 6.

[m] ואחר עורי נקפו זאת That great critic Michaelis in his *notes on the Prelections* (p. 211. 8vo.) reads *abher alius*, instead of *abhar post*, *postquam*; and נקפה *nikpah laceratio*, instead of נקפו. His translation is, *Alia erit cutis mea, hæc laceratio*, i. e. hæc mea cutis, mera jam laceratio (qualis esse in elephantiasi solet) alia tunc nova fiet. He observes from Schultens, that the verb נקף in Arabic signifies *the laceration of the skin*. Mr. Heath remarks, that נקפה in hebrew is used for *a rent* in Isaiah iii. 24. But I see no occasion to change נקפו which may as well be rendered *is torn*, as יהדפהו *jehdepuhu (they shall drive*

in its present state, torn and mangled by his ulcerous disease, with the advantageous renovation of it at the resurrection. By *seeing God* he means, I apprehend, seeing God with the visual organ of the new resurrection body: for he says *in my flesh*, that is, in my body ⁿ, *I shall see God*. When it is said, that Nadab and Abihu and seventy of the Elders of Israel *saw the God of Israel*, it is explained of a visible representation of the divine majesty: *and* there was *under his feet, as it were a paved work of a sapphire stone, and as it were the body of heaven in* his *clearness* °. Job expected to behold the glorious visible representation in which the Deity will manifest himself when he shall come to raise and judge the dead. This, I think, is the *face*, and *likeness*, or representation, of God which the Psalmist also hoped to behold; Psalm xvii. 15. *As for me, I shall behold thy face in righteousness: I shall be satisfied, when I awake, with thy likeness.*

Ver. 27. *Whom I shall see, even mine eyes*, &c.] This is not superfluous repetition. It is a more emphatical and explicit declaration of his faith, that in a *re-embodied state* he should see the glory of God.

on my side ᵖ, *and not estranged* ᑫ] By the former expression *on my side*, or *for me*, he means the protection and blessing which he shall receive from God in the future judgment. By the latter expression he represents God's present seeming alienation from him. Astonishing is the force of a good conscience, that could enable him, under such prodigious discouragements, to entertain a confidence in God so sublime as this.

my

---

drive him) be rendered *he is driven*, chap. xviii. 18. If however a nominative, or agent, must be supplied, it may be *worms*; which worms *have thus torn*. נִקְּפוּ in Arabic signifies, *rosus à tereti ne*, *worm-eaten*. Vid. Castell. Lex. זֹאת is an adverb *thus, so, in this manner*, Gen. xliv. 10. as Mr. Heath observes.

ⁿ Castellio, *ex meo corpore*.

° Exod. xxiv. 10, 11.

ᵖ לִי *for me*, *on my side*. Psal. lvi. 10. xciv. 16 cxviii. 6. Mr. Heath.

ᑫ זָר *estranged*. It is rendered *a stranger* ver. 15. It may however be the participle of the verb זוּר which is translated ver. 17. *is strange*. Comp. Ps. lxix. 8. (heb. 9.) It signifies in the Targum on Ps. xliv. 19. *aversus, alienated in affection*.

my reins, &c.] This phrase denoteth vehement and almost insupportable desire. It is equivalent to the Psalmist's language, *My soul fainteth for thy salvation*[r]. The word there rendered *fainteth*, is the same which is here translated *are consumed*.

It will, perhaps, be asked, how Job knew all the foregoing particulars. I answer, The prophecy of Enoch[s] revealed a future judgment. The murder of Abel suggested the idea of a reward for the righteous in another world: and Enoch's translation led directly to the belief, that good men will enjoy the felicity of that better world in an embodied state. That prophecy and those facts, we may reasonably suppose, were preserved in the Abrahamic family. Job's descent from that family, or connexions with it, might bring him to an acquaintance with all these important truths. His own observations on the unequal distributions of Providence here, confirmed his faith: and the testimony of conscience to his integrity, assured him of his own glorious interest in these great futurities.

If the above explication of this passage does not satisfy the reader, I must refer him to the excellent defence of it by Mr. Peters in his *Critical Dissertation*.

---

[r] Psal. cxix. 81.   [s] Jude, ver. 14, 15.

APPENDIX.

NUMBER IV.

An attempt to restore the original text *in* chap. xxxvi. 14.

IN this passage, as it stands in the present hebrew text, *a word is manifestly missing*[1], which is however preserved in the Septuagint version.

תמת בנער נפשם
וחיתם [ ] בקדשים

Αποθανοι τοινυν εν νεοτητι η
ψυχη αυτων :
Η δε ζωη αυτων [τιτρωσκομενη]
υπο αγγελων.

First, The lost word, answering to τιτρωσκομενη, I take to be חללה *confossa*. For חלל is rendered by LXX. τετρωμενος *confossus* in Numb. xxxi. 19. Joshua xi. 6, in the Aldine and Complutensian editions.

Secondly, Instead of *kedeshim the unclean*, LXX. read *kedoshim the holy beings*: for they render it αγγελων *the angels*, as the word with those vowels signifies chap. v. 1. xv. 15. compared with iv. 18. See also Dan. iv. 17. 23. (Heb. ver. 14, 20.) and Jude ver. 14.

The text thus restored, and the translation, will be as follows;

תמת בנער נפשם
וחיתם [חללה] בקדשים

Their breath dieth in youth,
And their life [is destroyed] by the holy beings.

Thus

---

[1] It is certain, says a learned and sensible writer, that several letters and some whole words of the old testament have been lost by the negligence of transcribers. *Essay for a new translation of the bible*, by R. H. 1702. p. 25.

The word עני is dropt in the hebrew Pf. xi. 4. but is preserved by the LXX. ως τω πτωχω. Also a whole hemistich is lost in Pf. xiii. 6. which likewise is found in LXX. as Bp. Lowth has remarked. See Merrick's Annotations, p. 15, 19.

Thus the correspondence between the two members of the period, so usual in the hebrew poetry, is recovered: For now חללה answers to תמת, as well as חיתם to נפשם. But still בקדשים does not tally with בנער. I am inclined therefore to follow Schultens, in translating בנער *cum excussione with shaking out*[1], i. e. with violence. *The holy* beings correspond to the *violence*, as they are the ministers of it. So then a violent death, inflicted by angels, is described in this passage. And now the translation will be,

Their breath dieth by violence,
And their life is destroyed by the holy beings.

The notion that the angels are employed by Providence to inflict death upon mankind, probably took its rise from the well-known destruction of Sodom and the cities of the plain by their ministry.

This notion is referred to, if I mistake not, chap. xxxiii. 22. *His soul draweth near to the grave, and his life to the destroyers,* that is, the destroying angels. The hebrew word is כממתים rendered by the Vulgate *mortiferis.* The Seventy indeed turn it εν αδη. But in their version, or rather paraphrase, of the first sentence of the next verse, we find traces of the same opinion: εαν ωσι χιλιοι αγγελοι θανατηφοροι, εις αυτων ȣ μη τρωση αυ͡ον, *Although there be a thousand angels who inflict death, let not one of them wound him.*

This notion kept its ground among the Jews. For in the *Apocryphal History of Susannah,* Daniel says to one of the two elders, ver. 55. *even now the angel of God hath received the sentence of God to cut thee in two;* and likewise to the other, ver. 59. *the angel of God waiteth with the sword to cut thee in two, that he may destroy thee.*

To conclude, This *sword of the destroying angel* is, I apprehend, alluded to in chap. xxxiii. 18. and xxxvi. 12. and in Psal. xxxv. 5, 6.

---

[1] In chap. xxxviii. 13. the verb נער in *Niphal* is rendered *to be shaken out,* and is there used of *a violent death* by the hand of human justice.

F I N I S.

CORRECTIONS.

page	line	for	read
3	19	credulity	credibility
8	28	Exod. xi.	Exod. ix.
25	25	π. 47.	π. 447.
29	29	fod	fhod
36	14	Mecca, in	Mecca, near
42	30	fun.	fur.
60	32	xxxiv. 14.	xiii. 18.
72	32	p. 99.	p 67.
74	3	fh..ll	fhalt
115	22	Patrocles	Patroclus
154	26	offices	office
173	31	veftitium	veftitum
249	29	xxviii. 9.	xxviii. 8.
292	32	aphærifes	aphærefis

p. 40. l. penult. Erafe chap. xxxvi. 24. and that whole citation, to the words *gaze upon* inclufively.
p. 77. l. 1. Erafe comma after *ear*.
p. 158. l. 6. Erafe comma after *bull*.

ERRATA in the Hebrew letters.

Pag.	lin.	pro	lege
44	28	(לך)	(לו)
54	29	פי	מי
126	31	קואנץ	מקנץ
214	23	דהמיסי	המיביך
233	28	חירפי.	חרפי
251	27	רישטבי	תשטמני

www.ingramcontent.com/pod-product-compliance
Lightning Source LLC
Chambersburg PA
CBHW030542300426
44111CB00009B/824